China and the International Human Rights Regime

Rana Siu Inboden examines China's role in the international human rights regime between 1982 and 2017 and, through this lens, explores China's rising position in the world. Focusing on three major case studies – the drafting and adoption of the Convention against Torture and the Optional Protocol to the Convention against Torture, the establishment of the UN Human Rights Council, and the International Labour Organization's Conference Committee on the Application of Standards – Inboden shows China's subtle yet persistent efforts to constrain the international human rights regime. Based on a range of documentary and archival research, as well as extensive interview data, Inboden provides fresh insights into the motivations and influences driving China's conduct and explores China's rising position as a global power.

Dr. Rana Siu Inboden is Distinguished Scholar with the Robert S. Strauss Center for International Security and Law at the University of Texas. She formerly worked on China policy at the US State Department and has consulted for a number of organizations implementing projects in China.

T0364227

China and the International Human Rights Regime

1982–2017

Rana Siu Inboden

CAMBRIDGE
UNIVERSITY PRESS

Shaftesbury Road, Cambridge CB2 8EA, United Kingdom

One Liberty Plaza, 20th Floor, New York, NY 10006, USA

477 Williamstown Road, Port Melbourne, VIC 3207, Australia

314–321, 3rd Floor, Plot 3, Splendor Forum, Jasola District Centre, New Delhi – 110025, India

103 Penang Road, #05–06/07, Visioncrest Commercial, Singapore 238467

Cambridge University Press is part of Cambridge University Press & Assessment, a department of the University of Cambridge.

We share the University's mission to contribute to society through the pursuit of education, learning and research at the highest international levels of excellence.

www.cambridge.org
Information on this title: www.cambridge.org/9781108744836

DOI: 10.1017/9781108888745

First published 2021
First paperback edition 2022

A catalogue record for this publication is available from the British Library

ISBN   978-1-108-84107-8   Hardback
ISBN   978-1-108-74483-6   Paperback

Cambridge University Press & Assessment has no responsibility for the persistence or accuracy of URLs for external or third-party internet websites referred to in this publication and does not guarantee that any content on such websites is, or will remain, accurate or appropriate.

For Will

Contents

Figures

Tables

Acknowledgments

When I first began to study China in earnest many years ago, China was much less developed economically but there was optimism that the country's trajectory would include not only economic growth but expanded political reform as well. China's growing openness to the world also fueled expectations that it would emerge as a responsible power that supported international order. Yet, while China's skylines and living standards have risen, political liberalization has stalled and under Xi Jinping China has pursued a nationalistic foreign policy and rebuffed human rights ideals. My hope is that this book contributes to our understanding of China and the factors that have thus far impeded its acceptance of human rights norms.

Some people will misconstrue my focus on China and human rights by assuming an anti-China bias. Yet, I was drawn to these issues because I think they are critical to securing a prosperous and stable future for China's citizenry. In an era where tension between the West and China is mounting, I wanted to avoid feeding into overly broad generalizations about China and its role in the world. Thus, throughout this book I endeavored for accuracy and rigor, including basing my work strongly on empirical evidence.

This book is based on the doctoral thesis that I completed at the University of Oxford. I am grateful to my supervisor Rosemary Foot, whose dedication and scholarship set a wonderful example for me in my own teaching and research. She consistently provided valuable guidance, pushed me to excel, and demonstrated her commitment to my success. During my time at Oxford, I benefited from academic camaraderie and friendship from David Blagden, Hoo Tiang Boon, Amy King, Nicola Leveringhaus, Carlotta Minnella, Sean Richmond, and Nina Silove. Other contacts and friends who helped in strategic ways include Ambassador Julia Chang Bloch, Christine Chung, Megan Reiss, Paul Haenle, Shi Tianjian, Alex Hall Hall, He Baogang, Emilie Kao, Katie Lee, Yawei Liu, Zhao Li, Rachel Hoff, Randy Schriver, Natalie Britton, Alice Siu, and Kate and Joel Harris. I am also thankful to a number of my former colleagues at the US Department of State, particularly Susan O'Sullivan, Mike Kozak, Kristen Silverberg, Mark Lagon, Lynn Sicade, and to a handful of others who due to political sensitivities should remain anonymous.

My research involved travel to numerous cities, from Geneva to Shanghai, where I benefited tremendously from the willingness of diplomats, scholars, activists, and UN/ILO officials to speak with me. Most of them requested anonymity so can't be acknowledged here, but I wish to express my deep thanks. They were generous with their time and insights, and several hosted me in their homes or showed hospitality to me in other ways. Their interviews were crucial in helping me to understand the complexity of the human rights regime and China's relationship with it. Moreover, their commitment and work to advance human rights around the world is laudable.

As I engaged in the lonely process of revising my dissertation with the hopes of publishing it as a book, I received helpful comments, encouragement and friendship from Felice Gaer, Andrea Worden, Titus Chen, Carl Minzner, Jennifer Salen, Eva Pils, Emily Finkelstine, Sophie Richardson, Jean-Philippe Beja, Katherine Wilshusen, Katrin Kinzelbach, Josh Eisenman, Perry Link, Ted Piccone, Amy Wages and Suzy Weatherford. I would also like to express my gratitude to two anonymous scholars who reviewed the manuscript and provided insightful suggestions and edits. I am grateful to Cambridge University Press, especially Lucy Rhymer, for seeing this book's contribution to the academic discipline, and Emily Sharp for her assistance.

A number of institutions and individuals provided help with my research, including the Interlibrary Services Department of the University of Texas Library, the librarians at the United Nations Library in Geneva, the New York office of Amnesty International, and the Shanghai Academy of Social Sciences. I acknowledge support for research expenses from the Oxford University China Centre, the Department of Politics and International Relations at Oxford University, and St. Cross College. I am grateful to have been a recipient of a Philanthropic Educational Organization (P.E.O.) Scholar Award. Aside from the financial support they provided, the P.E.O. women in Austin were also incredibly supportive, especially in affirming the value of my research. Bobby Chesney, the director of the Robert S. Strauss Center for International Law and Security at the University of Texas at Austin, has made the Strauss Center a welcoming professional home for me.

I also want to thank and acknowledge the doctors and nurses at St. David's North Austin Medical Center, especially Dr. Gras and

Dr. Meritt and my ICU nurses, who cared for me when I suffered a rare and usually fatal medical complication. I thank them for working tirelessly to sustain my life and prevent damage to my brain and organs. Without a full recovery, I would never have been able to complete this book.

I am grateful to have the support of a warm and loving family. I am grateful for parents who consistently nurtured my academic interests. Cyrus and Phyllis, my father and step-mother, have been steadfast in their support and love. They have been supportive of my educational and career endeavors beginning with sending me to Punahou School in Honolulu and then being the first to purchase this book . Although my mother, Winona, did not live to see me begin my career, she encouraged my love of the written word and my zeal for international relations. My Chinese-American family in Hawaii has loved and encouraged me, even when they did not fully understand my academic pursuits. I thank my grandmothers, my sister and Aunty Audrey–who has always loved and treated me like a daughter. I thank my loving in-laws, Bill and Connie Inboden, who supported me in this, and in so many other things. I also thank them for the gift of their son – who is the best man I know.

It was in the halls of the US State Department where I not only became interested in the issues explored in this book but where I met and fell in love with my husband, Will. I dedicate this book to him, as he has been a source of love, affection, encouragement, companionship, and protection, including accompanying me on numerous research trips. His scholarship, character, leadership, and faith are a constant guide and inspiration to me. He is a reminder to me that "Every good gift and every perfect gift is from above, coming down from the Father of lights."

Soli Deo Gloria.

Abbreviations

ACFTU	All-China Federation of Trade Unions
APT	Association for the Prevention of Torture
CASS	Chinese Academy of Social Sciences
CAT	Convention against Torture
CCAS	Conference Committee on the Application of Standards of the International Labour Organization
CCP	Chinese Communist Party
COE	Committee of Experts on the Application of Standards of the International Labour Organization
CRG	Cross Regional Group
ECOSOC	Economic and Social Council
GA	General Assembly
GRULAC	Group of Latin American and Caribbean Countries
IB	institution-building
ICCPR	International Covenant on Civil and Political Rights
ILC	International Labour Conference
ILO	International Labour Organization
ISHR	International Service for Human Rights
LMG	Like-Minded Group
MFA	Ministry of Foreign Affairs
NAM	Non-Aligned Movement
NGOs	nongovernmental organizations
OHCHR	Office of the High Commissioner for Human Rights
OIC	Organization of the Islamic Conference
OPCAT	Optional Protocol to the Convention against Torture
PRC	People's Republic of China
R2P	responsibility to protect
ROC	Republic of China
SPT	Subcommittee on the Prevention of Torture

UN	United Nations
UNCHR	UN Commission on Human Rights
UNHRC	UN Human Rights Council
UPR	Universal Periodic Review
USSR	Union of Soviet Socialist Republics
WTO	World Trade Organization

1   Introduction

Prior to China's entry into the United Nations (UN) in 1971, there was fierce debate about its anticipated behavior and impact. Proponents of Chinese membership argued that integration into the UN would ultimately change or "civilize" the People's Republic of China (PRC) while skeptics countered that the "the UN is not going to serve as a reform school for Peking," and that China was likely to attempt to alter the international system.[1] When Chinese Communist Party (CCP) leaders failed to challenge the existing global order and eventually adjusted their own priorities and goals to fit into it and even benefit from the prevailing international order, the PRC's behavior alleviated concerns of destructive behavior. Yet, the larger question of China's longer-term impact on and role in international regimes remains an open question. Even if the PRC has not acted as a spoiler of the international system, are there subtle yet significant ways that it has pursued change toward international regimes?

This question becomes more pressing and salient with China's ascendance and rising weight in global politics, especially given indications that it is shedding its earlier status quo posture and shifting to a more assertive one. As scholar Elizabeth Economy noted in a June 2018 speech, PRC President Xi Jinping "put the world on notice: China has its own ideas about how the world should be run and is prepared, as he put it, to 'lead in the reform of global governance.'"[2] Scholars have begun

---

[1] Lincoln P. Bloomfield, "China, the United States, and the United Nations," *International Organization* 20, no. 4 (Autumn 1966): 665. For an example of an argument favoring PRC admission into the UN, see Richard Nixon, "Asia After Vietnam," *Foreign Affairs* 46, no. 1 (October 1967): 111–125.

[2] Elizabeth Economy, "Xi's Assertive Superpower Plans," *The Wall Street Journal*, July 21–22, 2018, and Alastair Iain Johnston "China in a World of Orders: Rethinking Compliance and Challenge in Beijing's International Relations, *International Security* 44, no. 2 (Fall 2019): 9–60. At the Fourth Plenum, the CCP leadership indicated that China would step up its global role, including the making of international norms. See "Communique of the Fourth Plenary Session of the Eighteenth Central Committee of CPC," China Change, www.china.org.cn/china/fourth_plenary_session/2014-12/02/content_34208801.htm, accessed December 28, 2018.

grappling with China's economic, military, and strategic global impact, yet little scholarly work has investigated its role in the area of human rights. Beijing's shift under Xi Jinping to a more proactive stance in the UN Human Rights Council (UNHRC), where it has championed resolutions that challenge the universality of human rights, privileges the power of the state over individual rights, and stresses development and economic rights over civil and political rights, provides some evidence that the PRC is shifting from a reactive stance to a more insistent one.[3] These developments underscore the import of this book.

As the title suggests, this book seeks to answer the question of China's role in and impact on the international human rights regime and the drivers of its behavior. In order to do so, it specifically asks whether the PRC acted as a maker, promoter, taker, constrainer, or breaker toward this international regime during the period from 1982, when it first began participating in the UN human rights regime, through 2017. While my inquiry is focused on China's behavior in the international human rights regime, my findings also provide insight into the broad questions of rising China's willingness to accept global order, its behavior in international regimes, and the human rights regime's future. Policy makers and scholars have wrestled with questions such as, Will a rising China threaten or accept the liberal international order? Is Beijing inclined to accept, adjust, or revamp existing international regimes? If either of the latter two, what are its strategies and motivations? This book also sheds light on the human rights regime, particularly questions such as, To what extent is the human rights regime contested? What is the likelihood the regime will endure? My findings provide relevant insight into these questions, and, therefore, have scholarly as well as policy relevance. If Xi Jinping moves China to a more muscular international posture, as he seems intent on doing, this book will help decipher China's possible intentions and vision for the human rights regime.

The question of China's role in the international human rights regime is worthy of study for a number of reasons. First, China's growing political and economic weight makes it a key actor whose behavior has the potential to influence positively or negatively the functioning of international regimes through its formal positions as well as its general behavior and interaction with other states. Moreover, any Chinese

---

[3] Ted Piccone, *China's Long Game on Human Rights at the United Nations* (Washington DC: Brookings Institute, 2018), www.brookings.edu/research/chinas-long-game-on-human-rights-at-the-united-nations, accessed September 24, 2018, and Yu-Jie Chen, "China's Challenge to the International Human Rights Regime," *NYU Journal of International Law and Politics* 51, (2019): 1179–1222.

success in enacting changes to this regime has impact beyond its borders since other states are held to the same human rights norms, standards, and procedures. Second, after a number of decades where it maintained a low profile in the human rights regime, the PRC appears to have jettisoned its earlier modest posture in favor of a more active and assertive role.[4] Signs of this shift include the PRC initiating action in the UNHRC, including a Presidential Statement on the right to health, resolutions on promoting human rights through "mutually-beneficial cooperation" and "the contribution of development to the enjoyment of human rights," and President Xi's January 2017 speech entitled "Work Together to Build a Community of Shared Future for Mankind." Further, China along with other countries has attempted to thwart the passage of rights-friendly Human Rights Council (HRC) resolutions it disagrees with, such as protecting human rights defenders and civil society.[5] These kinds of actions fuel concern that China's growing influence is contributing to "the end times of human rights."[6] Moreover, the US decision to withdraw from the UNHRC in 2018 created greater opportunity for the PRC to pursue its priorities and vision. This book's investigation into the PRC's priorities, preferences, and stances in the regime provides insight into the way a more muscular China is likely to behave and the kinds of changes it is likely to pursue. Third, the PRC's acceptance of international human rights norms appears to lag behind other regimes, such as those governing finance and arms control. Thus, human rights may represent an issue area where there is wide divergence between China, a one-party authoritarian state, and the international regime. Because the PRC is an unlikely supporter of the human rights regime, studying its behavior in this issue area has the potential to provide insight on the ability of international regimes to shape, and even alter, state behavior. Fourth, previous scholarship focused primarily on domestic compliance and the application of the international human rights regime to China, particularly after the

---

[4] See, for example, Aaron Friedberg, "Rethinking China: Competing with China," *Survival* 60, issue 3 (Summer 2018): 7–64, and Josh Roggin, "Inside China's 'Tantrum' Diplomacy at APEC," *The Washington Post*, November 20, 2018. Several diplomats described China as primarily acting defensively in the human rights regime. Interview with North American diplomat, July 30, 2012, Washington DC, and interview with North American diplomat, May 24, 2011, Geneva, Switzerland.

[5] "China Rising," Universal Rights Group, www.universal-rights.org/blog/china-rising-review-37th-session-un-human-rights-council/, accessed August 3, 2018.

[6] Stephen Hopgood, "The Endtimes of Human Rights," in *Debating the Endtimes of Human Rights*, eds. Doutje Lettinga and Lars van Troost (Amsterdam: Amnesty International Netherlands, 2014): 11.

1989 Tiananmen Square crackdown.[7] While these works provided insight into whether and how the regime might be changing China, they neglected the question of the PRC's possible impact on the human rights regime. The approach taken in this book has the benefit of treating Beijing as more than a passive actor in an inevitable process of being drawn closer into and in greater compliance with the international human rights regime and captures the two-way process of interactions between the state and the international regime.

This book's line of inquiry is also worthwhile because it helps answer a puzzle. China's entry into the human rights regime and voluntary participation in many of the regime's activities are surprising for a variety of reasons.[8] First, according to a number of sources, including foreign governments, UN experts, and human rights organizations, the Chinese government commits serious and systematic human rights abuses.[9] Beijing has also shielded rights-abusing allies, including North Korea and Syria, from international scrutiny. Thus, Beijing's voluntary participation in the human rights regime exists alongside actions that appear to contradict the substance of the regime.[10] Second, unlike other international regimes, such as the World Trade Organization where China stands to gain reciprocal benefits, participation in the human rights regime does not result in tangible material benefits. Thus, it is not immediately obvious why China participates in the human rights regime or how it benefits from participation. Third, there is an inherent tension between China's political system and the principles undergirding

---

[7] Examples include Ann Kent, *China, The United Nations, and Human Rights: The Limits of Compliance* (Philadelphia: University of Pennsylvania Press, 1999); Rosemary Foot, *Rights Beyond Borders: The Global Community and the Struggle over Human Rights in China* (Oxford: Oxford University Press, 2001); and Na Jiang, *China and International Human Rights: Harsh Punishments in the Context of the International Covenant on Civil and Political Rights* (New York: Springer, 2014).

[8] For similar observations, see Yuchao Zhu, "China and International Human Rights Diplomacy," *China: An International Journal* 9, no. 2 (September 2011): 220, and Rana Mitter, "An Uneasy Engagement: Chinese Ideas of Justice and Order in Historical Perspective," in *Order and Justice in International Relations*, eds. Rosemary Foot, John Lewis Gaddis, and Andrew Hurrell (Oxford: Oxford University Press, 2003), 227.

[9] For a scholarly account, see Eva Pils, *Human Rights in China: A Social Practice in the Shadows of Authoritarianism* (Oxford: Polity Press, 2018).

[10] For reasons countries participate in the human rights regime, see Oona Hathaway, "Do Human Rights Treaties Make a Difference?" *Yale Law Journal* 111, no. 8: 1935–2042; Emilie Hafner-Burton and Kiyoteru Tsutsui, "Human Rights in a Globalizing World: The Paradox of Empty Promises," *American Journal of Sociology* 110, no. 5 (1373–14110; Heather Smith-Cannoy, *Insincere Commitments: Human Rights Treaties, Abusive States, Citizen Activism* (Washington DC: Georgetown University Press, 2012), and James Vreeland, "Political Institutions and Human Rights: Why Dictatorships Enter into the United Nations Convention against Torture," *International Organizations* 62: 65–101.

the human rights regime. As scholar Rosemary Foot put it, unlike other international regimes, "participation in the rights regime poses particular threats to an authoritarian government because of the domestic political transformation that full adherence to international standards entails."[11] Yet, rather than shunning the human rights regime, Beijing has ratified five of the seven major human rights instruments; contributed to the drafting of a number of human rights treaties; joined the United Nations Commission on Human Rights (UNCHR), now the UNHRC or HRC; and submitted to international human rights monitoring by participating in the Universal Periodic Review and providing reports to a number of human rights treaty bodies.

This book also contributes to existing scholarship. It updates the literature on international regimes by applying a fresh approach and considering China's behavior using a spectrum of possible state roles, including maker, promoter, taker, constrainer, and breaker. It also adds to our study of China's multilateral behavior and the human rights regime. I examine the PRC's role in the context of three distinct case studies that include the drafting of the Convention against Torture (CAT) and the Optional Protocol to the Convention against Torture (OPCAT), negotiations to replace the UN Commission on Human Rights with a new body, and participation in the International Labour Organization's (ILO) Conference Committee on the Application of Standards (CCAS), a committee that holds states accountable to ratified conventions.

I argue that China played varied roles in the regime including acting as a taker and a constrainer during CAT and OPCAT, respectively, a constrainer during the establishment of the HRC, and a taker in the ILO's CCAS. My findings also unveil PRC strategies and its relative success in instances when it acted as a constrainer. In order to explain these varied roles, I argue that China's posture was influenced by four explanatory factors that included the PRC leadership's animosity toward external human rights scrutiny, Chinese officials' concern with its international image, the Chinese government's ideas that prioritize state sovereignty and the import of local conditions over the regime's authority and scope, and the Chinese government's degree of familiarity with the human rights regime. By doing so, this book not only documents the PRC's actions and positions, it also provides insight into the how and why of China's behavior. The year 2017, where my research concludes, is a natural inflection point, especially since, as noted earlier, there are

---

[11] Foot, *Rights Beyond Borders*, 2.

indications that the PRC is shifting toward a more assertive and confident posture and departing from Premiere Deng Xiaoping's dictum to "keep a low profile." Consequently, observers warn that "Beijing is making significant headway in upending international norms on political and human rights."[12] These trends make it an opportune time to assess the PRC's role in and impact on the regime, the factors that incline the PRC toward a more cooperative posture, and the issues and principles that the PRC has championed or resisted within the regime.

This chapter is organized as follows. The next section defines the possible roles a state can play within a regime and discusses these roles in the context of China's interactions with the human rights regime. I then discuss the explanatory factors that best account for the PRC's posture toward the regime. The final section introduces the chapters and summarizes my findings.

International Regimes and State Roles

International regimes have been defined as arising from converging state expectations about particular issues. As scholar Stephen Krasner defined them, regimes comprise "principles, norms, rules, and decision-making procedures around which actor expectations converge in a given issue-area."[13] There are some key differences between the human rights regime and other international regimes that are worth noting. First, the human rights regime does not govern an issue where reciprocity is a critical feature and lack of compliance can tangibly damage other states' economic or security interests. Consequently, arguments about the regime processes that potentially shape state beliefs, expectations, and understanding of acceptable behavior that are largely based on mutual

[12] Economy, "Xi's Assertive Superpower Plans," *The Wall Street Journal*, July 19, 2018. See also Carl Minzer, *End of an Era: How China's How Authoritarian Revival Is Undermining Its Rise* (Oxford: Oxford University Press, 2018).

[13] Stephen D. Krasner, ed., *International Regimes* (Ithaca, New York: Cornell University Press, 1983), 2. Krasner elaborated that "[p]rinciples are beliefs of fact, causation and rectitude. Norms are standards of behavior defined in terms of rights and obligations. Rules are specific prescription or proscriptions for action. Decision-making procedures are prevailing practices for making and implementing collective choice." See also Thomas Risse and Kathryn Sikkink, "The Socialization of International Human Rights Norms into Domestic Practices: Introduction," in *The Power of Human Rights: International Norms and Domestic Change*, eds. Thomas Risse, Stephen C. Ropp, and Kathryn Sikkink (Cambridge: Cambridge University Press, 1999), 20–25, and Katrin Kinzelbach, "Resisting the Power of Human Rights: The People's Republic of China," in *The Persistent Power of Human Rights: From Commitment to Compliance*, eds. Thomas Risse, Stephen C. Ropp, and Kathryn Sikkink (Cambridge: Cambridge University Press, 2013).

gains or benefit may be less applicable. For example, whether the PRC complies with human rights norms does not affect other states' interests directly – although noncompliance may ease normative human rights pressure on other countries. Thus, arguments about the power of international regimes that stress state cooperation, reciprocal gains, and interstate trust may be less salient to the field of human rights and the human rights regime might be less powerful in altering state behavior and beliefs.[14] At the same time, it should be noted that because the human rights regime does not rely on reciprocity as other regimes do such as trade and arms control, noncompliance alone is unlikely to destroy the regime. Second, the human rights regime lacks strong enforcement tools and its power is based more on symbolism, reputation, and moral suasion. Finally, a number of scholars argue that the human rights regime remains highly contested and may even be undergoing challenges, which might provide states with greater latitude in their role and behavior within the regime, including making it easier to pursue changes toward the human rights regime.[15]

Before discussing state roles vis-à-vis the regime, it is critical to establish what constitutes the core of the human rights regime. While international human rights protection can be defined broadly to encompass other aspects of humanitarian and human rights protection, including action by the UN Security Council related to intervention, peacekeeping, and the responsibility to protect, and other international bodies that govern migration and refugees, such as the International Organization for Migration, I focus primarily on the UN's human rights bodies that are aimed at safeguarding the rights outlined in the Universal Declaration of Human Rights. Thus, I argue that there are four core pillars of the human rights regime: an interstate forum where states can debate human rights, take collective action, such as adopting treaties and declarations, and address country-specific human rights abuses; universally accepted norms and standards articulated in the Universal Declaration of Human Rights and international human rights treaties that elaborate and specify those rights; treaty bodies that monitor state compliance with ratified human rights treaties and issue findings; and the system of special procedures, which features independent experts focused on particular human rights issues, such as human rights defenders, torture, and religious freedom. The totality of the human rights regime includes other

---

[14] These arguments are most often associated with Robert Keohane and Joseph Nye and the neoliberal institutionalist school.
[15] Philip Alston, "The Populist Challenge to Human Rights," *Journal of Human Rights* 9 (2017): 1–15, and Stephen Hopgood, *The Endtimes of Human Rights* (Cornell: Cornell University Press, 2013).

Maker	Promoter	Taker	Constrainer	Breaker

Figure 1.1 Possible state roles

complementary bodies and mechanisms, such as the Office of the High Commissioner for Human Rights, who serves as the UN's chief official for human rights, and the HRC's Universal Periodic Review process. Yet, I define the above four pillars as the core of the regime because of the unique role they play in holding states accountable, making human rights specific and actionable and preventing or halting human rights violations. My intention is not to demote other elements of the regime but to provide a definition of the core of the regime that helps differentiate among the five regime roles states play and helps situate state action vis-à-vis the regime. For example, a state intent on acting as a breaker would take aim at these core components of the regime.

While there is ongoing scholarly debate about the power of international regimes to alter state behavior, states can be understood as playing a primary role in establishing regimes as well as altering them. In this vein, Krasner conceived that states can play a number of roles toward the regime, including "maker," "breaker," or "taker."[16] I borrow from Krasner's typologies and expand on them by developing other possible state roles, including "constrainer," in which a state seeks to weaken the regime or prevent it from developing further and "promoter," whereby a state introduces reforms to strengthen and expand the regime. In determining which of these roles to play states are likely driven by a variety of factors, including their beliefs and ideas or self-interest. The advantage of applying these typologies to this inquiry is that it helps us view PRC behavior along a spectrum that is attentive to state agency and captures not just the regime's ability to alter state behavior but also the ways a state might seek to influence a regime. Because most international regimes comprise a variety of bodies and mechanisms, it is possible that a state might simultaneously play different roles in various parts of a regime. The roles as presented in this section are ideal categories with actual state behavior likely running along a continuum. In some cases, drawing a distinction is difficult as differences among these roles might be subtle. The spectrum of these roles is represented in Figure 1.1 and explicated in the following section.

[16] Stephen D. Krasner, "United States Commercial and Monetary Policy: Unraveling the Paradox of External Strength and Internal Weakness," in *Between Power and Plenty: Foreign Economic Policies of Advanced Industrial States*, ed. Peter J. Katzenstein (Madison, Wisconsin: The University of Wisconsin Press, 1983), 52.

Makers

At one end of the spectrum are regime makers. These states are strong supporters of the regime and are therefore willing to expend the effort to create the regime. A maker state may need to establish an entirely new regime or because the process of building a regime is lengthy maker states might be involved in later stages after some initial regime components have already been instituted. For example, even though the UN had adopted a Declaration against Torture in the mid-1970s, Sweden acted as a maker of the regime by proposing CAT several years later and advancing a draft primarily because of its conviction that combatting torture required the force of an internationally legally binding instrument. While promoter states, which are defined in the next section, pursue more incremental changes and improvements to the regime, maker states propose substantively novel and robust additions to the international regime.

This is a demanding role that requires leadership, negotiating and lobbying skills, diplomatic experience, and familiarity with the international system. Maker states likely also need a degree of credibility among other nations. Costa Rica's activities as a maker with regard to OPCAT are illustrative of the challenges of this role. In order to secure the passage of OPCAT, Costa Rica prodded the UN to take action on a proposed draft, engaged in shrewd negotiating with states, and lobbied others to win support for adoption. As human rights scholars have documented, the states that spearheaded the creation of the human rights regime had to build international consensus over a number of years as they exhorted and persuaded others of the necessity of constructing the regime and worked with other similarly minded countries.[17] A maker state might continue its efforts to strengthen the regime by acting as a promoter once the work of erecting the core of the regime has been completed. Given the effort and initiative required, makers would likely be motivated by a strong commitment to the principles underlying the regime that could be based on beliefs and values or material self-interest, or a combination of the two.[18] Unlike other regimes, makers of the human rights regime do not necessarily have to be geopolitically important or possess particular material resources, such as advanced weaponry or a large domestic market, and small states have shown a remarkable degree of activism in creating the human rights regime.

---

[17] See, for example, Glendon, *A World Made New,* 2001.
[18] Stephen Krasner, "Sovereignty, Regimes and Human Rights," in *Regime Theory and International Relations,* ed. Volker Rittberger (Oxford: Clarendon Press, 1993), 152.

Some scholars, particularly those who subscribe to realist-inspired views, have predicted that rising powers like China will seek to alter international regimes in accord with their interests and agenda.[19] In contrast to these arguments, in the case studies that form this book, China did not act as a maker and tended toward lower-profile roles. However, as noted previously, there are indications that the PRC may be emerging as a more prominent actor and for much of the period covered by this book China was still only a rising power.

Promoter

An additional category not included in Krasner's typologies is "promoter." Like makers, states that act as promoters are supportive of the regime and they work to strengthen and further develop it, including expanding the regime's breadth and authority. For example, in 2009, the thirty-seven countries that sponsored HRC resolution 12/2, which called for greater state cooperation with UN human rights mechanisms, acted as promoters of the regime. However, in contrast to makers, the commitment, activism, and effort of promoter states is more measured. While they might not be sufficiently motivated to do the heavy lifting of constructing the regime, such as creating new bodies or norms, they might speak in favor of it and urge other states to back the regime. During the establishment phase of a regime, they could support maker states in their quest to construct the regime but would not play as active a role. The line between makers and promoters can be somewhat blurry as the intent of their activities is similar. One key distinction is that makers are focused on more momentous additions to the regime rather than merely strengthening the existing architecture. For example, the activities of the EU and Organization of Islamic Conference states that worked to secure passage of a 2018 HRC resolution on Myanmar can be classified as makers of the regime because the resolution stipulated the creation of an international, impartial, and independent mechanism

---

[19] See, for example, A.F.K. Organski and Jacek Kugler, *The War Ledger* (Chicago: University of Chicago Press, 1980); Robert Gilpin, *War and Change in World Politics* (Cambridge: Cambridge University Press, 1981); and Paul Kennedy, *The Rise and Fall of the Great Powers* (Vintage Books, New York, 1989). The underlying ontological orientation of much of this work sees rising powers as dissatisfied with the existing system. Examples of China-specific work include Aaron L. Friedberg, *A Contest for Supremacy: China, America, and the Struggle for Mastery in Asia* (New York: W. W. Norton & Company, 2011); Michael Pillsbury, *The Hundred-year Marathon: China's Secret Strategy to Replace America as the Global Superpower* (New York: Henry Holt and Company, 2015); and Martin Jacques, *When China Rules the World: the End of the Western World and the Birth of a New Global Order* (New York: The Penguin Press, 2009).

(IM) to "collect, consolidate, preserve and analyse evidence of the most serious international crimes and violations of international law" in light of the severe treatment of the Rohingya, a Muslim minority group in Myanmar: 2018 HRC resolution on.[20] This IM marked the first time the regime had created this type of body and tasked it with preparing files to facilitate and expedite fair and independent future criminal proceedings.[21]

After a regime has been created, promoter states back strengthening the regime, such as additions or changes to reinforce, expand, and fortify the regime. Along these lines, in the UNHRC, Norway has spearheaded a resolution affirming the role of human rights defenders, and also extending the mandate of the special rapporteur on the situation of human rights defenders.[22] Promoters could also ensure that sufficient resources are provided to keep the regime functioning effectively. For example, a promoter of the UN's human rights special procedures would ensure that this part of the regime receives adequate funding. Promoters do not need to possess the same resources as makers, such as diplomatic skill, but will often have some means to bolster the regime or they might cooperate with other states. For example, Ireland, which has championed the role of civil society, worked with a core group of countries, including Chile, Japan, Sierra Leone, and Tunisia, to secure passage of a 2016 HRC resolution endorsing the role of independent civil society in protecting human rights. The PRC did not act as a promoter of the human rights regime in any of the case studies examined in this book.

Taker

Regime takers are satisfied with the regime and accept existing regime arrangements, including procedures as well as substantive norms. Even if they have a weak commitment to the regime or are not comfortable with particular aspects of the regime, these states are generally content with the status quo and not motivated to pursue change. Thus, states acting as takers do not challenge the regime and their behavior is generally in

---

[20] Universal Rights Group, *The Human Rights Council in 2018: Leadership, Resolve and Cooperation at the UN's Main Human Rights Body* (Geneva: Universal Rights Group, 2019): yourhrc.org/wp-content/uploads/2018/12/yourHrc_end_of_year_report_2018. pdf

[21] "UN Independent International Fact-Finding Mission on Myanmar Advances Accountability and Initiates New Investigations," UN Office of the High Commissioner for Human Rights, March 14, 2019, www.ohchr.org/EN/NewsEvents/ Pages/DisplayNews.aspx?NewsID=24334&LangID=E.

[22] Interview with European diplomat, June 22, 2016, Geneva.

compliance with the regime – at least procedurally if not substantively. Some taker states might comply only minimally, such as fulfilling procedural requirements for reporting, without conforming on a more substantive level. As described in Chapter 3, China's behavior with regard to CAT shows that it generally met reporting requirements but domestic practices remain riddled with the problem of torture. Although this might seem to be the most passive of the five roles, takers must still devote resources to bringing their practices into compliance. Some states may adopt the role of taker because the regime does not harm their interests or pose a threat to them even if they are not enthusiastic supporters. Scholars of international regimes theorize that in order to avoid controversy small states and newcomers to the regime are more likely to adopt the posture of a taker.[23]

Takers might also benefit from the arrangements under the regime and may even adjust their policies in order to maximize their gains.[24] During the establishment phase of the regime, taker states would be neutral actors who would not detract from efforts to create the regime but would also not be prone to assist in the working of erecting it. In both the drafting of CAT and the proceedings of the ILO's CCAS, the PRC acted as a taker. However, even as a taker in ILO's CCAS, as detailed in Chapter 5, the PRC's actions did not always uphold the principles underlying the regime as it used this venue to defend allies coming under scrutiny for reported labor rights violations. As demonstrated by the PRC's behavior in the CCAS, delineating the border between takers and constrainers can be difficult in the case of a state that accepts extant procedures and mechanisms yet manipulates them. As mentioned above, takers might be lukewarm toward the regime but are still not inclined to pursue reform. Also, as Beijing did, takers might instrumentally adjust their behavior to benefit from the regime's arrangements. Because these typologies run along a spectrum, Beijing's CCAS actions can be viewed as edging very close to the behavior of a constrainer. China has often sought to give the veneer of accepting the extant regime while still failing

---

[23] Oran R. Young, "International Regimes: Toward a New Theory of Institutions," *World Politics* 39, no. 1 (October 1986), 120, and Alastair Iain Johnston, *Social States: China in International Institutions, 1980–2000* (Princeton: Princeton University Press, 2008), 33.

[24] Krasner, "United States Commercial and Monetary Policy," 52. The point about benefiting from a regime is similar to Kim's observation that China adopted a "system-exploiting" posture. See Samuel Kim, "China's International Organization Behavior," in *Chinese Foreign Policy: Theory and Practice*, eds. Thomas W. Robinson and David Shambaugh (Oxford: Clarendon Press), 46, and Samuel Kim, "Thinking Globally in Post-Mao China," *Journal of Peace Research* 27, no. 2 (May 1990): 193.

to conform and even when it has accepted the regime this book shows that the substance of its behavior did not always uphold the regime.

Constrainer

States that act to limit or circumscribe the regime can be described as constrainers. They are dissatisfied with the regime yet are not completely opposed to it. A constrainer resists attempts to strengthen the regime or seeks to alter the existing regime by rolling back the regime's authority or detracting from existing mechanisms and procedures. A key difference between constrainers and breakers is that the former attempts to introduce more limited change by working within the existing regime while leaving the core of the regime intact. For example, constrainer states might seek changes to rules and procedures or thwart the application of particular procedures, but would leave the underlying normative framework and the regime's central mechanisms and bodies unscathed. In some cases, constrainers will seek to conceal their behavior. For example, as outlined in Chapter 4, beginning in the late 1990s, a group of authoritarian countries within the UNCHR proposed changes to the regime under the guise of reform yet the thrust of their proposals would have enervated the regime. Prior to Xi Jinping's assumption of power, Beijing's penchant was similar in seeking to obscure its aim of constraining the regime.

In order to be effective, a constrainer must be able to affect changes within the system or succeed in impeding the application of particular procedures and rules. If its influence is limited, a constrainer might work in cooperation with other similarly minded states.[25] A constrainer state might aspire to results more akin to a breaker but might determine that it is more realistic to pursue gradual modifications, which may be the case with China. As shown in the subsequent chapters, during both the drafting of OPCAT and the establishment of the HRC, China acted as a constrainer as it sought not only to prevent strengthening the regime but also to weaken it. During the Institution-Building phase of the HRC, which spanned 2006 through 2007, Beijing clearly acted as a constrainer as it attempted to hamper the HRC's ability to pass resolutions focused on a single country. As will be explained below, regime breakers are more extreme in their actions and intentions. It is possible that over time a state could continually pursue constraining actions that cumulatively have a much more deleterious effect than initially obvious.

---

[25] Oran R. Young, "International Regimes: Problems in Concept Formation," *World Politics* 32, no. 3 (April 1980), 354.

Breaker

Breaker states do not support the regime and their dissatisfaction drives them to challenge or oppose it with the intent of destroying it. This is a challenging role since breakers are attempting to unravel international consensus on a given issue area. A breaker state might begin by violating the regime's rules and procedures. Yet, unlike other regimes, such as those governing the nonproliferation of weapons, a state's noncompliance in the human rights regime might not be as damaging to the international regime. Breakers might continue to participate in the regime until they have succeeded in developing an alternative to it or in destroying the original regime. In addition to noncompliance or non-cooperation, a breaker would mount more direct efforts to delegitimize or discredit the regime, particularly voicing strong opposition or attempting to start a competing regime. To be successful a breaker needs to be able to persuade a sufficient number of states of the rightness of its position.

Given the extent of the changes a breaker would pursue, this is a high bar and a state would have to be significantly discontent to venture into this territory. Many states might be pacified with constraining the regime. Unlike constrainers, a regime breaker seeks more extensive changes to undermine, and in some cases eviscerate, the regime. Delineating the boundary between constrainer and breaker is a hard call and is largely a matter of the degree of activism, the extent of the state's resistance, and the extent to which its proposed modifications detract from the regime and unravel the core of the regime. Breakers and constrainers both share a dissatisfaction with the status quo. Surprisingly, even when the PRC came under intense scrutiny from different parts of the human rights regime after 1989, in the case studies comprising this book it did not act as a breaker. As will be discussed in the next section, this may be due to the tempering influence of some of the explanatory factors. Moreover, China may have been satisfied with attempting to constrain the regime.

Explaining PRC Posture toward the Human Rights Regimes

While the PRC's role varied between taker toward CAT and the ILO's Conference Committee to a constrainer vis-à-vis OPCAT and the UNHRC, the factors that determined its role remained constant, and included the Chinese government's fixation with averting international criticism of its human rights violations, its concern with a positive international image, the Chinese leadership's views that favored state sovereignty and the importance of local conditions over the international regime's authority and scope, and its degree of familiarity with the human rights regime. Aside from these four determinative factors, I offer a secondary factor – the PRC's ability and willingness to cooperate with other countries – as another influence on its conduct. I describe this as a secondary factor because unlike the four explanatory factors, which strongly determined the PRC's particular role, the influence of this secondary factor was much more subtle. While it did not dictate the role Beijing adopted, it had two important effects as it moderated the PRC's behavior and reinforced its human rights views. Because of the limited influence of nonstate actors in China these variables center on the Chinese government. These factors and the secondary influence are expanded more fully in the following section and their relative weight in each of the case studies is discussed more thoroughly in Chapter 6.

The Chinese Government's Antipathy for International Scrutiny of Its Human Rights Practices

The strongest explanatory factor shaping China's posture toward the regime was its deep-seated distaste for scrutiny of its record. Reflecting the depth of this concern, the PRC reacted vigorously when attention was directed at its human rights record and, as outlined in Chapter 2, it worked to avoid, counter, and prevent UN resolutions, statements or expressions of concern from other countries, and critical mention by UN officials and experts. It might seem obvious to state that countries dislike human rights scrutiny or criticism, but the CCP leadership is unusually sensitive and reacts strongly to deflect and push back against negative attention. This highly reactive response is due in part to the unique threat that external human rights criticism represents for authoritarian countries like China. For the Chinese leadership in particular, this distaste for scrutiny reflects not only reputational concerns but also their ongoing perception that negative international human rights attention could damage the PRC's material interests, domestic stability, and the CCP's continued rule.[26]

---

[26] These image concerns might be grounded in a Chinese cultural emphasis on face or *mianzi,* which refers to a sense of dignity, prestige, social standing, status, respect, or how one is perceived by others. Interview with Chinese international relations scholar, June 11, 2012, Beijing, China; interview with PRC Ministry of Foreign Affairs, June 6, 2012, Beijing, China; interview with Chinese scholar, July 12, 2013, Beijing, China; and interview with Chinese scholar, June 2, 2012, Shanghai, China. On Chinese "face" see, Lu Xun, "On 'Face,'" translated by Yang Xianyi and Gladys Yang, *Selected Works of Lu*

In international relations, while concern with reputation or image is often associated with social constructivism, I argue that in addition to concerns about the way other nations view it, the PRC's aversion to human rights scrutiny is also related to economic and strategic interests. The Chinese leadership's experience when they faced international condemnation after the 1989 Tiananmen crackdown taught them that a negative international human rights image could have a direct bearing on their material interests. After Tiananmen, the PRC faced diplomatic isolation and sanctions that resulted in political and economic losses as China suffered a two-year decline in its credit rating, foreign investment, export orders, and tourism; a weakening of its negotiating position on a range of issues, such as trade, resulting in Chinese concessions on market access and intellectual property rights; diminished opportunities to raise concerns about Taiwan, which weakened the PRC's ability to block arms sales to Taiwan; and the possibility of losing US Most Favored Nation trade status.[27] It has been estimated that China lost $11 billion in bilateral aid during the four years after the June 4 crackdown.[28] Prior to 1989, the PRC had been attentive to its external image but after 1989, human rights criticism became a lightning rod that the Chinese leadership responded to with vehemence. This variable became much more powerful after Tiananmen. Although the PRC overcame the sanctions and stigma of Tiananmen and is a rising power that has experienced robust economic growth and expanding political influence, Chinese leaders likely recall their weakened position after Tiananmen, and view international human rights scrutiny as potentially damaging to PRC national interests. Even though UN statements and resolutions are declaratory and carry no specific sanctions or material penalties, Beijing's vehement opposition and efforts to prevent them indicates the Chinese leadership's concerns about the ramifications of negative human rights attention.

Hsun (Beijing: Foreign Language Press 1959):129–132; and David Yau-Fai Ho, "On the Concept of Face," *American Journal of Sociology* 81, no. 4 (1976): 867–884.

[27] See Ming Wan, *Human Rights in Chinese Foreign Relations: Defining and Defending National Interests* (Philadelphia: University of Pennsylvania Press, 2001), 7; Andrew Nathan, "China and the International Human Rights Regime," in *China Joins the World: Progress and Prospects*, eds. Elizabeth Economy and Michel Oksenberg (New York: Council on Foreign Relations Press, 1998), 147; and James Seymour, "Human Rights in Chinese Foreign Relations," in *China and the World: Chinese Foreign Policy Faces the New Millennium*, ed. Samuel S. Kim (New York: Westview Press, 1998): 225.

[28] Rosemary Foot, "China and the Tian'anmen Bloodshed of June 1989," in *Foreign Policy: Theories, Actors, Cases*, 2nd edition, eds. Steve Smith, Amelia Hadfield and Tim Dunne (Oxford: Oxford University Press, 2012), 339.

The CCP leadership likely views international human rights criticism as a potential threat to their continued rule for several reasons.[29] First, the Chinese leadership's legitimacy is largely dependent on continued economic growth, which has largely been driven by foreign economic relationships – the very relationships that could be jeopardized by a blemished human rights image as happened following the Tiananmen Square crackdown. Second, as a one-party authoritarian political system, the CCP leadership finds external criticism threatening because they believe it could weaken their political legitimacy and embolden domestic opposition.[30] As a Chinese scholar suggested, "[T]he Chinese leadership fears that something small, like international criticism, could lead to something big such as domestic challenges to its rule, and that 'external criticism could mobilize domestic civil society.'"[31] The Chinese government has continually framed external human rights scrutiny as damaging to internal stability and cohesion.[32] For example, the Ministry of State Security has characterized human rights attention from Western countries, particularly the United States, as intended "to cultivate so-called democratic forces within socialist countries and to stimulate and organize political opposition using catchwords like 'democracy,' 'liberty,' or 'human rights.'"[33] In a similar vein, in response to Secretary Clinton's

---

[29] Because the CCP government is unaccustomed to domestic criticism, it might also be more sensitive to external human rights scrutiny. Interview with PRC scholar, July 9, 2013, Beijing, China.

[30] On the CCP government's sense of vulnerability, see Robert Weatherley, *Politics in China Since 1949: Legitimizing Authoritarian Rule* (Routledge: New York, 2006) and Andrew J. Nathan and Andrew Scobell, *China's Search for Security* (New York: Colombia University Press, 2012), 342.

[31] Interview with Chinese scholar, June 9, 2012, Macau, China. Similar points also made by other scholars, including interview with PRC scholar, May 26, 2012, Chengdu, China. Along these lines, the PRC's spending on internal "stability maintenance" exceeds its defense budget. Michael Martina, "China Withholds Full Domestic-security Spending Figure," *Reuters*, March 4, 2014, www.reuters.com/article/us-china-parliament-security/china-withholds-full-domestic-security-spending-figure-idUSBREA240B720140305, accessed March 29, 2018.

[32] As scholar Robert Weatherley put it, "The worldwide condemnation of this event … convinced the CCP that the outside world … was trying to conquer China once again … Instead of seeking to change China from the barrel of a gun, the West was attempting to change China from the inside by imposing an alien political culture and belief system, namely Western democracy and rights, on to a country with a completely different way of thinking and behaving." Robert Weatherley, *Making China Strong: The Role of Nationalism in Chinese Thinking on Democracy and Human Rights* (London: Palgrave McMillan, 2014), 142.

[33] Zhang Liang (comp.), Andrew Nathan and Perry Link, eds. *The Tiananmen Papers: The Chinese Government's Decision to Use Force Against Their Own People—In Their Own Words* (New York: Public Affairs, 2001), 338. For an example of a PRC statement to this effect, see PRC Embassy, "US Report Distorts Human Rights Status in China," news release, October 10, 2003, www.china-embassy.org/eng/zt/zgrq/t36687, accessed July 5, 2018.

2011 remarks raising concern about human rights, the PRC retorted that this was an attempt to foster unrest in China and "alleged that U.S. human rights concern was intended to split and suppress China."[34] The effort Chinese leaders put into muffling human rights criticism and the striking patterns of reciprocal protection with other countries outlined in Chapter 5 further testify to the PRC's deep sensitivity in this regard.

In this book's case studies, the desire to avoid negative human rights attention affected Chinese behavior in several distinct ways. The PRC was particularly inclined to act as a taker when the regime did not focus on its human rights record or a particular body or mechanism lacked the means to employ selective scrutiny on individual countries. Consequently, because the ILO's Committee on the Application of Standards paid minimal attention to China's labor rights violations, the PRC was content to accept the CCAS's arrangements for monitoring. Conversely, the PRC acted as a constrainer when the regime spotlighted its human rights abuses or had the potential to do so. As elaborated in Chapter 4, the PRC acted as a constrainer toward the HRC and staked out a provocative position in an attempt to weaken the international regime's use of country-specific resolutions. Along these lines, the PRC also appeared to respond most strenuously to bodies and mechanisms that enjoyed a more prominent stature within the UN and that generated greater public attention. For example, although it had an aversion to other forms of human rights scrutiny, such as treaty body reviews or negative attention from the special procedures, the PRC was most antagonistic toward negative attention in the UN's political human rights bodies, which comprise China's peers. In particular, PRC leaders particularly abhorred UNCHR resolutions – arguably the strongest form of censure in the human rights regime.

Chinese Concern with Its International Image

The PRC's posture toward the international human rights regime was also strongly influenced by a drive to cultivate a positive international image. This preoccupation with image is somewhat related to the first explanatory factor, the PRC's efforts to avert human rights scrutiny, but encompasses much more. It captures at a much broader level the PRC's efforts to burnish its international reputation and project an image as an

---

[34] "China Hits Out at US Human Rights Comments," *People's Daily Online*, May 14, 2011, www.english.people.com.cn/90001/90776/90883/7379780.html, accessed March 29, 2018.

engaged, agreeable, and cooperative international actor that is in good standing in international regimes.[35] This objective was partly based on the belief that a positive global image was strategically useful – even if the benefits might be diffuse or indirect.[36] Image as defined here is closely related to the concept of status or reputation, which captures the way in which a state is viewed by other states.[37] While other countries also value a positive image, PRC leaders have shown a particular sensitivity to theirs and have devoted significant resources and energy into projecting a positive image. As one observer put it, "Without claiming that China cares *more* about its image than other states, it is reasonable to assert that image considerations weigh heavily on the minds of Chinese decision-makers."[38] China's image concerns appear to be fueled by its years as a pariah state in the 1950s and 1960s, its experience following the Tiananmen Square crackdown, an aspiration to great responsible power status, and attempts to assuage concerns about its rise.[39]

In an effort to portray itself as cooperative and agreeable, beginning in the era of reform and opening, the PRC stepped up its engagement with a variety of international regimes as it became involved in nearly every international policy arena and made some commitments, such as acceding to certain arms control requirements and becoming a supporter and

---

[35] This is idea is related to Fung's use of the term status. See Courtney Fung, *China and Intervention at the UN Security Council: Reconciling Status* (Oxford: Oxford University Press, 2019).

[36] Simon Rabinovitch, "The Rise of an Image-Conscious China," *China Security* 4, no. 3 (Summer 2008). The importance Beijing attaches to a positive image was also noted by a PRC diplomat. Interview with PRC Ministry of Foreign Affairs official, June 6, 2012, Beijing, China. A Chinese scholar noted that image may have become important to the PRC leadership because they believe "that they can best achieve their goals through a positive image." Interview with Chinese international relations scholar, June 8, 2012, Guangzhou, China. Johnston and Evans pointed out that image can have instrumental value, even if the benefits are diffuse and vague. Alastair Ian Johnston and Paul Evans, "China and Multilateral Security Institutions," in *Engaging China: The Management of an Emerging Power* (Routledge: New York, 1999), 251–253.

[37] See, for example, Johnston, *Social States*, 90–91. Premier Deng Xiaoping highlighted this concern on the eve of Gorbachev's June 1989 visit when the Tiananmen Square protests were growing and the welcoming ceremonies for Gorbachev had to be diverted to another location. Deng stated, "We have to maintain our international image. What do we look like if the Square is a mess?" Zhang, *The Tiananmen Papers*, 148.

[38] Rabinovitch, "The Rise of an Image-Conscious China," 33.

[39] See, for example, Samuel Kim, *China, the United Nations and World Order* (Princeton: Princeton University Press, 1979), 117–125, 196, and 210, and Johnston, *Social States*, 90–91. After 1989, the PRC created an external communications office in 1990, sponsored cultural exchange activities, and hired public relations firms. Rabinovitch, "The Rise of an Image-Conscious China," 34 and 37. On aspiration to great responsible power status, see also Rosemary Foot, "Chinese Power and the Idea of a Responsible State," *The China Journal* 45 (January 2001): 8 and 15.

participant in international peacekeeping.[40] In the human rights regime, Chinese officials devoted significant energy, resources, and attention in trying to depict the PRC as a supportive and compliant actor, even though its record on substantive conformity and cooperation is deeply marred. Along these lines, its 1991 White Paper claimed that "[t]he Chinese government has always submitted reports on the implementation of the related conventions, and seriously and earnestly performed the obligations it has undertaken."[41] In later years, the PRC White Papers also highlighted that "to date, [the PRC has] acceded to 21 international human rights conventions, and has taken every measure to honor its obligations under those conventions" and claimed that during the HRC's Universal Periodic Review process it participated in a "serious and highly-responsible attitude [and] gave a detailed account of its human rights accomplishments."[42]

In the case studies examined as part of this book, this image concern had a moderating effect as the PRC tended toward a less assertive and more cooperative role. As outlined in Chapters 3 and 4, respectively, even when it acted as a regime constrainer as it did during the creation of OPCAT and the UNHRC, Beijing attempted to do so without taking a prominent position or drawing attention to its efforts. Moreover, in

---

[40] A number of scholars have pointed to the effect of image as resulting in more cooperative and restrained behavior. See Margaret M. Pearson, "China in Geneva: Lessons from Chan's Early Years in the World Trade Organization," in *New Directions in the Study of China's Foreign Policy*, eds. Alastair Iain Johnston and Robert S. Ross (Stanford, California: Stanford University Press, 2006); Johnston and Evans, "China's Engagement with Multilateral Security Institutions," 248–249 and 252–253; Michael Swaine and Alastair Iain Johnston, "China and Arms Control Institutions," in *China Joins the World: Progress and Prospects*, eds. Elizabeth Economy and Michel Oksenberg (New York: Council on Foreign Relations, 1999), 108 and 115; and Alastair Iain Johnston, "International Structures and Chinese Foreign Policy," in *China and the World: Chinese Foreign Policy Faces the New Millennium*, 4th edition, ed. Samuel S. Kim (Boulder, Colorado: Westview, 1998), 77.

[41] Information Office of the State Council, *Human Rights in China 1991* (Beijing: Information Office of the State Council, 1991), section X. Similar point made by interview with PRC scholar, June 13, 2012, Beijing, China.

[42] Information Office of the State Council, *Progress in China's Human Rights Cause in 2003* (Beijing: Information Office of the State Council, 2004), section VIII and Information Office of the State Council, *Human Rights in China 2010* (Beijing: Information Office of the State Council, 2010), section VII. For similar statements see; "Opening Statement by Ambassador Li Baodong, Head of the Chinese Delegation at the Fourth Session of the HRC Working Group on UPR, 2009/02/10," Permanent Mission of the People's Republic of China to the United Nations at Geneva, www.china-un.ch/eng/hom/ t536333.htm, accessed July 6, 2018, and "Statement by H.E. Ambassador Liu Zhenmin, Deputy Permanent Representative of China to the United Nations, at the Third Committee of the 64th Session of the General Assembly on Report of the Human Rights Council, 2009/10/29," Permanent Mission of the PRC to the UN, www.china-un .org/eng/chinaandun/socialhr/rqwt/t623503.htm, accessed September 1, 2014.

several instances, a desire to avoid damage to its international image also appeared to cause Beijing to back away from a controversial or insistent position – or venturing into the territory of a regime breaker. Thus, in 1984, during the final stages of the drafting of CAT, image concerns caused PRC officials to retreat from their opposition to universal jurisdiction, and therefore preserve the PRC's role as a taker. Similarly, the PRC abandoned efforts to introduce restrictive rules to the use of country resolutions during the UNHRC Institution-Building Process in order to avert damage to its image. Thus, this explanatory factor prevented China from being more obstructionist or engaging in the kind of behavior that a regime breaker might display.

The Beijing Government's Human Rights Preferences and Beliefs

The Chinese government's preexisting ideas about the delineation between the state and the international human rights regime strongly influenced the PRC's posture toward the regime.[43] This seems like an obvious statement to make because ideas matter. However, unlike other international regimes, where there is evidence that the PRC's ideas shifted and became more receptive to international norms, its views on international human rights monitoring have proven to be less malleable. Even prior to the establishment of the PRC in 1949, China had its own discourse and conception of human rights, and despite the CCP government's growing involvement with the international human rights regime, it has retained key tenets of its own thinking.[44] In particular, two key elements of the Chinese conception about the nexus between the international human rights regime and the state have proven to be deeply ingrained and have played a strong role in determining the PRC's posture toward the regime. First, Beijing was quick to claim that the regime was infringing on state sovereignty. Second, Beijing's positions often reflected a degree of resistance to the universality of human rights standards based on the import of particular national, developmental, and local conditions. These preexisting Chinese ideas were partially shaped by the

---

[43] On PRC human rights views, see Stephen C. Angle, *Human Rights and Chinese Thought: A Cross-Cultural Inquiry* (New York: Cambridge University Press, 2002); Robert Weatherley, "The Evolution of Chinese Thinking on Human Rights in the Post-Mao Era," *Journal of Communist Studies and Transition Politics* 17, no. 2 (June 2001); Marina Svensson, *Debating Human Rights in China: A Conceptual and Political History* (Lanham, MD: Rowman and Littlefield Publishers, Inc., 2002); and Robert Weatherley, *The Discourse of Human Rights in China: Historical and Ideological Perspectives* (New York: St. Martin's Press, 1999).

[44] See Svensson, *Debating Human Rights in China*, and Eva Pils, *Human Rights in China*, 13–31.

legacy of Confucianism and Marxism, but can also be attributed to the influence of Maoist thought and perhaps more recently Xi Jinping's vision.[45] The remarkable consistency in PRC views throughout the decades covered in this book is a key finding. In the concluding chapter, I discuss some of the potential reasons for the stubbornness of these ideas.

In the following section, I explicate two key features of the Chinese government's thinking about human rights that not only shaped PRC behavior but also enjoyed a high degree of consensus among CCP government entities.[46] While the Chinese government is not a unitary actor, among the entities with responsibility for China's human rights diplomacy there exists strong ideational consensus on human rights. The constellation of key PRC government agencies whose mandates pertain to China's external human rights policy is broad but I focus in particular on the speeches and remarks by the top PRC leadership, publications, documents, and statements issued by the Ministry of Foreign Affairs, which is responsible for China's conduct in the UN, and the State Council, which issues the Chinese government's human rights white papers.

While these views do appear to reflect genuinely held beliefs, it must be acknowledged that Chinese leaders also deployed these ideas instrumentally. This makes it difficult to weigh protestations made on principle versus instances when Beijing invoked these arguments in an attempt to thwart human rights criticism and resist normative pressure.[47] For example, the PRC articulated these ideas prior to 1989, especially in the UN where CCP leaders delivered statements suggesting that sovereignty was inviolable, but these assertions became much more forceful after Tiananmen and were often used in response to human rights censure. Further, after 1989, PRC leaders cited these ideas with greater vigor and frequency. Thus, it is likely that it was convenient for Beijing to

---

[45] Carl Schmitt, sometimes referred to as "the crown jurist of the Third Reich," has gained currency in China. Pils, *Human Rights in China*, 29–30.

[46] In Ambassador Wu Hailong's contribution to the Universal Rights Group blog he complained about interference in internal affairs, naming and shaping and other "confrontational approaches" while insisting on the need to "bear in mind the different social and cultural backgrounds of States." See "Reflections on the Human Rights Council: the Way Forward by H.E. Ambassador Wu Hailong," Universal Rights Group, www.universal-rights.org/blog/reflections-on-the-human-rights-council-the-way-forward/, accessed October 28, 2019.

[47] For a similar point, see Svensson, *Debating Human Rights in China*, 307. Svensson notes that "[t]he CCP has at times made skillful use of the human rights concept purely out of strategic considerations." In fact, Kent suggests that in the mid 1990s when it faced significant human rights scrutiny, the PRC resurrected the noninterference doctrine after it had waned in Chinese rhetoric. Kent, *China, the United Nations, and Human Rights*, 72.

use even sincerely held ideas opportunistically in response to the regime's growing focus on its marred record. As will be further elaborated later, these Chinese views found easy alignment with a number of other non-Western countries, especially the Like-Minded Group – comprising primarily authoritarian countries.

Prioritizing State Sovereignty over Regime Authority

Beijing's inclination toward a Westphalian definition of state sovereignty meant that Chinese leaders favored safeguarding sovereignty at the expense of the international regime's reach. Thus, when there was a tension between the two, Chinese leaders favored protection of state sovereignty and had a low tolerance for the regime's interference in internal affairs.[48] This belief was reflected in Premier Deng Xiaoping's 1974 address to the UN General Assembly, "We hold that in both political and economic relations, countries should base themselves on … mutual respect for sovereignty and territorial integrity … We hold that the affairs of each country should be managed by its own people."[49] As noted previously, China's experience during the nineteenth century, when it was forced to grant market access and foreign-ruled concession areas, left it with a high degree of sensitivity toward threats to national sovereignty and foreign interference. CCP leaders have embraced a version of sovereignty that hews close to the definition laid out by the 1648 Peace of Westphalia, which stressed each nation's sovereign rule over its territory and domestic affairs and advanced the principle of noninterference, particularly that external actors should respect the state's domestic jurisdiction.

Even prior to the 1989 Tiananmen Square protests, the CCP noted a tension between sovereignty and the international human rights regime's norms and monitoring. In a 1982 article the CCP's journal *Red Flag* stated that "the so-called international character of human rights advocated is based on [the] theory of considering individuals as subjects of

---

[48] On PRC sovereignty views, see Allen Carlson, "More Than Just Saying No: China's Evolving Approach to Sovereignty and Intervention Since Tiananmen," in *New Directions in the Study of China's Foreign Policy*, eds. Alastair Iain Johnston and Robert S. Ross (Stanford: Stanford University Press, 2006), 217–241; Shan Wenhua, "Redefining the Chinese Concept of Sovereignty," in *China in the New International Order*, eds. Gungwu Wang and Yongnian Zheng (New York: Routledge, 2008); and Allen Carlson, *Unifying China, Integrating with the World* (Stanford, California: Stanford University Press, 2005).

[49] *Speech by Chairman of the Delegation of the People's Republic of China, Teng Hsiao-ping, at the Special Session of the U.N. General Assembly* (Beijing: Foreign Languages Press, 1974), 18.

international law and thus setting the principle of state sovereignty against the principle of human rights" and asserted that "human rights must be subordinate to the principle of state sovereignty and cannot be superior to the principle of state sovereignty."[50] Later, in the aftermath of Tiananmen, this tension between PRC views and the regime's reach fueled Deng's words that "[t]his turmoil has taught us a lesson the hard way, but at least we now understand better than before that the sovereignty and security of the state must always be the top priority."[51] Two years later, the PRC's 1991 human rights white paper offered a similarly vigorous defense of sovereignty, stating that

China has firmly opposed any country making use of the issue of human rights to sell its own values, ideology, political standards and mode of development, and to any country interfering in the internal affairs of other countries on the pretext of human rights, the internal affairs of developing countries in particular, and so hurting the sovereignty and dignity of many countries. Together with other developing countries, China has waged a resolute struggle against all such acts of interference, and upheld justice by speaking out from a sense of fairness. China has always maintained that human rights are essentially matters within the domestic jurisdiction of a country.[52]

PRC diplomats persisted in reiterating these views within the human rights regime. For example, PRC representative Zhang Yishan stated in 1996 at the UN Commission on Human Rights that "[t]he sovereign equality of States and non-interference in their internal affairs were principles enshrined in the Charter of the United Nations and were inviolable."[53] Even in the face of the brutal Khmer Rouge genocide, in

---

[50] Shen, Baoxiang and Wang Chengquan, and Li Zerui, "*Guanyu guoji lingyu de renquan wenti*" [On the Question of Human Rights in the International Arena] *Hong Qi* [Red Flag], no. 8 (1982): 103–104.

[51] Quoted Zhang, *The Tiananmen Papers*, 358.

[52] Information Office of the State Council, *Human Rights in China 1991*. For similar views see Li Buyun and Wang Xiujing, "*Renquan guoji baohu yu Guojia Zhuquan*" [The International Protection of Human Rights and State Sovereignty] *Faxue Yanjiu* [Legal Research] 4 (1995): 19–23, and Zhou Qi, "*Renquan waijiao zhong de lilun wenti*" [Theoretical Issues in Human Rights Diplomacy], *Ouzhou* [Europe]1[1999]: 4–15.

[53] UN Commission on Human Rights, "Summary Record of the 33rd Meeting," April 16, 1996, E/CN.4/1996/SR.33, paragraph 2. For similar statements, see "Ambassador He Yafei, interview by Swiss Newspaper *Le Temps*," Permanent Mission of the PRC to the UN, September 7, 2011, www.china-un.ch/eng/hom/t856087.htm, accessed November 4, 2018; "Statement by Ambassador Wang Min at the Third Committee of the Sixty-sixth Session of the United Nations General Assembly on Human Rights," Permanent Mission of the PRC to the UN, October 26, 2011, www.china-un.org/eng/dbtxx/WMdsjl/WANGminhuodong/t871084.htm, accessed November 4, 2018, and "Statement by Ambassador Wang Min at the Third Committee of the 67th Session of the General Assembly on Human Rights," Permanent Mission of the PRC to the UN, November 8, 2012, www.china-un.org/eng/hyyfy/t987111.htm, accessed November 4, 2018. Similar views expressed in interview with PRC scholar, June 13, 2012, Beijing,

1997 the PRC stated that the "question of Pol Pot is Cambodia's internal affair" and "should be decided by the Cambodians themselves without foreign interference." [54] In a similar vein, during a 2011 special session of the HRC on Syria, Ambassador He Yafei asserted that "the future of Syria should be determined by its people rather than being dictated by outside forces ... We believe ... [external] initiatives ... must fully respect the sovereignty, independence and territorial integrity of Syria."[55]

These views on sovereignty have translated into PRC government positions that favor stronger state control over the application of the human rights regime's mechanisms, procedures, and its composition and restricting the regime from taking certain actions, such as resolutions. Beijing also took positions that relegated the international regime to advisory services or capacity building and treated states as the primary actors in the regime while limiting the ability of individuals to directly access the regime's procedures and mechanisms and seeking to place limits on the authority of UN officials and experts.[56] The PRC also prefers monitoring that involves state-provided reporting rather than relying on information provided by civil society or investigative visits by international experts.[57] This state-centered approach meant that the PRC often stressed the state's primary role and responsibility in the implementation of measures to improve human rights without

---

China, and interview with PRC Ministry of Foreign Affairs official, June 6, 2012, Beijing, China.

[54] Quoted in James Seymour, "Human Rights in Chinese Foreign Policy," in *China and the World*, 4th ed., ed. Samuel S. Kim (Boulder, CO: Westview Press, 1998), 229. See also Barbara Crosette, "Beijing Says It Won't Go Along with Creation of Pol Pot Tribunal," *New York Times*, June 24, 1997.

[55] "Statement by Ambassador He Yafei at the Special Session of the Human Rights Council on the Human Rights Situation in Syria," PRC Ministry of Foreign Affairs, August 22, 2011, www.fmprc.gov.cn/mfa_eng/wjb_663304/zwjg_665342/zwbd_665378/t851126.shtml, accessed July 3, 2018.

[56] As Nathan noted, "China argued that since states, not individuals, are the subjects of international law, the rights of individuals cannot be used as a justification for mutual interference. China argued that problems that outsiders might label as human rights violations are precisely such internal affairs – matters of domestic Chinese law and not the business of foreigners to condemn or fix it." Andrew Nathan, "China and International Human Rights," in *China Joins the World: Progress and Prospects*, eds. Elizabeth Economy and Michel Oksenberg (Council on Foreign Relations: New York, 1999), 211. For PRC statement affirming the primary role of states, see UN Economic and Social Council, "Commission on Human Rights, Fifty-first session, Summary Record of the 44th Meeting," March 3, 1995, UN Doc. E/CN.4/1995/SR.44, paragraph 69.

[57] Mo Jihong, "A New Perspective on Relations between Human Rights' Covenants and China," in *Construction within Contradiction: Multiple Perspectives on the Relationship Between China and International Organizations*, ed. Wang Yizhou (Beijing: China Development Publishing House, 2003), 212. Similar points made in interview with Chinese scholar, June 1, 2012, Shanghai, and interview with Western European diplomat, June 28, 2011, New York.

acknowledging that frequently it is the government that is the perpetrator of human rights violations. This defense of sovereignty and the government's role should not be construed as a strong belief that governments should commit themselves to human rights protection but rather that the international regime should have an attenuated role.

A hallmark of the PRC's human rights views that is based on its definition of sovereignty is a belief that a strong state whose sovereignty is not violated forms the foundation for the realization and protection of human rights.[58] According to a Chatham House report, "in the Chinese conception, sovereignty is presented as the cornerstone of or precondition for all rights."[59] While Western thinking often envisions human rights as protecting people from the encroachments of an abusive state, Chinese government leaders believe that a powerful government protects society from chaos, instability, and upheaval.[60] Moreover, in the Chinese conception individual human rights are considered to be derived from the state, and are not considered to be inherent to the individual or absolute.

The Import of Differing National, Cultural, and Developmental Conditions

While the PRC has occasionally indicated a rhetorical acceptance of the universality of human rights, even prior to 1989 it also argued that human rights vary based on different social and political systems, levels of economic and cultural development, religious tradition, and national customs and habits.[61] A January 1989 article by a government-affiliated scholar asserted that

[t]he theory, legal provisions and actual conditions of a country concerning human rights or civil rights depend on the country's political system, government policies, economic development level, spiritual life and cultural characteristics, as well as historical geography, educational level, and

---

[58] See, for example, Robert Weatherley, *Making China Strong: The Role of Nationalism in Chinese Thinking on Democracy and Human Rights* (New York: Palgrave MacMillan, 2014), 153.

[59] Sonya Sceats and Shaun Breslin, *China and the International Human Rights System*, (London: Chatham House, 2012), 7. Similar point made in Andrew Nathan, "Sources of Chinese Rights Thinking," in *Human Rights in Contemporary China*, ed. R. Randle Edwards, Louis Henkin, and Andrew Nathan (New York: Colombia University Press, 1986), 154.

[60] Angle, *Human Rights and Chinese Thought*, 249, and Weatherley, *The Discourse of Human Rights in China*, 3.

[61] Svensson, *Debating Human Rights in China*, 262; Katrin Kinzelbach, "Will China's Rise Lead to a New Normative Order?," *Netherlands Quarterly of Human Rights*, 30, no. 3, (2012), 308, and Xue, *Chinese Contemporary Perspectives on International Law*, 150.

democratic traditions. Since the national conditions of different countries vary widely, an objective observation of the human rights situation of a country cannot be separated from the country's political, economic, and cultural conditions.[62]

A month after the Tiananmen crackdown, this argument was made again in a July 1989 *Renmin Ribao* article that asserted that human rights protections "are constrained by the country's political system, economic relations, cultural traditions, habits and customs, and many other factors. Thus, there is … no universally applicable … model of human rights for all of humanity."[63]

In the post-Tiananmen era, Chinese officials have continued to utter similar views. While they occasionally mouthed support for the universality of human rights, more often their statements resembled Premier Li Peng's 1992 UN Security Council words that "[a] country's human rights situation should not be judged in total disregard of its history and national conditions.[64] Thus, Beijing has often conditioned its acceptance of the international human rights regime with assertions, such as "Given the diverse social conditions prevailing in States and their varied historical backgrounds, the implementation of human rights principles could not be divorced from consideration of each country's specific situation."[65] In 2000 Foreign Minister Tang Jiaxuan elaborated further that

[t]he human rights conditions of a country are up to the people of that country to assess and improve. Since people live under different circumstances, the form in which human rights are embodied changes with these circumstances and with

---

[62] See also Tian Jin, "*Guoji renquan huodong de fazhan he cunzai zhengyi de wenti*" [The development of international human rights activities and some controversial issues] *Guoji wenti yanjiu* [Journal of International Studies], no. 1 (January 1989): 4–7.

[63] Shi Yun, "*Shei shi renquan de zhenzheng hanweizhe?*" [Who are the true defenders of human rights?], *Renmin Ribao* (July 7, 1989). For similar PRC scholarly views, see also Li Buyun, "Constitutionalism and China," in *Democracy and the Rule of Law in China*, ed. Yu Keping (Leiden: Brill, 2010), 217. See also Liu Hainian, "Human Rights Perspectives in Diversified Cultures," in *Human Rights: Chinese and Dutch Perspectives*, eds. Peter R. Baehr, Fried van Hoof, Liu Nanlai, and Tao Zhenghua (The Hague: Martinus Hijhoff Publishers, 1996), 17.

[64] UN Security Council, "Provisional Verbatim Record of the Three Thousand and Forty-sixth Meeting," January 31, 1992, UN Doc. S/PV.3046, paragraphs 92–93. For a similar statement see UN Commission on Human Rights, "Forty-eighth session, Summary Record of the 28th Meeting," April 2, 1992, UN Doc. E/CN.4/1992/SR.28, paragraphs 63–65.

[65] UN Commission on Human Rights, "Summary Record of the 33rd Meeting," April 16, 1996, UN doc. E/CN.4/1996/SR.33, paragraph 3. For similar statements, see UN Security Council, "Provisional Verbatim Record of the Three Thousand and Forty-sixth Meeting," January 31, 1992, UN Doc. S/PV.3046, paragraphs 92–93, and UN Economic and Social Council, Commission on Human Rights, fortieth session, "Summary Record of the 28th Meeting," April 3, 1992, UN Doc. E/CN.4/1992. SR.28, pages 64–66.

time. Therefore, how to protect and promote human rights depends on the actual conditions and specific needs of a country. To arbitrarily impose a fixed set of human rights rules, regardless of the differences in the specific environment and reality, will not serve the interests of any country.[66]

When the PRC presented its candidacy for a seat on the HRC in 2006, it reiterated that it

respects the universality of human rights ... [but also that] The Chinese Government holds that owing to differences in social systems, level of development, religious and cultural background as well as historical tradition, it is natural for countries to differ on human rights issues ... The Chinese Government holds that the Human Rights Council should respect the historical, cultural and religious backgrounds of different countries and regions.[67]

These beliefs meant that Beijing frequently advanced arguments based on cultural relativism, which is not compatible with some of the key principles underlying the international human rights regime, particularly the idea that because of the inherent worth and dignity of all human beings there are international standards that should apply to all people and nations. Instead, the PRC often championed "Asian values" as it did in the lead-up to the 1993 Vienna World Conference, where it referenced the "diverse and rich cultures and traditions" of the Asian region as part of the Bangkok declaration.[68] These views also informed Beijing's preference for larger human rights bodies with broad regional representation based on the premise that this more adequately represents the diversity of views and traditions in the world. Moreover, Beijing's emissaries often pushed for the inclusion of language that specifically noted the salience of national, cultural, developmental, and domestic conditions in the realization of human rights.

Degree of Familiarity with the Regime

The Chinese government's familiarity with the regime, which, as would be expected, has increased over time, has also influenced its role vis-à-vis the regime. This explanatory factor encompasses Beijing's substantive understanding of human rights norms as well as its exposure to regime

---

[66] UN General Assembly, "Fifty-fifth session, 12th plenary meeting," September 13, 2000, UN. A/55/PV.12, page 7.

[67] United Nations General Assembly, "Aide Memoire," April 13, 2006, www.un.org/ga/60/elect/hrc/china.pdf, accessed March 20, 2017. For a more recent similar statement, see United Nations General Assembly Third Committee, "Seventieth Session, 47th Meeting," November 16, 2015, UN Doc. GA/SHC/4154.

[68] Michael Davis, "Chinese Perspectives on Human Rights," in *Human Rights and Chinese Values: Legal, Philosophical, and Political Perspectives*, ed. Michael C. Davis (Oxford: Oxford University Press, 1995), 3.

procedures and venues and its familiarity with the functioning of the regime. In addition, the PRC's willingness to engage in a broader array of regime activities, such as signing treaties, interacting with UN special procedures and holding a seat in the UN Commission on Human Rights, and subsequently the UNHRC, expanded the PRC's exposure to the regime. Moreover, after the 1989 Tiananmen Square crackdown the PRC experienced the application of the regime's monitoring mechanisms, when special procedures, treaty bodies, and other member states increased scrutiny of China's human rights violations.

As might be expected during the early years of the PRC's involvement with the regime, it was inclined toward the unassuming role of taker and as the PRC's familiarity with the regime grew, its ability, willingness, and interest in playing roles beyond taker increased.[69] The inclination to act as a taker may have been particularly pronounced due to China's period of isolation from the UN and international regimes from 1949 to 1971. China's own words when it joined the UN indicated its limited experience and knowledge. Premier Zhou Enlai stated: "We do not have too much knowledge about the United Nations and are not too conversant … it means that caution is required and that we must not be indiscreet and haphazard."[70] During the PRC's early years in the regime, its inexperience meant that the PRC was strongly inclined to act as a taker of the regime. As elaborated in Chapter 3, this cautious posture was evident during the drafting of CAT in the 1980s, when the PRC did not speak in the drafting group during the first two years of its participation and quickly backed away from its resistance to universal jurisdiction.

Yet, even with increased levels of familiarity, this variable did not necessarily cause the PRC to take a more assertive role in the regime. For example, despite over three decades of experience in the ILO CCAS and a high degree of familiarity with this part of the regime, it remained a taker. However, when the other, more powerful variables inclined the PRC to act as a constrainer, greater familiarity with the regime meant

---

[69] Ann Kent, "China and the International Human Rights Regime: A Case Study of Multilateral Monitoring, 1989–1994," *Human Rights Quarterly* 17, no. 1 (February 1995), 7.

[70] Quoted in Ann Kent, *Beyond Compliance: China, International Organizations and Global Security* (Stanford, Stanford University Press, 2007), 48–49. These sentiments were echoed by Chinese diplomats. Ambassador Ch'en Ch'u at his debut in the First Committee stated, "As we begin to participate in the work of the UN there will be a period of learning for us, so that we may understand the actual workings of the UN." Expressing similar sentiments, Ambassador Fu Hao in the Special Political Committee said that China "hoped for the assistance and co-operation of its colleagues" because it "was not yet familiar with the procedures in the UN." Quoted in Kim, *China, the United Nations and World Order*, 110.

that Beijing had at its disposal diplomat acumen, substantive knowledge, and mastery of the regime's rules. Thus, this explanatory factor was weaker than the three others and was more powerful in constraining the PRC when it was a novice in the regime.

The PRC Government's Ability and Willingness to Work with Other Countries

In addition to the above explanatory variables, the PRC's ability and willingness to cooperate with other countries that shared its human rights views acted as a secondary influence. While other scholarship uncovered evidence of general collaboration among authoritarian countries, my findings add a new dimension showing mutual aid and coordination in multilateral institutions.[71] Chapter 3 captures the start of this behavior in the late 1990s when the PRC began joining statements made by Cuba, Algeria, Egypt, Saudi Arabia, Sudan, and Syria as these countries began working together to resist the proposed draft OPCAT. As noted earlier, unlike the explanatory variables outlined above, this was not a determinative variable, meaning that it did not govern which of the five state roles the PRC adopted. It had a subtler influence on the manner in which the PRC acted out its particular role.

In numerous instances, this variable had a moderating influence on the PRC's behavior. When China was able to work with a group of like-minded countries it often preferred to sign onto the group's statements and adopt a more modest posture as it allowed other countries to take a more vocal role in representing the group's views. In these instances of collaboration with a similar-minded group of nations, the PRC delegation often refrained from making its own national-level statement or when it did make its own statement it noted that its views were represented or aligned with a group of other countries. For example, during the OPCAT negotiations in the 1990s, Beijing's ability to sign onto the statements made by Cuba, Algeria, Egypt, Saudi Arabia, Sudan, and Syria allowed Chinese diplomats to adopt a lower profile while allowing other countries in the group to take more visible stances. The countries that Beijing cooperated with were primarily non-Western, developing world countries that held similar human rights views, particularly defending state sovereignty, insisting on the salience of unique national, cultural, and developmental conditions, and disputing the use of

---

[71] For scholarship on other forms of collaboration among authoritarian countries, see Christian von Soest, "Democracy Prevention: The International Collaboration of Authoritarian Regimes," *European Journal of Political Research* 54 (2015): 623–638.

country-focused human rights scrutiny. In the late 1990s, these countries coalesced in the UNCHR as the "Like-Minded Group" (LMG) and included Algeria, Bangladesh, Belarus, Bhutan, Cuba, Egypt, India, Indonesia, Iran, Malaysia, Myanmar, Nepal, Pakistan, the Philippines, Russia, Sri Lanka, Sudan, Syria, Venezuela, Vietnam, and Zimbabwe. This group was active in the UNCHR until 2006 when the Council was established and the coalition disbanded. In 2011, the group reemerged in the HRC and although the states affiliating with the group are not fixed, the group claims fifty-two members.[72]

At the same time, and in contrast to the modulating influence of this cooperation, the existence of this group of countries espousing similar human rights views appears to have reinforced a number of PRC views, such as defending state sovereignty and asserting that human rights are contingent and based on differing conditions. Scholars have observed that the position and influence of other states can shape a state's posture toward a regime.[73] By voicing similar positions, defending the PRC when it came under scrutiny after 1989, and serving as a kind of peer group, this group of countries appears to have eased the regime's normative pressure. Instead, this chorus of voices appears to have reinforced Chinese human rights views. For example, as detailed in Chapter 3, during the decade-long OPCAT negotiations, Beijing's opposition to the proposed inspection visits underwent little change. Similarly, as detailed in Chapter 4, many of the positions the PRC maintained in the UNCHR in the 1990s persisted during discussions about dissolving the Commission in favor of the Council. In both instances, the PRC's views were shared by other countries, especially the LMG.

China's preference to cooperate with this group of countries is consistent with its behavior in other international regimes and reflects other facets of Chinese foreign policy, particularly its identification with the developing world and inclination toward a low-profile posture. Since joining the UN in 1971, the PRC consistently aligned with or defended the developing world and its continued cooperation with these countries in the human rights regime appeared to deepen their affinity. When

---

[72] The Universal Rights Group, "The Like Minded Group (LMG): Speaking truth to power," www.universal-rights.org/blog/like-minded-group-lmg-speaking-truth-power/, accessed April 4, 2018. For background on the LMG, see Philip Alston, "Reconceiving the Human Rights Regime: Challenging Confronting the New UN Human Rights Council," *Melbourne Journal of International Law* 7, no. 1 (2006): 185–224, and Rana Siu Inboden, *Authoritarian States: Blocking Civil Society Participation in the United Nations* (Austin, Texas: Robert S. Strauss Center for International Security and Law, 2019).

[73] Martha Finnemore and Kathryn Sikkink "International Norm Dynamics and Political Change," *International Organization* 52, no. 4 (October 1998): 887–917.

China came under human rights pressure after 1989, it capitalized on its long-standing courtship of the developing world. As elaborated in Chapter 2, these countries eventually formed a reservoir of support for the PRC in the Commission on Human Rights, and later the Council. In addition, numerous scholars have observed the PRC's preference to play a low-profile role in the international arena, which Deng Xiaoping encouraged with his post-Tiananmen admonition to *taoguang yanghui*, which translates into hide brightness and nourish obscurity.[74] This dictum has been interpreted to mean that the PRC should maintain a low profile and avoid controversy.[75] For example, even though the PRC has often supported and identified with the developing world, China has also been careful not to assume a leadership role. Yet, there has been debate about whether China's rise and Xi Jinping's leadership is leading China to abandon Deng's cautious words in favor of a more assertive posture.

Methodology and Structure

The chapters that follow are based on case studies covering a period from 1982 through 2017 and are presented chronologically. This chronological approach is intended to reveal shifts over time and the evolution of China's behavior toward the regime. The period covered in this book – from 1982 through 2017 – spans over three decades and includes the periods before and after the 1989 Tiananmen Square crackdown as well as China's shift from a novice in the regime to its emergence as a more active participant and rising power. The earliest case studies document China as a regime novice, when it was finally admitted to the UN in the early 1980s, and subsequently Deng Xiaoping's open-door policy and pragmatic foreign policy approach, which meant that it became more receptive to international regimes. By covering the period through 2017, this book covers the periods before and after the 1989 Tiananmen Square crackdown and is also attentive to China's rising power, which became much more pronounced after the 2008 Beijing Olympics.

---

[74] See Kim, *China the United Nations and World Order*, 114, 117, 128, 196, and 210.

[75] Dingding Chen and Jianwei Wang, "Lying Low No More?: China's New Thinking on the Tao Guang Yang Hui Strategy," *China: An International Journal* 9, no. 2 (September 2011): 195–216. By numerous accounts, this low-profile posture began to shift shortly after the Beijing Olympics in 2008. See Aaron L. Friedberg, "The Sources of Chinese Conduct: Explaining Beijing's Assertiveness," *The Washington Quarterly* 37, no. 4 (Winter 2015): 133–150, and Yong Deng, "China: The Post-Responsible Power," *The Washington Quarterly* 37, no. 4 (Winter 2015): 117–132.

This book addresses varied components of the human rights regime, including the drafting sessions for two torture conventions, the establishment of the UNHRC, which serves as the UN's primary venue for addressing human rights, and part of the ILO's system for monitoring state compliance with ratified treaties. My case studies possess a number of strengths. First, the following chapters investigate PRC behavior with regard to a range of human rights issues, including torture and labor rights. This captures the PRC's response to parts of the regime that embody civil and political rights and economic, social, and cultural rights. Second, I also cover varied settings, such as drafting groups comprising roughly thirty to forty individuals representing interested states and nongovernmental organizations (NGOs) and high-profile negotiations over replacing the UNCHR with a new human rights body. Finally, in the chapters that follow I examine China's behavior in institutions with different characteristics and approaches to human rights monitoring and protection, including an ILO Committee that meets during the annual International Labour Conference (ILC) to publicly question states with reported lapses in compliance with ratified treaties, the creation of an international treaty to combat torture, the establishment of a system of inspection visits with the goal of preventing torture, as well as the UN's primary human rights bodies, where UN member states discuss and review human rights abuses.

While these case studies cumulatively form a representative picture of Chinese conduct in the human rights regime, they do not capture the totality of China's behavior. This is worth noting since there are instances in which the PRC has displayed greater intransigence.[76] For example, in 2017 the PRC organized the South–South Human Rights Forum, which resulted in the "Beijing Declaration," a document that advanced the importance of national conditions and elevated social and economic rights over political rights.[77] Along these lines scholar Katrin Kinzelbach posited, "As China emerges as a great power ... rather than seeking to demonstrate compliance, Beijing rebukes its international critics with increasing confidence."[78] In a similar vein, as Brookings Institution

[76] See, for example, Human Rights Watch, *The Costs of International Advocacy, China's Interference in United Nations Human Rights Mechanisms* (New York: Human Rights Watch, 2016), www.hrw.org/report/2017/09/05/costs-international-advocacy/chinas-interference-united-nations-human-rights.

[77] Johnston, "China in a World of Orders," 33–34.

[78] Katrin Kinzelbach, "Resisting the power of human rights: the People's Republic of China," in *The Persistent Power of Human Rights: From Commitment to Compliance*, eds. Thomas Risse, Stephen C. Ropp and Kathryn Sikkink (Cambridge: Cambridge University Press, 2013), 164.

scholar Ted Piccone argued, since 2016 China has been advancing regressive resolutions in the HRC that use innocuous-sounding phrases, such as dialogue and win–win cooperation, in an attempt to weaken international human rights norms.[79] Yet, the general pattern of the PRC's conduct is similar to this book's findings with the PRC shifting between offering resistance to efforts to strengthen international protection mechanisms while at the same time being flexible in not holding up progress, especially when there was international consensus. As will be shown in the subsequent chapters, the PRC often operated near the boundary of taker and constrainer of the regime.

China has been particularly resistant to making commitments that would limit its policy options or allow the international regime to hold the PRC government accountable for its domestic human rights conditions. For example, China is not a party to the International Criminal Court (ICC), the International Convention for the Protection of all Persons from Enforced Disappearance (ICPED), or the Ottawa Convention, also known as the Mine Ban Treaty, which aims to prohibit "the use, stockpiling, production, and transfer of anti-personnel landmines."[80] China's stance on the ICPED, which was adopted by the UN General Assembly in 2006, is somewhat surprising given that this treaty is similar to CAT and other international human rights treaties that Beijing has been a party to for decades and that center on state-provided reporting – Beijing's preferred form of monitoring as opposed to opening up its borders to independent investigators. At the same time, this stance is expected given Beijing's use of enforced disappearances and the use of such disappearances to silence and cower activists especially under Xi Jinping's rule.[81] Even though the PRC has ratified similar treaties, including CAT, the International Covenant on Economic, Social and Cultural Rights, the Convention on the Rights of Persons with Disabilities, the Convention on the Elimination of Discrimination against Women, the Convention on the Elimination of Racial Discrimination, and the Convention on the Rights of the Child, China's reviews before these

[79] Piccone, *China's Long Game* and Chen, "China's Challenge to the International Human Rights Regime."

[80] "Statement at the 2nd Review Conference of the Ottawa Convention by H.E. Mr. Cheng Jingye," Embassy of the People's Republic of China in the United States, www.china-embassy.org/eng/xw/t646934.htm, accessed December 2, 2019.

[81] See Edward Wong, "From Virginia Suburb, a Dissident Chinese Writer Continues His Mission," *New York Times*, February 12, 2012, www.nytimes.com/2012/02/26/world/asia/yu-jie-dissident-chinese-writer-continues-his-work-in-us.html and Alex W. Palmer, "'Flee at Once': China's Besieged Human Rights Lawyers," *The New York Times*, www.nytimes.com/2017/07/25/magazine/the-lonely-crusade-of-chinas-human-rights-lawyers.html, accessed October 9, 2019.

treaty bodies have increasingly involved tough questioning and greater scrutiny of its lapses. Consequently, the PRC has likely become much more resistant to this form of monitoring.

The PRC has also complained about UN efforts to protect individuals reporting human rights abuses arising from state reprisals. In November 2015, the PRC delegation complained that

we have noted the adoption of what is known as the Guidelines against Intimidation and Reprisals (aka the San Jose Guidelines) by the meeting of the chairs. China is of the view that the primary responsibility for protecting individuals from intimidation and reprisals lies with each State party as it concerns the State party's treaty obligations. Therefore, such guidelines should be formulated through consultations involving State parties, instead of being unilaterally decided by the meeting of the chairs of treaty bodies ... there are inconsistencies between parts of the Guidelines, and the provisions of the treaties concerned.[82]

Although the PRC couched its arguments in the context of respecting the authority of the state, this stance challenges the entirely valid premise that individuals reporting human rights abuses to the UN can be targeted by the government, that they deserve protection from retribution, and that as the potential perpetrator the government in question is not a fair arbiter. Thus, the PRC's insistence on making the international regime deferential to states stands in contrast to the concerns from human rights experts.

In addition, Beijing has taken actions to hold back the strengthening of the international regime, often invoking its position that the regime should not inhibit domestic sovereignty. For example, the PRC along with other states opposed UN initiatives to strengthen the treaty body system, including seeking to use a code of conduct to place constraints on the independent experts serving on committees to hold governments accountable.[83] Yet, the PRC framed these complaints as being intended to avoid burdening states, ensuring the treaty bodies avoid going beyond

---

[82] Permanent Mission of the People's Republic of China to the UN, "Statement by Liang Heng of (sic) Chinese Delegation at the Third Committee of the 70th Session of the GA under Agenda Item Implementation of Human Rights Instruments, 2015/11/05," www .china-un.org/eng/lhghyywj/t1312398.htm, accessed October 24, 2019.

[83] "Views of the Chinese Government regarding the human rights treaty body strengthening process," UN Doc. HRC/NONE/2011/184, available at www2.ohchr.org/english/bodies/ HRTD/docs/submissions2011–12/states/ChinaSubmission.doc (China Letter). The PRC also sought to restrict civil society participation in the treaty body reviews, including excluding NGOs without formal UN consultative status, preventing the treaty bodies from publicizing NGO information without the consent of the country under review and barring treaty bodies from citing information from NGOs in their concluding observations.

their mandates and averting politicization and selectivity. Chinese diplomats veiled these attempts with euphemistical words, stating, "Treaty bodies should ... conduct their work with the support of the conference of States (sic) parties under the principles of objectivity, impartiality and independence ... and help States (sic) parties implement the treaties more effectively through constructive dialogue carried on an equal footing."[84] However, Beijing's aim appeared to be hampering the regime's ability to scrutinize state parties with greater rigor.

Beijing has also vacillated between resistance and some openness on international efforts related to the responsibility to protect (R2P), which obligates the international community to protect populations from genocide, war crimes, ethnic cleansing, and crimes against humanity.[85] In this vein, during the negotiations over the Rome Statute that created the ICC in 2002 the PRC offered stiff resistance to the body's prosecutorial authority and the definition of "crimes against humanity" but ultimately did not block the creation of the court."[86] While the PRC has customarily opposed UN Security Council resolutions reprimanding other countries for humanitarian crises or massive rights violations, it has been flexible in select cases. For example, Beijing initially refused to support UN Security Council action on Sudan, but eventually abstained and allowed referral to the ICC rather than exercising its veto power.[87] Beijing qualified this action with a statement from Ambassador Ma Zhaoxu that read:

The Government of the Sudan has made active efforts to maintain peace and stability in Darfur and has played a vital role. It is our belief that the Security Council and the international community should continue to fully respect the Government's leadership in the Darfur issue, strengthen communication and coordination with the Sudanese Government and listen attentively to its views and suggestions.[88]

---

[84] Permanent Mission of the People's Republic of China to the UN, "Statement by Liang Heng of (sic) Chinese Delegation at the Third Committee of the 70th Session of the GA under Agenda Item Implementation of Human Rights Instruments."

[85] See Zhu Lijiang, "Chinese Practice in Public International Law: 2006," *Chinese Journal of International Law* 6, no. 2 (2007): 475–506.

[86] Joel Wuthnow, "China and the ICC," *The Diplomat*, December 7, 2012, thediplomat .com/2012/12/china-and-the-icc/, accessed September 29, 2019.

[87] "China and Russia block UN action after 'bloody massacre' in Sudan," *South China Morning Post*, June 5, 2019, www.scmp.com/news/world/africa/article/3013179/china-and-russia-block-un-action-after-bloody-massacre-sudan, accessed September 30, 2019.

[88] Permanent Mission of the PRC to the UN, "Statement by Ambassador Ma Zhaoxu at the Security Council on the African Union–United Nations Hybrid Operation in Darfur 2019/06/27, www.china-un.org/eng/hyyfy/t1680549.htm, accessed October 21, 2019.

On Libya, the PRC relented and not only softened its stance guarding sovereignty and championing noninterference but voted in support of a 2011 Security Council resolution.[89] Beijing's position on this matter has been attributed to support for Security Council action from the Arab League and even the Libyan Ambassador to the UN, who called for the international community's support.[90] In contrast to these actions, Beijing has opposed censuring Venezuela and Syria, even blocking efforts by European countries to pass a mild, nonbinding Security Council statement condemning Syria's violent crackdown on protesters. Although the PRC has been cautious in using its veto as a P5 member, of the thirteen vetoes it has exercised since joining the UN, seven of them have been used to stymie resolutions on Syria, where the government has unleashed massive attacks on civilians since 2011. Further indicating Beijing's difficulty in countenancing the international community's responsibility to protect has been its position, often made in tandem with Russia, that seeks to minimize human rights as part of peacekeeping operations.[91]

While acknowledging examples of greater PRC resistance to broad international efforts to protect people from these massive human rights crises, my case study selection is sound and justifiable. They are diverse and cumulatively highly representative of the PRC's behavior in the international human rights regime. Moreover, they are sufficiently granular in that they provide meaningful insight into PRC behavior and its stances toward the components of the regime. Chapter 2 further situates China's behavior within the international human rights regime.

Following this introductory chapter, Chapter 2 provides a brief over-view of the UN human rights regime and Chinese human rights views. The main substance of this chapter is an overview of China's experiences with and participation in the human rights regime. Because the subsequent chapters cover a wide range of the regime's bodies and procedures, this chapter seeks to provide background on China's interactions with a wide range of the regime's components, including the treaty bodies and special procedures. Chapter 2 begins with China's first foray into the

[89] "China's Vote On Libya Signals Possible Shift," *Wall Street Journal*, February 28, 2011, www.wsj.com/articles/SB10001424052748703933404576170793783265986, accessed December 2, 2019.

[90] Julian Borger, "Libya no-fly resolution reveals global split in UN," *The Guardian*, March 18, 2011, www.theguardian.com/world/2011/mar/18/libya-no-fly-resolution-split, accessed September 30, 2019. Also, in the 1990s, the PRC agreed to the establishment on international criminal tribunals on Rwanda and the former Yugoslavia. These tribunals paved the way for the creation of the ICC.

[91] Courtney Fung, *China and Intervention at the UN Security Council: Reconciling Status* (Oxford: Oxford University Press, 2019), 7.

regime in the early 1980s beginning with the UN Commission on Human Rights and traces the PRC's growing engagement with the regime, including China's ratification of a range of human rights treaties and acceptance of visits by select UN special procedures. Crucially, it examines the post-Tiananmen period, when after 1989 the PRC faced international opprobrium and human rights scrutiny not only in the UNCHR where other states tried to pass resolutions on China's record, but also from other parts of the regime. It details Beijing's strategies to mitigate negative human rights attention. This broader background provides the context for the subsequent chapters.

Chapter 3 examines China's role in the drafting and adoption of the Convention against Torture and Other Cruel, Inhuman or Degrading Treatment or Punishment and OPCAT. This chapter provides insight into China's behavior within a more intimate group, working toward consensus to establish the first international convention on combatting torture and a subsequent second working group established to create a preventive UN monitoring mechanism with extensive visiting powers. By covering the drafting of two different international agreements that occurred nearly a decade apart, this chapter illuminates China's evolving posture as it shifted from a novice acting as a taker during the CAT negotiations to a more experienced regime participant attempting to constrain the regime during the negotiations over OPCAT. China's behavior during the adoption process of OPCAT also reveals the moderating influence of image as it offered less resistance as the Optional Protocol advanced to larger UN bodies. This chapter also documents the emergence in the late 1990s of a group of countries with shared views about resisting the kind of visiting authority envisioned in OPCAT, and the PRC's cooperation with this group. I also briefly discuss the PRC's interactions with the Committee against Torture to demonstrate that even though the PRC has been a taker toward this body it is not necessarily in substantive compliance with this convention.

Chapter 4 examines China's role during the establishment of a new body to replace the UN Commission on Human Rights. In order to provide context, the first section investigates China's behavior in the UNCHR, which it joined in 1982, and the impact of Tiananmen as a watershed event that altered the PRC's relationship with the regime. I examine Beijing's positions in reforming the UN human rights body and replacing the Commission with the Council beginning with the first reform proposals in 2004 to the final stage when HRC members engaged in an Institution-Building Process from 2006 through 2007. Because the Institution-Building Process encompassed reviewing a wide range of human rights procedures, including the individual petition system and the special procedures, this chapter provides an unparalleled glimpse into the PRC's posture toward a broad array of the regime's mechanisms. This chapter shows how the PRC sought to constrain the regime while seeking to minimize negative attention. It also chronicles the emergence of the Like-Minded Group in the mid to late 1990s where this group advanced proposals to weaken the regime that they touted as reforms .

Chapter 5 investigates China's participation in the ILO's CCAS, where its taker behavior can be attributed mainly to the lack of scrutiny it received from this Committee. PRC representatives first began attending the annual sessions of the ILC and the CCAS sessions in 1984 and have participated continuously since then. This chapter illuminates PRC behavior in a public body comprising member states responsible for holding their peers accountable to their commitments under ratified international labor conventions. This chapter unveils an instrumental aspect of Beijing's behavior, exposing that beginning in the late 1990s the PRC began using this venue to speak in defense of friendly countries during their reviews before the ILC. By analyzing the votes and statements of these countries in the UNCHR and HRC, I show that Beijing appears to have benefited from reciprocal treatment as these countries frequently voted against resolutions on China's record and offered protective statements during the PRC's Universal Periodic Review before the HRC. This behavior suggests that even though the PRC was a taker in this Committee, its actions did not necessarily uphold the principles undergirding the regime.

Chapter 6 parses the explanatory factors that account for the PRC's role as a constrainer and taker in the human rights regime. It discusses each of the case studies and assesses the relative weight of each of the variables. It also explores Beijing's cooperation with other like-minded countries as a secondary influence on its behavior. It argues that the two most prominent explanatory variables were the CCP government's antipathy for scrutiny of its record and its preexisting ideas that stressed state sovereignty and local conditions, which caused Beijing to take positions that limited the authority and scope of the human rights regime. At the same time, I show that image concerns had an important restraining effect, inclining the PRC toward more cooperative stances.

The concluding chapter reviews China's constrainer and taker roles and discusses the implications of my findings. I consider the relevance of my findings regarding China's rise, its behavior within international regimes more generally, and the fate of the human rights regime. I argue that the continued strength of image concerns as a moderating influence will be crucial in determining Beijing's future role in international regimes. Although I demonstrate that the PRC and other nations, especially countries belonging to the Like-Minded Group, contested various elements of the human rights regime, the regime's lack of meaningful sanctions means that these countries may be less inclined to mount a challenge but are likely to block efforts to strengthen the regime.

This book is based on qualitative research involving semistructured interviews and documentary research. The breadth and diversity of my interview subjects is a particular strength of this book. I conducted over seventy interviews with UN and ILO officials, foreign diplomats, human rights NGO representatives, and Chinese academics and policy makers. These interviews were conducted from 2010 through 2019. I benefited from especially good access to UN and ILO officials and diplomats from North America and Western Europe. Although interviews with diplomats from other regions can be difficult to obtain, I was also able to interview numerous diplomats from the Middle East, South Asia, and East Asia, as well as UN officials coming from non-Western countries. My access to individuals from these nations is important because many of these countries are ones that often aligned and cooperated with China. These interviews provided me with further insight into PRC behavior, especially its "behind the scenes" conduct in nonpublic venues and the functioning of the Like-Minded Group.

During the summer of 2012, I completed interviews in China with scholars, government representatives, and party officials. My interviews with scholars included academics affiliated with organizations, such as the Chinese Academy of Social Sciences, a government-organized think tank; the Central Party School; and the China Society for Human Rights, a government-affiliated NGO; as well as scholars at China's leading universities in Beijing, Shanghai, Guangzhou, Hong Kong, and Macau. I was also fortunate in gaining good access to a number of key Chinese government officials, including a former ambassador and two Ministry of Foreign Affairs officials at the deputy director-general level. In addition to the Ministry of Foreign Affairs, I was able to interview officials with the Ministry of Labor and Social Security, which has the primary responsibility for the PRC's interactions in the ILO.

In terms of written sources, this work draws primarily on English language sources but is also complemented by Chinese language sources. In particular, I utilized official UN and ILO documents, including records from drafting meetings for CAT and OPCAT; sessions of the UN Commission on Human Rights and the UNHRC, including position papers submitted by China available via the HRC extranet; and over twenty-five years of reports from the ILO CCAS. The HRC extranet is a semipublic website where country position papers, meeting summaries, and other reports are housed and is intended primarily for diplomats and

UN officials. Although scholars can request access to the site, few have combed through the records on the HRC Institution-Building Process, which provided a rich source of information on Chinese positions. The records of a variety of NGOs have also proven to be indispensable. I was extremely fortunate that Amnesty International's New York office allowed me to access its records on the establishment of the UNHRC. These documents, which are not generally available to the public, tracked state positions on various issues relating to the proposed Council, and were especially helpful in identifying China's positions during the early phase of the HRC negotiations. The Geneva-based NGO, the International Service for Human Rights, also issued detailed reports on the Institution-Building Process of the UNHRC, which provided me with extremely useful information on state positions.

PRC sources in both Chinese and English, including government documents such as white papers on human rights, government statements, press releases, and other public documents, have also been utilized. In addition, news reports from *Renmin Ribao* and *Xinhua* have proven to be useful sources. Scholarly works in Chinese, including journals, books, and memoirs, have provided me with a greater understanding of PRC positions and motivations. For example, the memoir of former PRC Foreign Minister Qian Qichen, *Ten Episodes in China's Diplomacy*, is a valuable source of Chinese views.

Despite my strenuous efforts to access all available sources, there are some limitations. Due to the opaque nature of the CCP rule, government sources, such as Ministry of Foreign Affairs records, particularly internal policy documents, for the time period under investigation are not available. Further, although I was able to interview a handful of Chinese government officials and a number of scholars, given the political environment in China, these interviewees were likely cautious and avoided revealing sensitive political information. Moreover, when I pursued interviews with Chinese citizens, in numerous instances I did not receive responses and a number of recipients declined an interview. In view of these limitations and the absence of more direct evidence on China's motivations, such as PRC policy documents, these explanatory factors have been inferred from its behavior.[92] I also scrutinized existing scholarship, publicly available documents, and the additional sources noted above to reach an informed understanding of key explanatory factors for PRC behavior.

---

[92] Similar point made by Nathan, "China and the International Human Rights Regime," 148.

2   China's Evolving Posture toward the International Human Rights Regime: 1949–2017

In order to provide a broader context for the chapters that follow, this chapter offers background on China's interactions in the human rights regime with a focus on key inflection points, Beijing's varied approach as it displayed both resistance and receptivity to this regime, and its strategies for mitigating human rights attention. By focusing on both the PRC's receptivity to select parts of the human rights regime and its resistance to others, this chapter alerts us to the components of the regime that have most rankled the Chinese leadership. I employ a chronological approach that is attentive to the evolution of Beijing's reactions, its expanding political and economic leverage, and shifts in its conduct, including indications that Xi Jinping is abandoning Beijing's previous low-profile, defensive posture in favor of a more activist stance. I conclude this chapter by outlining the CCP government's strategies to resist human rights scrutiny, which were largely successful because of the resolve, energy, and resources Beijing employed. These strategies alert us to possible tactics China used as a potential maker, promoter, taker, constrainer, or breaker of the regime.

This chapter begins with a brief description of the structure and content of the human rights regime. This is followed by a synopsis of the CCP government's human rights views that builds on the discussion in Chapter 1. It then outlines China's interactions with and posture toward the regime, especially the effect of decisive episodes such as the 1989 Tiananmen Square crackdown. Because the chapters that follow cumulatively cover a wide range of the regime's bodies and mechanisms, this chapter seeks to provide a broad introduction to these components of this regime and China's relationship with them. The final section of this chapter chronicles Beijing's determined application of a number of strategies to deter and deflect scrutiny of its human rights record.

The Creation of the International Human Rights Regime

The first steps toward establishing the international human rights regime began in 1946 when UN member states created the UN Commission on

Human Rights (UNCHR or Commission), which was called for by the UN Charter. This was followed by the adoption of the Universal Declaration of Human Rights (UDHR) two years later in 1948.[1] UN member states differed over how to maintain the equilibrium between protecting state sovereignty and enabling strong international mechanisms. As an example of this tension, even though the UN had begun to receive a flood of individual petitions from people around the world reporting human rights violations, in 1947 the Economic and Social Council (ECOSOC), the UNCHR's parent body, ruled that the Commission had no power "to take any action in regard to any complaints concerning human rights."[2] It was only gradually that the Commission's authority was expanded and it began to play a role in standard setting through human rights treaties and as a venue to raise human rights concerns. Despite the Commission's contributions, there were also shortcomings and over time complaints that it was "politicized" grew. As recounted in Chapter 4, mounting grievances led to the creation in 2006 of a new charter body to replace the UNCHR.[3]

Cold War politics and ideological differences hampered further development of the human rights regime until 1966 when the UNCHR adopted two foundational covenants, the International Covenant on Civil and Political Rights (ICCPR) and the International Covenant on Economic, Social and Cultural Rights (ICESCR). These two covenants elaborated the rights in the UDHR, provided for implementation measures, bound states that ratified the covenants to compliance through periodic reporting, and established treaty bodies comprising independent experts to review state reports and preside over an in-person examination of each state party. After these foundational covenants came into

---

[1] On the drafting of the UDHR, see Mary Ann Glendon, *A World Made New: Eleanor Roosevelt and the Universal Declaration of Human Rights* (New York: Random House, 2001). Due to resistance from a number of states, the proposal that the Commission be composed of independent experts instead of member states was rejected. Howard Tolley, *The U.N. Commission on Human Rights* (New York: Westview Press, 1987), 36–40.

[2] This decision was made by both the Commission and its parent body, the Economic and Social Council (ECOSOC). The UN Secretary-General was at least charged with providing the UNCHR with a list of petitions even if they were not acted on. Philip Alston, "The Commission on Human Rights," in *The United Nations and Human Rights: A Critical Appraisal*, 1st ed., ed. Philip Alston (Oxford: Clarendon Press, 1995), 129–130.

[3] The UNCHR and UNHRC are referred to as charter bodies because this kind of entity is called for in the UN Charter. Amnesty International bemoaned that "membership is too often used to shield the Commission members from human rights scrutiny instead of to protect and promote human rights." Amnesty International, *2005 Commission on Human Rights: The UN's Chief Guardian of Human Rights?* (New York: Amnesty International, 2005), www.amnesty.org/en/library/info/IOR41/001/2005/en, accessed September 4, 2013.

force in 1976, UN member states further expanded the regime by adopting a series of additional treaties, including conventions covering discrimination of women (1981), religious intolerance (1981), torture (1987), the rights of the child (1990), and the rights of persons with disabilities (2006). While these treaties were welcome additions, they have limited means to address noncompliance and rely primarily on moral pressure or the "mobilization of shame" to motivate states to comply.

The UNCHR also established a system of "special procedures" that relied on independent experts, sometimes referred to as mandate holders, who are given the authority to monitor and promote human rights related to specific countries or issue areas, such as human rights defenders, freedom of expression, and torture.[4] The initial step toward the creation of the special procedures began in 1967 when ECOSOC passed resolution 1235, which authorized the Commission "to examine information relevant to gross violations of human rights and fundamental freedoms," including studying "situations which reveal a consistent pattern of violations of human rights."[5] Although the first special procedures that were established were an Ad Hoc Working Group of Experts on South Africa and a Special Rapporteur on Apartheid, resolution 1235 provided the legal basis for other special procedures for handling issues beyond racial discrimination and specifically enabled the Commission to "consider the question of the violation of human rights ... in all countries."[6] In the following decades, several thematic special procedures addressing important human rights abuses and enjoying global reach were added, including the Working Group on Enforced or Involuntary Disappearances (1980), the Special Rapporteur on Summary or Arbitrary Executions (1982), the Special Rapporteur on Torture (1985), the Special Rapporteur on Religious Intolerance (1986), and the Working Group on Arbitrary Detention (1990). While the process of establishing special procedures has been ad hoc and

---

[4] For background on the special procedures, see Miko Lempinen, *Challenges Facing the System of Special Procedure of the United Nations Commission on Human Rights* (Turku, Finland:: Institute for Human Rights, Åbo Akademi University, 2001); Amnesty International, *United Nations Special Procedures: Building on a Cornerstone of Human Rights Protection* (New York: Amnesty International, 2005), www.amnesty.org/en/documents/ior40/017/2005/en/, accessed September 1, 2017; and Meghna Abraham, *A New Chapter for Human Rights* (Geneva: International Service for Human Rights and Friedrich Ebert Stiftung, 2006), 40–41.

[5] UN Economic and Social Council Resolution 1235, "Question of the violation of human rights and fundamental freedoms, including policies of racial discrimination and segregation and apartheid, in all countries, with particular reference to colonial and other dependent countries and territories," June 6, 1967, accessed July 27, 2018.

[6] Ibid.

contingent on the political will of states, the number of rapporteurs and working groups has grown to include thirteen country-specific mandates and forty-three thematic ones, which employ investigative visits, urgent appeals, direct communications, and public statements. The special procedures have been praised as "the crown jewel" of the human rights regime in part because unlike treaty bodies their jurisdiction is not constrained by a state's willingness to ratify particular treaties and as independent experts they are thought to enjoy a degree of freedom from the politics that often plague bodies comprising member states.[7]

The UN developed other entities and procedures to monitor and protect human rights. In 1946, under the Commission on Human Rights, a Sub-Commission on the Prevention of Discrimination and Protection of Minorities, composed of independent experts, was established as a subsidiary body that undertook research, engaged in preparatory work on new human rights treaties, made recommendations, and considered resolutions.[8] As will be further detailed in Chapter 4, a group of states that included China challenged the Sub-Commission and beginning in the 1990s worked to diminish its authority with the result that it has been transformed into an Advisory Committee with diluted power and autonomy, acting only at the direction of the HRC.[9] The Sub-Commission and later the Advisory Committee have also been a part of the adjudication process for the individual complaints procedure. The groundwork for the complaints procedure was laid in 1970 when ECOSOC adopted resolution 1503, which instituted a confidential complaint procedure and authorized the Commission to deal with communications that demonstrated a consistent pattern of gross human rights violations.[10] While this procedure was retained during the transition from the Commission to the Council in 2006, it is a lengthy, cumbersome process and the intention was never to provide for individual redress but simply to bring to the Commission's attention patterns of massive human rights violations.[11]

---

[7] Paul Gordon Lauren, *The Evolution of International Human Rights: Visions Seen* (Philadelphia: University of Pennsylvania Press, 2003), 254.

[8] In 1967 the UNCHR authorized the Sub-Commission to address government human rights abuses during the Sub-Commission's annual session. This led to the number of countries spotlighted by the Sub-Commission during its sessions increasing from ten in 1977 to seventy-two in 1967. Foot, *Rights beyond Borders*, 37. On the Sub-Commission's work, see Abraham, *A New Chapter for Human Rights*, 51–60. It was renamed in 1999 as the Sub-Commission on the Promotion and Protection of Human Rights.

[9] UN Human Rights Council, "Institution Building of the United Nations Human Rights Council," A/HRC/Res/5/1, paras. 70–84.

[10] Abraham, *A New Chapter for Human Rights*, 62.

[11] In addition to the requirement that domestic remedies be exhausted and violations "reliably attested," the process is confidential, involves a two-stage review that often takes eighteen months or longer, and aside from the Commission being informed of the

The International Labour Organization (ILO), which was established through the Treaty of Versailles in 1919 to secure fair, safe, and just labor conditions for workers, is another component of the human rights regime and in 1946 it became a specialized UN agency.[12] As the ILO began setting international labor standards and requiring state reporting, it realized that it needed a dedicated monitoring process and set up a formal supervisory system, including commissions of inquiry, to respond to emerging conditions as well as standing bodies of experts, such as the Committee on the Freedom of Association.[13] As part of this effort, it also established the Conference Committee on the Application of Standards in 1926, which includes government, labor, and employer representatives, and is examined in Chapter 5.[14]

As the human rights regime was gradually developed and international human rights standards gained acceptance and prominence, governments – especially liberal democracies – began to include human rights as part of their foreign policies both multilaterally in the UN and bilaterally in their relationship with other countries. The growing importance of human rights in foreign policy meant that a number of states also incorporated human rights into their bilateral interactions with China. As the next section will demonstrate, this development meant that after the 1989 Tiananmen Square crackdown, China faced human rights pressure from within the human rights regime and from other states.

Chinese Views on International Human Rights

This section provides a brief overview of the Chinese government's ideas about human rights, which is helpful in understanding its behavior in the regime and areas where the PRC's ideas might diverge from the substance of the human rights regime.[15] Chapter 1 outlined two distinctive

countries being examined there is little publicity. Between 1970 and 2005 only fifty-five countries were considered by the Commission. Abraham, *A New Chapter for Human Rights*, 64.

[12] For an overview of some of the limitations of the ILO, see Jan Klabbers, "Marginalized International Organizations: Three Hypotheses Concerning the ILO," in *China and the ILO Fundamental Principles and Rights at Work*, eds. Ulla Liukkunen and Chen Yifeng (New York: Wolters Kluwer, 2014), 182–184.

[13] Victor-Yves Ghebali, *The International Labour Organisation: A Case Study on the Evolution of U.N. Specialised Agencies* (Dordrecht, Netherlands: Martinus Nijhoff Publishers, 1989), 235.

[14] Ibid., 221.

[15] Although some scholars have cautiously voiced more liberal ideas, their influence is limited. For an overview of these voices, see Weatherley, *The Discourse of Human Rights in China*, 132–149, and Mab Huang, "Universal Human Rights and Chinese Liberalism," in *Human Rights and Asian Values: Contesting National Identities and Cultural*

elements of the PRC's human rights thinking – the primacy of state sovereignty and the salience of national, developmental, social, and cultural particularities – which strongly influenced Beijing's role in the regime. This chapter elaborates other elements of the PRC's human rights views that may have had less of a determinative impact on the particular role Beijing adopted vis-à-vis the regime but are still relevant to its conduct. A number of these views were formed prior to 1989 and reflect Confucian, Mencian, and Communist influences as well as Chinese conceptions about the role of the government and the relationship between authorities and the individual and individual rights and responsibilities.[16] There is also an instrumental aspect to Beijing's human rights arguments and positions. In the wake of the 1989 crackdown Chinese officials devised counterarguments to deflect human rights scrutiny and even those beliefs that were preexisting and deeply seeded were invoked and deployed instrumentally to refute human rights scrutiny.

A number of PRC human rights views are grounded in Chinese conceptions of the state, the collective, and the individual. As discussed in Chapter 1, the PRC views a strong state as central to the realization of human rights while Western thinking often regards the state skeptically, as the potential abuser of individual freedoms. Related to this elevated view of the government is the Chinese focus on the duty and obligations of the individual to the state and on the state as grantor of rights.[17] In the Chinese view "the duty of loyalty and obedience [to the state from the individual] was fundamental, whereas the right to receive benevolent treatment [from the state] was secondary or derivative," not absolute.[18] In contrast, in the Western conception individual human rights are considered to be inherent rather than bestowed by the state. While liberal democracies tend to emphasize individual worth and dignity, Chinese thought considers individual freedom as secondary to collective imperatives, such as security and public order.[19] Thus, the CCP government

Representations in Asia, eds. Michael Jacobsen and Ole Bruun (Richond, Surrey: Curzon Press, 2000).

[16] See, Angle, *Human Rights and Chinese Thought*.

[17] For PRC statement, see UN Commission on Human Rights, "Summary Record of the 52nd Meeting," April 22, 2005, UN Doc. E/CN.4/2005/SR.52, para. 75.

[18] Daniel C. K. Chow, "How China Uses International Trade to Promote Its View of Human Rights," *The George Washington International Law Review* 45 (2013): 103–124, and Weatherley, *Making China Strong*, 153–155.

[19] Zhou Wei, "The Study of Human Rights in the People's Republic of China," in *Human Rights and International Relations in the Asia Pacific*, ed. James T. H. Tang (London: Pinter, 1995), 88 and 90. The PRC has also asserted that security is a fundamental

prioritizes stability, economic growth, and increasing welfare in the aggregate even if this means diminished individual human rights protections and individual freedoms, such as limiting freedom of expression and assembly and clamping down on independent civil society. Scholar Yuchao Zhu captured this tension between Beijing's utilitarian approach and individual human rights protection by noting that the PRC leadership "claimed that *guoquan* (the right of a nation or sovereignty) is more important than *renquan* (human rights), and *shengcun quan* (right of subsistence) is more fundamental than political freedom."[20] The PRC's statist views also translate into positions that regard the state, not the individual, as the subject of the human rights regime, meaning that the actors in the regime should be states, not individuals.[21]

The CCP government also harbors an underlying distrust of external human rights scrutiny and views human rights attention as being politically motivated and insincere. Even prior to the 1989 Tiananmen crackdown, this view was manifest in PRC statements, news reports, and journal articles.[22] For example, Premier Deng Xiaoping asserted in 1979 that "[some domestic groups] have raised such sensational slogans as 'Oppose Hunger' and 'Give us human rights,' inciting people to hold demonstrations and deliberately trying to get foreigners to give worldwide publicity to their words and deeds."[23] In a similar vein, a 1984 PRC news article decried the use of "human rights" by the superpowers to intervene in the internal affairs of another state and specifically accused the US government of using human rights for political purposes.[24] Beijing has persisted in this view and labeled international attempts to

---

human right and stability is a precondition for other rights. Sceats and Breslin, *China and the International Human Rights System*, 9 and 24.

[20] Zhu, "China and International Human Rights Diplomacy," 223.

[21] Stephen C. Angle and Marina Svensson, eds., *The Chinese Human Rights Reader: Documentary and Commentary 1900–2000* (New York: M. E. Sharpe, 2001), xxi–xxii, and Weatherley, *Making China Strong*. This state-centric view means a PRC government focus on how human rights might serve the nation, not the individual.

[22] A 1979 article in the official Party journal, *Red Flag*, stated that "'human rights' is always a bourgeois slogan ... there are some with ulterior motives who energetically praise the bourgeois slogan of human rights; not only do they lack a Marxist spirit but their sense of patriotism has also disappeared into thin air." Xiao Weiyun, Luo Haocai, Wu Xieying, "Makesi zenmeyang kan 'renquan' wenti" [How Marxism Views the Human Rights Question], *Hongqi* [*Red flag*], no. 5 (1979): 43–48.

[23] Bureau for the Compilation and Translation of Works of Marx, Engels, Lenin and Stalin, *Selected Works of Deng Xiaoping (1975–1982), Vol. II*, (Beijing: Intercultural Press, 1984), 182.

[24] Liu Fengming, "Human Rights Law and Its International Implementation," *Zhongguo Fazhi Bao* [*China Legal Daily*] July 18, 1984, p. 4.

monitor its human rights practices as "a pretext for ulterior motives" to weaken and contain China, subvert its socialist system, and embolden separatist actors.[25] A Chinese Academy of Social Sciences scholar, speaking in 2013, accused the West of using human rights "as a tool to block China's rise and suppress" it.[26] Expressing similar views, a former PRC ambassador claimed that the PRC is not opposed to the notion of international human rights but that the "problem is ... with the West using human rights to interfere in internal affairs."[27] These views are also reflected in the CCP government's use of human rights criticism as a tool to use against adversaries, which it did as early as the 1930s and 1940s when the CCP maligned Chiang Kai-shek for repression.[28] In a similar vein, Chinese diplomats used their participation in the UNCHR in the 1980s as a forum to disparage their adversaries, namely, the Soviet Union and Vietnam, for trampling on the rights of the Afghan and Cambodian peoples.[29] Moreover, Beijing has often responded to scrutiny by attacking the record of the country expressing human rights concerns and along these lines in the late 1990s began to publish a critical report on human rights in the United States.

Another central tenet of Beijing's conception of human rights that predates the 1989 Tiananmen crackdown is an emphasis on economic, social, and cultural rights over civil and political rights.[30] Along these lines, the PRC advanced the view that economic rights and economic development are the foundation for the realization of other human rights.[31] As the Chinese government's 1991 white paper stated,

---

[25] UN General Assembly, "12th Plenary Meeting," September 13, 2000, UN Doc. A/55/PV.12, p. 7. See also PRC Ministry of Foreign Affairs Policy Research Office, *Zhongguo Waijiao 1997* (Beijing: World Knowledge Press, 1997), 713.

[26] Interview with Chinese Academy of Social Sciences scholar, July 12, 2013, Beijing, China.

[27] Chen Jian (former PRC Ambassador to the UN and former UN Undersecretary), interview by author, June 11, 2012, Beijing, China.

[28] In December 1936, Mao called for Chiang to release all political prisoners and "guarantee the freedoms and rights of the people." Mao Tse-tung, *Selected Works of Mao Tse-tung Volume 1* (Pergamon: London, 1965), 255–262. In 1944, Mao referred to the "autocratic Kuomintang leaders" and criticized the lack of "political reform." Mao Tse-tung, *Selected Works of Mao Tse-tung Volume 3* (Pergamon: London 1965), 179–184.

[29] Tian Peizeng, ed., *Gaige Kaifang yilai de Zhongguo Waijiao* [*China's Diplomacy since Reform and Opening*] (Beijing: Shijie Zhishi Chubanshe [World Affairs Press], 1993), 569.

[30] Dingding Chen, "Explaining China's Changing Discourse on Human Rights," *Asian Perspectives* 29, no. 3 (2005): 169, 176.

[31] Weatherley, *The Discourse of Human Rights in China*, 115, and "Renquan shouxian shi renmin shengcun quan guojia duli quan," ["Human Rights Are Primarily the People's Right to Subsistence and National Independence"] *Renmin Ribao* [*People's Daily*] April 15, 1991, p. 1.

"the right to subsistence is the most important of all human rights, without which the other rights are out of the question."[32] In 1992, in the UNCHR, the PRC elaborated that

the very essence of the concept of human rights lay in the right to survive and flourish ... The path to follow towards achieving human rights in a country therefore encompassed social progress, social stability and economic development. Experience and history proved, in fact, that in most developing countries, including China, the most pressing matter was to resolve problems of food, housing, employment, education and health care. As pointed out by the leaders of some developing countries, a hungry man was not a free man. Consequently, human rights and fundamental freedoms could only be guaranteed in the context of substantial growth of the national economy and improvements in the livelihood of the population.[33]

In order to advance these ideas, the PRC championed a right to development and argued that economic and social rights should have at least equal standing relative to civil and political rights.[34] In this vein, in 2003 the Ministry of Foreign Affairs' annual publication on the PRC's foreign affairs asserted that

[e]conomic and social development is the basis for the full realization of human rights. Poverty is a major obstacle for enjoying human rights. International society must attach great importance to economic, social, cultural rights, and the right to development and help the majority of developing countries to eliminate poverty and realize development.[35]

---

[32] Information Office of the State Council of the PRC, *Human Rights in China 1991*, Section X, Active Participation in International Human Rights Activities.

[33] UN Economic and Social Council, "Commission on Human Rights, Forty-eighth session, Summary Record of the 28th Meeting," April 3, 1992, E/CN.4/1992/SR.28, paragraph 65. The PRC has also trumpeted its record in improving the livelihood of its population to deflect negative human rights attention. See, for example, Information Office of the State Council of the PRC, *Progress in China's Human Rights Causes in 1996* (Beijing: Information Office of the State Council, 1996), Section I, People's Rights to Subsistence and Development.

[34] Svensson, *Debating Human Rights in China*, 252. For example, see UN Commission on Human Rights, "Summary Record of the 33rd Meeting," April 16, 1996, UN Doc. E/CN.4/1996/SR.33, paragraph 3.

[35] PRC Ministry of Foreign Affairs Policy Research Office, *Zhongguo Waijiao 2003* [China's Foreign Affairs 2003], (Beijing: *Shijie Zhishi Chubanshe*, 1998), 345. See also Information Office of the State Council, *China's Progress in Poverty Reduction and Human Rights* (Beijing, Information Office of the State Council, 2016). For similar statement, see "Statement by H.E. Ambassador Sha Zukang, on behalf of the Like-Minded Group, at the 61st Session of the Commission on Human Rights, March 14, 2005," PRC Statement, UN Commission on Human Rights, Geneva, March 14, 2005, www.china-un.ch/eng/rqrd/t187353.htm, accessed March 24, 2018, and "Statement by Ambassador Wang Min at the Third Committee of the Sixty-sixth Session of the United Nations General Assembly on Human Rights (Agenda Item 69 6 &c)," Permanent Mission of the PRC to the UN, www.china-un.org/eng/dbtxx/WMdsjl/WANGminhuodong/t871084.htm, accessed March 25, 2018.

The lack of human rights attention on the PRC's record prior to 1989 may have softened some of the differences between Chinese thinking and a number of principles undergirding the human rights regime. However, after 1989, when the Chinese government came under international condemnation for its use of violence to end popular protests, this divergence became much more pronounced and Beijing sought to deflect human rights attention by developing counterarguments and utilizing some of the views outlined in this section instrumentally to challenge external human rights scrutiny. As part of this effort, Beijing voiced a preference for "thematic" approaches to human rights rather than singling out particular countries; even-handed, nonselective monitoring in which all countries receive the same attention and countries are not singled out regardless of human rights abuses; and "cooperation" and "dialogue" as opposed to "confrontation," a term the PRC developed to give country-specific resolutions a negative gloss. The PRC also appealed to sovereignty concerns by insisting that external human rights monitoring, even mere expressions of concern, should be governed by "mutual respect" and "equality."[36] The next section will focus on China's relationship with the international human rights regime, including detailing the world's reaction to the 1989 Tiananmen Square crackdown and Beijing's response. After 1989, China's relationship with the international human rights regime was marked by tension and antagonism and Chinese leaders deployed a number of strategies to deter and deflect human rights attention.

China's Interactions with the Human Rights Regime

This section chronicles China's engagement with the international human rights regime, noting in particular areas of Chinese resistance and turning points, as well as examples of Beijing's willingness to accept or become involved with parts of the regime. By detailing China's experience in facing scrutiny in the post-Tiananmen period, this section provides background on the regime's monitoring mechanisms that most riled the CCP leadership. It also demonstrates that even after 1989 the PRC not only remained in the regime but continued the trend begun in the 1980s of expanding its participation. As this section will show, while the 1989 Tiananmen demonstrations lasted for six weeks, its legacy would endure for decades as international civil society, foreign

---

[36] These phrases were included in the 1991 PRC white paper. Information Office of the State Council, *Human Rights in China 1991*, Section X, Active Participation in International Human Rights Activities.

governments, and international experts serving in the UN human rights regime were more aware of China's ongoing human rights violations. The development of the international human rights regime outlined previously in this chapter meant that there were a number of international monitoring mechanisms that could be applied to China.

China's foray into the human rights regime began in the early 1980s when it shifted from avoiding human rights matters in the UN and dismissing human rights as "bourgeois" and antithetical to Marxism to casting UN votes in favor of resolutions on Afghanistan and Chile and cautiously entering into the regime first as an observer in the UNCHR and then a member in 1982.[37] As part of a broader opening to international regimes that was brought about by Deng's policy of reform and opening, Beijing gradually increased its participation in the human rights regime throughout the 1980s. These actions included sending its first delegation to the annual International Labour Conference in 1983, ratifying seven human rights treaties, including conventions on the discrimination of women, the elimination of racial discrimination and torture, and beginning to report to and appear before the relevant treaty bodies to review compliance.[38] Beijing's initial posture was cautious and low-profile, which may have been due to its limited previous exposure to the regime. Moreover, due to the confines of PRC rule there was very limited familiarity with human rights as discussion and scholarship on human rights was severely restricted prior to the early 1990s.[39] In spite of this limited familiarity and its status as a novice in the regime, the PRC displayed some promising signs of receptivity and its rhetoric became increasingly affirmative, such as stating that "the two covenants [the

---

[37] This contrasts with the 1970s in which it eschewed human rights matters, even absenting itself during General Assembly votes on resolutions on the creation of the post of UN Human Rights Commissioner and the human rights situations in Chile, El Salvador, and Guatemala. Foot, *Rights Beyond Borders*, 73; Kim, *China, the United Nations, and World Order*, 126; and Kent, *China, the United Nations and Human Rights*, 43.

[38] By the end of 1986, the PRC had joined nearly 400 international organizations, ratified and acceded to over 130 conventions, and entered nearly all the UN specialized institutions. Nianlong Han, ed., *Diplomacy of Contemporary China* (Hong Kong: New Horizon Press, 1990), 469–70. In contrast, prior to the 1980s, China had joined only eight of the UN's seventeen agencies and limited its involvement to organizations that were primarily technical, scientific, and educational. Kim, *China, the United Nations and World Order*, 402, and Kim, "China and the United Nations," 45.

[39] The PRC itself noted its limited familiarity, stating in 1974 that "the Universal Declaration of Human Rights ... had been adopted ... prior to the founding of the People's Republic of China. It was therefore necessary for [the Chinese] Government to examine its contents." Quoted in Kim, *China, the United Nations and World Order*, 485. On limited human rights discussion and study, see Svensson, *Debating Human Rights in China*, 233–234, 261, and Zhou, "The Study of Human Rights in the People's Republic of China," 83–84.

ICCPR and ICESR] have played a positive role in realizing the purposes and principles of the UN Charter concerning respect for human rights. The Chinese government has consistently supported these purposes and principles."[40] Beijing's openness to the regime prior to 1989 was likely eased by the lack of international scrutiny of China's human rights practices.[41] Even though the UN General Assembly had passed resolutions on the PRC's treatment of Tibetans during the 1960s and the US Congress and NGOs continued to draw attention to human rights concerns in Tibet, after gaining UN membership in 1971 China faced limited scrutiny within the UN and its initial reviews before the treaty bodies were mild and uneventful.[42] The international community may also have been inclined toward a more lenient attitude because of the positive impression that Deng's open-door policy had created.

Despite the PRC's growing involvement with the regime, it also displayed ambivalence toward civil and political rights and placed some limits on the reach of the regime as it opted out of all the voluntary articles of the Convention against Torture, which meant that when it ratified this convention in 1988 it rejected the Committee against Torture's ability to receive interstate and individual complaints of torture or to initiate a confidential inquiry in response to reports of systemic use of torture. This mixture of receptivity and hesitance was evident in the PRC's 1988 statement that "China has no objection to the United Nations expressing concern in a proper way over consistent and large-

---

[40] Information Office of the State Council, *Human Rights in China 1991*, Section X, Active Participation in International Human Rights Activities. A series of PRC articles indicated some openness, such as a 1982 article in the CCP journal *Red Flag*, which stated that "socialism and human rights are one." Shen Baoxiang, Wang Chengquan, and Li Zerui, "*Guanyu guoji lingyu de renquan wenti*" [On the Question of Human Rights in the International Arena], *Hong Qi* [Red Flag] 8 (1982): 47–48. See also Li Zerui, "A Theoretical Study of International Human Rights Law," in *Zhongguo Guojifa Niankan* [Chinese Yearbook of International Law] (Beijing: China Translation and Publishing Corp, 1983), 96–97, and Yu Keping, "*Renquan yinlun: jinian Faguo 'Ren yu gongmin quanli xuanyan' xiang shi 200 zhounian*" [An Introduction to Human Rights: Commemorating the 200th Anniversary of the French 'Declaration of the Rights of Man and Citizen'], *Zhengzhixue yanjiu* [Political Science Research], no. 3 (1989): 30–35.

[41] Roberta Cohen, "People's Republic of China: The Human Rights Exception," *Human Rights Quarterly* Vol. 9, No. 4 (November 1987), 447–549, and Susan Shirk, "Human Rights: What About China?" *Foreign Policy* 29 (Winter, 1977–1978), 109–127.

[42] Kent, *China, the United Nations and Human Rights*, 45–46 and 56. See, for example, UN Committee on the Elimination of Discrimination against Women, "Summary Record of the 33rd Meeting," April 9, 1984, UN Doc. CEDAW/C/SR.33, paragraph 27, and UN General Assembly, "Report of the Committee on the Elimination of Racial Discrimination, Forty Second Session," 1987, UN Doc. A/42/18, paragraph 329–338. As noted by Foot, during this period China was accorded "sympathetic treatment … based on the scale of the economic reforms taking place and the problems it faced." Foot, *Rights Beyond Borders*, 98.

scale human rights violations in a given country, but it opposes the interference in other countries' internal affairs under the pretext of defending human rights."[43]

When the Chinese leadership used force to end widespread demonstrations calling for democratic political reform on June 4, 1989, its actions halted domestic unrest but fueled international scrutiny of its human rights abuses and resulted in isolation and sanctions that caused significant material and reputational damage. As scholar Thomas Robinson noted, "Internationally, Tiananmen vitally affected China's relations with many other states, all of whom reacted with revulsion and disgust at the wanton and immoral slaughter of so many ordinary and innocent Chinese citizens and the unnecessary incarceration of so many others in Beijing and other Chinese cities."[44] Western countries, particularly the United States, and the EU imposed sanctions that included suspending weapons sales; freezing military and high-level diplomatic exchanges; halting cooperative bilateral aid and development programs, such as civilian nuclear cooperation; and opposing World Bank and Asian Development Bank lending.[45] Consequently, China experienced substantial political and economic losses including a two-year decline in foreign investment, export orders, tourism, and its credit rating; lack of access to international lending estimated at $2.3 billion; a weakened negotiating position on a range of issues that resulted in Chinese concessions on market access and intellectual property rights; diminished opportunities to raise concerns about Taiwan, which weakened the PRC's ability to block arms sales; and a freeze in bilateral aid from a number of countries estimated at $11 billion.[46] This crisis was jarring to Chinese leaders who could not comprehend the international opprobrium they were facing at a time that they were correcting some of

---

[43] Quoted in *Kent, China, the United Nations and Human Rights*, 34–35.

[44] Thomas W. Robinson, "Chinese Foreign Policy from the 1940s to the 1990s," in *Chinese Foreign Policy: Theory and Practice*, ed. Thomas W. Robinson.

[45] Foot, *Rights Beyond Borders*, 123–125, and Foot, "China and the Tian'anmen Bloodshed of June 1989," 338–339.

[46] The $2.3 billion figure is for World Bank lending for 1989–1990. See David Zweig, "Sino-American Relations and Human Rights: June 4 and the Changing Nature of a Bilateral Relationship," in *Building Sino-American Relations: An Analysis for the 1990s*, ed. William T. Tow (New York: Paragon House, 1991), 70–71, 75. During the previous year, Beijing borrowed $1.3 billion from the World Bank. James Mann, *About Face: A History of America's Curious Relationship with China, From Nixon to Clinton* (New York: Vintage Books, 1998), 197. The $11 billion estimate is based on four years of bilateral aid. See Foot, "China and the Tian'anmen bloodshed of June 1989," 339. On the PRC's diminished political and economic leverage, see Wan, *Human Rights in Chinese Foreign Relations*, 7; Nathan, "China and the International Human Rights Regime," 147, and Seymour, "Human Rights in Chinese Foreign Relations," 225.

the worst abuses of the Maoist system.[47] In order to break out of isolation, the PRC launched a diplomatic campaign that began with courting non-Western countries to normalize relations and making select human rights concessions, including lifting martial law, which cleared the way for rapprochement with Western countries. Beijing's success meant that by the end of 1991 the PRC had largely recovered its diplomatic and economic relationships.[48]

While the PRC leadership managed to overcome the immediate domestic and international crisis resulting from the crackdown, this was the beginning of longer-term scrutiny in the regime. In August 1989, just two months after the Tiananmen Square crackdown, the experts on the UNCHR Sub-Commission adopted a resolution on China that marked the first time this body censured a UN Security Council P5 member.[49] The Sub-Commission resolution passed despite PRC claims that "not a single person had been killed by the army" and heavy-handed lobbying that included hounding African delegates in their hotel rooms and warnings that votes could result in damaged bilateral economic interests.[50] Other countries, particularly industrialized democratic countries, began to use their seats on the Commission on Human Rights to put forward resolutions on the PRC's human rights practices. For example, at the February–March 1990 UNCHR session, Australia, Canada, and Sweden initiated a draft resolution that was sponsored by eighteen countries, including the United States.[51] Although Chinese diplomats marshaled the votes for a "no-action" motion, a procedural maneuver that prevented consideration of the UNCHR resolution, the margin was slim with seventeen in favor, fifteen against, and eleven abstentions.[52] This narrow victory was secured through aggressive PRC lobbying of developing world countries and sending a large delegation to Geneva and dispatching the foreign minister. This strategy yielded results as a number of Third World diplomats cited political solidarity, diplomatic pressure, and economic aid in explaining their votes' resolution.[53] In 1990, in order to avoid a PRC veto on the Gulf War in the

---

[47] Andrew J. Nathan, "China and International Human Rights: Tiananmen's Paradoxical Impact," in *The Impact of China's 1989 Tiananmen Massacre*, ed. Jean-Philippe Beja (New York: Routledge, 2011), 210.

[48] Philip Baker, "Human Rights, Europe and the People's Republic of China," *The China Quarterly* No. 169 (March 2002), 50.

[49] Quoted in Kent, *China, the United Nations and Human Rights*, 57.

[50] Kent, *China, The United Nations and Human Rights*, 57–59 and Foot, *Rights Beyond Borders*, 119–120.

[51] Kent, *China, The United Nations, and Human Rights*, 60.

[52] Foot, *Rights Beyond Borders*, 121, and Kent, *China, the United Nations and Human Rights*, 61–62.

[53] Foot, *Rights Beyond Borders*, 141.

UN Security Council, the Sub-Commission and the UNCHR did not introduce resolutions on the PRC. However, in 1991, the Sub-Commission passed a resolution on Tibet that the PRC discounted as "null and void."[54] The PRC also faced scrutiny from other parts of the human rights regime.[55] For example, the UN Special Rapporteur on Torture, who had already raised a number of Tibetan cases prior to 1989, continued to do so and sent an urgent appeal to the PRC on June 13 expressing concern about the large number of detentions following the 1989 crackdown.[56] The UN Special Rapporteur on Extrajudicial, Summary or Arbitrary Executions not only inquired about unrest and hundreds of deaths in Tibet in the spring of 1989, but also sent four cables to the PRC in June 1989 voicing concern about the violent crackdown and continued use of excessive force and urged Chinese leaders to exercise restraint.[57] In a similar vein, in 1990, the Committee against Torture expressed concerns about reports of torture involving Tibetans and other ethnic minorities, coercive or violent implementation of family planning policies, extrajudicial detention, and the lack of an investigative mechanism for reported incidents of torture.[58]

During the 1990s, Beijing continued to face human rights scrutiny from other countries, and the special procedures and the treaty bodies, which became more rigorous in their reviews of China after 1989.

---

[54] Quoted in Kent, *China, the United Nations, and Human Rights*, 65. See also ibid., 62–63. There were some indications of sustained Western concern as the Danish and German legislatures also held major hearings on human rights conditions in Tibet. Seymour, "Human Rights in Chinese Foreign Policy," 228.

[55] See Foot, *Rights Beyond Borders*, 117–118.

[56] UN Economic and Social Council, "Question of the Human Rights of All Persons Subjected to Any Form of Detention or Imprisonment, Torture and Other Cruel, Inhuman or Degrading Treatment," January 23, 1989, UN Doc. E/CN.4/1989/15, paragraphs 24–29, and UN Economic and Social Council, "Question of the Human Rights of All Persons Subjected to Any Form of Detention, or Imprisonment, Torture and Other Cruel, Inhuman or Degrading Treatment or Punishment," December 18, 1989, UN Doc. E/CN.4/1990/17, paragraphs 41–44.

[57] UN Economic and Social Council, "Report by the Special Rapporteur," January 23, 1990, UN Doc. E/CN.4/1990/22, paragraphs 83–113. This attention from the special procedures continued; see UN Economic and Social Council, "Report of the Working Group on Arbitrary Detention," January 21, 1992, UN Doc. E/CN.4/1992/20, paragraph 14; UN Economic and Social Council, "Report of the Working Group on Arbitrary Detention," January 12, 1993, UN Doc. E/CN.4/1993/24, paragraph 12; UN Economic and Social Council, "Report of the Working Group on Arbitrary Detention," October 5, 1994, UN Doc. E/CN.4/1995/31/Add.1; UN Economic and Social Council, "Report of the Working Group on Arbitrary Detention," December 21, 1994, UN Doc. E/CN.4/1995/31, paragraph 7.

[58] See UN Committee against Torture, "Report of the Committee against Torture," 1990, UN Doc. A/45/44 and UN Committee against Torture, "Summary Record of the 51st meeting," May 4, 1990, UN Doc. CAT/C/SR.51.

A number of countries also persisted in using the UN as a venue to register concern about China's human rights violations, and during the 1990s the PRC faced a UNCHR resolution every year except for 1991 and 1998.[59] Although the resolution carried no penalties or sanctions and Third World support enabled the PRC to defeat the resolutions, the resolution's power was symbolic and the mere introduction of a resolution was embarrassing to Beijing.[60] The PRC's distaste for the resolution was clear as it lambasted the sponsors, impugned their motivations as being intended to harm the PRC, and dismissed these efforts as interference in its domestic affairs.[61] Due to the PRC's strenuous lobbying, the only year it lost the no-action motion and the resolution came to floor for a vote was 1995 when Russia voted against the no-action motion. However, when the resolution was taken up by the Commission, Russia switched its vote to shield China from censure and the resolution failed by one vote. After this close call, the PRC redoubled its efforts to build a reservoir of support, especially appealing to non-Western countries with arguments emphasizing their shared identity as developing countries and lavishing diplomatic attention and aid on some countries, especially those in Africa.[62] These efforts appeared to bear fruit and in subsequent years Beijing secured the votes needed to defeat UNCHR resolutions by more comfortable margins.[63] China also benefited from its earlier efforts to champion developing world causes. A Southeast Asian diplomat suggested that these countries may have been more inclined to shield the PRC because of its "consistent

---

[59] Rosemary Foot, "Bush, China and Human Rights," *Survival* 45, no. 2 (Summer 2003), 175. After the breakdown of President Clinton's effort to link Most-Favored Nation trading status with the PRC's human rights record in the mid 1990s, use of a UNCHR resolution was one of the remaining US points of leverage.

[60] As noted in a Human Rights Watch report, the resolution "is a curiously potent tool ... given that it is an unenforceable statement that carries no penalties or obligations. But ... even to table a resolution for discussion is considered by many countries, China among them, a major loss of face. Human Rights Watch, *Chinese Diplomacy, Western Hypocrisy, and the U.N. Human Rights Commission* (New York: Human Rights Watch, 1997), www .hrw.org/report/1997/03/01/chinese-diplomacy-western-hypocrisy-and-un-human-rights-commission, accessed June 5, 2010.

[61] Foot, *Rights Beyond Borders*, 178.

[62] Human Rights Watch, *Chinese Diplomacy, Western Hypocrisy, and the U.N. Human Rights Commission*. For example, during the period between the 1995 and 1996 UNCHR annual sessions, Vice Premier Li Lanqing visited six African countries, five of which were slated to be UNCHR members, and the PRC Minister of Foreign Trade and Economic Cooperation visited seven African countries, six of which were going to be on the Commission. See also David H. Shinn and Joshua Eisenman, *China and Africa* (Philadelphia: University of Pennsylvania Press, 2012), 96.

[63] In 1996 developing world support was critical in preventing the passage of a UNCHR resolution on China. Peter Van Ness, "China and the Third World: Patterns of Engagement and Indifference," in *China and the World: Chinese Foreign Policy Faces the Millennium*, ed. Samuel Kim (Boulder, Colorado: Westview Press, 1998), 159.

support of developing countries, especially on human rights issues," which he explained meant that PRC diplomats championed the importance of economic development and other issues of importance to the developing world.[64]

In other ways, 1995 proved to be a high mark for external focus on the PRC's record as a number of the special procedures, which had already begun focusing on Chinese human rights abuses earlier in the 1990s, intensified their scrutiny.[65] In their annual reports that year the UN Working Group on Arbitrary Detention, the Special Rapporteur on Torture, and the Special Rapporteur on Freedom of Religion made critical mention of China.[66] The Special Rapporteur on Religious Freedom and Belief, who was the first special procedure mandate holder allowed to visit China, noted that his November 1994 visit revealed "that Chinese authorities are trying to restrict and repress all religious activities ... [official] structures ... and were at the same time reducing authorized religious activities across the whole of China," including Tibet, which "continues to encounter grave difficulties as far as religious tolerance is concerned."[67] The PRC also faced rigorous treaty body reviews in the 1990s. For example, the Committee against Torture used its 1996 review to voice concern about reports of torture, particularly "repeated violations of human rights in Tibet, the systemic use of force against peaceful demonstrations in Tibet and acts of religious and racial discrimination against the population in general" as well as the nationwide use of reeducation through labor.[68]

---

[64] Interview with Southeast Asian diplomat, November 9, 2011, London, United Kingdom.

[65] Even prior to 1995, the special procedures had been monitoring PRC human rights practices. For example, in 1994, the Special Rapporteur on Torture sent four urgent appeals and thirty-four queries of alleged torture. UN Commission on Human Rights, "Question on the Human Rights of All Persons Subjected to Any Form of Detention or Imprisonment, in Particular: Torture and Other Cruel, Inhuman or Degrading Treatment or Punishment," January 6, 1994, UN Doc. E/CN.4/1994/31, paragraphs 146-172.

[66] Foot, *Rights Beyond Borders*, 182. UN Economic and Social Council, "Report of the Working Group on Arbitrary Detention," January 12, 1993, UN Doc. E/CN.4/1993/24, paragraph 12; UN Economic and Social Council, "Report of the Working Group on Arbitrary Detention," October 5, 1994, UN Doc. E/CN.4/1995/31/Add.1; UN Economic and Social Council, "Report of the Working Group on Arbitrary Detention," December 21, 1994, UN Doc. E/CN.4/1995/31, paragraph 7.

[67] UN Economic and Social Council, "Report of the Special Rapporteur," UN Doc. E/CN.4/1995/91, December 22, 1994, page 119.

[68] UN Committee against Torture, "Report of the Committee against Torture, General Assembly Official Records," 1996, UN Doc. A/51/44, paragraphs 138–150. In 1996, the Committee on the Elimination of Racial Discrimination expressed concerns about Tibet and Xinjiang and asked detailed questions about Han migration to those regions. UN, "Consideration of Reports Submitted by State Parties under Article 9 of the Convention,

The PRC intensified its efforts to counter UNCHR resolutions, which it succeeded in doing in 1997 when EU resolve to continue sponsorship of the resolution crumbled. Beijing abhorred this highly public tool and devoted significant resources toward ridding itself of this annual battle as it applied economic and political muscle, employed counterarguments, alleged that the resolution violated the ideals of cooperation and dialogue, and offered a quid pro quo that if the usual sponsors of the resolution would abandon this form of UN action the PRC would engage in bilateral human rights dialogue with them.[69] The lure of the burgeoning Chinese economy provided fertile ground for this PRC strategy and in 1997 France broke from the EU's policy of cosponsoring resolutions and Germany, Italy, Spain, and Greece followed suit.[70]

In 1997, even though the EU had withdrawn support, Denmark agreed to sponsor the resolution. The PRC responded by threatening that it would take "a rock that [it] will smash down on the Danish government's head" and stated that it would exclude Danish corporations from future contracts.[71] In order to make the lesson clear, the PRC also penalized other supporters of the resolution, cancelling high-level visits with the Netherlands, Austria, Ireland, and Luxembourg.[72] Even though individual EU countries could still support a resolution, this marked the end of the EU's policy of backing a resolution as a bloc and most EU countries downplayed UN action and made closed-door bilateral human dialogue the cornerstone of their efforts to address the PRC's human rights violations.[73] Consequently, after 1997 and for the remainder of the Commission's existence until 2006, support for the resolution was inconsistent even though by numerous accounts bilateral human rights discussions produced limited results. While the United States accepted Beijing's offer to engage in bilateral human rights dialogue, it insisted on a "results-based dialogue" in which it agreed to forego a resolution in the Commission only if the PRC made human rights improvements and increased cooperation, including allowing visits by

Concluding Observations of the Committee on the Elimination of Racial Discrimination," September 27, 1996, UN Doc. CERD/C/304/Add.15, paragraphs 112–114.

[69] Katrin Kinzelbach, *The EU's Human Rights Dialogue with China* (New York: Routledge, 2015), 32.

[70] Ibid., 27, 40.

[71] Quoted in Seymour, "Human Rights in Chinese Foreign Relations," 231.

[72] Shen Guofang, China's Foreign Ministry spokesman at the time, issued an explicit warning: "If Denmark insists on doing this it will end up the biggest loser. [...] I can say relations will be severely damaged in the political and economic trade areas." Quoted in Kinzelbach, *The EU's Human Rights Dialogue with China*, 35.

[73] Foot, *Rights Beyond Borders*, 204–206.

international human rights experts and releasing individual prisoners. Thus, from the late 1990s until the Commission was dissolved in 2006, citing insufficient progress on human rights, the United States tabled resolutions in 1999, 2000, 2001, 2002, and 2004.[74]

After the Human Rights Council replaced the Commission in 2006, human rights attention on the PRC eased further. While Beijing was subject to routine monitoring through the HRC's Universal Periodic Review (UPR) process and other countries occasionally voiced concern, it did not face the specter of a resolution in the Council, even from the United States.[75] Moreover, even though Beijing proved to be an increasingly uncooperative and difficult dialogue partner, the EU did not revisit use of the resolution and continued to make bilateral human rights dialogue the centerpiece of its human rights policy with China.[76] Although the PRC's human rights record has been examined every four years under the UPR process, as detailed in Chapters 4 and 5, it worked hard to limit scrutiny and recruit allies to make bland or praiseworthy comments in an effort to drown out negative statements. When it did face occasional negative attention in the Council it reacted vigorously. The case of Cao Shunli, a human rights defender who had drawn attention to the Chinese government's failure to allow civil society inputs in the UPR process, generated significant international concern. In 2014 when an NGO attempted to have a moment of silence for Cao, who died in police custody, the PRC used global demarches and entreaties in Geneva to marshal the votes to deny the NGO the right to be silent during its allotted speaking time.[77] Likewise, China protested angrily with demarches and threats in response to a 2016 joint statement in the Human Rights Council signed by twelve countries expressing

[74] Although the PRC was prevailing in the resolution vote by comfortable margins, in 2003 and 2005 it agreed to a range of steps to avert a UNCHR resolution, including inviting the UN Special Rapporteur on Torture to visit, ratifying the ICESCR, signing the ICCPR, and releasing prisoners Xu Wenli, Rebiya Kadeer, and a number of Tibetan Buddhists. Adam Ereli, Deputy Spokesman, US State Department Daily Press Briefing, March 17, 2005, Washington DC, 2001-2009. state.gov/r/pa/prs/dpb/2005/43603.htm, accessed June 3, 2018.

[75] China benefited when the Bush administration withdrew from the Council to protest the low bar for membership and even after the Obama administration reengaged with the Council it failed to consider resolutions on China.

[76] Beijing's representatives at the dialogue refused to accept lists of prisoners of concern, resisted the inclusion of NGO participants, approached the dialogue with a "frosty and aggressive" attitude, and snubbed EU efforts to hold the dialogue twice a year. Kinzelbach, *The EU's Human Rights Dialogue with China*, 109, 143, 149–151, 180, and 189. Shen Yongxiang, the PRC head of the delegation, even openly "laughed at the EU's concerns." Ibid., 140–141.

[77] Human Rights Watch, *The Costs of International Advocacy, China's Interference in United Nations Human Rights Mechanisms*, 86–88 and 94–96.

concern about troubling PRC human rights practices.[78] Chinese lobbying, pressure tactics, and economic leverage appear to have persuaded some countries to abandon even these occasional expressions of concern. For example, in 2017 Greece blocked an EU statement that would have expressed concern regarding Chinese human rights violations.[79]

Although China did not consistently face UN resolutions after 1997, other parts of the human rights regime, such as the special procedures, continued to monitor its human rights practices. While the CCP government's willingness to allow visits by special rapporteurs responsible for education, torture, food, discrimination against women, and foreign debt and poverty provided opportunities to urge compliance, during a number of these visits Chinese authorities surveilled UN experts and officials, attempted to restrict their movements and meetings, and interfered with access to independent civil society actors.[80] Further, Beijing engaged in prolonged negotiations over the terms of the visit and appeared to cherry-pick the special procedures that were invited as it preferred ones that it thought would be likely to issue favorable findings.[81] For example, before the 2005 UN Torture Rapporteur's visit, the PRC insisted that he could meet with PRC authorities only "on an equal footing and in the spirit of mutual respect" and resisted the usual terms of reference for visits.[82] These investigative trips were opportunities to document human rights abuses and develop recommendations in an effort to prod Beijing toward greater conformity with international standards. For example, the Rapporteur on Torture found that torture was "widespread" and forwarded twenty-four recommendations, such as video or audio taping of police questioning and abolishing reeducation through the labor system.[83] In addition, a number of mandate holders issued joint press

---

[78] Ibid., 86–90.

[79] Robin Emmott and Angeliki Koutantou, "Greece Blocks EU Statement on China Human Rights at U.N.," *Reuters*, June 18, 2017, www.reuters.com/article/us-eu-un-rights/greece-blocks-eu-statement-on-china-human-rights-at-u-n-idUSKBN1990FP, accessed July 24, 2018. For other examples, see Thorsten Benner et al., *Authoritarian Advance: Responding to China's Growing Political Influence in Europe* (Berlin: Global Public Policy Institute and Mercator Institute for China Studies, 2018), 16 and 17.

[80] Human Rights Watch, *The Costs of International Advocacy*, 60-65.

[81] Ibid., 63. Interview with UN official, March 17, 2017, via Skype.

[82] Kinzelbach, "Will China's Rise Lead to a New Normative Order?" 316.

[83] UN News Center, "Torture, Though on Decline, Remains Widespread in China, UN expert reports," December 2, 2005, www.un.org/apps/news/story.asp?NewsID=16777#.WmoB5rpFzSE, accessed January 25, 2018, and UN Economic and Social Council, "Civil and Political Rights, Including the Question of Torture and Detention," March 10, 2006, UN Doc E/CN.4/2006/6/Add.6. The Special Rapporteur on Religion visited in 1994, the Special Rapporteur on Education visited in 2003, the Working Group on Arbitrary Detention visited in 1997 and 2004, and the Special Rapporteur on Torture visited in 2005.

statements that drew attention to specific cases or abuses. For example, between 2014 and 2017, the UN Rapporteur on the Situation of Human Rights Defenders partnered with other mandate holders to issue eight press statements on China, including one that called for a full investigation into the death of Cao Shunli, whose inadequate medical care in detention led to her death.[84] Beijing was vehement in denouncing these findings and expressions of concern.

There was a dissonance in Beijing's behavior toward human rights treaties as it voluntarily signed some key treaties and submitted to reporting requirements while also rebuffing others, disputing the treaties bodies' concerns and attempting to place limits on their authority. For example, while Beijing ratified a handful of fundamental ILO treaties and eight of the nine core UN human rights treaties, it is among a group of less than thirty countries that refuses to ratify the ICCPR and when it acceded to the ICESCR it made a reservation that Article 8, which recognizes the right of workers to form or join a trade union and their right to strike, could only be implemented in conformity with PRC law, which explicitly denies this right to workers. Further, several of the treaty bodies flagged serious human rights concerns and questioned CCP government officials about widely documented human rights violations. In this vein, during its first ICESCR review in 2005, the Committee queried Beijing about the inability of North Korean refugees to access refugee determination procedures, the discriminatory household registration system, and the reeducation through labor system.[85] Even the Committee on the Rights of the Child, which Beijing may have hoped would be more lenient, used their 2005 review to question Chinese officials about discrimination against children of ethnic minority rights groups, such as Tibetans and Uighurs; restrictions on religious freedom for children, including the whereabouts of Gedhun Choekyi Nyima, whom the Dalai Lama recognized as the eleventh Panchen Lama in 1995; and the refoulement of children from North Korea who face harsh

---

[84] "OHCHR Latest News," UNOHCHR, www.ohchr.org/EN/NewsEvents/Pages/News Search.aspx?MID=SR_HR_Defenders, accessed July 23, 2018.

[85] UN ECOSOC, "Concluding observations of the Committee on Economic, Social and Cultural Rights," May 13, 2005, UN Doc. E/C.12/1/Add.107. See also UN Committee against Torture, "Report of the Committee against Torture, Twenty-third Session (November 8–19, 1999) Twenty-fourth Session (May 1–19, 2000)," 2000, UN Doc. A/55/44; UN Committee on the Elimination of Racial Discrimination, "Report of the Committee, Fifty-eighth Session (March 6–23, 2001) Fifty-ninth session (July 30–August 17 2001)," 2001, UN Doc. A/56/18, paras 231-255; and United Nations, "Concluding observations of the Committee against Torture, China," December 12, 2008, UN Doc. CAT/C/CHN/CO/4.

punishment and imprisonment on repatriation.[86] In turn, the PRC insisted that these reviews should be a "discussion" rather than an appraisal of state compliance and sought to relegate the treaty bodies to providing advisory services rather than monitoring compliance. In this vein, Chinese diplomats argued that "the consideration of implementation reports of state parties by human rights treaty bodies is a process of dialogue and exchange of views on an equal footing between the relevant treaty bodies and states [sic] parties."[87] Further, as a 2017 Human Rights Watch report detailed, the PRC has made inappropriate contact with UN treaty body experts and staff, obstructed civil society participation with China's treaty body reviews, resisted established treaty body working methods, refused to provide information, and challenged the authority of the treaty bodies.[88]

While Beijing has long contained its actions in the human rights regime to defending itself from the kind of scrutiny described above, more recently, and particularly under President Xi, who came to power in 2013, the PRC has assumed a more assertive posture as it has begun to spearhead initiatives and offer stronger resistance to normative human rights pressure. This shift appeared to correspond with its expanding political and economic power and increased confidence following the 2008–2009 financial crisis and the 2008 Beijing Olympics but became more pronounced after 2013. In addition to a more muscular global role, Xi has also presided over tightening domestic political control, including characterizing universal human rights, constitutional democracy, media independence, and civic participation as subversive and threatening to

---

[86] United Nations Committee on the Rights of the Child, "Concluding observations: China (including Hong Kong and Macau Special Administrative Regions)," November 24, 2005, UN Doc. CRC/C/CHN/CO/2. See also UN Committee on the Rights of the Child, "Concluding Observations of the Committee on the Rights of the Child: China," June 7, 1996, UN Doc. CRC/C/15/Add.56.

[87] "Statement by Tian Ni, Adviser of the Chinese Delegation, on 'Implementation of Human Rights Instruments' (Item 71a) at the Third Committee of the 60th Session of the General Assembly 2005/10/24," Permanent Mission of the People's Republic of China to the UN, www.china-un.org/eng/chinaandun/socialhr/rqwt/t218125.htm, accessed June 22, 2018. See also "Statement by Mr. Ren Yisheng, Advisor of the Chinese Delegation, on Item 18: Effective Functioning of Human Rights Mechanisms at the 57th Session of the Commission on Human Rights (April 19, 2001, Geneva) 2004/04/16," Permanent Mission of the People's Republic of China to the United Nations at Geneva, www.china-un.ch/eng/gjhyfy/hy2001/t85139.htm, accessed June 22, 2018; and "Statement by Ms. Zhang Dan, Counsellor of the Chinese Delegation, at the Third Committee of the 63rd Session of the General Assembly, on the Report of the Human Rights Council 2008/10/30," Permanent Mission of the People's Republic of China to the UN, www.china-un.org/eng/chinaandun/socialhr/rqwt/t521159.htm, accessed June 22, 2018.

[88] Human Rights Watch, *The Costs of International Advocacy*, 42–58.

the CCP's hold on power.[89] PRC diplomats also no longer merely acted defensively to deflect human rights attention but began to use the Human Rights Council to propagate their views through HRC presidential statements and resolutions. For example, in June 2017, the HRC adopted a China-led resolution on the "Contribution of Development to the Enjoyment of All Human Rights," which the *People's Daily*, the mouthpiece of the Chinese Communist Party, celebrated as a blow to the West's monopoly of international human rights discourse.[90] Other countries voiced concern with the resolution, such as the United States, which voted against it with the explanation that "[w]e recognize the role development can have in contributing to the enjoyment of human rights. But all development, including sustainable development, needs to respect human rights. We reject any suggestion that development goals could permit countries to deviate from their human rights obligations and commitments. To this end, we continually encourage all states to implement their human rights obligations and commitments, regardless of level of development."[91] More recently, at the March 2018 HRC session China initiated a resolution that called for "mutually beneficial cooperation" on human rights issues that other diplomats and NGO representatives warned could be used to erode support for country-specific scrutiny, privilege a state-centric approach that marginalizes certain populations, and weaken the UPR and the special procedures ability to spotlight human rights abuses.

China's Strategies in the Human Rights Regime

China's evolution from a passive novice that faced intense scrutiny after 1989 to a growing force in the Human Rights Council calls for a discussion of its strategies in the regime. During most of this period, Beijing's main objective in the human rights regime was preventing and resisting attention on its record. As outlined in the previous section, liberal democracies, UN officials and experts, and human rights organizations

---

[89] Chris Buckley, "China Takes Aim at Western Ideas," *New York Times*, August 19, 2013; Chris Buckley and Andrew Jacobs, "Maoists in China, Given New Life, Attack Dissent," *New York Times*, January 4, 2015.

[90] "China's Party Paper Trumpets U.N. Rights Resolution as Combating West's Monopoly," *Reuters*, June 24, 2017, www.reuters.com/article/us-china-rights-un-idUSKBN19F0A8, accessed July 24, 2018.

[91] "Explanation of Position on Resolution on the Contribution of Development to the Enjoyment of all Human Rights," Mission of the United States, Geneva, Switzerland, June 22, 2017, geneva.usmission.gov/2017/06/23/explanation-of-position-on-resolution-on-the-contribution-of-development-to-the-enjoyment-of-all-human-rights-ahrc35l-33/, accessed July 24, 2018.

have expressed concern about rights abuses in China. PRC diplomats deployed a number of strategies in the aftermath of Tiananmen and over time honed them and developed additional measures to combat scrutiny. The PRC was largely successful because of the energy and resources it devoted to this task as well as its growing economic and political weight. This discussion draws attention to the kind of tactics the PRC may have used as it assumed various roles, as examined in the subsequent chapters.

Employing Political and Economic Clout

Beijing learned as early as 1990 that it could use its political clout to shield itself from scrutiny and by the early to mid 1990s, it realized that its burgeoning economy was a source of economic leverage as well. In 1990, when the United States and its allies sought to avoid a PRC veto on the Gulf War and the Sub-Commission and the UNCHR decided to forego China resolutions, CCP leaders realized that in exchange for cooperative behavior in the Security Council and on general foreign policy issues they could avoid such resolutions.[92] Chinese leaders also underscored to the United States their ability to be helpful on other issues, such as non-proliferation, Cambodia, and North Korea.[93] In the early 1990s as the Chinese economy gained steam, it capitalized on foreign economic interest, particularly access to the Chinese market and the possibility of major purchases, to compel other countries to deprioritize human rights.[94] For example, in 1990 Beijing agreed to buy seventy-two Boeing airplanes and made a major US wheat purchase.[95] This taught the United States and other countries that downplaying human rights, including foregoing UNCHR resolutions and other forms of human rights pressure, could benefit bilateral economic ties with the PRC. For example, in 1995, Italian prime minister Berlusconi told the Dalai Lama that he was "caught between the importance of maintaining [Chinese] trade relations and protecting human rights."[96] As noted earlier, in 1997, when

---

[92] Kent, *China the United Nations and Human Rights*, 62–63. As Foot noted, "The Chinese leadership quickly realized that it could use its weight within the global system to defy certain of the international demands and explore those underlying weaknesses in the global human rights regime." Foot, *Rights Beyond Borders*, 148.
[93] Foot, *Rights Beyond Borders*, 140.   [94] Mann, *About Face*, 284.
[95] Foot, *Rights Beyond Borders*, 140.
[96] James Reilly, "China's Unilateral Sanctions," *The Washington Quarterly* 35, no. 4 (Fall 2012) 123. After leaders from France, the United States, and Japan met with the Dalai Lama, those countries experienced an average 12.5 percent drop in their exports to China for two years. Andreas Fuchs and Nils-Hendrik Klann, "Paying a Visit: The Dalai Lama Effect on International Trade," *Journal of International Economics* 91 (2013): 164–177.

Denmark tabled a China resolution in the UNCHR, Beijing announced that in retaliation it would take "a rock that [it] will smash down on the Danish government's head" and is reported to have excluded Danish companies from contracts.[97] The PRC also punished the United States for supporting the 1997 resolution and rewarded the EU for backing away from UNCHR action by passing over Boeing and announcing a $1.5 billion Airbus purchase.[98] Two years later, Beijing appeared to reward France for not raising human rights during President Jiang's 1999 trip to France by announcing that it would buy twenty-eight Airbus jets.[99]

More recently, as China became the world's second largest economy and its global influence grew, it was in an even greater position to exercise its mushrooming leverage to mute criticism. In 2010, after the Oslo-based Nobel Committee awarded jailed Chinese political dissident and writer Liu Xiaobo the Nobel Peace Prize, the PRC put Norway in a "deep freeze" diplomatically and economically, including restrictions that are thought to have led to a decline in Norwegian salmon imports to China.[100] Because of Beijing's economic muscle and growing importance regionally and globally, the United States sought Beijing's cooperation in managing tensions between India and Pakistan, the six-party talks with North Korea, and the Global War on Terror.[101] The importance of PRC cooperation was reflected in US Secretary of State Clinton's February 2009 statement that even though she would raise human rights with China she insisted that "our pressing on those issues can't interfere with the global economic crisis, the global climate change crisis and the security crisis."[102] Beijing's fierce response to human rights scrutiny

---

[97] The PRC cancelled high-level visits and Danish exports declined by approximately half a billion Danish krone. Kinzelbach, *The EU's Human Rights Dialogue with China*, 37, and Paul Lewis, "China Warns Denmark on Resolution," *New York Times*, April 8, 1997.

[98] Seth Faison, "China to Buy 30 Planes for $1.5 Billion From Airbus Industrie," *New York Times*, May 16, 1997, www.nytimes.com/1997/05/16/business/china-to-buy-30-planes-for-1.5-billion-from-airbus-industrie.html, accessed January 3, 2018. The lure of the Chinese economy was such that when President Clinton attempted to link China's MFN status with human rights in the mid 1990s, his efforts failed in part because the US business community and members of his cabinet lobbied against it. Foot, *Rights Beyond Borders*, 162–163.

[99] Kinzelbach, *The EU's Human Rights Dialogue with China*, 67.

[100] Interview with Western European diplomat, August 29, 2016, via Skype.

[101] Foot, "Bush, China and Human Rights," 168, 179.

[102] Jane Perlez and Sharon LaFraniere, "Chinese Dissident Is Released from Embassy, Causing Turmoil for U.S.," *New York Times*, May 2, 2012, https://www.nytimes.com/2012/05/03/world/asia/chen-guangcheng-leaves-us-embassy-in-beijing-china.html?pagewanted=all, accessed June 5, 2018. See also "How Do You Get Tough on Your Banker?" and *Washington Post* op-ed, "Hillary Clinton's Silence on Chinese Human Rights," February 24, 2009, http://www.washingtonpost.com/wp-dyn/content/article/2009/02/23/AR2009022302412.html, accessed June 5, 2018.

meant that other countries often anticipated its wrath and practiced "preemptive obedience."[103] For example, when the United States delivered a 2016 joint statement signed by twelve countries, at least one country reported that it declined to sign the statement because it feared damage to the atmospherics for an upcoming visit with the PRC.[104] In a similar vein, Greece blocked the EU from delivering a statement at the Human Rights Council at the June 2017 session, which the PRC noted with satisfaction.[105]

Courting Non-Western Countries and the Developing World

In the aftermath of Tiananmen, the PRC quickly realized that support from the developing world was critical to recovering its diplomatic standing and defeating UNCHR resolutions and devised a number of strategies to secure their assistance. In order to break out of its post-Tiananmen diplomatic freeze, the PRC increased contact with non-Western countries and established official diplomatic relationships with countries that it had previously not recognized, including Singapore, Indonesia, South Korea, and Saudi Arabia.[106] Beijing's progress in establishing diplomatic relationships with these countries was a critical part of China's return to normalized relationships within the international community.

Beijing also saw that building Third World support would be critical to defeating resolutions in the UNCHR.[107] Even though Chinese leaders had been championing Third World causes since joining the UN, the backing of the developing world was initially tepid and at the 1990 UNCHR the PRC's no-action motion passed by a slim margin of victory with seventeen in favor, fifteen opposed, and eleven abstaining. Subsequently, the PRC was more attentive to recruiting developing

---

[103] Kinzelbach, *The EU's Human Rights Dialogue with China*, 70. The term "preemptive obedience" was used in a report on China's effort to expand its global influence. Benner et al., *Authoritarian Advance*, 2.

[104] Interview with European diplomat, June 24, 2016, Geneva, Switzerland.

[105] Robin Emmott and Angeliki Koutantou, "Greece Blocks EU Statement on China Human Rights at the U.N." *Reuters*, June 18, 2017, https://www.reuters.com/article/us-eu-un-rights/greece-blocks-eu-statement-on-china-human-rights-at-u-n-idUSKBN1990FP, accessed July 24, 2018. See also Benner et al., *Authoritarian Advance*, 16.

[106] Foot, *Rights Beyond Border*, 139. Beijing particularly made overtures to countries in the Asia Pacific, many of which were eager to establish beneficial economic relations.

[107] As noted by Foot, developing world diplomats cited political and economic considerations in their support for the PRC during the 1990 UNCHR session, including "They are our friends," "They send us economic aid," and "They are bringing political pressure on our government." Foot, *Rights Beyond Borders*, 141.

world votes and deployed economic largesse, diplomatic attention, and rhetorical arguments to marshal greater Third World support. For example, in the year after Tiananmen, Chinese foreign aid increased from \$223.5 million in 1989 to \$374.6 million.[108] Along these lines, the PRC's 1991 human rights white paper highlighted that it "always upheld justice and made unremitting efforts to safeguard the right of third world counties to national self-determination and to stop massive infringement of human rights" and touted its support for the right to development as reflecting its commitment to developing world causes.[109] The PRC's statement at the 1993 Vienna World Conference, which referenced the problems of colonialism, racism, apartheid, foreign invasion and occupation, and "the struggle for survival," also appeared to be crafted to appeal to the developing world.[110] While these strategies bore some fruit and the PRC found greater support in the UNCHR, it again intensified these efforts after 1995 when the no-action motion failed and the resolution came within a vote of passing.[111] Following this close call, CCP leaders strategically visited countries that were UNCHR members or would be joining the Commission and lavished them with diplomatic attention, aid, loans, and trade opportunities.[112] As a result, at the spring 1996 UNCHR session all of the African countries visited by CCP leaders voted for China's no-action motion. The PRC also stepped up efforts to appeal to Third World solidarity and consistently framed the UNCHR resolution as targeted at not merely itself but the whole of the developing world.[113] In this vein, PRC Ambassador Wu Jianmin asserted in

[108] Lin, T., "Beijing's Foreign Aid Policy in the 1990s: Continuity and Change," *Issues and Studies*, 32, no. 1, (1996): 32–65.

[109] Information Office of the State Council, *Progress of Human Rights in China, 1995*, Section X, Working Hard to Promote the Healthy Development of International Human Rights Activities.

[110] See Fried van Hoof, Asian Challenges to the Concept of Universality: Afterthoughts on the Vienna Conference on Human Rights," in *Human Rights: Chinese and Dutch Perspectives*, eds. Peter Baehr, Fried van Hoof, Liu Nanlai and Tao Zhenghua (The Hague: Martinus Nijhoff Publishers, 1996), 4–10.

[111] Foot, *Rights Beyond Borders*, 176. The PRC is reported to have circulated a memo to developing countries on the UNCHR threatening to cut off aid if they did not support the no-action motion. Kent, *China, the United Nations, and Human Rights*, 65.

[112] Human Rights Watch, *Chinese Diplomacy, Western Hypocrisy, and the U.N. Human Rights Commission*. For example, during the period between the 1995 and 1996 UNCHR annual sessions, Vice Premier Li Lanqing visited six African countries, five of which were slated to be UNCHR members, and the PRC Minister of Foreign Trade and Economic Cooperation visited seven African countries, six of which were going to be on the Commission.

[113] Information Office of the State Council, *The Progress of Human Rights in China, 1995*, Section X. The PRC's 1995 white paper characterized the introduction of country-specific resolutions on China as Western arrogance and the successful defeat of the

1996 that "under agenda item 10, 67 countries, almost all developing countries had been 'put in the dock' since 1992."[114] Likewise, in 2004, the PRC complained that "agenda item 9 had been distorted by certain Western countries, which used it to humiliate the developing countries and trample on their sovereignty through acrimonious attacks, arrogance and prejudice ... developing countries were not inveterate human rights violators."[115] These efforts paid dividends as the PRC defeated UNCHR resolutions by more comfortable margins and these countries later offered positive or soft-ball comments during China's UPR in the Human Rights Council.

Promoting Chinese Views and a Counternarrative

Almost immediately after the 1989 crackdown, the PRC began asserting its own human rights narrative and developed counterarguments that framed its opposition to human rights scrutiny as being based on principles such as noninterference with state sovereignty. For example, just days after the June 4 crackdown Premier Deng Xiaoping asserted that "China will never accept interference by other countries in its internal affairs ... The only solution is peaceful coexistence and cooperation of all countries with different social systems ... not interference in other countries' internal affairs and provoking disorders."[116] Beijing also turned to

resolutions as "a victory not only for China, but also for the vast number of developing countries."

[114] Quoted in the *New York Times*, April 24, 1996, p. A12. Kent noted that the PRC rallied the developing world with the refrain that "You could be next." Kent, *China, the United Nations and Human Rights*, 71.

[115] UN Economic and Social Council, "Commission on Human Rights, Sixtieth session, Summary Record of the 21st Meeting," April 1, 2004, UN Doc. E/CN.42004/SR.21, paragraph 54. See also UN Commission on Human Rights, "Summary Record of the 62nd Meeting," April 23, 2001, UN Doc. E/CN.4/2001/SR.62, paragraph 58; UN General Assembly, Third Committee, "Summary Record of the 32nd Meeting," February 9, 2011, UN Doc. A/C.3/65/SR.32, para 62; UN Commission on Human Rights, "Summary Record of the 56th Meeting," December 13, 2000, UN Doc. E/CN.4/2000/SR.56, paragraph 74; UN Commission on Human Rights, "Summary Record of the 50th Meeting," December 9, 2005, UN Doc. E/CN.4/2004/SR.50, paragraph 35; UN Commission on Human Rights, "Summary Record of the 21st Meeting," April 1, 2004, UN Doc. E/CN.4/2004/SR.21, paragraph 56; and UN Commission on Human Rights, "Summary Record of the 20th Meeting," April 8, 2005, UN Doc. E/CN.4/2005/SR.20, paragraph 17, and "Statement by Ambassador Wang Min at the Third Committee of the Sixty-Sixth Session of the United Nations General Assembly on Human Rights (Agenda Item 69 6 & c)," Permanent Mission of the PRC to the UN, www.china-un.org/eng/dbtxx/WMdsjl/WANGminhuodong/t871084.htm, accessed March 28, 2018.

[116] Bureau for the Compilation and Translation of Works of Marx, Engels, Lenin and Stalin, *Selected Works of Deng Xiaoping*, Vol. III, 348–49. See also Guo Jisi, "Opposing Using the Human Rights Issue as an Excuse to Interfere in Internal Affairs," *Renmin Ribao*, January 12, 1990, p. 7; Deng Xiaoping, "Deng Hails Armymen," *Beijing Review*,

Chinese scholars to develop rebuttals. As part of this strategy, the PRC government hosted the first domestic conference on human rights in September 1990 and established the China Society for Human Rights as a government-organized NGO in 1993.[117] The PRC's inaugural 1991 white paper featured some of these arguments, including making a case for Chinese human rights accomplishments; insisting that more attention be paid to economic rights and that the right to subsistence is the "most important" of all rights; arguing that state sovereignty is critical for the protection of human rights, especially given China's suffering at the hands of imperial aggressors; asserting the import of specific national, cultural, social, and developmental conditions; and favoring nonselective human rights monitoring in which all countries are treated equally instead of being subjected to country-specific monitoring.[118] Along these lines, in the introduction to its 1995 white paper on human rights the PRC touted that "[n]ational economic and social development in China has advanced by leaps and bounds ... The Chinese people's life has improved greatly."[119]

The PRC continued to adjust and augment these arguments and from the early 1990s onward gave resolutions on its human rights record a negative gloss by referring to them as "confrontation" and "naming and shaming" while calling for "cooperation and dialogue" and emphasizing "mutual respect."[120] Beijing also impugned the motives of those voicing

June 12–25, 1989; and Shi Yun, "Shei Shi Renquan de zhensheng hanweizhi?," [Who Are the True Defenders of Human Rights?], *Renmin Ribao*, July 7, 1989.

[117] Wei, "The Study of Human Rights in the People's Republic of China," 83–86 and 87–88, and Seymour, "Human Rights in Chinese Foreign Relations," 222. Svensson notes that in November 1989 the CCP Central Propaganda Department began convening meetings with scholars where they stressed the "urgency" of human rights scholarship to counter Western criticism. Svensson, *Debating Human Rights*, 267–268. For examples of PRC scholarship, see Dong Yunhu, *"Zhongguo renquan fazhan de yige zhongyao lichenbei"* (An Important Milestone in China's Human Rights Development), *Ren Quan* [Human Rights], no. 1 (2002): 25; Meng Chunyan, *"Jianchi Makesizhuyi renquanguan, fandui zichan jieji renquanguan"* [Insist on the Marxist View of Human Rights, Oppose the Bourgeois View of Human Rights], *Renmin Ribao* [People's Daily], September 17, 1990, and Guangbo Zhang, *"Jianchi Makesizhuyi renquanguan"* [Insisting on the Marxist View of Human Rights] *Zhongguo Faxue* [Chinese Legal Science] 4, no. 10 (1990).

[118] Information Office of the State Council, *Human Rights in China 1991* and Foot, *Rights beyond Borders*, 145.

[119] Information Office of the State Council, *The Progress of Human Rights in China, 1995*, Foreword.

[120] For PRC statement to this effect, see UN Commission on Human Rights, "Summary Record of the 44th Meeting," March 3, 1995, UN Doc. E/CN.4/1995/SR.44, paragraph 63–70. In its 1995 white paper the PRC endorsed the use of "dialogue and exchanges in the sphere of human rights," and ranted about the "anti-China proposals, [and] wantonly interfering in China's internal affairs." Information Office of the State

concern about Chinese human rights violations as being driven by animus rather than sincere concern. In this vein, the Chinese government described the UNCHR resolution as a "move ... designed [to] provide a forum for those with ulterior motives to continue their slandering of China in order to interfere in China's internal affairs."[121]

Advancing "Reform"

The PRC's vociferous complaints about the negative attention it received expanded into reformist efforts with the mid 1990s serving as a turning point. After the 1995 no-action motion failed in the UNCHR and a number of special procedures made critical mention of the PRC in their reports, Beijing responded with a 1995 statement that "the Commission was in need of comprehensive reform ... including streamlining the agenda, giving equal treatment to the two categories of human rights, reducing the Commission's workload, standardizing the participation of non-governmental organizations and eliminating selectivity."[122] This PRC statement fit within a broader effort to criticize certain parts of the regime and dilute the regime's monitoring capabilities under the guise of "reforms." The next year China made a similar statement and also called for geographic redistribution of seats and insisted that the UNCHR "should include more developing countries."[123] In 1997, the PRC again called for reform, especially prioritizing the developing world interests, including increasing their proportional representation and ridding the Commission of confrontation, meaning country-specific resolutions, in exchange for more cooperative forms of human rights monitoring.[124]

Council, *Progress of Human Rights in China, 1995*, Section X, Working Hard to Promote the Healthy Development of International Human Rights Activities.

[121] Similarly, Liu Hainan, a Chinese Academy of Social Sciences Scholar, asserted that "[d]ue to the dominance of some Western powers, the commission was turned into an instrument for them to interfere in the domestic affairs of other countries." Xing Zhigang, "Official Seeks Fresh Start for Rights Body," *China Daily*, June 22, 2006, www.chinadaily.com.cn/ 2006-06/22/content_623010.htm, accessed September 12, 2017.

[122] UN Economic and Social Council, "Commission on Human Rights Fifty first session, Summary Record of the 44th meeting," March 3, 1995, UN Doc. E/CN.4/1995/SR.44, paragraphs 63–66.

[123] See, for example, UN Commission on Human Rights, Summary Record of the 33rd Meeting, April 16, 1996, UN Doc. E/CN.4/1996/SR.33, para 1–6, and Wan, *Human Rights in Chinese Foreign Relations*, 113. This position likely reflected its realization that it benefited from the expansion of the Commission in 1991 from forty-three to fifty-three members with a growing number of seats going to the Africa, Asia, and Latin America.

[124] Kent, *China, the United Nations, and Human Rights*, 75.

The PRC along with similarly minded countries turned their reformist efforts toward the UNCHR's Sub-Commission which had passed resolutions on China in 1989 and 1991.[125] Beginning in the mid 1990s, these countries successfully eroded the Sub-Commission's authority through a series of resolutions that stripped this body of the authority to consider country situations being dealt with by the Commission, pass country or thematic resolutions that contained specific reference to individual countries, and initiate its own studies and research.[126] The PRC along with other authoritarian countries also made a "concerted push ... to eliminate all country-specific resolutions" in the UNCHR.[127]

Beijing also assailed other parts of the regime, including the special procedures and the treaty bodies. In 1995, the PRC protested that "[i]n some cases ... working groups were acting beyond the scope of their mandate; they were refusing to give serious consideration to replies from Governments, failing to respect sovereign judicial decisions, and reaching hasty decisions. Such methods cast doubt on the impartiality of those working groups."[128] Similarly, in 2005 China decried that the UN Special Rapporteur on Torture's trip report was "short on factual grounds and does not conform to reality" and assailed the credibility by stating that "within short two weeks and a trip to only three cities, the rapporteur may jump to conclusions."[129] In a similar vein, as treaty body scrutiny of China grew, the PRC responded with criticism. For example, in 1996, the PRC complained that "some treaty bodies addressed issues

---

[125] Following the Sub-Commission's 1991 resolution, PRC representative Zhang Yishan criticized the Sub-Commission as politicized and duplicating the work on the UNCHR and accused it of making "wanton attacks on the domestic affairs of sovereign states." Quoted in Kent, *China, the United Nations and Human Rights*, 63.

[126] See UNCHR, "Summary Record of the Fiftieth Meeting," December 11, 2000, UN Doc. E/CN.4/2000/SR.50, paragraph 74; UNCHR, "Work of the Sub-Commission on the Promotion and Protection of Human Rights," April 26, 2000, resolution 2000/83; UNCHR, "Enhancing the Dffectiveness of the Mechanisms of the Commission on Human Rights," April 26, 2000, decision 2000/109; UNCHR, "The Work of the Sub-Commission on the Promotion and Protection of Human Rights Commission on Human Rights," April 24, 2003, resolution 2003/59; UNCHR, "The Work of the Sub-Commission on the Promotion and Protection of Human Rights," April 20, 2005, Resolution, 2005/53. See also Kent, *China, the United Nations, and Human Rights*, 64, 74–75.

[127] Alston, "Reconceiving the UN Human Rights Regime: Challenges Confronting the New UN Human Rights Council," 196.

[128] UN Economic and Social Council, "Commission on Human Rights, Fifty-first session, Summary Record of the 44th Meeting," March 3, 1995, UN Doc. E/CN.41995/SR.44, paragraph 67.

[129] NBC News, "China Denies U.N. Claim of Widespread Torture," December 9, 2005, http://www.nbcnews.com/id/10347827/from/RS.1/#.WmoE_LpFzSE, accessed January 25, 2018. For similar PRC complaints, see Sceats and Breslin, *China and the International Human Rights System*, 13.

outside their terms of reference or duplicated the work of other bodies."[130]

Cooperation with Similarly Minded Countries

As discussed in Chapter 1, beginning in the mid to late 1990s, the PRC began to more explicitly work with a group of countries that shared its human rights views. These countries organized as the "Like-Minded Group" (LMG) and the group was initially composed of nineteen countries including Algeria, Bangladesh, Belarus, Bhutan, Cuba, Egypt, India, Indonesia, Iran, Malaysia, Myanmar, Nepal, Pakistan, the Philippines, Sri Lanka, Sudan, Vietnam, and Zimbabwe. In 1997, this group began offering joint statements opposing country-specific human rights monitoring; privileging dialogue and cooperation over confrontation; challenging the universality of human rights; emphasizing the right to development; and stressing state sovereignty at the expense of robust monitoring.[131] Although there is no particular ideology that connects them, the group's views closely aligned with China's, and several LMG member countries noted these views were already widely shared among these nations. As a diplomat hailing from an LMG member country put it, the PRC did not have to persuade other countries because "there was a meeting of the minds" on these issues.[132] While China was not described as the principal or permanent leader of the group, LMG participants and observers acknowledge China as one of the "core member countries" and from 2004 through 2006, the PRC served a turn

---

[130] UN Economic and Social Council, "Commission on Human Rights, Fifty-second session, Summary Record of the 16th Meeting," April 2, 1996, UN Doc. E/CN.4/1996/SR.16, paragraph 15.

[131] Alston, "Reconceiving the UN Human Rights Regime," 204–205. For examples of the group's statements, see UN Commission on Human Rights, "Summary Record of the 16th Meeting," March 30, 2004, UN Doc. E/CN.4/2004/SR.16, paragraph 53; UN Commission on Human Rights, "Summary Record of the 16th Meeting," November 8, 2005, UN Doc. E/CN.4/2005/SR.16, paragraph 36; UN Commission on Human Rights, "Rationalization of the Work of the Special Procedures System," April 10, 1997, UN Doc. E/CN.4/1997/L.86, and UN Commission on Human Rights, "Rationalization of the Work of the Commission," March 9, 1999, UN Doc. E/CN.4/1999/120. LMG views also detailed by a number of interviews, including diplomats from LMG countries. Interview with Latin American diplomat, June 1, 2011, Geneva, Switzerland; interview with Western European diplomat, May 26, 2011, Geneva, Switzerland; interview with former human rights NGO representative, May 26, 2011, Geneva, Switzerland; and interview with Southeast Asian diplomat, May 25, 2011, Geneva, Switzerland.

[132] Interview with Southeast Asian diplomat, May 25, 2011, Geneva, Switzerland.

as spokesperson for this group.[133] During this time, Ambassador Sha Zukang, speaking for the LMG, stated in 2005 that

[s]ince the end of the Cold War, the Commission had adopted over 100 country-specific resolutions that had almost all been directed against developing countries, leaving the impression that human rights problems existed only in those countries, and that developed countries had a perfect record ... Tabling of resolutions on country situations had therefore become a privilege of the strong and powerful, and it was not surprising, therefore, that those who had found themselves in the dock were often developing countries.[134]

More recently, at the March 2014 HRC session Egypt delivered a statement that an LMG participant described as the group's "charter."[135] Egypt's statement argued for the primacy of the state's responsibility to govern over "external imposition or external vision" or "attempts of some to impose ... values and ... social and legal standards"; the salience of the unique circumstances and the challenges facing each nation; rejecting the use of outside criticism, "politicization," and "double standards" without "understanding our daily problems"; and defending the right to development as an "inalienable right."[136] While the group's membership is not fixed, since 2011 the membership appears to have expanded and the group claims fifty-two members.[137] As detailed in Chapter 5, China and some of these countries have also cooperated by speaking in defense of each other in the HRC during the UPR process.

---

[133] Comments on the PRC role based on interview with former Middle Eastern diplomat, May 25, 2011, Geneva, Switzerland, and interview with Southeast Asian diplomat, May 25, 2011, Geneva, Switzerland. The interview with the Middle Eastern diplomat revealed that Egypt initiated the group and played a strong leadership role, even describing Egyptian diplomats as the "chief" of the LMG. Other countries also helped lead and organize the group at different times and membership of the LMG was not fixed. Other countries playing a leadership role included Egypt, Pakistan, and Malaysia.

[134] UN Commission on Human Rights, Sixty-First session, "Summary Record of the 20th Meeting," April 8, 2005, UN Doc. E/CN.4/2005/SR.20, paragraph 14.

[135] "The Like-Minded Group (LMG): Speaking Truth to Power," The Universal Rights Group, www.universal-rights.org/blog/like-minded-group-lmg-speaking-truth-power/, accessed April 4, 2018.

[136] UN Web TV, "Egypt, High-Level Segment - 8th Meeting, 25th Regular Session Human Rights Council," March 5, 2014. http://webtv.un.org/meetings-events/human-rights-treaty-bodies/chairpersons%E2%80%99-meeting/watch/egypt-high-level-segment-8th-meeting-25th-regular-session-human-rights-council/3296881104001?page=2, accessed July 26, 2018.

[137] "The Like-Minded Group (LMG): Speaking Truth to Power," The Universal Rights Group. An analysis of the group's statements reveals that fifty-one countries have signed onto the group's statements; twenty-one of them have signed ten or fewer. See Rana Siu Inboden, *Authoritarian States: Blocking Civil Society Participation in the United Nations* (Austin, Texas: Robert S. Strauss Center for International Security and Law, 2019).

Creating a Semblance of Human Rights Cooperation

The PRC has also sought to craft an image as an active and cooperative regime participant that is in good standing within the regime. This public relations effort stemmed from a desire to deflect human rights scrutiny as well as China's broader goal to project a positive global image. The language China used in multilateral venues or public documents portrayed it as much more cooperative than its record warrants. Along these lines, PRC government statements and publications drew attention to its activities, commitments, and procedural compliance. For example, the 1991 PRC white paper on human rights highlighted its ratification of treaties and noted that "[t]he Chinese government has always submitted reports on the implementation of related conventions, and seriously and earnestly performed the obligations it has undertaken."[138] Likewise, the PRC's 2003 white paper on human rights asserted that "China has all along been supportive of and actively participated in activities in the field of human rights sponsored by the United Nations."[139] In a similar vein, in 2009, it claimed that China participated in the UPR process with a "serious and highly-responsible attitude."[140] Similarly, when it sought HRC membership, Beijing stated that "it respects the universality of human rights and supports the UN in playing an important role in the protection and promotion of human rights" and detailed its myriad activities in the regime.[141] Yet, the actions that Beijing pointed to were primarily procedural, such as submitting reports or undergoing periodic reviews, and did not necessarily amount to substantive compliance, which by numerous accounts is deeply flawed.[142] Moreover, a number of its actions in the regime appear to have a symbolic or public relations motivation rather than being intended to bring about meaningful improvement in its practices.

Conclusion

This background on the international human rights regime, China's interactions with the regime, and Chinese strategies sets the context for

---

[138] Information Office of the State Council, *Human Rights in China, 1991.*

[139] Information Office of the State Council, *Progress in China's Human Rights Cause in 2003,* Section VIII, International Exchanges and Cooperation in Human Rights.

[140] Information Office of the PRC State Council, *Progress in China's Human Rights in 2009* (Beijing: Information Office of the PRC State Council, 2009).

[141] United Nations General Assembly, "Aide Memoire," April 13, 2006, www.un.org/ga/60/elect/hrc/china.pdf.

[142] For an example of PRC statements, see "FM Spokesman on China's Efforts to Promote Human Rights," *People's Daily,* November 21, 2000, www.china.org.cn/english/2000/Nov/4323.htm, accessed May 25, 2017.

the examination of the PRC's role in various parts of the human rights regime that follows. As has been shown, the creation of the international regime and its continued expansion meant that after the 1989 Tiananmen Massacre there were a number of procedures that were applied to China. Beijing responded with an approach that married participation and engagement with resistance and reformist efforts as well as vigorous assertion of its own human rights views. Thus, while this chapter traced China's shift from its Mao-era suspicion and dismissal of human rights to its willing entry and broader engagement with the regime and even cooperation with a number of procedures, it also demonstrates the limits of the PRC's acceptance of the regime and its intense aversion to human rights monitoring that spotlighted its violations.

In the post-Tiananmen era, Chinese diplomats expanded and honed their strategies. They continued to use a familiar mixture of diplomatic and economic muscle to deter attention from other countries; courting the developing world for support; espousing China's own views and a counternarrative; seeking to weaken regime mechanisms in the guise of "reforms"; cooperating with other countries with regard to shared grievances; and attempting to create the appearance of human rights cooperation without making substantive changes to bring the PRC's practices into compliance. These arguments and strategies formed the basis of the PRC's response to counter negative human rights attention that it would continue to rely on in later years as well and informed the tactics the PRC used as it acted out its various roles.

3 China, the Convention against Torture, and the Optional Protocol to the Convention against Torture: 1982–2002

China's conduct as a taker in the drafting and adoption of the Convention against Torture (CAT or the Convention) and later as a constrainer during the drafting of the Optional Protocol to the Convention against Torture (OPCAT or the Optional Protocol) illustrates the PRC's evolving posture toward the international human rights regime. The change from the more passive role of taker to an increasingly assertive one was largely the result of Beijing's experience in facing international opprobrium following the 1989 Tiananmen Square crackdown, which resulted in China's distaste for scrutiny of its record. This chapter shows how China benefited from the emergence in the late 1990s of a group of countries that resisted OPCAT and began jointly advancing positions in the drafting group affirming state sovereignty and the importance of each country's particular conditions, history, and traditions in the realization of human rights. Beijing's ability to work with this group and sign group statements helped obscure its resistance to OPCAT.

The Convention and the Optional Protocol are worthy of examination because they illuminate China's behavior in reference to what has been regarded as a peremptory norm involving harm to the person. In addition, they are important pillars of the international movement against torture that resulted from years of vigorous advocacy and prolonged negotiations. CAT, which was hailed as affirming that torture was "no longer acceptable in the eyes of the international community," bound state parties to implementation measures and led to the creation of a committee of experts responsible for reviewing state party compliance.[1] Created nearly two decades later, the Optional Protocol complemented CAT by establishing a body of independent experts who would conduct

---

[1] UN General Assembly, "93rd Plenary Meeting," December 11, 1984, UN Doc. A/39/PV.93, p. 11. For an analysis of CAT, see Andrew Byrnes, "The Committee against Torture," in *The United Nations and Human Rights: A Critical Appraisal*, ed. Philip Alston (Oxford: Clarendon Press, 1992), 509–511.

inspection visits to places of detention.[2] Both instruments were created through processes that began with negotiations over a draft by working groups and culminated in adoption by the UN General Assembly.[3] The working groups, which comprised between twenty and thirty government representatives, operated on the basis of consensus, meaning that votes were rarely taken and the discussions were intended to reach broad agreement.[4] Following the working group negotiations, the draft was considered by a series of UN bodies wherein state delegations could offer support, propose changes, or oppose adoption. During the negotiation and adoption process, states in favor of the proposed instrument had to sometimes accept concessions that watered down elements of the original draft.

The first half of the chapter focuses on CAT and the second half on the Optional Protocol. Each section begins with an introduction to the Convention, including a description of the drafting and negotiation process. The section that follows documents China's behavior in the drafting groups and the UN bodies that adopted both treaties. The creation of CAT and OPCAT provides an excellent opportunity to examine the PRC's behavior in smaller drafting groups largely comprising state representatives as well as in a variety of UN bodies, such as the UN Commission on Human Rights (UNCHR) and the General Assembly. Because the PRC signed CAT (but not OPCAT), I briefly address PRC compliance under CAT to underscore its continued tepid acceptance of it.

The Convention against Torture: Origins, Drafting, and Adoption

When the UN General Assembly adopted CAT in 1984, human rights activists and supportive states realized their goal of an international

---

[2] Malcolm Evans and Claudine Haenni-Dale, "Preventing Torture? The Development of the Optional Protocol to the UN Convention against Torture," *Human Rights Law Review* 4, no. 1 (2004), 20.

[3] J. Herman Burgers (Chairperson-Rapporteur of the Working Group, 1982–1984), interview by author, August 31, 2010, The Hague, Netherlands, and Evans and Haenni-Dale, "Preventing Torture?," 20.

[4] Evans and Haenni-Dale, "Preventing Torture?," 26; J. Herman Burgers and Hans Danelius, *The United Nations Convention against Torture: A Handbook on the Convention against Torture and Other Cruel, Inhuman or Degrading Treatment or Punishment* (London: Martinus Nijhoff Publishers, 1988), 26, and 32; and Burgers, interview. See also Association for the Prevention of Torture and the Inter-American Institute for Human Rights, *Optional Protocol to the United Nations Convention against Torture and Other Cruel, Inhuman or Degrading Treatment or Punishment: A Manuel for Prevention* (San Jose/Geneva: Inter-American Institute of Human Rights and the Association for the Prevention of Torture, 2005), 52.

convention prohibiting torture.[5] Although the UN had adopted the hortatory Declaration on Torture in 1975, advocates campaigned for a binding instrument with provisions for implementation and monitoring. In support of this goal, in 1977 Sweden proposed that the UN General Assembly convene a working group under the Commission on Human Rights and put forward a draft. In 1978, the diplomats comprising the drafting or working group began meeting on an annual basis for approximately one week prior to the spring UNCHR meeting and made some headway during the first several years. However, numerous areas of dispute remained. The Soviet Union and a number of other countries, including Eastern Bloc nations and some African and Asian states, contested elements of the draft, including the definition of torture and the authority of the proposed Committee against Torture.[6] In 1984, despite ongoing disagreement, J. Herman Burgers, the Dutch chairperson, decided to move the draft forward to the UNCHR. He did so because he believed that the group had "reached the limits of what it could accomplish in trying to find consensus"[7] and unease was growing among supporters of the Convention that delaying the process further might put the entire instrument in jeopardy or result in a weakened Convention.[8]

As the draft Convention moved through a succession of UN bodies in 1984, a number of states resisted it and pressed for changes. The Soviet Union and several other Warsaw Pact countries expressed reservations about Article 19, which addressed the Committee's authority to comment on state reports, and Article 20, which outlined the Committee's

---

[5] Ann-Marie Bolin Pennegard, "Overview Over Human Rights—the Regime of the UN," in *International Human Rights Monitoring Mechanisms: Essays in honor of Jakob Th. Moller*, eds., Gudmundur Alfredsson, Jonas Grimheden, Bertran G. Ramcharan, and Alfred de Zayas (The Hague: Martinus Nijhoff Publishers, 2001). For a discussion of advocacy efforts, see Matthew Lippman, "The Development and Drafting of the United Nations Convention against Torture and Other Cruel, Inhuman or Degrading Treatment or Punishment," *Boston College International and Comparative Law Review* 17, no. 2 (1994), 275–335; Ann Marie Clark, *Diplomacy of Conscience: Amnesty International and Changing Human Rights Norms* (Princeton, New Jersey: Princeton University Press, 2001); and Hilde Reiding, *The Netherlands and the Development of International Human Rights Instruments* (Antwerp: Intersentia, 2007).

[6] There was a need to reconcile a number of NGO- and state-sponsored drafts. Reiding, *The Netherlands and the Development of International Human Rights Instruments*, 79 and 83–84.

[7] UN Commission on Human Rights, 40th Session, "Summary Record of the 32nd meeting," March 6, 1984, UN Doc. E/CN.4/1984/SR.32, paragraphs 62–65, and Burgers and Danelius, *The United Nations Convention against Torture*, 100.

[8] Reiding, *The Netherlands and the Development of International Human Rights Instruments*, 80–85.

ability to launch an inquiry.[9] Despite their ongoing concerns, these countries did not oppose moving the draft forward to the Commission on Human Rights, the Economic and Social Council (ECOSOC), and the Third Committee of the General Assembly, which consider these kinds of human rights matters before they are brought to the UN General Assembly. The naysayers did not mount any challenges in the UNCHR or ECOSOC, which adopted the Convention by consensus. However, in the Third Committee, where social, humanitarian, and cultural issues are addressed, the Soviet Union, several Eastern Bloc countries, and a number of African and Asian states persisted in voicing opposition to Articles 19 and 20.[10] The Soviet Union led a number of these countries in proposing amendments to the aforementioned articles, including restricting the Committee's ability to put forward prescriptive comments in response to state reports and not requiring state parties to allow the Committee to launch an inquiry following reports of systematic torture. In order to break the impasse, CAT supporters agreed to several concessions that restricted the Committee to offering only "general comments" in response to state reports and allowed states to opt out of the inquiry procedure.[11] Once agreement on these changes was reached, the UN Third Committee adopted the resolution by consensus and the meeting "broke in[to] spontaneous applause."[12] The compromises made in the Third Committee paved the way for UN member states to adopt CAT by consensus in the UN General Assembly.[13]

The Convention bound state parties to specific responsibilities to prevent and combat torture by taking "effective legislative, administrative, judicial or other measures to prevent acts of torture in any territory under its jurisdiction."[14] The Convention also established the Committee against Torture, comprising ten experts elected by state parties and

---

[9] Burgers and Danelius, *The United Nations Convention against Torture*, 101.

[10] Burgers and Danelius, *The United Nations Convention against Torture*, 102–103.

[11] There were also minor changes made to the inquiry procedure, including emphasizing the importance of consultation and cooperation with the state party in the inquiry process. Reiding, *The Netherlands and the Development of International Human Rights Instruments*, 87–88. For the official record, see UN General Assembly, "Torture and Other Cruel, Inhuman or Degrading Treatment or Punishment: Report of the Third Committee," December 7, 1984, UN Doc. A/39/708, and UN General Assembly, "Summary Record of the 44th Meeting," November 19, 1984, UN Doc. A/C.3/39/SR.44, paragraphs 48–52, 56, and 60.

[12] Burgers and Danelius, *The United Nations Convention against Torture*, 106. The Soviet Union was particularly concerned that the Committee not be given the authority to determine noncompliance.

[13] Ibid. For the official record, see UN General Assembly, "93rd Plenary Meeting," December 10, 1984, UN Doc. A/39/PV.93.

[14] Article 2.

responsible for monitoring implementation of obligations, primarily by reviewing mandatory periodic state reporting and presiding over a public examination with state representatives.[15] Under Articles 21 and 22, states were given the option of allowing the Committee to consider interstate and individual complaints of torture.[16] As noted earlier, at the behest of a group of countries led by the Soviet Union, Article 20, which empowered the Committee to initiate an inquiry in response to reliable reports of systematic torture, was made into a voluntary article.[17]

China and the Convention against Torture

The PRC delegation, which had become a member of the Commission on Human Rights only in 1982, joined the CAT drafting group that same year and continued to participate until the Convention was completed in 1984. The drafting group had been meeting annually since 1978 and had already made some headway by the time Chinese representatives began attending these sessions. Although they were in attendance, PRC diplomats were not active participants in the drafting or adoption process and maintained a low profile as they offered few statements in the drafting group and remained silent during the adoption process. The PRC appeared to be unfamiliar and cautious as it did not voice opinions on a number of contentious issues being debated, including issues that fellow communist countries were challenging. J. Herman Burgers, chair of the working group from 1982 to 1984, noted that "China did not play a very active role, either obstructionist or cooperative."[18] Documentary sources, including the UN reports of the working group and a detailed account of the drafting process written by the two chairpersons of the working group, confirm this quiescent role.[19]

---

[15] Article 19.
[16] The reporting requirement and the consideration of individual and interstate complaints were similar to procedures in previous human rights treaties. The interstate procedure outlined in Article 21 is based on reciprocity.
[17] Article 28 allows a state party to declare that it does not recognize the Committee's competence to undertake an inquiry as outlined in Article 20. This inquiry procedure, which can include an investigative visit if agreed to by the state party, had not been featured in previous human rights instruments.
[18] J. Herman Burgers (Chairperson-Rapporteur of the Working Group, 1982–84), email correspondence with author, April 8, 2010.
[19] UN General Assembly, "Report of the Working Group on a Draft Convention against Torture and Other Cruel, Inhuman or Degrading Treatment or Punishment," March 5, 1982, UN Doc. E/CN.4/1982/L.40; UN General Assembly, "Report of the Working Group on a Draft Convention against Torture and Other Cruel, Inhuman or Degrading Treatment or Punishment," February 28, 1983, UN Doc. E/CN.4/1983/L.2; and UN Economic and Social Council, "Report of the Working Group on a Draft Convention

Initially, Chinese diplomats attended the drafting group sessions without making any statements or voicing support for or disagreement with the issues being discussed.[20] It was not until 1984, the final year of the drafting group, that the Chinese representatives made several statements, such as supporting the inclusion of a list of situations under which torture might be likely to occur, with specific reference to apartheid, racial discrimination, and genocide, which were human rights issues that already aligned with the PRC's existing ideas. Specifically, the PRC delegate stated that "although he agreed to the final text in a spirit of compromise, he would have preferred the listing of examples in paragraph 2, such as a state policy of apartheid, racial discrimination or genocide."[21] The PRC likely raised these points because apartheid, racial discrimination, and genocide were issues that resonated with the developing world. The inclusion of this proposed list would not have strengthened the Convention and Beijing's position appeared to be a maneuver to make common cause with the developing world. It was ultimately not accepted in the final text.

More significantly, at the 1984 session, the Chinese delegation opposed the language on universal jurisdiction.[22] Human rights scholar Jack Donnelly explains that universal jurisdiction meant that

State Parties are required to prosecute alleged torturers who are their nationals, who tortured victims who are their nationals, who committed torture in their territory, or who simply are found in their territory and then are not extradited to a State that has established criminal jurisdiction over the offense. And they may hold any torturer pending further proceedings, whatever the circumstances surrounding the offense.[23]

against Torture and Other Cruel, Inhuman or Degrading Treatment or Punishment," February 20, 1984, UN Doc. E/CN.4/1984/L.2. Because some of the UN reporting does not refer to country delegations by name, interviews and secondary literature, including a monograph by the two chairpersons of the drafting group, were used to supplement these records. As chairpersons of the working group, the authors' description of the drafting process could be considered a firsthand account.

20 For the 1982 session, see the UN General Assembly, "Report of the Working Group on the Draft Convention against Torture," March 5, 1982, UN Doc. E/CN.4/1982/L.40, and Burgers and Danelius, *The United Nations Convention against Torture*, 77–84. For the 1983 discussion see UN General Assembly, "Report of the Working Group on the Draft Convention against Torture," February 28, 1983, UN Doc. E/CN.4/1983/L.2, and Burgers and Danelius, *The United Nations Convention against Torture*, 84–91.

21 UN General Assembly, "Report of the Working Group on a Draft Convention against Torture," February 20, 1984, UN Doc. E/CN.4/1984/L.2, paragraph 25.

22 UN General Assembly, "Report of the Working Group on a Draft Convention against Torture," February 20, 1984, UN Doc. E/CN.4/1984/L.2, paragraph 25, and Burgers and Danelius, *The United Nations Convention against Torture*, 91–99.

23 Jack Donnelly, "The Emerging International Regime against Torture," *Netherlands International Law Review* 33, no. 1 (Spring 1986), 4.

Proponents of CAT argued that this clause was essential in order to give the Convention implementation powers and ensure that there would be no "safe havens" for torturers and that those who commit torture would be held accountable.[24] In contrast to its more flexible position in favor of an illustrative list of situations in which torture might occur, the Chinese delegation was firmer in its opposition to universal jurisdiction. The PRC representative stated that "it considered the current formulation of the draft articles concerned [on universal jurisdiction] not entirely satisfactory."[25] Further, according to an account by J. Herman Burgers and Hans Danelius, who served as the chairpersons of the working group, at the 1984 session "all delegations except the Chinese delegation were prepared to accept the current text."[26] It was uncharacteristic for the novice Chinese delegation to take such a divisive stand, especially when it was the only holdout. PRC diplomats were finally persuaded to accept this clause after informal consultations with the chairperson, which led to their realization that they were the only state disputing this language.[27] Despite China's concern with this article, it yielded in order to avoid being isolated or hindering progress.

As the draft moved through the UN adoption process, the PRC maintained a low profile, neither blocking nor explicitly supporting it. During debate in the Third Committee when key compromises were negotiated, China's representatives did not express their positions on a number of controversial and significant issues.[28] When the Soviet Union led a group of countries in successfully pushing to make the inquiry function optional and restricting the kinds of comments the Committee against Torture could make in response to state reports, China remained on the sidelines of these critical discussions.

On balance, the PRC's posture in the drafting and adoption of CAT was that of a taker. Aside from the single instance when it resisted the universal jurisdiction clause and its suggestion to include a reference to

[24] See UN General Assembly, "Report on the Working Group on the Draft Convention against Torture," March 5, 1982, UN Doc. E/CN.C/1982/L.40, paragraph 22.

[25] UN General Assembly, "Report of the Working Group on a Draft Convention against Torture," February 20, 1984, UN Doc. E/CN.4/1984/L.2, paragraph 28.

[26] Burgers and Danelius, *The United Nations Convention against Torture*, 94–95. See also UN Economic and Social Council, "Report of the Working Group on a Draft Convention against Torture and Other Cruel, Inhuman or Degrading Treatment or Punishment," UN Doc. E/CN.4/L.2, paragraphs 26–36.

[27] Burgers, interview.

[28] Burgers and Danelius, *The United Nations Convention against Torture*, 101–106; UN General Assembly Third Committee, "Summary Record of the 44th meeting of the Third Committee," November 19, 1984, UN Doc. A/C.3/39/SR.44; and UN General Assembly, "Record of the 93rd Meeting of the 39th Session of the General Assembly," December 10, 1984, UN Doc. A/39/PV.93.

apartheid, racial discrimination, and genocide, Beijing generally participated without seeking to shape the outcome. Even when PRC representatives expressed views against universal jurisdiction, as soon as it became clear that they were obstructing progress, they retreated and allowed the draft to move forward. This guarded acceptance of the Convention continued after CAT became a reality and the PRC became a state party.

The PRC further demonstrated its willingness to accept the regime and act as a taker when it signed CAT in 1986 and then ratified it in October 1988. However, despite its ratification, there were also limits to Beijing's acceptance of this treaty and it exempted itself from key optional provisions that allowed the Committee to launch an inquiry, receive individual complaints, and consider complaints from other states. It is one of only fourteen state parties that have opted out of Article 20, which allows the Committee to initiate a confidential inquiry in response to reports of systematic use of torture. This put the PRC in the company of Afghanistan, Equatorial Guinea, Eritrea, Israel, Fiji, Kuwait, Laos, Mauritania, Pakistan, Saudi Arabia, Syria, the United Arab Emirates, and Vietnam in refusing to grant the Committee this authority.[29] Further, the Chinese government did not enable the other optional clauses as it did not recognize the Committee's authority outlined in Articles 21 and 22, which enable the Committee to receive interstate and individual complaints.[30] The only procedure that it bound itself to was the reporting requirement, which was the one mandatory provision for state parties.

The PRC's degree of compliance with reporting and its conduct during its reviews show that even as a taker, it has exhibited some resistance. Even though it has submitted reports, it has often been late and it has at times been resistant to providing critical data. For example, even though the reporting period is four years, there was a seven-year gap from

[29] This list is accurate as of October 9, 2017. "Committee against Torture, Confidential inquiries under article 20 of the Convention against Torture," UN Office of the High Commissioner for Human Rights, www.ohchr.org/EN/HRBodies/CAT/Pages/Inquiry Procedure.aspx, accessed indicators.ohchr.org, accessed October 9, 2017.
[30] One hundred states have not accepted the Committee's competence to receive interstate communications outlined in Article 21. Ninety-six other states have not accepted the Committee's competence to receive communications from individuals as outlined in Article 22. As of June 2017, 162 countries had signed, ratified, or acceded to the Convention. UN General Assembly, "Report of the Committee against Torture, 51st–52nd sessions," May 2014, UN Doc. A/69/44, Annex III, and "Convention against Torture and Other Cruel, Inhuman or Degrading Treatment or Punishment," United Nations Treaty Collection, https://treaties.un.org/Pages/ViewDetails.aspx?src=IND&mtdsg_no=IV-9&chapter=4&lang=en, accessed July 30, 2018.

April 1999 until February 2006, when China finally submitted its third report, which was three years late.[31] Similarly, after its February 2006 report, it did not submit another report until June 2013.[32] Scholar Ann Kent described the PRC delegation's response to its first appearance before the Committee against Torture in the early 1990s by noting in particular that

[t]he Chinese representatives were reported to have been visibly upset by Committee members' reaction to its report, which was subsequently privately described as 'completely inadequate.' They were undoubtedly aware that the request to provide a supplementary report was not a regular occurrence. Their general reaction was astonishment that ten Committee members could question the condition of 1.2 billion Chinese citizens.[33]

Along these lines, PRC officials displayed a "basic failure to understand and accept the norms, principles, rules, and obligations flowing from its accession" and they asked for explanations on procedures and appeared baffled by the Committee's response to its first report.[34] Moreover, the PRC's reviews have involved tough questions and incomplete PRC answers and follow-up, which further indicate that the PRC has not fully embraced this Convention.

More recently and in a similar vein, the PRC's 2015 review was characterized by sharp questioning from UN experts, nonresponsive answers from PRC officials, and lack of follow-up on previous recommendations.[35] For example, Committee member Felice Gaer questioned CCP (Chinese Communist Party) government officials about reported abuses, such as the refoulement of North Koreans and the Hong Kong police's use of force in response to peaceful demonstrations. She also expressed concern about the PRC government's incomplete responses to the Committee's questions and reports that PRC authorities prevented

---

[31] "Reporting Status for China," UN Office of the High Commissioner for Human Rights, tbinternet.ohchr.org/_layouts/TreatyBodyExternal/Countries.aspx?CountryCode=CHN& Lang=EN, accessed October 9, 2017.

[32] Ibid.

[33] Kent, *China, the United Nations, and Human Rights*, 95–97. The official UN reporting, particularly the comments and questions from the Committee, demonstrated the inadequacy of China's reporting. See United Nations, "Committee against Torture, Fourth Session, Summary Record of the 51st Meeting," May 4, 1990, UN doc. CAT/C/SR.51, paragraphs 36–52. See also UN General Assembly, "Report of the Committee against Torture, 47th–48th sessions," June 2012, UN Doc. A/67/44.

[34] Kent, *China, the United Nations and Human Rights*, 96 and 105.

[35] See Nick Cummings-Bruce, "China Faces Sharp Questioning by U.N. Panel on Torture," *New York Times*, November 17, 2015, www.nytimes.com/2015/11/18/world/asia/china-faces-sharp-questioning-by-un-panel-on-torture.html?_r=0, accessed June 2, 2017, and UN Committee against Torture, "Concluding Observations on the fifth periodic report of China," February 3, 2016, UN. Doc CAT/C/CHN/C/5.

seven Chinese citizens from departing the country in order to attend the CAT review in Geneva.[36] Reflecting on this behavior, a Committee member noted:

[W]hen we then look at the substance in the constructive dialogue, it was not as constructive as the start might have indicated ... Because ... a lot of replies [from the Chinese government] were simply not given. A lot of replies to the questions provided were either evaded or they were denied, referring to state secrets. And we had a large number of questions that in terms of statistics—in terms of complaints, executions, and investigations—that were never replied to, or at least not replied in a satisfactory manner.[37]

More importantly, China's substantive conformity with CAT remains problematic. While the Chinese government has taken some steps to combat torture, including making torture illegal under domestic law, providing legal means to seek compensation in instances of state use of torture, and changing criminal laws to exclude evidence obtained through torture, implementation and enforcement are weak, and serious problems remain. Consequently, following a 2005 investigative visit, the UN Special Rapporteur on Torture found that "[t]hough [torture is] on the decline, particularly in urban areas ... torture remains widespread in China."[38] In this vein, scholar Katie Lee asserted that the PRC's ratification of CAT "had some impact on China's de jure compliance but very little, if any, direct impact on de facto compliance."[39] Further, Chinese officials have displayed resistance to normative pressure to comply with the Convention. For example, at the November 2015 review before CAT, Chinese officials not only admitted to the use of interrogation chairs but defended this practice. As a CAT member noted:

[36] United Nations Committee against Torture, "Fifty-sixth session, Summary record of the 1368th meeting," November 20, 2015, UN Doc. CAT/S/SR.1368, paragraphs 59, 63, 64, 89, and 92.

[37] Interview with CAT expert member by author, October 5, 2016, via Skype.

[38] UN Commission on Human Rights, "Report of the Special Rapporteur on Torture, Manfred Nowak, Mission to China," March 10, 2006, UN Doc. E/CN.4/2006/6/Add.6, p. 2. The Rapporteur also noted the necessity of further steps, including broadening the definition of torture under Chinese law to comply with international standards, establishing an independent body to investigate complaints of torture, and making torture by law enforcement officials a specific criminal act under domestic law. He also called for procedural safeguards and noted that "[t]he situation is aggravated by lack of self-generating and/or self-governing social and political institutions including a free and investigatory press, citizen-based independent human rights monitoring organizations, independent commissions visiting places of detention, and independent, fair and accessible courts and prosecutors."

[39] Katie Lee, "China and the International Covenant on Civil and Political Rights: Prospects and Challenges," *Chinese Journal of International Law* 6, no. 2 (2007), 455–456.

[T]he interrogation chairs are present in all police stations where people are being interrogated when they are suspected of a crime. And they are fixated in hands and feet, and they can sit there with no time limitation ... And apparently the [PRC] delegation—I was surprised—they were not even ashamed about it. They acknowledged that this interrogation chair existed, and their argument, which was even more surprising, was that it is to prevent escape—which is ridiculous, from a police station—or suicide—which is also ridiculous in a situation where you have a number of police officers or interrogators interrogating a suspect ... I would have thought that any government would have been ashamed or tried to deny it, or say, "Well, we'll do something about it, because obviously it's in conflict with the convention, etc." But they didn't.[40]

Thus, despite some efforts toward procedural compliance, such as submitting reports and participating in an examination before the Committee against Torture, a number of PRC government policies and practices contravene the Convention.

Moreover, even though the PRC has not renounced its ratification, it has been resistant to the treaty body's authority. Beginning in the 1990s Beijing voiced positions that the reviews by treaty bodies, including CAT, should be limited to "an exchange of views on an equal footing."[41] PRC officials portrayed treaty bodies as advisory bodies rather than being authorized to monitor state compliance. Thus, Beijing's taker posture could be shifting to one that is defiant toward the regime's authority. As will be shown in the section that follows, Chinese officials adopted a much more assertive and consequential role when UN member states began discussions over OPCAT in 1992.

The Optional Protocol to the Convention against Torture: Origins, Drafting, and Adoption

The genesis of the Optional Protocol arises from the work of Jean-Jacques Gautier, a Swiss banker and founder of the Swiss Committee against Torture, a nongovernmental organization. During the mid-1970s, in the midst of the discussions over CAT, Gautier began calling for the creation of an international body to conduct preventive visits, which was largely based on the model of the International Committee of the Red Cross, which was premised on opening places of detention to inspection visits.[42] At this time CAT was not yet a reality and as support for this idea grew, several competing approaches were proposed,

[40] Interview with CAT expert member by author, October 5, 2016, via Skype.
[41] Quoted in Kinzelbach, "Will China's Rise Lead to a New Normative Order?" 316.
[42] Evans and Haenni-Dale. "Preventing Torture?" 22 and 25. Ann-Marie Bolin Pennegard, "An Optional Protocol, Based on Prevention and Cooperation," in *An End*

including a draft based on Gautier's vision.[43] However, other human rights activists were concerned that including such an ambitious system of visits might complicate and impede passage of CAT. They felt that achieving a convention that first outlawed torture, provided for specific implementation measures, and established a monitoring system was a critical first step toward combating torture. Thus, other activists convinced Gautier to withdraw his draft with the understanding that a system of preventive visits would form the basis of a separate and complementary Optional Protocol after the passage of CAT was secured.[44] Finally, in 1991, based on a draft proposed by Costa Rica, the idea for an Optional Protocol was reintroduced at the UNCHR and a working group convened the following year.

The drafting process involved ten years of prolonged negotiations that spanned 1992 until 2002 and was marked by discord, conflict, and resistance efforts by the "coalition of the unwilling."[45] As with the CAT drafting group, the OPCAT working group usually met for a week or two prior to the annual UNCHR session. The Costa Rican draft, which formed the basis of discussions, proposed to create a Subcommittee that would have a "near unrestricted right of access to places of, and persons in, detention."[46] This novel approach provoked discomfort among some nations, which had misgivings about an international entity with far-reaching visiting authority and about allowing such extensive access.[47] Differences over the proposed Optional Protocol fueled "mounting levels of polarization between States, who supported the establishment of a solid preventive mechanism for visits and those resolved to either weaken its scope or to block it all together" and the drafting process dragged on as nations struggled to reach consensus.[48] In 1999, at the seventh annual session, the protracted negotiations caused the chairperson to stress to the

to Torture: Strategies for its Eradication, ed. Bertil Duner (London: Zed Books, 1998), 40–49.

[43] Clark, *Diplomacy of Conscience*, 67.

[44] Pennegard, "An Optional Protocol, Based on Prevention and Cooperation," 41–43.

[45] Claudine Haenni-Dale (APT Secretary General, 1995–2001), interview by author, June 2, 2010, Geneva, Switzerland. Haeeni-Dale was a key NGO participant and later advisor to Judge Odio-Benito.

[46] Association for the Prevention of Torture and the Inter-American Institute for Human Rights, *Optional Protocol*, 44.

[47] Haenni-Dale, interview, and Pennegard, interview.

[48] Association on the Prevention of Torture and the Inter-American Institute for Human Rights, *Optional Protocol*, 44 and 52. Ann-Marie Bolin Pennegard (chairperson of the informal working group, 1994–1999), interview by author, August 31, 2010, Brussels, Belgium. From 1994 to 1999, in an effort to achieve greater progress, the working group also convened an informal group under the leadership of Pennegard. See also Evans and Haenni-Dale, "Preventing Torture?" 26–27.

diplomats in the working group "the urgent need to conclude the work on the draft optional protocol without further delay" and the representative for the Association for the Prevention of Torture (APT), a nongovernmental organization, to lament that the "enormous mistrust among the delegations had killed all spirit of cooperation as well as the expectations of the international community."[49] After seven years, OPCAT supporters were "frustrated that the negotiations had stalled."[50]

It was also at the seventh session, in 1999, that Cuba, Algeria, Egypt, Saudi Arabia, Sudan, Syria, and China initiated more explicit cooperation in the form of joint statements and written submissions as a group.[51] As will be detailed in the following section, the thrust of these interventions emphasized state sovereignty, including calling for language affirming domestic legislation; the import of cultural, national, and other domestic conditions; and limitations on the proposed Subcommittee's access and authority. A Western diplomat speculated that these countries may have resorted to strengthened cooperation because "things were not moving in their direction, so in order to influence the outcome they had to cooperate more openly against some aspects" of OPCAT.[52] Another Western European diplomat described this group of countries as "the usual suspects" who seek to hold back the strengthening of the regime.[53] In a similar vein, another diplomat participant described these countries as "a group of spoilers who simply didn't want OPCAT" to become a reality.[54] In contrast, a former diplomat who represented a country in the group of resistors defended the

[49] For the chairperson's remarks, see UN Economic and Social Council, "Report of the Working Group on the Draft Optional Protocol to the Convention against Torture and Other Cruel, Inhuman, or Degrading Treatment or Punishment on its Seventh Session," March 26, 1999, UN Doc. E/CN.4/1999/59, paragraph 22. For the APT's statement, see UN Economic and Social Council, "Report of the Working Group on the Draft Optional Protocol to the Convention against Torture and Other Cruel, Inhuman, or Degrading Treatment or Punishment on its Seventh Session," March 26, 1999, UN Doc. E/CN.4/1999/59, paragraph 107.

[50] Cecelia Jimenez (former program officer for the Association for the Prevention of Torture and participant in the Working Group, 1998–2002) interview by author, June 2, 2010, Geneva, Switzerland.

[51] For examples of this group's position, see UN Economic and Social Council, "Report of the Working Group on the Draft Optional Protocol to the Convention against Torture and Other Cruel, Inhuman or Degrading Treatment or Punishment," December 2, 1999, E/CN.4/2000/58, paragraph 63. Costa Rican diplomat Christian Guillermet speculated that the joint written submission requiring state consent and limiting the places the Subcommittee could visit was drafted by Saudi Arabia. Christian Guillermet (Costa Rican diplomat, who participated in the working group, 1998–2002), interview by author, June 8, 2010, Geneva, Switzerland.

[52] Pennegard, interview.

[53] Interview with Western European diplomat, June 28, 2011, New York.

[54] Interview with Western European diplomat, July 26, 2010, Copenhagen, Denmark.

actions of these countries and explained that these nations had an "alternate vision" from the "myopic" view advanced by the supporters of OPCAT, which he noted were primarily Western countries.[55] The former diplomat elaborated that this informal group in OPCAT was the precursor to the Like-Minded Group, a more formal group that was active in the Commission on Human Rights.[56] The issues this group of countries first began championing in OPCAT were similar to the themes that the Like-Minded Group rallied around.

As the drafting process entered its ninth year, some proponents of the Optional Protocol had become concerned that further sessions would be fruitless and that the proposed instrument might not be adopted.[57] The discussions were mired by the same intractable differences, and discord permeated the drafting group's sessions. At this juncture, Mexico disrupted negotiations by introducing a new draft that took a different approach. Mexico's draft gave primacy to a national-level body and a diminished role for the international Subcommittee, which was relegated to providing support and supervision to the national-level entity. In a nod to the original version, the Mexican draft gave states the option of allowing the international Subcommittee to conduct visits. This dramatically different proposal disarmed some of the resistant countries who had not wanted to see a strong international entity, yet it alarmed a number of the supporters of the original draft, including Sweden, which on behalf of the European Union offered a counterdraft that elevated the importance of the proposed international Subcommittee and granted a more limited role to national counterparts. At this point, the negotiations were "on a knife-edge" and "some [participants] believed that no further progress was possible and the session ended in considerable disarray."[58]

With the goal of producing a consensus document, at the end of the tenth session Judge Odio Benito, who had served as chairperson for the first session and had resumed this role at the eighth session, put forward a compromise draft. This version blended national and international approaches by establishing an international body, which took the lead in conducting inspection visits, complemented by independent monitoring by national bodies.[59] At around this time, some of the proponents of

[55] Interview of former Middle Eastern diplomat, May 25, 2011, Geneva, Switzerland.
[56] Interview of former Middle Eastern diplomat, May 25, 2011, Geneva, Switzerland.
[57] Association for the Prevention of Torture and the Inter-American Institute for Human Rights, *Optional Protocol*, 49.
[58] Evans and Haenni-Dale, "Preventing Torture?" 27.
[59] UN Economic and Social Council, "Report of the Working Group on the Draft Optional Protocol to the Convention against Torture and Other Cruel, Inhuman or Degrading Treatment or Punishment," February 20, 2002, UN Doc. E/CN.4/2002/78, paragraph

Table 3.1 *UN voting on the Optional Protocol to the Convention against Torture*[a]

	For	Against	Abstain
Commission on Human Rights	29	10	14
Economic and Social Council	35	8	10
Third Committee	104	8	37
General Assembly	127	4	42

[a] For voting in the UNCHR, see UN Commission on Human Rights, "Report of the 58th Session, Supplement No. 3," March 18–April 26, 2002, UN Doc. E/2002/23, paragraph 335. For ECOSOC voting, see UN Economic and Social Council, "Provisional Summary Record of the 38th Meeting," November 12, 2002, UN Doc. E/2002/SR.38, paragraph 89. For the Third Committee voting record, see UN General Assembly, "Human rights questions: implementation of human rights instruments," October 28, 2002, UN Doc. A/C.3/57/L.30. For voting in the General Assembly see UN General Assembly, "Resolution Adopted by the General Assembly, Resolution 57/199 Optional Protocol to the Convention against Torture," January 9, 2003, A/RES/57/199.

OPCAT also acknowledged that there might be an important role for a national mechanism since an international body lacked the capacity and resources to conduct a sufficient number of worldwide visits per year with the result that some countries might go for long periods of time without a visit.[60] Unlike the Mexican draft, Odio Benito's draft contained no opt-in clause for visits by the international body and acceptance of both international and national mechanisms was compulsory. Despite continued resistance from some countries, Odio Benito believed that "sufficient ideas and proposals had been put on the table over the past ten years" and pressed to move the draft to the Commission.[61]

In 2002, as the draft made its way through the UN, including the UNCHR, the ECOSOC, the Third Committee, and the General Assembly, the countries most opposed to it attempted to block adoption, forcing a vote rather than the UN's preferred method of adoption by consensus. Table 3.1 captures the voting outcomes. Aside from Cuba, China, Algeria, Egypt, Syria, and Sudan, the United States also sought to prevent passage and explained that "certain specific provisions conflicted in part with the United States Constitution ..." and "in view of the country's federal system of government, the regime established by the

78. State parties were required to allow international visits and also establish or maintain an independent national body that would also conduct visits. Evans and Haenni-Dale, "Preventing Torture?" 27–28, and Haenni-Dale, interview.
[60] Haenni-Dale, interview, and Jimenez, interview.   [61] Haenni-Dale, interview.

draft would be considered overly intrusive."[62] At the April 2002 session of the UNCHR, Cuba led a number of countries seeking to squelch the Optional Protocol by calling for continued deliberations and introducing a no-action motion.[63] Following prolonged debate, this effort failed by a vote of twenty-eight against, twenty-one in favor, and four abstaining, and the draft survived.[64] The next hurdle was the ECOSOC where in July 2002 the United States submitted an amendment to reopen discussions on the draft, which was rejected with twenty-nine votes against, fifteen in favor, and eight abstaining.[65] After this hostile amendment was defeated, ECOSOC member states voted in favor of moving the Optional Protocol forward with thirty-five countries voting in favor, eight against, and ten abstaining.[66] In the Third Committee, Japan's effort to delay the vote for twenty-four hours failed with eighty-five countries against, twelve in favor, and forty-three abstaining.[67] The United States again attempted to stymie passage by introducing an amendment that OPCAT expenses be funded exclusively by the contributions of state parties, which failed as ninety-eight states voted in opposition, eleven voted in support, and thirty-seven abstained.[68] Following this, supporters of OPCAT were able to garner sufficient votes for passage by the Third Committee.[69] Finally, in December 2002 the proponents of the Optional Protocol prevailed and the General Assembly voted to adopt OPCAT.[70] Given that the UN prefers to adopt human rights instruments by consensus, which is thought to convey broad international legitimacy and widespread acceptance, the repeated votes and tense debate indicate

---

[62] UN Economic and Social Council, "Provisional Summary Record of the 38th Meeting," November 12, 2002, UN Doc. E/2002/SR.38, paragraph 87.

[63] UN Commission of Human Rights, "Report of the 58th Session, Supplement No. 3," March 18–April 26, 2002, UN Doc. E/2002/23, paragraph 335. Cuba withdrew its amendment to continue the working group and then introduced the no-action motion.

[64] Cuba's no-action motion failed by twenty-eight against, twenty-one for, and four abstentions. China, Cuba, Japan, Libya, Malaysia, Nigeria, South Korea, Saudi Arabia, Sudan, and Syria voted against OPCAT. UN Commission on Human Rights, "Report of the 58th Session, Supplement No. 3," March 18–April 26, 2002, E/2002/23, paragraph 339. See also Association for the Prevention of Torture and Inter-American Institute for Human Rights, *Optional Protocol*, 54.

[65] Association for the Prevention of Torture, *Optional Protocol*, 55.

[66] UN Economic and Social Council, "Summary Record of the 38th Meeting, November 2002," UN Doc. E/2002/SR.38, paragraphs 68–70 and 89.

[67] Association for the Prevention of Torture and Inter-American Institute for Human Rights, *Optional Protocol to the Convention against Torture*, 55.

[68] Ibid., 56.

[69] UN General Assembly Third Committee, "Report of the 57th Session of the Third Committee of the General Assembly," October 28, 2002, UN Doc. A/C.3/57/L.30.

[70] UN General Assembly, Resolution 57/199, "Optional Protocol to the Convention against Torture and Other Cruel, Inhuman or Degrading Treatment or Punishment," December 18, 2002, UN Doc. A/RES/57/199.

ongoing resistance to OPCAT. Even though the voting was contentious, OPCAT proponents felt that adoption by vote was preferable to shelving the draft.

When the UN General Assembly adopted OPCAT, it established a system of preventive on-site inspections by national and international bodies. The international body – the Subcommittee on the Prevention of Torture (SPT or Subcommittee) – was given the authority to visit "any place under [the state party's] jurisdiction and control, where persons are or may be deprived of their liberty."[71] The ten members of the SPT were to be elected by states and were to serve in their personal capacities, not as state representatives. The Optional Protocol required the SPT to determine visits by lot and produce confidential postvisit reports that addressed areas for improvement. This report was intended primarily for the state in question with a focus on specific steps that could be taken to prevent or halt torture, and would only be made public with the consent of the Committee against Torture, if they felt that this step was necessary in order to elicit state cooperation.[72] OPCAT also mandated that state parties maintain, designate, or establish an independent national-level entity that conducts inspection visits, makes recommendations, and produces an annual report that states are to publish and disseminate.[73]

China and the Optional Protocol to the Convention against Torture

In contrast to its muted conduct vis-à-vis CAT, China adopted the more consequential role of constrainer during the drafting and adoption of OPCAT. PRC representatives attended the annual working group sessions every year, where they proposed specific text and voiced positions on a number of controversial issues. Although the substance of its contributions sought to dilute the draft and other participants recalled Beijing's attempts to thwart progress, the PRC sought to obscure its resistance and therefore acted with restraint. These efforts paid off as other participants described China as not being among the more uncooperative states and other participants characterized the PRC delegation as "not being excessively vocal," "somewhat low-key,"[74] "active, yet not

---

[71] Article 4.
[72] Evans and Haenni-Dale, "Preventing Torture?" 46. Under Article 1, if a state party refuses to cooperate with the Subcommittee or take steps to make improvements, the Subcommittee can request that the CAT make a public statement or publish the Subcommittee's report. Under Articles 11 and 13, although the SPT may propose a follow-up visit, the state party is not obligated to accept such a visit.
[73] Articles 11, 17, 19, 20, and 23.   [74] Pennegard, interview.

always taking the floor,"[75] "not a major actor,"[76] "cautious," "active, yet not taking the lead," "not necessarily obstructive,"[77] and "not excessively vocal."[78] Along these lines, a Western European diplomat noted that although China was against OPCAT "they were certainly not the most active, even in the negative sense. They took the floor at times but were never in the lead against something but rather supported the ideas of other resistant countries."[79] In a similar vein, an NGO participant noted that although China "may have been in on some of the blocking efforts," it did not appear to be "spearheading the group" or "to be leading the strategy of this group of countries."[80] Judge Odio Benito, the chairperson responsible for the final draft, described China as "more passive" and "always maintain[ing] some sort of low profile."[81]

Even as the substance of its contributions sought to roll back the original vision for OPCAT, the PRC employed a number of strategies to limit damage to its image. First, instead of making lone statements or spearheading opposition, when possible it signed onto statements made by a group of like-minded countries or referenced the position of other countries. As noted earlier, beginning in 1999, during the seventh session, an informal group of countries comprising Cuba, Algeria, Egypt, Saudi Arabia, Sudan, Syria, and China coalesced, and began to issue joint statements.[82] After this group's emergence, the PRC preferred to affiliate with the group's stance rather than make its own national-level statements, allowing Chinese diplomats to adopt a more modest profile. Second, when possible, the PRC let other countries take vocal, prominent positions. Beijing benefited from the presence and activism of other countries, such as Cuba, Algeria, and Egypt, which shared similar views and were more strident in their objections.[83] As an NGO participant

---

[75] Haenni-Dale noted that China did not try to derail the discussions.
[76] Guillermet, interview. He noted that while the PRC was not the most difficult countries, during the later sessions China became more active, expressed disagreement, and urged that torture efforts focus more on CAT, such as relying on the state reporting procedure.
[77] Jimenez, interview.
[78] Interview with Western European diplomat, July 26, 2010, Copenhagen, Denmark.
[79] Interview with Western European diplomat, June 28, 2011, New York.
[80] Haenni-Dale, interview.
[81] Odio Benito, correspondence with author. On a similar note, Debra Long, who served as the APT representative to the OPCAT negotiations, described China as "not that engaged in the negotiations." Debra Long (APT representative and participant from 2000 to 2002), email correspondence with author, May 11, 2011.
[82] Haenni-Dale, interview.
[83] Pennegard noted that Mexico, Cuba, Nigeria, and Egypt were obstructionist. Pennegard, interview. Jimenez cited Algeria, Cuba, and Egypt and Saudi Arabia as uncooperative. Jimenez, interview. Similarly, Long noted that "other states were more vocal in expressing their disapproval." Long, correspondence. None of these interview subjects mentioned China as being among the most difficult delegations.

opined, "While China was not generally obstructive and maintained a low profile, this is relative because there were other countries that were definitely much more difficult and obstructive."[84] Another participant also noted that "China was not in a position that it had to block [because] there were other countries doing it for them."[85] While there is some speculation that Beijing may have tried to "influence things from behind," there is no evidence that it organized or led the group's efforts or that Chinese diplomats had to work to persuade others to adopt these positions.[86] Rather, there appears to have been a meeting of the minds and these countries already had misgivings about the proposed OPCAT. Moreover, their emergence as the Like-Minded Group signifies that aside from skepticism toward OPCAT, they held broadly similar views. The PRC's third strategy was to act cautiously during the adoption process, especially in UN bodies with larger audiences. Thus, although the PRC voiced misgivings about OPCAT and offered acerbic statements in the UNCHR, it did not sponsor formal action, such as no-action motions or amendments, to derail the Optional Protocol. Moreover, once action moved to larger UN bodies, including the Third Committee and the General Assembly, it adopted a lower profile and no longer voiced opposition.

As will be detailed, despite Beijing's measured disposition, the substance of its contributions sought to dilute the original draft. Throughout the drafting sessions, PRC representatives expressed views on some of the most divisive elements, taking the following key positions:

- insisting that in addition to ratification prior state consent for a visit to a country was necessary and that states should have leeway to refuse or postpone a visit
- calling for limits on the places the Subcommittee would be authorized to visit within a country and giving states the latitude to refuse access to a particular facility
- seeking to allow states to elect the Subcommittee members and refuse the inclusion of a particular individual expert on a country visit
- challenging the use of additional experts to assist the Subcommittee during country visits
- underscoring the import of state sovereignty and seeking the inclusion of language affirming respect for domestic legislation
- stressing that the state in question should be allowed to make comments and modifications to the Subcommittee's postvisit report and

[84] Jimenez, interview.   [85] Haenni-Dale, interview.
[86] Interview with Western diplomat, June 28, 2011, New York.

seeking to limit the kinds of recommendations the SPT could put forward, such as by arguing that the recommendations must be "feasible"

- opposing selective attention and arguing for universal monitoring in which the SPT conducts visits on a rotational system rather than focusing on particular countries

The majority of these positions were often at odds with human rights advocates and proponents of a robust OPCAT and paralleled the substance of the contributions from overtly obstructive countries, such as Egypt, Algeria, and Cuba.[87] The essence of its statements caused a member of the UN Committee against Torture who attended the OPCAT working group sessions for a number of years to describe China as "negatively active" and note that it sought to weaken provisions of the original draft.[88] Offering a softer assessment, one of the working group chairpersons observed that "China did not play, at any moment, a positive role during the whole process" and further that it was generally "not very cooperative."[89]

Among the issues that caused the most acrimony within the working group was the degree of access to be granted to the Subcommittee. Proponents of OPCAT argued that in order to be effective, the SPT needed far-reaching access with little leeway for state parties to refuse access to both the country and the specific places of detention. Yet, some countries, including China, held deep reservations about giving the Subcommittee such a high degree of access, which they characterized as tantamount to an open invitation to conduct inspection visits. The PRC was among the delegations that argued for more restrictive language, preferring to constrain the SPT's visiting authority while giving states greater control.[90] As a participant noted, the PRC had issues with the "places to be visited ... very difficult for China was the article on when the Sub-Committee was visiting how freely it could move around, including for interviews with detainees."[91]

More specifically, under discussion were the questions of whether prior consent from the state was required, the kinds of places to be visited, and reasons that a state could use to delay or refuse a visit. Some participants

---

[87] Haenni-Dale, interview and Jimenez, interview.
[88] Bent Sorensen (former member of the Committee against Torture) interview by author, July 26, 2010, Copenhagen, Denmark.
[89] Judge Elizabeth Odio Benito (Chairperson of the Working Group, 1992 and 2002–2002), correspondence with author, June 23, 2010.
[90] Pennegard described this as of one China's main concerns. Pennegard, interview.
[91] Pennegard, interview.

were concerned that too much prior notification would diminish the effectiveness of the visits while resisters used arguments such as allowing states
sufficient time to make preparations in order to provide the Subcommittee
the requisite information, resources, and access to place limits on the SPT's
access. China and other countries insisted that ratification did not equal a
standing invitation and urged that explicit state consent be required prior to
a visit.[92] At the fifth session in 1997, the PRC representative, along with
Mexico and Cuba, argued that explicit state consent beyond ratification
should be required before a visit. The PRC delegate stated that "while
recognizing the importance of the Sub-Committee being allowed to exercise its functions ... [it] felt that the principles of non-intervention and prior
consent were ... important and must have their place in the text."[93] By
invoking the term "non-intervention," Beijing's diplomats framed their
arguments as protecting state sovereignty, a principle that they contended
was at risk of being violated. Several years later, in 1999, Beijing reiterated
this point insisting that "all missions or visits should be conducted only with
the prior consent of the State concerned."[94] At the same session, Chinese
representatives also sought to give the government in question greater
leeway by putting forward a broad range of loosely defined acceptable
reasons to postpone a visit, arguing that "the list of exceptional circumstances [in which a visit might be delayed] should be comprehensive and
even exhaustive" and proposed adding considerations such as the "health
status of the person to be visited, urgent interrogation for a serious crime,
and serious natural disaster."[95] Yet, these situations, especially health concerns and interrogation, are instances in which external monitoring can be
useful to ensure adequate protections of detained individuals. Moreover,
there was concern that countries could invoke these situations as excuses to
delay or refuse an unwanted visit. China along with a handful of other
countries were dogged in their opposition, and also clarified that states
should be able to reject an entire visit to the country as well as visits to
particular areas and places of detention. At the session in 1999, China

[92] Guillermet, interview.
[93] UN Economic and Social Council, "Report of the Working Group on a Draft Optional
Protocol to the Convention against Torture and Other Cruel, Inhuman or Degrading
Treatment or Punishment," December 23, 1996, UN Doc. E/CN.4/1997/33,
paragraphs 31–32 and 34.
[94] UN Economic and Social Council, "Report of the Working Group on the Draft Optional
Protocol to the Convention against Torture and Other Cruel, Inhuman or Degrading
Treatment or Punishment," December 2, 1999, UN Doc. E/CN.4/2000/58,
paragraph 65.
[95] UN Economic and Social Council, "Report of the Working Group on the Draft Optional
Protocol to the Convention against Torture," March 26, 1999, UN Doc. E/CN.4/1999/
59, paragraph 60.

signed onto a joint statement and a written submission by Cuba, Egypt, Saudi Arabia, Sudan, and Syria. The joint statement "underlined that the objections ... [to a visit by the SPT] were to be decided by the State Party and should apply to a particular part of a visit but also, as appropriate, to a whole visit."[96] On the related issue of the places the SPT would be allowed to visit within a country, China sought to limit the Subcommittee's access and worked with other countries to advance this position. During the eighth session in 2000, China associated with a statement made by Cuba on behalf of Algeria, Egypt, Saudi Arabia, Sudan, and Syria that argued for greater limits on the kinds of places the Subcommittee could visit and proposed restrictive language.[97] These countries insisted that the scope of places included in the draft was "too wide, controversial and undefined, and raised many problems relating to national security and domestic affairs."[98]

The final version of the Optional Protocol reflected a compromise. States were not specifically allowed to reject or postpone a visit to a country but were permitted to object to a visit to a particular place of detention "on urgent and compelling grounds of national defense, public safety, natural disaster, or serious disorder."[99] In an attempt to prevent misuse of this clause, it was noted that a state of emergency "shall not be invoked ... as a reason to object to a visit."[100] At the same time, accession to OPCAT functioned as prior consent and the SPT was allowed to visit "any place under [the state's] jurisdiction and control where persons are or may be deprived of liberty" with no exceptions for states to defer or refuse a visit to the country. Further, "deprived of liberty" was defined broadly as "any form of detention or imprisonment or the placement of a person in a public or private custodial setting, from which this person is not permitted to leave at will by order of any judicial, administrative or other authority."[101]

Beijing also sought to strengthen state influence over the composition of the Subcommittee.[102] As a participant in the drafting group put it, the PRC insisted "that states should ... select the SPT experts and took positions to make the state as forceful as possible."[103] Specifically, the PRC objected to allowing the Committee against Torture to select the Subcommittee members, arguing that other treaties granted states this

[96] Ibid. and UN Economic and Social Council, "Report of the Working Group on the Draft Optional Protocol to the Convention against Torture and Other Cruel, Inhuman or Degrading Treatment or Punishment," December 2, 1999, UN Doc. E/CN.4/2000/58, paragraph 52.

[97] UN Economic and Social Council, "Report of the Working Group on a Draft Optional Protocol to the Convention against Torture and Other Cruel, Inhuman or Degrading Treatment or Punishment," December 2, 1999, UN Doc. E/CN.4/2000/58, paragraph 63.

[98] Ibid., paragraph 63.   [99] Article 14.   [100] Article 14.   [101] Article 4.

[102] Pennegard, interview.   [103] Sorenson, interview.

authority. Along these lines, in 1997, the Chinese representative asserted that "the method of election of the proposed body should adhere to the general procedures followed by other human rights bodies. Accordingly, he felt that it was not appropriate for the Committee against Torture to be involved in the composition of the Subcommittee" and that instead states should elect the Subcommittee.[104] This position was incorporated into the final document and thus states nominate and elect SPT members.[105] Although state selection of SPT members sounds innocuous, it can allow states to veto individuals who they suspect would favor vigorous monitoring or be willing to spotlight states for serious violations.

The PRC also opposed the use of non-SPT experts to assist Subcommittee members on visits and sought to restrict their ability to serve on country visits. In particular, the PRC challenged the necessity of experts, sought to give states influence over the selection process, and attempted to restrict the immunities and privileges to be granted to experts.[106] While OPCAT supporters as well as members of the Committee against Torture maintained that non-SPT experts were needed because their specialized knowledge could be useful and would augment the Subcommittee's capabilities, this was among the litany of issues that the PRC countered.[107] In reaction to the original draft, which allowed the Subcommittee to select experts to serve on missions without state involvement, the PRC pressed for enhanced state control. During the 1994 discussions, Beijing proposed text for Articles 10 and 11 that gave state parties greater say over the use and selection of experts, including giving states veto power over particular individuals. The proposed text read, "In exceptional cases, the Subcommittee may, after full consultations with, and having obtained permission of the State Party concerned, invite advisers in the personal name of members of the Subcommittee who will carry out the missions/visits to assist them in the missions/visits."[108] During the 1995 session, the Chinese

---

[104] UN Economic and Social Council, "Report of the Working Group on the Draft Optional Protocol on the Draft Optional Protocol to the Convention against Torture and Other Cruel, Inhuman or Degrading Treatment," December 23, 1996, UN Doc. E/CN.4/1997/33, paragraph 57.

[105] Articles 6 and 7.   [106] Pennegard, interview.

[107] For the views of Amnesty International, which supported the use of experts, see UN Economic and Social Council, "Report of the Working Group on the Draft Optional Protocol to the Convention against Torture and Other Cruel, Inhuman or Degrading Treatment or Punishment," December 12, 1994, UN Doc. E/CN.4/1995/38, paragraphs 39–44.

[108] UN Economic and Social Council, "Report of the Working Group on the Draft Optional Protocol to the Convention against Torture and Other Cruel, Inhuman or Degrading Treatment or Punishment," December 12, 1994, UN Doc. E/CN.4/1995/38, page 19. See also UN Economic and Social Council, "Report of the Working Group

representative even argued that "the need for experts to assist a mission was dubious."[109] In 1997, the PRC again reiterated a similar position that "the number of experts should be limited and that experts should only be used in exceptional cases after permission had been obtained from the State concerned. Experts proposed by the State Party to be visited should be considered on a priority basis when selecting experts from the list."[110] The PRC continued to press that "it was important for the State Party concerned to be able not only to oppose the inclusion of a specific expert in a mission, but also to express its objection to the number of experts."[111] Reflecting the hostility the PRC harbored toward the use of outside experts, Chinese diplomats also expressed "reservations on the facilities, privileges and immunities provided to the advisers" serving as experts with the SPT on a country visit.[112] During the drafting session in 1997, the PRC argued that "experts on missions should not enjoy the same privileges and immunities as members of the Subcommittee."[113] The inclusion of immunities, which is similar to the immunities extended to diplomats, was intended to protect the Subcommittee and privileges were meant to give the Subcommittee the kind of access and treatment that would facilitate a visit. China was not alone and Mexico and Cuba delivered similar comments at the same session suggesting that states should be able to unconditionally reject an expert.[114] Beijing's efforts to influence the final draft met with some success and OPCAT "leans toward the sensibilities of states since experts can be excluded [by states] without any particular justification being

on the Draft Optional Protocol to the Convention against Torture and Other Cruel, Inhuman or Degrading Treatment or Punishment," January 25, 1996, UN Doc. E/CN.4/1996/28, paragraphs 23 and 26.

109   UN Economic and Social Council, "Report of the Working Group on the Draft Optional Protocol to the Convention against Torture and Other Cruel, Inhuman or Degrading Treatment," January 25, 1996, UN Doc. E/CN.4/1996/28, paragraph 26.

110   UN Economic and Social Council, "Report of the Working Group on a Draft Optional Protocol to the Convention against Torture and Other Cruel, Inhuman or Degrading Treatment or Punishment," December 2, 1997, UN Doc. E/CN.4/1998/42, paragraph 48.

111   Ibid., paragraph 52.

112   UN Economic and Social Council, "Report of the Working Group on the Draft Optional Protocol to the Convention against Torture and Other Cruel, Inhuman or Degrading Treatment or Punishment," January 25, 1996, UN Doc. E/CN.4/1996/28, paragraph 132.

113   UN Economic and Social Council, "Report of the Working Group on a Draft Optional Protocol to the Convention against Torture and Other Cruel, Inhuman or Degrading Treatment or Punishment," December 2, 1997, UN Doc. E/CN.4/1998/42, paragraph 137.

114   Ibid., paragraph 49.

given" and experts were not explicitly granted immunity and privileges in the final text.[115] This compromise and the limiting of immunities and privileges to members of the Subcommittee reflected PRC preferences.

China also opposed selective attention by the SPT and insisted on universal, nonselective human rights monitoring. In this regard, the PRC delegation opposed allowing the SPT to focus on particular states and insisted on a regular rotational schedule for country visits.[116] In 1999, China signed on to a statement made by Cuba on behalf of Algeria, Egypt, Saudi Arabia, Syria, and Sudan, which insisted that "the protocol should be based on non-discriminatory regular visits to all State Parties, avoiding any possibility of selectivity."[117] OPCAT advocates hoped that the SPT might be given the authority to conduct follow-up, ad hoc visits in cases where a routine visit revealed serious concerns. Yet, the PRC was among those delegations opposing any follow-up, ad hoc visits. These views shaped the final text, which precluded selective attention by requiring that regular visits be established by lot. Further, while the SPT can propose an additional trip subsequent to a regular visit, the state in question is not required to accept such a visit.

Throughout the negotiations, the PRC, along with other countries, pushed for the inclusion of the language referencing respect for domestic law, framing their arguments as upholding state sovereignty.[118] Some human rights advocates were concerned that inclusion of this language might be used to interfere with the SPT's work or that incorporating such a reference could be used by states to resist the Subcommittee's recommendations or findings. The PRC and other nations issued a salvo of insistent statements. In 1997, following an Egyptian proposal to include reference to national legislation, China "expressed full support for the proposal [made by Egypt], stating that nothing should interfere with

---

[115] Evans and Haenni-Dale, "Preventing Torture?" 30.

[116] UN Economic and Social Council, "Report of the Working Group on the Draft Optional Protocol to the Convention against Torture and Other Cruel, Inhuman or Degrading Treatment or Punishment," December 2, 1999, UN Doc. E/CN.4/2000/58, paragraph 64.

[117] Ibid., paragraphs 63–67.

[118] UN Economic and Social Council, "Report of the Working Group on the Draft Optional Protocol to the Convention against Torture and Other Cruel, Inhuman or Degrading Treatment," March 26, 1999, UN Doc. E/CN.4/1999/59, paragraphs 35–49, and UN Economic and Social Council, "Report of the Working Group on the Draft Optional Protocol to the Convention against Torture and Other Cruel, Inhuman or Degrading Treatment," December 2, 1999, UN Doc. E/CN.4/2000/58, paragraph 58.

State sovereignty."[119] During the same session, the PRC, along with Cuba and Egypt, "expressed the opinion that national laws must be respected."[120] Again, in 1999, China joined Algeria, Cuba, Egypt, Saudi Arabia, Sudan, and Syria in submitting a shared position statement that read:

> The importance of referring to national legislation has to be clearly and positively reflected in the following legal context: (i) national legislation is absolutely necessary to complement and implement the provisions of the protocol ... (iii) in the absence of a clear reference to national legislation ... [the] Subcommittee may be seen as a 'supranational' body ... so that it could enjoy a situation of party and judge at the same time, or at least, exercise a unilateral faculty of interpretation of the State's national legislation.[121]

During this same session, the Chinese representative also proposed language for Article 12 that read, "The provisions of this Protocol shall be applied in accordance with domestic law consistent with international obligations of states."[122] At the following session, held in 2001, China signed onto a statement delivered by Cuba on behalf of the Algeria, Cuba, Egypt, Saudi Arabia, Sudan, and Syria, which again argued for an article affirming national legislation.[123] Despite these efforts, OPCAT does not include such a reference.

Again reflecting positions that sought to elevate the state and constrain the Subcommittee, China also sought to strengthen state influence in the preparation of the Subcommittee's postvisit report and limit the kinds of recommendations and comments the Subcommittee could issue.[124] While proponents of a robust version of OPCAT contested that this

---

[119] UN Economic and Social Council, "Report of the Working Group on a Draft Optional Protocol to the Convention against Torture and Other Cruel, Inhuman or Degrading Treatment," December 2, 1997, UN Doc. E/CN.4/1998/42, paragraph 69.

[120] Ibid., paragraph 75.

[121] UN Economic and Social Council, "Report of the Working Group on the Draft Optional Protocol to the Convention against Torture and Other Cruel, Inhuman or Degrading Treatment or Punishment," March 26, 1999, UN Doc. E/CN.4/1999/59, paragraph 49.

[122] Ibid., paragraphs 36 and 43. During the same session, Egypt proposed language similar to China's. Ibid., paragraph 38.

[123] UN Economic and Social Council, "Report of the Working Group on the Draft Optional to the Convention against Torture and Other Cruel, Inhuman or Degrading Treatment," December 2, 1999, UN Doc. E/CN.4/2000/58, paragraph 64.

[124] UN Economic and Social Council, "Report of the Working Group on the Draft Optional Protocol to the Convention against Torture and Other Cruel Inhuman or Degrading Treatment or Punishment," March 26, 1999, UN Doc. E/CN.4/1999/59, paragraphs 71–79, and UN Economic and Social Council, "Report of the Working Group on the Draft Optional Protocol to the Convention against Torture and Other Cruel, Inhuman and Degrading Treatment or Punishment," February 20, 2002, UN Doc. /CN.4/2000/58, paragraphs 46–50.

might open the door to state interference with the SPT's independence and authority, the PRC put forward a variety of positions to strengthen state influence. For example, in 1996, it proposed specific text for Article 14 that would allow states to "make comments and modifications" to the SPT report and asserted that in "its preparation of its report, the Subcommittee shall give fair and equitable consideration to the comments and modifications offered by the State Party concerned."[125] Beijing persisted and several years later supported language that restricted the Subcommittee to making only "feasible" recommendations.[126] While this adjective might sound harmless, it could potentially be used to reject SPT recommendations based on the premise that they did not meet this standard. These views were not incorporated into OPCAT, which does not require the SPT to consult with the state over the report and does not restrict the kinds of recommendations the SPT can suggest.[127] Further, under Article 1, if a state party refuses to cooperate with the Subcommittee or take steps to make improvements in conformity with the SPT's recommendations, the Subcommittee can request that the Committee against Torture make a public statement or publish the Subcommittee's report.

In 2001, when Mexico presented its controversial draft that favored national mechanisms over the international Subcommittee, China and a number of other countries endorsed it and praised the prominent role accorded national bodies and the much diminished mandate for the international body.[128] For example, China, the United States, and Egypt argued that "national and regional mechanisms should take the leading role in visiting places of detention."[129] According to a diplomat in the working group, the PRC responded positively to the Mexican draft

[125] UN Economic and Social Council, "Report of the Working Group on a Draft Optional Protocol to the Convention against Torture and Other Cruel, Inhuman or Degrading Treatment or Punishment," January 25, 1996, UN Doc. E/CN.4/1996/28, paragraph 39.
[126] UN Economic and Social Council, "Report of the Working Group on the Draft Optional Protocol to the Convention against Torture and Other Cruel, Inhuman or Degrading Treatment or Punishment," March 26, 1999, UN Doc. E/CN.4/1999/59, paragraph 78.
[127] Evans and Haenni-Dale, "Preventing Torture?," 49.
[128] Haenni-Dale, interview and UN Economic and Social Council, "Report of the Working Group on a Draft Optional Protocol to the Convention against Torture and Other Cruel, Inhuman or Degrading Treatment or Punishment," March 13, 2001, UN Doc. E/CN.4/2001/67.
[129] UN Economic and Social Council, "Repot of the Working Group on a Draft Optional Protocol to the Convention against Torture and Other Cruel, Inhuman or Degrading Treatment or Punishment," February 20, 2002, UN Doc. E/CN.4/2002/78, paragraph 39.

because it reflected the PRC view that "human rights [should be treated] as a national issue to be dealt with by the Chinese people themselves."[130] As has been noted previously, the PRC contests approaches that elevate the authority and role of the international human rights regime and seeks to relegate international mechanisms to providing capacity-building and advisory services. The PRC – along with Cuba, Egypt, and Syria – voiced support for the approach embodied in the Mexican draft and attempted to demote the international body to a lesser role by arguing that "the main function of the international mechanism should be to provide technical and financial support to national mechanisms The visiting functions should mainly be entrusted to the national mechanism."[131] In this vein, the PRC delegation "suggested that the international mechanism could participate in the visits to places of detention carried out by the national mechanisms but should not have the leading role."[132]

In response to the chairperson's compromise draft, which retained a robust role for the international Subcommittee while also establishing national-level bodies that would undertake complementary activities, China expressed opposition and called for continued discussions.[133] The PRC representative offered platitudinous words, noting the chairperson's hard work and the headway the working group had made. Yet, the PRC attempted to stymie progress by "questioning the necessity of setting up a global mechanism" since interested states could become party to the European Convention on the Prevention of Torture, which was a regional mechanism that employed a similar approach of investigative visits by experts. The PRC elaborated that

the Chairperson's draft reflected 10 years of hard work ... States still held differing views, such as on the mandate of the subcommittee ... There had been little change with regard to the role of national legislations (sic); the differences had not been reconciled. The delegation suggested that the Chairperson should seek compromises on the issues with which some States still had difficulties ... The delegation reiterated its support for an effective mechanism to prevent torture ... Noting its willingness to cooperate with the Chairperson and other delegations, the delegate of China called for further consultations.[134]

The PRC closed its statement by noting that the positions of Egypt, Russia, Saudi Arabia, and the United States, which all offered resistance

---

[130] Guilermet, interview.
[131] UN Economic and Social Council, "Report of the Working Group on the Draft Optional Protocol to the Convention against Torture and Other Cruel, Inhuman or Degrading Treatment of Punishment," December 2, 1999, UN Doc. E/CN.4/2002/78, paragraph 16.
[132] Ibid., paragraph 22.   [133] Ibid., paragraph 76.   [134] Ibid., paragraphs 74–76.

to OPCAT, to some extent also reflected China's views.[135] Despite the objections from China and these other countries, the chairperson proceeded to move the draft to the UNCHR.

During 2002, when the draft was considered in the smaller UN bodies, such as the fifty-three-member Commission on Human Rights and the fifty-four-member UN ECOSOC, the PRC's strategy of varying its behavior based on the audience and size of the venue was evident. In these smaller UN bodies, China firmly opposed the draft and spoke out against it. At the same time, it did not spearhead its own blocking efforts but instead supported the actions of other resistant nations. Thus, when Cuba introduced a no-action motion in an attempt to delay action in the Commission, PRC Ambassador Sha Zukang joined Saudi Arabia in endorsing Cuba's proposition and disparaged the chairperson's decision to move the draft forward as "arbitrary" and the text as "unbalanced." He claimed that the PRC was not opposed to the Optional Protocol in principle, yet he warned that there would be "negative consequences" if the proposed draft were pushed through.[136] China matched its acerbic words by joining twenty other countries voting in favor of Cuba's unsuccessful no-action motion, which failed when twenty-eight countries voted against it.[137] When OPCAT came up for a vote in the Commission, the PRC along with ten other countries voted against it, while twenty-nine states voted to adopt and fourteen abstained.[138] In ECOSOC, China backed a US amendment aimed at blocking adoption by reopening discussion on the proposed text.[139] PRC representative Zhang Yishan declared that the Optional Protocol should be "the product of consensus" and that "the concerns of some [States] had been ignored and a controversial vote on the Optional Protocol had been forced through."[140]

---

[135] Ibid., paragraphs 74–76.
[136] UN Commission on Human Rights, "Report of 50th meeting of the 58th Session," July 30, 2002, UN Doc. E/CN.4/2002/SR.50, paragraph 18 (translated from French). The Cuban delegation proposed both an amendment seeking to extend the mandate of the working group and a no-action motion.
[137] Other countries that voted in favor of Cuba's motion include Bahrain, Cuba, India, Indonesia, Japan, Libya, Malaysia, Nigeria, Pakistan, South Korea, Russia, Saudi Arabia, Sudan, Swaziland, Syria, Thailand, Togo, Uganda, Vietnam, and Zambia. Cuba's motion was rejected by twenty-eight votes against and twenty-one for, with four abstentions. UN Commission on Human Rights, "Report of the 58th Session," March 18–April 26, 2002, Supplement No. 3, UN Doc. E/CN.4/2002/23, paragraph 337.
[138] Other countries voting against the resolution include Cuba, Japan, Libya, Malaysia, Nigeria, South Korea, Saudi Arabia, Sudan, and Syria. Ibid., paragraph 339.
[139] UN Economic and Social Council, "Provisional Summary Record of the 38th Meeting," November 12, 2002, UN Doc. E/2002/SR.38, paragraphs 68–70 and 85. China was among the fifteen countries voting in favor of the US amendment, which failed with twenty-nine countries voting against and eight abstaining.
[140] Ibid., paragraph 78.

Zhang called for continuing negotiations to reach a version "that would be acceptable to all" and along with fourteen other countries voted in favor of the failed US amendment.[141] As shown in Table 3.3, when the chairperson's draft came up for a vote, China joined seven other countries in voting against what turned out to be a successful resolution that enjoyed the support of thirty-five ECOSOC member states.[142]

Once action shifted to the more expansive UN bodies, particularly the Third Committee and the General Assembly, both of which comprise all UN members states, Chinese representatives shifted tactics and played a less visible role. As a Western European diplomat noted, "China was one of the countries that was opposed" to the Optional Protocol and during the adoption process it belonged to the "difficult camp along with Cuba, the U.S. and Japan" but once the resolution reached the larger New York-based UN bodies "China was no longer out in front" and was "not particularly difficult."[143] Along these lines, the PRC refrained from making statements in opposition, but still voted in favor of other countries' attempts to prevent passage of OPCAT. The PRC may have adopted this subtler position as it saw that the active blocking efforts of other countries were futile. Moreover, by backing away from resistance, the PRC benefited from being able to appear more moderate and cooperative than the countries that continued to oppose OPCAT, including the United States and Japan. As a Western European diplomat noted, at this stage, "Apart from its voting positions, China did not go out and lobby against" OPCAT.[144] In the Third Committee, the PRC was among twelve countries that voted in favor of Japan's unsuccessful motion to defer action on the resolution for twenty-four hours but abstained on the failed US amendment to require that OPCAT expenses be financed only by the contributions of state parties.[145] The Chinese delegation joined Cuba, Israel, Japan, Nigeria, Syria, the United States,

---

[141] For quote, see ibid., paragraph 78. For vote, see Ibid., paragraphs 68–70 and 85. China was among the fifteen countries voting in favor of the US amendment to extend the mandate of the working group, which failed with twenty-nine countries voting against and eight abstaining. Aside from China, the other countries voting in favor of the US amendment included Australia, Cuba, Egypt, Ethiopia, India, Iran, Japan, Libya, Nigeria, Pakistan, Russia, Sudan, Uganda, and the United States.

[142] Ibid., paragraph 89. Australia, Cuba, Egypt, Japan, Libya, Nigeria, and Sudan also voted against the resolution, which was adopted by thirty-five votes with ten abstentions.

[143] Interview with Western European diplomat, May 26, 2011, Geneva, Switzerland.

[144] Interview with Western European diplomat, May 26, 2011, Geneva, Switzerland.

[145] UN General Assembly, "Fifty-seventh Session, Report of the Third Committee," December 3, 2002, UN Doc. A/57/556/Add.1, paragraphs 6–18.

and Vietnam in voting against OPCAT in the Third Committee.[146] Once the Optional Protocol reached the General Assembly and the draft gained even more backers, China abandoned overt opposition efforts. The PRC likely pursued this strategy of tempering its remarks and refraining from initiating blocking action because they saw that the active efforts of other states, including Cuba and United States, to sabotage OPCAT were failing and therefore surmised that continued opposition was fruitless and would only earn it a blemished image. The PRC no longer spoke in opposition and abandoned even voting in support of efforts to delay or block OPCAT. Rather than voting against as it did earlier, Beijing abstained while the Marshall Islands, Nigeria, Palau, and the United States voted against the resolution.[147]

The PRC's persistent efforts to shape OPCAT shows that the PRC sought to act as a constrainer of this part of the human rights regime as it attempted to roll back the proposed draft offered by Costa Rica and then sabotage adoption. However, even as the PRC endeavored to constrain the regime it did so with restraint. Although the Chinese delegation took firm positions on a range of issues and argued for its views to be incorporated, it was careful to avoid the appearance of being obstructive, especially once more expansive UN bodies began to consider the draft. As a result of this restrained opposition, other participants described the PRC as not being among the most difficult countries. For example, Judge Odio Benito described the Chinese delegation as "more passive as they always maintained some sort of low profile."[148] As noted previously, the PRC's opposition was obscured by more visible detractors as well as the emergence of a group of countries offering similar resistance. This group of countries, which initially comprised Algeria, Cuba, Egypt, Syria, Sudan, and China, has been described as the precursor to the more formal Like-Minded Group, which stresses greater respect for state

---

[146] United Nations, "General Assembly to be asked to Adopt Protocol on Torture Convention, Setting Up Inspection Regime for Implementation of Its Terms," press release, November 7, 2005. For a summary of the meeting see UN General Assembly, "Human Rights Questions: Implementation of Human Rights Instruments," December 3, 2002, UN Doc. A/57/566/Add. 1, paragraphs 7–9. Japan's motion to defer action was rejected by a vote of eighty-five to twelve, with forty-three abstentions. The Third Committee adopted OPCAT by a vote of 104 in favor, 8 against, and 37 abstentions.

[147] UN General Assembly, Resolution 57/199, "Optional Protocol to the Convention against Torture and Other Cruel, Inhuman or Degrading Treatment or Punishment," December 18, 2002, A/RES/57/199.

[148] Odio Benito, correspondence.

Table 3.2 *PRC and other states voting on the Optional Protocol to the Convention against Torture*[a]

UN Body	Number of country participants	For	Against	Abstain
Commission on Human Rights	53	29	10 (China)	14
Economic and Social Council	54	35	8 (China)	10
Third Committee	All UN members	104	8 (China)	37
General Assembly	All UN members	127	4	42 (China)

[a] For voting in the UNCHR, see UN Commission on Human Rights, "Report of the 58th session, Supplement No. 3," March 18–April 26, 2002, UN Doc. E/2002/23, paragraph 335. For ECOSOC voting, see UN Economic and Social Council, "Provisional summary record of the 38th Meeting," November 12, 2002, UN Doc. E/2002/SR.38, paragraph 89. For the Third Committee voting record, see UN General Assembly, "Human Rights Questions: Implementation of Human Rights Instruments," October 28, 2002, UN Doc. A/C.3/57/L.30. For voting in the General Assembly, see UN General Assembly "Resolution Adopted by the General Assembly, Resolution 57/199 Optional Protocol to the Convention against Torture," January 9, 2003, A/RES/57/199. Also, see Association for the Prevention of Torture and the Inter-American Institute for Human Rights, Optional Protocol.

sovereignty over international monitoring, the importance and salience of cultural and national particularities, and the use of dialogue and cooperation as opposed to more selective attention, such as country-specific action.[149]

In the final denouement, Beijing's effort to act as a constrainer of the regime and influence OPCAT met with only partial success and this outcome was achieved only because of a chorus of similar views coming from Algeria, Cuba, Egypt, Syria, and Sudan. Despite the combined efforts of China and these other countries to dilute the draft or derail adoption, these states had only modest success and the final version of OPCAT provided for a more robust visiting mechanism than they preferred. For example, states cannot reject a Subcommittee visit but can only deny access to a particular facility on "urgent and compelling grounds of national defense, public safety natural disaster or serious disorder."[150] The main intent of OPCAT – to establish an international monitoring body to undertake preventive visits – was preserved to the displeasure of the PRC and other like-minded states. Further, despite the

---

[149] Jimenez, interview.   [150] Article 14.

high priority China and other countries placed on sovereignty, they failed to secure reference to respect for national legislation or strengthen state influence over the content of the postvisit report. However, Beijing and the position of other resisters on the use of experts was partially reflected in the Optional Protocol. While experts can be included in missions, they were not granted the immunities and privileges enjoyed by the SPT, and states are allowed to reject an expert. Of the issues raised by the Chinese delegation, only their preference on giving states the authority to elect the Subcommittee and monitoring based on universality, specifically non-selective visits, were accepted without modification. On all of these issues, China consistently associated with the same group of countries whose diplomats trumpeted similar positions and the impact that these countries had on the final text reflect their joint efforts. Because of the divergence between the PRC's preferences and OPCAT, it has not become a signatory. China has good company as the Optional Protocol has been ratified or acceded to by only eighty-three countries. Further, two other P5 members, the United States and Russia, have not signed the Protocol.[151] In the context of OPCAT's relatively low accession rate, Beijing's has not been a significant outlier and its absence has not detracted from the work of the Subcommittee.

Conclusion

The PRC evolved from a quiescent novice acting as a taker during the CAT negotiations to a more consequential participant attempting to dilute the draft of the Optional Protocol. When China entered the CAT negotiations in 1982, it had also become a new member of the UNCHR that same year. Given its limited skills, diplomatic relationships, and expertise, the PRC likely determined that it was most prudent to adopt the safe and less controversial role of taker. Moreover, it was a latecomer to the talks as the CAT discussions had already been going on since 1978. As a result, Chinese diplomats attending the discussions in the 1980s were reserved and tentative in their participation. While a number of divisive issues remained open to debate, the PRC delegation offered no statements during its first two years and it was not until 1984 that Chinese diplomats made interventions, particularly on universal jurisdiction. Despite its reservations when it became aware that it was the lone holdout it dropped its opposition and allowed CAT to proceed.

---

[151] "Optional Protocol to the Convention against Torture (OPCAT) Subcommittee on the Prevention against Torture," UN OHCHR, www.ohchr.org/EN/HRBodies/OPCAT/Pages/OPCATIndex.aspx, accessed October 16, 2017.

As the draft Convention was debated in various UN bodies and the Soviet Union led a group of nations seeking to make various elements voluntary, Chinese delegations remained silent and offered neither support nor opposition as the UN finally adopted the Convention by consensus.

In contrast, when states began considering the draft Optional Protocol in the early 1990s, Beijing experienced the fallout from the 1989 Tiananmen square crackdown, and Beijing was much more inclined to attempt to constrain the regime. This changed role was evident in not only the frequency of PRC interventions but also its tone and specificity. Chinese diplomats made numerous interventions, speaking in the working group every year, suggesting specific text to the articles under discussion, and articulating clear arguments. Yet, whenever possible Beijing tended toward a low-profile role to obscure its opposition and limit reputational damage. Along these lines, Chinese diplomats showed dexterity within the drafting group as they worked with and through other nations to advance their views. The thrust of Beijing's positions, which were shared by a handful of other countries that were described as resisters of OPCAT, sought to limit the SPT's access, enable the state to postpone or object not only to a visit to the country but to specific areas and facilities, and tip the balance of control toward states by allowing them to select the Subcommittee and exercise influence over postvisit reporting. Because only some of its positions were accepted, as the OPCAT draft moved through the UN bodies, Chinese diplomats continued to express deep reservations. However, Beijing's representatives also showed restraint as they never initiated overt blocking attempts and once the draft moved to the UN's larger bodies, they no longer offered strong verbal opposition.

An important aspect of China's evolution within the human rights regime was its realization that it behooved them to work with other countries. While Chinese diplomats remained aloof from other delegations in the CAT working group in the 1980s, in the OPCAT drafting group they affiliated themselves with Cuba, Algeria, Egypt, Saudi Arabia, Sudan, and Syria and with these countries attempted to prevent passage of OPCAT and circumscribe the Subcommittee's remit. Given their shared views, these countries began making collective statements in the OPCAT working group in the late 1990s and China signed onto every statement. The presence of these other nations allowed Beijing to deploy a number of strategies that helped it limit damage to its international image. First, in the drafting group when other countries were already voicing similar concerns, Chinese diplomats toned down their opposition. Second, the PRC preferred to cooperate with Cuba, Algeria, Egypt, Saudi

Arabia, Sudan, and Syria in putting forth joint statements and once it signed onto these statements it often did not make national-level statements. Third, as adoption proceeded and OPCAT was taken up by a range of UN bodies, the PRC moderated its conduct and muted its opposition of the draft. At this stage, as other states persisted in their resistance, the PRC took a different tactic. It did not initiate action but sometimes supported other countries' attempts to sabotage passage of OPCAT.

These different roles were partly a function of its growing familiarity as well as the impact of Tiananmen, which left Beijing with strong reservations about a strengthened regime. The PRC's changed roles also reflect key differences in the approaches contained in CAT, which relies on state reporting, and OPCAT, which would authorize the Subcommittee to undertake preventive visits with broad access to domestic facilities. While the PRC and its human rights allies were only modestly successful in shaping the final outcome, as the following chapter will show they became much more organized and coalesced as the Like-Minded Group and have been active in the UNCHR and the UN Human Rights Council.

4   China and the Establishment of the Human Rights Council: 2004–2007

This chapter parses China's posture and positions during the negotiations to replace the UN Commission on Human Rights (UNCHR or Commission) with the UN Human Rights Council (HRC or Council), a process that began in 2004 and culminated in 2007. The Commission and the Council are often described as "political" entities because they comprise government officials representing UN member states. This composition means these are ideal venues to observe the Chinese government's behavior in the human rights regime. Moreover, China had a particularly strong incentive to attempt to influence the outcome because institutional UN reform occurs infrequently and this was a rare opportunity to shape the entity that would replace the Commission, which had served as the principal UN body for human rights for nearly six decades. Because the final stage of HRC reform, the Institution-Building (IB) Process, addressed a number of the regime's mechanisms, including the complaint procedure, the Sub-Commission on the Promotion and Protection of Human Rights (Sub-Commission), and the special procedures, this chapter provides a unique view into PRC positions on a broad array of the regime's components. Throughout this process, China acted as a constrainer as it sought to hold back the Council from emerging as a more robust and forceful entity than the Commission. The majority of Beijing's positions were shared by a number of other states and together they were able to influence the outcome, including opposing the establishment of criteria for Council membership, expanding representation for non-Western countries, and securing election by simple majority rather than a two-thirds vote of the General Assembly (GA). Yet, Beijing failed to secure its most important objective – the elimination of country resolutions. China's actions to impede the strengthening of the HRC reflect the PRC's evolution within the UN human rights regime as well as the importance the Council and previously the Commission play in protecting human rights.

The first section of this chapter provides a description of the growing international disillusionment with the Commission and then outlines the

112

process of UN human rights institutional reform. The second section expands on the background provided in Chapter 2 on China's participation in the regime by detailing Beijing's experiences with the Commission and the Sub-Commission. By doing so, it provides a useful context for Beijing's positions on the HRC. The third section examines the PRC's positions, behavior, and strategies during the multiple stages of the negotiations to establish the HRC.

The PRC can best be described as a constrainer because it sought to limit or hold back the strengthening of this part of the regime. In a similar vein, other observers and scholars have argued that states, including China, sought to weaken the regime or had a "negative reform agenda."[1] I classify China as a constrainer as opposed to a breaker because even though Beijing challenged numerous aspects of the regime, its efforts were confined to weakening but not entirely hollowing out the regime. As outlined in Chapter 1, these terms run along a spectrum with a breaker attempting to cause much more serious damage to the regime.

Replacing the UN Commission on Human Rights

During its sixty-year existence, the Commission made a number of positive contributions, including giving international human rights greater precision and substance and serving as the UN's primary body to address human rights. Nevertheless, the Commission's deficiencies, particularly the inclusion of rights-abusing governments as members and the Commission's failure to consistently spotlight egregious abuses, led to criticism and growing calls for reform. For example, in 2001 Human Rights Watch labeled the UNCHR a "rogues' gallery of human rights abusers."[2] In 2004, US Ambassador Richard Williamson called for reforms, particularly introducing membership criteria, so that the Commission would "not be allowed to become a protected sanctuary

---

[1] Meghna Abraham, *Building the New Human Rights Council: Outcome and Analysis of the Institution-Building Year* (Geneva: Friedrich Ebert Stiftung, 2008), http://library.fes.de/pdf-files/bueros/genf/04769.pdf, accessed September 11, 2017, 24. Abraham does not specifically point to China as the most destructive but her description of China's proposals puts China in this camp.

[2] Human Rights Watch, "U.N. Rights Body Admits Abusive Members," press release, May 3, 2001, http://pantheon.hrw.org/legacy/english/docs/2001/05/03/sudan135_txt.htm, accessed August 5, 2011. See also Robin Wright, "U.S. Shocked by Loss of Seat on U.N. Rights Panel but Vows to Stay Active," *Los Angeles Times*, May 5, 2001. For background on the UNCHR, see Howard Tolley Jr., *The U.N. Commission on Human Rights* (Boulder, Colorado: Westview Press, 1987), 98–100 and 187–189, and Philip Alston, "The Commission on Human Rights," in *The United Nations and Human Rights: A Critical Appraisal*, 1st edition, ed. Philip Alston (Oxford: Oxford University Press, 1992).

for human rights violators who aim to pervert and distort its work."[3] Former UN High Commissioner Mary Robinson, lamented that "[i]t was ... deeply frustrating to see [the Commission's] work increasingly undermined by block voting and procedural maneuvers that prevented some of the world's worst human rights violators from being held to account for their abuses."[4] For many, the final straw came with the election of Libya as UNCHR chair in 2003 and Sudan's membership in 2005, which coincided with ongoing atrocities in Darfur. Yet, even though criticism was nearly unanimous, these complaints stemmed from drastically different concerns. For example, in 2002 PRC Ambassador Sha argued that

[t]he Commission on Human Rights ... should have been a forum for countries to have exchange of views and dialogue in the field of human rights on an equal footing ... Unfortunately, it has turned into a battlefield for ideological confrontations ... almost all country-specific resolutions adopted under this item are targeted against developing countries. This has left people with a false impression that human rights problems are the 'patent' of developing countries while developed countries are impeccable."[5]

These grievances meant that China and a group of like-minded countries often protested the use of country-specific resolutions and special procedure mandates. They claimed that country-focused attention reflected politicization, unfair and selective attention, and confrontation rather than cooperation.

Although disillusionment with the Commission had been growing for years, a threshold of support for reform was reached finally after the UN High-Level Panel Report on Threats, Challenges and Change (HLP or Panel) and the Secretary-General's *In Larger Freedom* report endorsed the creation of a new UN human rights body.[6] The 2004 HLP report recommended that the UN dissolve the Commission and create a

---

[3] U.S. Department of State, "U.S. Proposes Reforms at U.N. Commission on Human Rights," news release, Washington File, March 19, 2004, usinfo.org/wf-archive/2004/040319/epf512/htm, accessed September 5, 2013.

[4] Mary Robinson, "Human Rights: A Needed UN Reform," *The New York Times*, March 2, 2006, www.nytimes.com/2006/03/02/opinion/human-rights-a-needed-un-reform.html, accessed July 11, 2017.

[5] "Statement by Ambassador Sha Zukang, Head of the Chinese Delegation, on Item 9 at the 58th Session of the Commission on Human Rights (8 April 2002)," Permanent Mission of the PRC to the UN at Geneva and Other International Organizations in Switzerland, www.china-un.ch/eng/rqrd/thsm/t85150.htm, accessed February 4, 2014.

[6] For examples of criticism, see Human Rights Watch, "U.N. Rights Body in Serious Decline," news release, April 25, 2003, www.hrw.org/news/2003/04/25/un-rights-body-serious-decline, accessed May 6, 2014. Freedom House also noted that "six of the eighteen most repressive governments, those of China, Cuba, Eritrea, Saudi Arabia, Sudan and Zimbabwe, are members of the Commission on Human Rights (CHR)."

Human Rights Council, which would have universal membership and be elevated from a subsidiary of the Economic and Social Council (ECOSOC) to a higher status, such as being on par with the UN Security Council.[7] UN Secretary-General Annan's March 2005 *In Larger Freedom* report offered further momentum for reform by noting that "the Commission's capacity to perform its tasks has been increasingly undermined by its declining credibility and professionalism ... As a result, a credibility deficit has developed, which casts a shadow on the reputation of the United Nations system as a whole."[8] In contrast to the HLP's proposal for a universal body, Annan recommended that the Commission be replaced "with a smaller standing Human Rights Council," which would either be a principal UN organ or a subsidiary of the GA and consist of members elected by two-thirds of the GA who "undertake to abide by the highest human rights standards."[9]

In response, UN member states engaged in multistage negotiations that started with the World Summit Outcome Document, which they hoped to use to unveil the proposed Council at the upcoming September 2005 World Summit, the largest ever gathering of world leaders at that time. Yet, member states espoused conflicting visions for the new body, resulting in divergence on key issues and protracted deliberations. Intractable differences over membership criteria, size, composition, election processes, organizational status, and functions prevented states from reaching substantive agreement. Thus, by the time the World Summit was convened, they could only agree to call on the President of the UN GA "to conduct open, transparent and inclusive negotiations, to be completed as soon as possible during the sixtieth session, with the aim of establishing the mandate, modalities, functions, size, composition, membership, working methods and procedures for the Council."[10]

Heeding this request, GA President Jan Eliasson of Sweden presided over discussions that involved "months of intense and difficult labor in the face of bitter criticism, delaying tactics and efforts at sabotage" and

---

Freedom House, "World's Worst Regimes Revealed," press release, March 31, 2005, www.freedomhouse.org/template.cfm?page=70&release=255, accessed April 6, 2012.

[7] UN General Assembly, "Report of the Secretary General's High-Level Panel on Threats Challenges and Change, A More Secure World, Our Shared Responsibility," December 2, 2004, UN Doc. A/59/565, http://www.un.org/en/peacebuilding/pdf/historical/hlp_more_secure_world.pdf, accessed September 8, 2017, paragraphs 285–291.

[8] UN General Assembly, "Report of the Secretary-General, In Larger Freedom: Toward Development, Security and Human Rights for All," March 21, 2005, UN Doc. A/59/2005, paragraph 182.

[9] Ibid., paragraph 183.

[10] UN General Assembly, Resolution 60/1, "2005 World Summit Outcome Document," October 24, 2005, UN Doc. A/RES/60/1, paragraph 160.

"significantly different visions of what the new Human Rights Council should be."[11] Due to ongoing disagreement on key issues, such as the frequency and duration of Council meetings, the agenda, the convening of special sessions, the details of the peer review process, and civil society involvement, the GA resolution that was adopted in March 2006 left a number of specific features of the Council unresolved.[12] However, countries that were opposed to a high bar for membership, such as requiring that members make certain human rights commitments, applying membership criteria, or establishing election by a two-thirds GA vote, succeeded in eliminating strict membership requirements and securing election by a mere majority vote of the GA.[13] The UN Secretary-General, the US government, and human rights groups expressed frustration that the most promising proposed features, particularly higher membership standards, had been stripped away.[14] A *New York Times* editorial noted that a "once-promising reform proposal has been so watered down that it has become an ugly sham, offering cover to an unacceptable status quo. It should be renegotiated or rejected."[15]

Mexican Ambassador Luis Alfonso de Alba, the first president of the newly established HRC, led Council members in year-long IB negotiations that spanned June 2006 through June 2007. These discussions were convened via six working groups as well as regular meetings with de Alba to resolve outstanding issues. These negotiations were hampered by many of the long-standing divisions that plagued the earlier stages for HRC reform and participants described the discussions as being impeded by "complete mistrust" and a "clash of ideas."[16] Yet, under

---

[11] Paul Gordon Lauren, "To Preserve and Build on its Achievements and to Redress its Shortcomings: The Journey from the Commission on Human Rights to the Human Rights Council," *Human Rights Quarterly* 29, no. 2 (2007): 333. Only the United States, Israel, and the Marshal Islands voted against the resolution. See also ibid., 332–335.

[12] UN General Assembly, Resolution 60/251, "Human Rights Council," April 3, 2006, UN Doc. A/RES/60/251.

[13] A human rights NGO representative noted that although the idea of criteria was laudable, it was difficult to develop appropriate metrics. For example, if ratification of human rights treaties had been used, this could have barred the United States since it has not ratified treaties on women's rights and children's rights. Interview with human rights NGO representative, August 23, 2017, via Skype.

[14] See Maggie Farley, "New U.N. Rights Panel is Proposed," *Los Angeles Times*, February 24, 2006.

[15] Editorial, "The Shame of the United Nations," *New York Times*, February 26, 2006. Traub described the Council as "an eviscerated version of the body Annan had proposed a year before."

[16] Husak noted the "complete mistrust" that impeded progress in the Working Group that he facilitated. Tomas Husak (Czech Ambassador to the UN in Geneva and special procedures Working Group Facilitator), interview by author, May 25, 2011, Geneva, Switzerland. Loulichki described the discussions as involving a "clash of ideas" and that

de Alba's leadership, the IB discussions eventually resolved many of the outstanding issues and succeeded in reviewing the special procedures, revamping the body of expert advisors and the complaint procedure, setting up the new Universal Periodic Review (UPR) process, and developing the Council's agenda, program of work, and rules of procedure. In the end, numerous compromises were forged, such as eliminating the mandates for the rapporteurs assigned to Cuba and Belarus and confining the UPR interactive discussion to states, which meant a more limited role for civil society.[17]

Scholars, diplomats, and human rights advocates have debated whether the Council is an improvement over the Commission. Meghna Abram offers a somber assessment, arguing that "[s]tates with a negative agenda have been very successful ... in articulating their vision for the Council," especially in stressing cooperation and dialogue as opposed to drawing attention to country-specific abuses.[18] Along these lines, a Western European diplomat described some states as so disillusioned that they "were ready to write off the Council."[19] These views stemmed from the fact that while there were some positive changes, such as increased meeting time, a number of other revisions appeared to be merely cosmetic and the Council fell short of initial hopes. Table 4.1 captures the organizational differences between the Commission and the Council.

The Council's record thus far has been mixed. A 2009 Freedom House report argued that "a small but active group of countries with very poor human rights records have so far succeeded in limiting the ability of the Council to protect human rights" and pointed to the Council's failure to "take timely action on some of the most egregious human rights abuses ... and its ability to address emerging global threats to fundamental human rights such as freedom of expression and freedom of association."[20] A number of observers are disheartened that the UPR,

---

his goal was to "dissatisfy the least number of people." Mohammed Loulichiki (former Moroccan Ambassador to the UN in Geneva and UPR Working Group Facilitator), interview by author, June 29, 2011, New York.

[17] Abraham, *Building the New Human Rights Council*, 4–5.

[18] Ibid., 45. For further background, there are several relevant chapters in M. Cherif Bassiouni and William A. Schabas eds. *New Challenges for the UN Human Rights Machinery: What Future for the UN Treaty Body System and the Human Rights Council Procedures?* (Cambridge: Intersentia, 2011).

[19] Interview with Western European diplomat, May 26, 2011, Geneva, Switzerland.

[20] Freedom House, *Special Report The UN Human Rights Council Report Card: 2007–2009* (Washington, DC: Freedom House, September 10, 2009), www.freedomhouse.org/report/special-reports/un-human-rights-council-report-card-2009-2010, accessed September 11, 2017, 1.

Table 4.1 *Key differences between the UN Commission on Human Rights and the UN Human Rights Council*

	The Commission on Human Rights	The HRC
Size	53 member states	47 member states
Organizational standing	Subsidiary body of the Economic and Social Council	Subsidiary body of the GA
Sessions	An annual six-week session, special sessions could be held but were never scheduled	Minimum three sessions per year with total duration of at least ten weeks; special sessions can be called by a vote of one-third of the members
Membership criteria	None	No hard criteria; however, states are encouraged to "take into account" the candidate country's contribution to the promotion and protection of human rights and their voluntary human rights pledges and commitments
Election process	States are nominated by regional blocs and voted on to the Commission by ECOSOC, requiring twenty-eight votes or a majority of members present and voting (fifty-four members). However, this was generally by "clean slates" in which there are generally not more candidates than seats	States are elected by secret ballot based on regional allocation by a simple majority of the GA, requiring 97 votes out of 192
Term limits	None	Two consecutive terms
Suspension of membership	None	A two-thirds majority needed to suspend a member for gross human rights violations
Geographical composition	African states, 15; Asian states, 12; Eastern European states, 5; Latin America and Caribbean states, 11; Western Europe and others, 10	African states, 13; Asian states, 13; Eastern European states, 6; Latin America and Caribbean states, 8; Western Europe and others, 7
Review of member states' human rights records	Member states often blocked attempts to review their own human rights records	All UN member states reviewed through the UPR process
Country-specific mechanism for urgent human rights crises	Country-specific resolutions and special procedures available	Country-specific resolutions and special procedures available; able to call a special session with support of one-third of the members

Table 4.1 (*cont.*)

	The Commission on Human Rights	The HRC
Special procedures	Existing system of country-specific and thematic special procedures	Continues the system of special procedures for both country and thematic special rapporteurs but during the IB Process the mandates for Cuba and Belarus were terminated

which was hailed as one of the Council's strengths because it requires all states to be routinely reviewed, has been manipulated by a number of countries and has fallen short of expectations. In 2008, the International Service for Human Rights, a Geneva-based nongovernmental organization (NGO), expressed

serious concern at the practice of some States which have been lining up [to speak during the UPR] only to praise their allies. This approach runs contrary to the agreed principle that the UPR should be conducted in an 'objective, transparent, non-selective, constructive, non-confrontational and non-politicized manner.' In this sense, the UPR has not lived up to the expectations of a move away from the 'politicisation' of the past. Indeed, in many cases, this 'politicisation' has seemed more pronounced than ever.[21]

Yet, a number of observers indicate that since around 2010, the Council became more effective at addressing country-specific abuses and note promising developments, such as the use of a resolution, commission of inquiry, and membership suspension, to spotlight human rights violations in Libya; special sessions on the Ivory Coast, Libya, and Syria; and the reinstatement of the mandate for the Rapporteurs on Iran and Belarus.[22] For example, scholars Ted Piccone and Naomi McMillen,

[21] "NGO Statement on Item 6 – Friday, 13 June 2008," International Service for Human Rights, http://olddoc.ishr.ch/lca/statements_council/otherngos/upr_statement_final_13_june_2008.pdf, accessed September 11, 2017. Similar complaint noted in Allehone Mulugeta Abebe, "Of Shaming and Bargaining: African States and the Universal Periodic Review of the United Nations Human Rights Council," *Human Rights Law Review* 9, no. 1 (2009), 19.

[22] Interview human rights NGO representative, May 31, 2011, Geneva, Switzerland and interview with human rights NGO representative/human rights scholar, May 26, 2011, Geneva, Switzerland. See also Suzanne Nossel, *Advancing Human Rights in the UN System, Working Paper* (New York: Council on Foreign Relations, 2012), www.cfr.org/sites/default/files/pdf/2012/05/IIGG_WorkingPaper8.pdf, accessed September 11, 2017.

writing in 2016, argued that "while Israel/Palestine continues to dominate country-specific human rights issues at the Human Rights Council,
recently states have begun to more robustly to address dire human rights
situations in other countries and regions through special reviews, inquiries and investigations."[23] Several observers acknowledged that US reen-
gagement with the Council in 2010 led to improvements in the HRC's
functioning.[24] However, citing the Council's bias against Israel, which
came up for discussion as a standing agenda item at every session, while
countries with serious human rights abuses such as Congo, Venezuela,
and Iran escaped censure, in 2018 the United States announced its
withdrawal.[25] Praise for the Council's focus on select countries is not
universally shared by all nations and some diplomats hailing from non-
Western, developing countries point to country-specific action as a defi-
ciency. A South Asian diplomat, speaking in 2011, noted,
"Unfortunately, over the last nine to ten months the Council is moving
toward the way of the Commission. There is a general atmosphere of
pointing fingers ... or you hold a special session in which you condemn.
We believe the best way is to engage and work cooperatively."[26]

These differing views meant that the HRC's five-year review in
2011 was characterized by drama and disagreement as a number of
countries belonging to the Western and Others Group (WEOG) pushed
for improvements such as requiring pledges from candidate countries to
take particular human rights steps and proposals for mechanisms to
better address country-specific situations, while some countries, including China, defended the status quo and successfully countered efforts to
strengthen the Council.[27] These disputes suggest ongoing division over

---

[23] Ted Piccone and Naomi McMillen, *Country-Specific Scrutiny at the United Nations Human Rights Council, Working Paper* (Washington DC: Project on International Order and Strategy, Brookings Institution, May 2016), www.brookings.edu/research/country-specific-scrutiny-at-the-united-nations-human-rights-council-more-than-meets-the-eye/, accessed September 11, 2017.

[24] Interview with Western European diplomat, May 26, 2011, Geneva, Switzerland, and interview with NGO representative, May 31, 2011, Geneva, Switzerland.

[25] Carol Morello, "U.S. withdraws from U.N. Human Rights Council over perceived bias against Israel," *The Washington Post*, June 19, 2018, www.washingtonpost.com/world/national-security/us-expected-to-back-away-from-un-human-rights-council/2018/06/19/a49c2d0c-733c-11e8-b4b7-308400242c2e_story.html?noredirect=on&utm_term=.470a012cb3e0, accessed July 2, 2018.

[26] Interview with South Asian diplomat, May 31, 2011, Geneva, Switzerland. Other non-Western diplomats expressed similar views. Interview with Southeast Asian diplomat, May 25, 2011, Geneva, Switzerland, and interview with South Asian diplomat, May 27, 2011, Geneva, Switzerland.

[27] Interview with South Asian diplomat, May 27, 2011, Geneva, Switzerland; interview with Western European diplomat, June 28, 2011, New York; interview with Western European diplomat, May 26, 2011, Geneva, Switzerland; interview with Western

the regime's substance and procedures, which may have meant that China had greater latitude in its attempts to constrain the regime.

China and the UN Commission on Human Rights

China joined the HRC negotiations with an attitude that was prefigured by its experiences with the UNCHR, including the Sub-Commission, where it faced scrutiny after the 1989 Tiananmen Square protests. The crackdown and the international condemnation that followed altered Beijing's relationship with the regime as Chinese officials found themselves facing intense international human rights criticism for the first time. In contrast, prior to 1989, during the 1980s, China's participation in the regime was without incident and it engaged cautiously in the UNCHR, acting primarily as a taker of this part of the regime.[28] As further elaborated in Chapter 2, after using force to end popular protests in June 1989, Beijing experienced UN censure, sanctions from Western governments, suspension of high-level bilateral contact, a freeze on World Bank and Asian Development Bank loans, and the cancellation of bilateral cooperation in a number of areas. PRC leaders developed a response that utilized a carrots and sticks approach that exploited its growing economic weight and political sway to rebuild its diplomatic standing and counter UNCHR resolutions.[29] In addition to muscular lobbying against UNCHR and Sub-Commission resolutions, the PRC assailed regime procedures that allowed for country-specific scrutiny and characterized country-specific resolutions as politicization and confrontation. This position countering country-level action was also championed by the Like-Minded Group (LMG), which coalesced in the UNCHR in the late 1990s and included the PRC.

Even prior to the LMG's emergence China along with some of these countries worked in concert to weaken the regime under the guise of reform. Among their first targets was the Sub-Commission on the Promotion and Protection of Human Rights, which was composed of independent experts and established in 1967 to "examine information relevant to gross violations of human rights and fundamental

---

European diplomat, June 28, 2011, New York, and interview with Southeast Asian diplomat, May 25, 2011, Geneva, Switzerland.

[28] Kent, *China, the United Nations and Human Rights*, 43. Kent does not specifically describe the PRC as a "taker." This description of China as a taker is based on my assessment of its posture at the time.

[29] Ibid., 77 and 114–118, and Foot, *Rights Beyond Borders*, 121–122.

freedoms."[30] Despite vigorous PRC lobbying, the Sub-Commission had passed resolutions on China's record in 1989 and 1991.[31] Consequently, in the early 1990s, the PRC began complaining about the Sub-Commission's politicization, overlap with the work of the Commission, neglect of the right to development, and "wanton attacks on the domestic affairs of sovereign states."[32] Subsequently, the PRC and other LMG countries used a series of resolutions to strip the Sub-Commission of the authority to consider country situations being dealt with by the Commission; deny it the ability to pass country or thematic resolutions that contained specific reference to individual countries; restrict its remit to conducting studies, research, and expert advice "at the request of the Commission"; and insist that it "should not undertake any new activity without the Commission's approval."[33] A number of these changes mirrored Chinese positions, including PRC delegate Ren Yisheng's 2000 statement that

the Sub-Commission should carry out studies and refrain from deliberating on human rights situations in specific countries ... the Sub-Commission should not adopt resolutions on country situations ... [it should] increase its efficiency by eliminating confrontation from its deliberations in the interests of dialogue and cooperation.[34]

China also took aim at UNCHR resolutions on its record. As detailed in Chapter 2, even though Beijing faced the introduction of UNCHR

---

[30] UN Economic and Social Council, Resolution 1235, "Question of the violation of human rights and fundamental freedoms, including policies of racial discrimination and segregation and of apartheid, in all countries, with particular reference to colonial and other dependent countries and territories," June 6, 1967, paragraph 2. Before 1999, it was known as the Sub-Commission on Prevention of Discrimination and Protection of Minorities.

[31] Because its members were not government representatives but independent experts, they are thought to be more resistant to lobbying and governmental pressure.

[32] Quoted in Kent, *China, the United Nations and Human Rights*, 63 and 74.

[33] See UN Commission on Human Rights, "Summary Record of the Fiftieth Meeting," December 11, 2000, UN Doc. E/CN.4/2000/SR.50, paragraph 74; UN Commission on Human Rights, "Work of the Sub-Commission on the Promotion and Protection of Human Rights," Resolution 2000/83, April 26, 2000; UN Commission on Human Rights, "Enhancing the effectiveness of the mechanisms of the Commission on Human Rights," Decision 2000/109, April 26, 2000; UN Commission on Human Rights, "The work of the Sub-Commission on the Promotion and Protection of Human Rights Commission on Human Rights," Resolution 2003/59, April 24, 2003; UN Commission on Human Rights, "The Work of the Sub-Commission on the Promotion and Protection of Human Rights," Resolution, 2005/53, April 20, 2005. See also Kent, *China, the United Nations, and Human Rights*, 64 and 74–75.

[34] UN Economic and Social Council, "Commission on Human Rights, Fifty-sixth session, Summary Record of the Fiftieth Meeting," December 11, 2000, UN Doc. E/CN.4/2000/SR.50, paragraph 73–74.

resolutions twelve times between 1990 and 2005, it defeated passage of the resolution by mobilizing non-Western, developing world support.[35] Chinese leaders accomplished this through diplomatic attention and economic incentives, particularly aid and trade. For example, in 1996, high-level PRC leaders visited all of the African countries that were on or would soon join the Commission on Human Rights, and the following year, China's no-action motion passed with the support of nearly every African nation on the UNCHR.[36] Yet, because the mere introduction of the resolution was an embarrassment for Beijing, Chinese diplomats continued to oppose the use of country-specific action. They framed these resolutions as reflecting Western arrogance and unfair treatment of developing countries. Along these lines, in 1993, the PRC lashed out against the sponsors of a resolution on PRC human rights practices and claimed that "[a]lmost all the sponsors [of the resolution] were Western countries, giving the false impression that only Western countries cared about human rights. China consistently supported the interests of the developing countries in the international arena, aiding with the poor against the rich."[37] The PRC sharpened its attack on country-specific scrutiny after 1995 when its no-action motion failed and the UNCHR resolution was defeated by only one vote.[38] As a result of this close call, the mid 1990s was a turning point in which the PRC initiated reformist efforts, which "coincided with a move by authoritarian states ... to challenge the UN monitoring mechanisms," including a "concerted push ... to eliminate all country-specific resolutions."[39] Along these lines, in 1995, PRC representative Zhang Yishan stated that

the Commission was in need of comprehensive reform ... his delegation had made a number of suggestions, including streamlining the agenda, giving equal treatment to the two categories of human rights, reducing the Commission's

---

[35] UNCHR resolutions were introduced in 1990, 1992, 1993, 1994, 1995, 1996, 1997, 1999, 2000, 2001, 2002, and 2004.

[36] Human Rights Watch, *Chinese Diplomacy, Western Hypocrisy, and the U.N. Human Rights Commission* (New York: Human Rights Watch, 1997), 6.

[37] UN Economic and Social Council, "Commission on Human Rights Forty-ninth session, Provisional Summary Record of the First Part of the 66th meeting," March 16, 1993, UN Doc. E/CN.4/1993/SR.66, paragraph 59.

[38] The no-action motion was a tactical maneuver that the PRC used to prevent a resolution on its record from being voted on; 1995 was the only year it did not pass.

[39] Phillip Alston, "Reconceiving the UN Human Rights Regime: Challenges Confronting the New UN Human Rights Council," *Melbourne Journal of International Law* 7, no. 1 (2006), 196. In explaining its support for resolutions on Israel and the Occupied Territories, China has justified this as a situation of unlawful occupation in which condemnation is legitimate. Sceats and Breslin, *China and the International Human Rights System*, 20.

workload, standardizing the participation of non-governmental organizations and eliminating selectivity.[40]

China's use of economic muscle and arguments favoring cooperation and dialogue convinced the EU to abandon support for China-focused resolutions after 1997. However, the United States persisted in using the resolution as a policy tool and when it introduced resolutions it was often joined by a handful of other supporting states.[41] As a result, the PRC continued its complaints about the UNCHR, especially the use of country-specific resolutions, and called for cooperation on the basis of mutual equality and respect; prioritizing developing world interests, including increasing their proportional representation in the UNCHR; and ridding the Commission of confrontation, meaning country-specific resolutions.[42] A chorus of countries hailing from the LMG voiced similar grievances and the PRC tailored its statements to appeal to these countries. For example, in 2005, the PRC alleged that Item 9, which provided the opportunity to raise country-specific concern,

had since turned into the most politicized and controversial item on the Commission's agenda. Since the end of the Cold War, the Commission had adopted over 100 country-specific resolutions that had almost all been directed against developing countries, leaving the impression that human rights problems existed only in those countries, and that developed countries had a perfect record ... Tabling resolutions on country situations had therefore become a privilege of the strong and powerful, and it was not surprising, therefore, that those who had found themselves in the dock were often developing countries.[43]

Beijing's actions and success with the no-action motion also appeared to set a precedent that further rendered the UNCHR ineffectual, and, after

---

[40] UN Economic and Social Council, "Commission on Human Rights Fifty-first Session, Summary Record of the 44th meeting," March 3, 1995, UN Doc. E/CN.4/1995/SR.44, paragraphs 63–66. In 1996, China also called for geographic redistribution of seats. See, for example, UN Commission on Human Rights, "Summary Record of the 33rd Meeting," April 16, 1996, UN Doc. E/CN.4/1996/SR.33, paragraphs 1–6.

[41] Baker, "Human Rights, Europe and the People's Republic of China," 57–59.

[42] Kent, *China, the United Nations, and Human Rights*, 75.

[43] UN Economic and Social Council, "Commission on Human Rights, Sixty-first session, Summary Record of the 20th meeting," April 8, 2005, UN Doc. E/CN.4/2005/SR.20, paragraphs 14–16. In 2004, the PRC made a similar complaint, when Ambassador Sha alleged that "agenda item 9 had been distorted by certain Western countries, which used it to humiliate the developing countries and trample on their sovereignty through acrimonious attacks, arrogance and prejudice. No country had a perfect human rights record. Developing countries were not inveterate human rights violators. The Commission had not mandated any State to serve as human rights judge." UN Economic and Social Council, "Commission on Human Rights, Sixtieth session, Summary Record of the 21st Meeting," April 1, 2004, UN Doc. E/CN.4/2004/SR.21, paragraph 54.

2002, other countries, including Zimbabwe, Cuba, and Belarus, also used this maneuver to prevent consideration of resolutions on their records.[44] China's grievances expanded to calls for "comprehensive reform," including "standardizing the participation of non-governmental organizations and eliminating selectivity," which for the PRC meant ridding the Commission of country-specific resolutions.[45] In place of country-focused scrutiny, Beijing advocated discussion without singling out individual countries and a thematic approach to human rights focused on particular kinds of human rights issues, not particular countries.[46] However, human rights advocates endorse spotlighting particular countries and point out that patterns of human rights violations often occur along national lines.

Although the PRC continued its tough rhetoric against country-specific resolutions, because of its success in using diplomatic pressure and economic leverage to prevent consideration of UNCHR resolutions on its record, it was comfortable with the Commission and hesitant when reform discussions emerged in 2004. Not only had PRC diplomats "mastered the art of human rights diplomacy within the existing UN structure," they also "had little difficulty in mustering the votes to pass no-action motions to thwart resolutions on its human rights record" and since the late 1990s were securing passage of the no-action motion by increasingly comfortable margins.[47] A Western European diplomat noted that China and other like-minded countries "had learned to control and manage" the UNCHR to avert scrutiny and were therefore "comfortable with the Commission." As a result, PRC diplomats were "nervous and resistant" when reform proposals emerged because they did not "want the new body to be more intrusive and powerful."[48] As a UN official put it, China was "satisfied with the status quo" because the

---

[44] Elvira Dominguez Redondo, "The Universal Periodic Review of the UN Human Rights Council: An Assessment of the First Session," *Chinese Journal of International Law* 7, no. 3 (2008), 723, and Kinzelbach, "Will China's Rise Lead to a New Normative Order?" 313.

[45] See UN Commission on Human Rights, "Sixty-first Session, Summary Record of the 20th Meeting," April 8, 2005, UN Doc. E/CN.4/2005/SR.20, paragraph 18. See also United Nations, "Commission on Human Rights Opens Sixty-First Session," press release, May 14, 2005, UN Doc. HR/CN/1107, www.un.org/News/Press/docs/2005/hrcn1107.doc.htm, accessed September 12, 2017.

[46] Kinzelbach, "Will China's Rise Lead to a New Normative Order?" 313.

[47] The Dui Hua Foundation, "The Commission on Human Rights: Another Round in 2006?" *Dialogue* 21 (Fall 2005), 1–3. For PRC positions, see, for example, United Nations, "Commission on Human Rights Opens Sixty-First Session," press release, March 14, 2005, UN Doc. HR/CN/1107, www.un.org/News/Press/docs/2005/hrcn1107.doc.htm, accessed September 12, 2017.

[48] Interview with Western European diplomat, July 23, 2012, New York

Commission was "no longer doing it damage, and was, therefore, hesitant about a new UN human rights body."[49]

China and the Creation of the UN Human Rights Council

Beijing's conduct throughout the HRC negotiations illustrates the extent to which it had become a participatory, skilled, and assertive actor in the regime with clearly defined positions and a predisposition to curb the authority and force of the regime. Unlike its quiescent behavior in the early 1980s during the Convention against Torture discussions, PRC diplomats engaged in the HRC negotiations in a more consequential manner and participated in every major discussion about the Council. As a former US government official remarked, China appeared to have "recognized that there was a substantial opportunity to de-fang the Commission, making the Council a less intrusive entity."[50] This was reflected in key PRC positions, including resisting membership criteria that would have excluded rights-abusing countries or election by a two-thirds GA vote; opposing country-focused approaches, including country-specific special procedures, special sessions, and resolutions; circumscribing certain mechanisms, such as the Sub-Commission, the 1503 complaint procedure, and the special procedures; restricting NGO participation or any binding follow-up as part of the UPR process; and endorsing a larger body with a greater allocation of seats for Asian and African countries – the very countries China drew support from. The thrust of Beijing's proposed positions, not all of which were accepted, attempted to dilute the Council from the more robust entity envisioned by Secretary-General Annan and other proponents of reform.

This section on China and the establishment of the HRC is organized into several subsections. I begin by discussing notable aspects of China's constrainer behavior. I then turn to outlining its behavior and positions during three key phases of the reform process, including announcing the Council as a September 2005 World Summit deliverable, securing its creation through the passage of a GA resolution, and determining a number of essential institutional features through the IB package. This chronological approach helps illuminate the evolution in Beijing's strategies and posture.

---

[49] Interview with UN official, June 29, 2011, New York.
[50] Interview with former US government official, October 27, 2010, Washington DC. Similar points made by interview with Western European diplomat, July 23, 2012, New York, and interview with Asia Pacific diplomat, September 28, 2011, Canberra, Australia.

Before parsing PRC conduct during the various phases of the reform process, it is worth calling attention to distinctive aspects of its conduct and strategies that were largely influenced by its overriding goals to keep a low profile and avoid being seen as a spoiler even in instances when it was acting to constrain the regime. These observations are evident throughout the following sections, which detail its behavior in greater detail. First, the PRC deliberately and assiduously worked to maintain a modest profile and resisted a prominent or leadership role.[51] Along these lines, China was described as rarely taking the lead on issues,[52] "not difficult,"[53] "not the most vocal,"[54] "not a ringleader,"[55] "playing it carefully and usually holding its fire,"[56] "careful and conservative,"[57] and "not fighting on the front lines."[58] As a North American diplomat put it, Beijing's diplomats "rarely put their heads above the parapet" in the regime.[59] In a similar vein, a Western European diplomat noted that "even when China is trying to kill something, they try to do so in a smooth and diplomatic way."[60] Second, the PRC preferred to let other countries take more prominent roles and once it knew that another country was championing an issue, it would hang back and quietly support those efforts. Beijing could afford to act with restraint because other countries such as Pakistan, Cuba, Russia, and Egypt shared its positions and were willing to be more vocal.[61] Instead, it appeared to

---

[51] Interview with former US government official, October 27, 2010, Washington DC; interview with North American diplomat, May 24, 2011, Geneva, Switzerland; interview with South Asian diplomat, June 3, 2011, Geneva, Switzerland; interview with Western European diplomat, May 26, 2011, Geneva, Switzerland; interview with North American diplomat, June 17, 2011, Washington DC; interview with Western European diplomat, June 13, 2011, Oslo, Norway; and interview with human rights NGO representative, August 16, 2017, via Skype. Sceats and Breslin noted that this passive posture was a source of frustration for some PRC allies, such as Russia. Sceats and Breslin, *China and the International Human Rights System*, 16.

[52] Interview UN official, June 29, 2011, New York; interview with former US government official, October 27, 2011, Washington DC, and interview with human rights NGO representative, August 16, 2017, via Skype.

[53] Interview with Western European diplomat, October 2, 2010, Stockholm, Sweden.

[54] Interview with Western European diplomat, June 13, 2011, Oslo, Norway.

[55] Interview with North American diplomat, June 17, 2011, Washington DC. China was said to rarely take minority positions and tries not to be "swamped in a vote." Similar observation from interview with UN official, June 29, 2011, New York, and interview with human rights NGO representative, August 16, 2017, via Skype.

[56] Interview with Asia Pacific diplomat, September 28, 2011, Canberra, Australia.

[57] Interview with North American diplomat, June 17, 2011, Washington DC.

[58] Interview with Asia Pacific diplomat, September 28, 2011, Canberra, Australia.

[59] Interview with North American diplomat, June 17, 2011, Washington DC.

[60] Interview with Western European diplomat, June 28, 2011, New York.

[61] Interview with Western European diplomat, July 23, 2012, New York, and interview with Asia Pacific diplomat, September 28, 2011, Canberra, Australia.

prefer "an invisible role in which China encouraged other autocratic governments or developing world governments to hold particular positions" while it acted as "a quiet power behind them."[62] Third, the PRC preferred to work with other countries, particularly the LMG. This helped to obscure its constraining attempts and allowed PRC diplomats to frame their positions as being aligned with other countries rather than solely a Chinese position. The HRC negotiations coincided with the PRC's turn serving as spokesperson for the LMG, which gave it a slightly more visible role, such as delivering statements.[63] Its rotational role as LMG spokesperson may have provided it with greater influence over the group's position papers and statements, yet it allowed it to couch these statements as representing a group of countries.[64] Fourth, although it preferred a more low-profile role, the PRC was willing to take a more prominent role and even hold up agreement at a critical stage when its key interests were at stake.[65] Former Pakistani Ambassador to the UN, Munir Akram, described China as playing "a kind of clever game" of not "put[ting] their chin out" except on issues of significant importance to it.[66] Similarly, a Western European diplomat observed that even though Beijing would "rather sit back and support others' efforts, China was willing to be vocal and take a strong stand on redlines."[67] Beijing's lone stance during the final hours of the IB Process when it sought to introduce rules to make it nearly impossible for the Council to employ country-specific resolutions is an example of this behavior. It reserved

---

[62] Interview with former North American diplomat, October 27, 2011, Washington DC.

[63] Ambassador Sha Zukang's biography specifically noted his role as "coordinator" of the LMG from 2004 to 2007, when he served as PRC Ambassador to the UN in Geneva. "The Biography of Sha Zukang Under-Secretary General for Economic and Social Affairs," United Nations, www.un.org/News/dh/infocus/SMG.asp?smgID=121, accessed June 11, 2011. While it does appear that the PRC was merely taking its turn serving as LMG spokesperson, it coincided with the tenure of Sha Zukang as Ambassador to the UN, who was often described as outspoken.

[64] It was during China's rotation as spokesperson that the LMG appeared to dissolve even though the PRC may have preferred that the group continue. A November 13, 2006, statement that the PRC initially drafted in the name of the LMG shows handwriting changing this to a China-only statement. Thus, Chinese diplomats may have drafted the statement with the expectation and hope that it would be delivered on behalf of the LMG, but found that LMG countries were less committed to continuing collaboration. After this there were no further LMG statements during the remainder of the IB process until the group reemerged in the HRC after 2011. "China," UN Human Rights Council Extranet, Institution-Building Working Groups, Working Groups, Working Group on Special Procedures, Expert Advice, and a Complaint Procedure doubt, Oral Statements, November 13, 2006, extranet.ohchr.org, accessed July 17, 2017.

[65] Interview with Western European diplomat, July 23, 2012, New York.

[66] Munir Akram (former Pakistani Ambassador to the UN), telephone interview material in private possession of author, January 16, 2012, Oxford to Geneva.

[67] Interview with former North American diplomat, October 27, 2011, Washington DC.

this strategy for issues of high interest when it had failed to secure its preferred outcome through lower-profile measures. Fifth, the PRC carefully tailored its conduct based on venue as Chinese diplomats took more vocal, assertive stances in smaller, less public gatherings while at the same time offering softer, cautiously worded, anodyne statements in larger, public venues with a broader audience. In this vein, a Western European diplomat described China as having "very strong views" against most of the proposed improvements, such as a high bar for membership and giving the HRC "greater [organization] status" on par with the Security Council but confined its strong interventions to non-public venues in order to avoid being "a prominently negative voice."[68] Finally, the PRC also adjusted its posture during each phase of reform, shifting from initial quiet resistance to becoming increasingly engaged and involved as the issues at stake were more critical. This pattern clearly emerges in the following sections that document the PRC's behavior in each stage of the HRC reform process.

The September 2005 World Summit Outcome Document

When discussions to replace the Commission on Human Rights first emerged in 2004 and the proposals advanced by the UN High-Level Panel and the Secretary-General were being debated, the PRC was initially wary and expressed resistance. As a UN official observed, Beijing "did not initially support" calls for a reformed UN human rights body and "appeared concerned about some of the proposals, such as membership criteria."[69] A former US government official suggested that Beijing's lukewarm response stemmed from a concern that the Council "might become something more intrusive and powerful than the Commission."[70] Thus, throughout the spring of 2005 the PRC voiced misgivings and used the discussions about reform as an opportunity to vent its oft-heard grievances. For example, in March 2005, China in its capacity as spokesperson for the LMG complained that the High-Level Panel Report

failed to address the problem of misuse of Item 9 and proliferation of country specific resolutions. In addition, the report should have highlighted the following concerns of the developing countries ... more emphasis on the promotion of economic social and cultural rights, and the right to development. Second, the UN Charter clearly stipulated that the way of promotion and protection of human

---

[68] Interview with Western European diplomat, July 23, 2012, New York.
[69] Interview with UN official, June 29, 2011, New York.
[70] Interview with former US government official, October 27, 2011, Washington DC.

rights is "to achieve international cooperation" … It's about time that members of the Commission do more to promote dialogue instead of confrontation, and have more soul-searching instead of finger-pointing.[71]

A month later, in Geneva in April 2005, Ambassador Sha asserted that the

LMG [Like-Minded Group] has noted the proposal to create a small-scaled human rights council (sic) to replace the present Commission. This is a new proposal … [that] does not stem from consultations among member states at the Commission on Human Rights, the ECOSOC and the General Assembly. Such a proposal requires thorough understanding and full discussion by the UN member states before it can be considered seriously. This is particularly so, because the proposal would create a new body within the UN system.[72]

As discussions about a new human rights body persisted through the summer, China continued to voice reservations and specifically took aim at proposals for a smaller body. For example, the PRC's June 2005 position paper on UN reform asserted that

[t]he UN human rights bodies must abide by the principle of equitable geographical distribution in their composition to ensure broad representation. To have a small 'Human Rights Council' to replace the Commission may not possibly overturn the serious 'credit deficit' in the human rights area.[73]

In June 2005, when UNCHR members met informally to discuss Annan's *In Larger Freedom* report, China again stated that "it was not yet convinced of the need to replace the Commission" and that the Commission should "not be dismissed lightly" and called for further "earnest discussions."[74] Although Beijing had called for reform for years, its goals and motivations were different from the main proponents of

---

[71] "Statement by H.E. Ambassador Sha Zukang, on Behalf of the Like-Minded Group, at the 61ˢᵗ session of the Commission on Human Rights, 2005/03/14" Permanent Mission of the PRC to the UN in Geneva, www.china-un.ch/eng/rqrd/thsm/t187353.htm, accessed August 20, 2017.

[72] "Statement by H.E. Ambassador Sha Zukang, on behalf of the LMG, at the Informal Meeting on Reform of the UN Human Rights Machinery, 2005/04/12" Permanent Mission of the PRC to the UN in Geneva, www.china-un.ch/eng/rqrd/thsm/t191364 .htm, accessed August 20, 2017.

[73] "Position Paper of the People's Republic of China on the United Nations Reforms, 1005/06/07," PRC Ministry of Foreign Affairs, www.china-un.org/eng/chinaandun/ zzhgg/t199101.htm, accessed August 5, 2011.

[74] UN Commission on Human Rights, "Commission on Human Rights Holds Informal Meeting on Secretary-General's Reform Proposals," news release, June 20, 2005, www .unog.ch/unog/website/news_media_archive.nsf/(httpNewsByYear_en)/ 80257631003154D9C12570F1004B621A?OpenDocument, accessed September 13, 2017. Amnesty International, "Cluster III and IV: Discussion of SG's report by member states—April 2005: Relevant Issues Summary" (Amnesty International New York office files), in author's possession; and Amnesty International, "Human Rights

reform. In this vein, the June 2005 PRC position paper elaborated that "[t]he essence of reform is depoliticizing human rights issues, rejecting double standards, reducing and avoiding confrontation and promoting cooperation."[75] Given these misgivings the PRC was among the delegations refusing to support the HRC as a deliverable to be announced at the September 2005 World Summit. Amnesty International's files indicate that "China and Russia consider it inappropriate to force a decision on this issue in the September Summit."[76] In a similar vein, a June 2005 *New York Times* article reported that, according to UN sources, "[o]nly China, of the major nations, has yet to lend its support."[77]

In keeping with its tendency to adopt a low-profile posture, a UN official noted that even though the PRC was resistant it "did not lead the charge" against the Council and sought to conceal its opposition.[78] In order to do so, it confined its opposition to smaller venues and avoiding being on record publicly as being opposed to the Council. According to John Bolton, former US Ambassador to the UN, Beijing did not "like to take a controversial public position" and preferred to express its more insistent positions privately.[79] He noted that as a result of this tendency "evidence of the PRC's role in the public record is hard to come by."[80] A Western European diplomat concurred that China was "careful to have less documentation" of its hostility toward the HRC.[81] Consequently, Beijing's misgivings were usually expressed during consultations involving only a limited number of state participants and UN officials. Along these lines, a former US government official recalled China's "vociferous" arguments against upgrading the status of the Council in smaller, private meetings, while Chinese public statements were bland, even offering vaguely supportive comments for reform.[82]

Council Matrix, last updated May 2, 2005" (Amnesty International New York office files), in author's possession.

[75] "Position Paper of the People's Republic of China on United Nations Reforms, 1005/06/07."

[76] Amnesty International, "Cluster III and IV: Discussion of SG's report by member states —April 2005: Relevant Issues Summary."

[77] See Tom Wright, "Swiss Take Lead Role in Seeking UN Rights Reform," *The New York Times*, June 30, 2005, www.nytimes.com/2005/06/30/world/europe/swiss-take-lead-role-in-seeking-un-rights-reform.html?mcubz=1, accessed August 16, 2017.

[78] Interview with UN official, June 29, 2011, New York.

[79] John Bolton, (former US Ambassador to the UN), interview by author, October 14, 2011, Washington, DC, United States.

[80] Bolton, interview.

[81] Interview with Western European diplomat, May 31, 2011, Geneva, Switzerland.

[82] Interview of former US government official, October 28, 2010, Washington DC. Similar observations offered by a former human rights NGO representative who noted that it is typical of China to offer resistance privately while releasing public statements that offer

Thus, the PRC's June 2005 public position paper stated that it "is in favor of and supports the reform of UN human rights bodies," even though it was still voicing resistance in private meetings.[83] As a result of these tactics, China's obstructive behavior was concealed, even though it was one of the last governments to agree to the Outcome Document.[84]

As the September 2005 World Summit approached, PRC representatives turned to their infrequent but often effective strategy of holding up progress at a late stage in order to obtain their preferred outcome. Even though the majority of states were already on board, China along with Russia and Pakistan withheld support until their misgivings were addressed. According to Ambassador Bolton, these three nations objected to some of the content of the draft World Summit Outcome Document "at the last minute, days before the September 14 deadline."[85] This intransigence reflected PRC redlines. As a UN official noted, China was "extremely focused" on removing language on membership standards or election by a two-thirds vote in the GA and opposing elevating the Council's organizational status to be on par with the Security Council.[86] Further, China – along with Russia and Pakistan – was described as resisting inclusion of language enabling the Council to censure a country in the case of "gross and continuous violations."[87] Only after their concerns were addressed and these ideas stripped from

general support. Former human rights NGO representative, email correspondence with author, August 23, 2011.

[83] "Position Paper of the People's Republic of China on the United Nations Reforms, 2005/06/07." See also "Statement by Ambassador Wang Guangya on the Report of the High-Level Panel, 27 January 2005," Permanent Mission of the PRC to the UN in New York, www.china-un.org/eng/xw/t181639.htm, accessed August 16, 2017. Despite the PRC's preference for a more expansive human rights body, according to three individuals involved with the UN High-Level Panel on Threats, Challenges and Change, the PRC did not influence the panel's recommendation for a universal human rights body. Lord David Hannay (member of the UN High Level Panel on Threats, Challenges and Change) interview by author, November 8, 2011, London, United Kingdom; Sebastian von Einsiedel (staff member, UN High-Level Panel on Threats, Challenges and Change), email correspondence with author, September 19, 2011; and Tarun Chabra (staff member, UN High-Level Panel on Threats, Challenges and Change), interview by telephone, September 10, 2011. Einsiedel identified Robert Badinter, one of the members of the High-Level Panel, as offering the idea for a universal human rights body.

[84] Interview with UN official, June 29, 2011, New York.

[85] Bolton, interview. Journalist James Traub similarly reported that in the lead-up to the September 2005 summit, "[t]he Chinese ... suddenly announced deep reservations about [numerous issues, including] the Human Rights Council." Traub, *The Best Intensions*, 373.

[86] Interview with UN official, June 29, 2011, New York. Similar comments from interview with former US government official, October 28, 2010, Washington DC, and interview with Western European diplomat, July 23, 2012, New York.

[87] Traub, *The Best Intentions*, 373.

the document did the PRC relent.[88] The success of these countries in defeating promising proposals endorsed by Annan and other advocates of reform led Amnesty International to complain that "[i]t is totally unacceptable that a small number of countries with deeply troubling human rights records led by China and Russia are being allowed to block the creation of a new, stronger, more effective and authoritative Human Rights Council."[89]

UN General Assembly Resolution 60/251

Despite China's initial hesitance, as it saw support for reform growing and the Council was included as a deliverable of the September 2005 World Summit, it moved from a wary attitude to a more engaged posture and advanced specific positions during the deliberations over a GA resolution. According to a UN official, "once China understood that the Commission was undermined and needed to be reformed, they were not going to stand in the way ... and began discussing specifics."[90] During this phase of reform, Beijing offered detailed positions and continued to attempt to constrain the regime and resist proposals to make the HRC a more forceful entity than the Commission. As with previous stages of HRC reform, even as the PRC acted as a constrainer it did so as discreetly as possible. As a Western European diplomat put it, even though China had deep reservations, it "was not out in front."[91] Ambassador Bolton described Beijing as preferring to "water down the resolution in private" and that the most promising elements of the Council were "stripped away behind the scenes."[92]

Beijing continued to oppose the proposals advanced by reform proponents, particularly membership standards and elevating the HRC's organizational status.[93] A diplomat who participated in the negotiations

---

[88] Interview with Western European diplomat, May 31, 2011, Geneva, Switzerland. Bolton, interview, and interview with UN official, June 29, 2011, New York.
[89] "In quotes: UN World Summit," BBC News, September 16, 2005, http/news.bbc.co .uk/2/hi/americas/4247296.stm, accessed January 2, 2013.
[90] Interview UN official, June 29, 2011, New York.
[91] Interview with Western European diplomat, May 31, 2011, Geneva, Switzerland.
[92] Bolton, interview. Similar description of the PRC being more direct in smaller venues from interview with UN official, June 29, 2011, New York.
[93] Interview with UN official, June 29, 2011, New York. The PRC also voiced its oft-heard grievances, including pushing to prioritize a right to development, giving more attention to economic, social, and cultural rights, and granting states greater authority and oversight over the regime, including the OHCHR. Amnesty International, "HRC Consultation, February 6, 2006" (Amnesty International New York office files), in author's possession.

recalled that "China was in favor of near universal membership" and that it "had very strong" views against human rights criteria for membership and election by a two-thirds majority.[94] According to Amnesty International records, the PRC responded to the draft resolution by arguing that "[a]ll UN members have the right to be candidates. There is no need for criteria … We should not exclude certain members."[95] Amnesty International files further describe Beijing as insisting that

we should expand and not shrink the size of the Council. We believe the Council should be composed of no less than 53 members elected by simple majority and ensure equitable geographic distribution. Asia has always been underrepresented. It is not about some losing and gaining seats. We are restoring equitable geographic distribution.[96]

These positions reflected proposals that Beijing had been making for years, including arguments dating from the mid-1990s that "the Commission was in need of comprehensive reform." More specifically, the PRC called for "a proportional increase in the members from under-represented regions and expansion of the Commission's membership to include all the Member States of the United Nations."[97] These positions on the HRC's composition were at least partly motivated by a desire to ensure that it and a number of the countries that shared its views and voted to protect it from scrutiny were not barred from the HRC. China continued to counter proposals that would have given the HRC the same organizational status as the UN Security Council, repeatedly asserting that the "Human Rights Council should be a subsidiary body of the GA" and further that "The Council shall report and recommend to the GA as its subsidiary body, while the GA shall decide whether it would convey

---

[94] Interview with Western European diplomat, July 23, 2012, New York.
[95] Amnesty International, "HRC Consultation, February 6, 2006."
[96] Ibid. PRC positions corroborated by interview with Western European diplomat, June 13, 2011, Oslo, Norway, and interview with former North American official, October 27, 2010, Washington DC. Similar PRC positions noted also in Amnesty International, "HRC Notes, February 7, 2006" (Amnesty International New York office files), in author's possession.
[97] UN Economic and Social Council, "Commission on Human Rights Fifty-first session, Summary Record of the 44th meeting," March 3, 1995, UN Doc. E/CN.4/1995/SR.44, paragraphs 63–66. Beijing had long complained of the need for redistribution of seats along geographic lines. See UN Commission on Human Rights, "Fifty-fifth Session, Summary Record of the 33rd Meeting," April 16, 1996, UN Doc. E/CN.4/1996/SR.33, paragraph 4. These positions are also corroborated by interviews with Western European diplomat, June 28, 2011, New York, and interview with Western European diplomat, May 31, 2011, Geneva, Switzerland. Similar PRC position against a smaller Human Rights Council from "Position Paper of the People's Republic of China on the United Nations Reforms, 2005/06/07."

relevant recommendations."[98] The opposition to elevating the HRC's status was in line with Beijing's broader efforts to prevent the Council from being a more robust entity than its predecessor.

Not surprisingly, Beijing also expressed concerns about enabling the HRC to spotlight particular countries for human rights violations by reiterating its disdain for country-specific resolutions and voicing concerns about the proposed UPR process.[99] In November 2005, PRC Ambassador Sha Zukang insisted that

[t]he Council should focus its work on national capacity building and technical assistance, provided upon request. The root causes of credibility deficit of CHR, which is characterized by politicization, double standards and selectivity should be stamped out. A thematic rather than a country specific approach to consideration of human rights issues should be applied to the Council. The Council should avoid naming and shaming that spoils the work of the current CHR. Therefore, the country specific review under Item 9 of CHR should either be abolished or applied strictly to address "gross and systemic violations" and certain criteria should be introduced in this regard to rationalize the consideration of country specific issues.[100]

According to Amnesty International records, in January, 2006, the PRC again took aim at country-level action by arguing that the "HRC should not do country-resolutions" but that it "could accept 2/3 vote [sic] [for passage of a resolution] as a bottom line for resolutions."[101] The next month, in February, 2006, Amnesty International records again describe China as insisting that in order to

eliminate politicization, transparent and clear criteria [for country-specific resolutions] is needed. There could be a 2/3 requirement for country-specific resolutions [in order to pass]. Finger pointing and political confrontation won't lead us anywhere. Dialogue should overcome challenges. If we inherit [sic] approach of values and dominance, it [the HRC] will have a birth defect.[102]

The PRC's proposed two-thirds vote for country resolutions was controversial and not widely supported because it would have nearly paralyzed

[98] "Statement by H.E. Ambassador Sha Zukang, on Behalf of the Like Minded Group, at the Meeting Between the President of the General Assembly and the Commission on Human Rights, 2005/11/25," Permanent Mission of the PRC to the UN in Geneva, www.china-un.ch/eng/rqrd/thsm/t223170.htm, accessed August 17, 2017.

[99] Kinzelbach, "Will China's Rise Lead to a New Normative Order?," 315.

[100] "Statement by H.E. Ambassador Sha Zukang, on Behalf of the Like Minded Group, at the Meeting Between the President of the General Assembly and the Commission on Human Rights, 2005/11/25," Permanent Mission of the PRC to the UN in Geneva.

[101] Amnesty International, "HRC Negotiations, January 11, 2006" (Amnesty International New York office files), in author's possession.

[102] Amnesty International, "Notes, February 2006" (Amnesty International New York office files), in author's possession.

the Council's ability to use country resolutions. Chinese diplomats also expressed some concern about the UPR, stating that "we had doubts about peer review. But to show flexibility ... we will not object to the review."[103] A former US government official conjectured that his Chinese counterparts were concerned that the UPR "could be used to focus on China's record."[104]

The PRC's receptivity to the Council grew as some of its views were accepted, particularly those positions that had backing from other countries, and it saw that support for the Council was growing, which made it unlikely that continued opposition would bear fruit.[105] Beijing was further mollified by the HRC's increase in the allocation of seats for Asia and Africa, which obtained twenty-six out of forty-seven seats, and only seven seats for Western European and Others Group countries. This arrangement had been agreed to earlier without strong PRC intervention yet benefited it since the countries it often drew support from gained greater representation.[106] Consequently, Ambassador Sha Zukang, stated that "[t]he resolution is not perfect, but it is a compromise that can be accepted by all UN members, so China hopes it can be adopted."[107] This willingness to back the resolution likely reflected the lack of membership criteria and election by only a majority of the GA rather than a two-thirds vote. Further, some themes that the PRC had regularly espoused, particularly dialogue and cooperation, were also incorporated into the GA resolution.[108] As a result, PRC Ambassador Zhang Yishan noted with satisfaction that "in its preamble and executive paragraphs, the draft resolution indicates on several occasions that human rights should be dealt with in an impartial and non-selective manner to avoid double standards and politicization, and promote genuine interactive dialogue and cooperation in the field of human rights."[109] After the passage of GA resolution 60/251, PRC Ambassador Zhang stated:

---

[103] Amnesty International, "HRC Consultation, February 6, 2006" (Amnesty International New York office files), in author's possession.

[104] Interview with former US government official, October 27, 2011, Washington DC.

[105] Interview with Western European diplomat, May 31, 2011, Geneva, Switzerland. As this interview subject noted, as momentum for the resolution grew, China "got on board" and started to support it.

[106] Sceats and Breslin, *China and the International Human Rights System*, 11.

[107] "China Calls for Adoption of New UN Rights Body," *Xinhua*, March 13, 2006, http://english.sina.com/china/1/2006/0313/69111.html, accessed November 1, 2014.

[108] Interview with Western European diplomat, June 13, 2011, Oslo, Norway.

[109] "Statement by Ambassador Zhang Yishan, Deputy Permanent Representative of China to the UN, after the Adoption of the Draft Resolution on Human Rights Council, 2006/03/15," Permanent Mission of the PRC to the UN, www.china-un.org/eng/chinaandun/socialhr/rqwt/t240623.htm, accessed August 5, 2011.

After more than 30 rounds of consultations in the past 5 months, the General Assembly has finally adopted the draft resolution on Human Rights Council [sic] today … This has been an arduous course full of disputes and challenges … The Chinese Delegation also wishes to indicate that L48 has failed to fully reflect the concerns of many developing countries, including China, over some issues. First, it does not provide effective [sic] guarantee to prevent the political confrontation caused by the country specific resolution, which has become a chronic disease of the Commission on Human Rights.[110]

Ambassador Zhang's statement offered a glimpse of China's priorities during the subsequent IB phase as it continued to attempt to constrain the regime, especially the use of country-specific human rights scrutiny.

Determining Key Institutional Issues through the Institution-Building Process

Once the Council was a reality and member states engaged in IB negotiations to determine remaining issues, China continued its constraining attempts. Chinese diplomats were active and engaged participants in the IB process and offered specific positions throughout the process.[111] A human rights NGO representative described the thrust of Beijing's stances as seeking "a dilution of the procedures, the role and the impact" of the HRC.[112] The IB negotiation phase spanned June 2006 through June 2007 and addressed significant parts of the regime. As a result, its conduct during this stage of the reform process provide unique insight into its positions on a broad range of components of the regime. PRC positions at this stage included

- challenging country-level action, including special procedures, resolutions, and special sessions;
- emphasizing greater state control over the special procedure mandate holders, including supporting a code of conduct to govern the behavior of these experts;
- restricting the Sub-Commission to serving only as an advisory body;
- opposing improvements to the 1503 complaint procedure;

---

[110] Ibid. PRC Foreign Minister Yang Jiechi echoed these sentiments, stating that "[p]olitical confrontation led to the [Commission's] credibility crisis." "Official seeks fresh start for rights body," *China Daily*, June 22, 2006, www.chinadaily.com.cn/china/2006-06/22/content_623010.htm, accessed July 1, 2014. See also UN Human Rights Council, "Summary Record of the 25th Meeting," December 6, 2006, UN Doc. A/HRC/2/SR.25, paragraph 44.

[111] Interview with Western European diplomat, June 28, 2011, New York; interview with Western European diplomat, May 26, 2011, Geneva, Switzerland; and interview with North American diplomat, June 27, 2011, New York.

[112] Interview with human rights NGO representative, August 16, 2017, via Skype.

- resisting proposals to strengthen the UPR through more frequent reviews and NGO involvement in the process, such as the ability to make recommendations and submit material as part of the UPR;
- making the UPR more deferential to states, such as objecting to binding follow-up and focusing the mechanism on state-provided reporting while resisting the inclusion of other forms of reporting.

These positions were advanced along with other countries, which, as with previous stages of the HRC reform process, was crucial to securing some of its preferred outcomes. Given that significant issues were being determined through the IB Process, it is not surprising that, as one participant noted, Chinese diplomats were "systematically participating in all the meetings."[113] As with the earlier stages of HRC reform, Beijing preferred to frame its positions as aligning with other countries and allow other countries with similar views to take more visible roles. Beijing deviated from its lower-profile posture only on issues where it had key imperatives or it surmised that its intervention was needed.[114] These tactics were partially successful in obscuring these efforts to resist strengthening the regime. Along these lines, a human rights NGO representative described China as "not the worst ... in the room [or] the most destructive country" because there were other countries taking more assertive roles and it appeared to be "letting others do the more aggressive job" of seeking to weaken the regime.[115] Yet, as shown throughout this subsection, the PRC was an assertive actor that advanced specific positions as it acted as a constrainer.

One of the targets of Beijing's constraining attempts was the 1503 procedure, which allowed individuals or groups to report rights abuses that "reveal a consistent pattern of gross and reliable attested" human rights violations.[116] During the IB discussions, Beijing "questioned

---

[113] Ibid.

[114] For example, because the discussions on the Sub-Commission were "going their way," a Western European diplomat surmised that the PRC refrained from taking a more outspoken position on this issue. Interview with Western European diplomat, May 26, 2011, Geneva, Switzerland. According to a Western European diplomat, "China was willing to be vocal on issues that were redlines, but on everything else it preferred to sit back and support other countries taking more prominent positions." Interview with Western European diplomat, July 23, 2012, New York. China's IB positions were shared by other more vocal countries namely, Algeria, Pakistan, Cuba, and Egypt are described as the more actively obstructionist countries. Interview with human rights NGO representative, August 16, 2017, via Skype.

[115] Interview with human rights NGO representative, August 16, 2017, via Skype.

[116] For background on the 1503 procedure, see Wade M. Cole, "Individuals v. States: The Correlates of Human Rights Committee rulings, 1979–2007," *Social Science Research* 40, no. 3 (2011), 985–1000.

whether the 1503 procedure is necessary to be retained"[117] and expressed "a concern that the 1503 procedure duplicates the work of the special procedures and treaty bodies."[118] China's challenge of the very existence of the procedure was not widely shared and as the discussions turned to the modalities of the complaint process Beijing sought to ensure the 1503 process remained lengthy and confidential. The already cumbersome nature of the process undermined this procedure as a meaningful tool and meant that as of 2005 only eighty-four countries had been examined under this procedure since it had first been instituted.[119] Under the Commission, complaints went through two stages of review that began with the Sub-Commission's Working Group on Communications, a body that comprised some of the experts from the Sub-Commission, followed by the Working Group on Situations, which comprised five government representatives from the UNCHR nominated by the regional group.[120]

The thrust of China's positions sought to maintain a narrow scope for admissible complaints, minimize pressure on states by limiting follow-up action, ensure confidentiality, secure government influence over the composition of the groups that reviewed the complaints, and prevent this procedure from being empowered to act as an early warning system to address "emerging consistent patterns" of abuse.[121] Even in cases of noncompliance from a state, the PRC insisted that the confidential nature of the process must be upheld.[122] It also consistently put forward arguments to retain restrictive language on inadmissible complaints, including anonymity, "manifestly political motivations and ... subject [that] is contrary to the provisions of the Charter of the United Nations" and situations in which domestic remedies had not been

[117] "China," UN Human Rights Council Extranet, Institution-Building Working Groups, Working Group on Special Procedures, Expert Advice, and a Complaint Procedure, oral statements, September 7–8, 2006, extranet.ohchr.org, accessed July 17, 2017.

[118] International Service for Human Rights, *Human Rights Council Working Group on Review of Mechanisms and Mandates: Review of the Complaint Procedure* (Geneva: International Service for Human Rights: 2007), 3.

[119] Abraham, *A New Chapter for Human Rights*, 65. Before the two working groups consider the complaint, the OHCHR does an initial review to exclude inadmissible complaints and processes between 5,000 and 220,000 every year.

[120] Ibid.

[121] International Service for Human Rights, *Human Rights Council Working Group Report Review of Complaint Procedure, 2nd Session (5–16 February 2007)* (Geneva: International Service for Human Rights 2007).

[122] "China," UN Human Rights Council Extranet, Institution-Building Working Groups, Working Group on Special Procedures, Expert Advice, and a Complaint Procedure, oral statements, December 6, 2006, extranet.ohchr.org, accessed July 17, 2017.

exhausted.[123] In a December 6, 2006, statement, China pushed for inclusion of the word "allegations" with the explanation that "many complaints brought to the attention of the procedure can only be defined as allegations since their reliability need (sic) to be provided."[124] In order to cast doubt on the veracity and motivation of some complaints, Beijing also sought to retain the phrase "political motivated (sic)."[125] It further resisted changes that would strengthen the procedure's ability to exert more pressure on states to respond to complaints. For example, PRC officials stated, "We do not support the link between UPR, and other coercive measures as a response to the so-called non-cooperation from a State."[126] Although Beijing framed these positions with arguments such as upholding the UN Charter, these positions clearly sought to protect states from scrutiny. Further, its spurious claims about the motives behind 1503 complaints appeared to be a ruse to protect the imperatives of even rights-abusing governments.

Beijing also sought to give states greater influence over the composition of both of the working groups examining complaints. The PRC argued that "experts of the first working group should be chosen from the new expert advisory body," which it insisted should comprise individuals elected by states.[127] The PRC further maintained that the second working group should comprise "members ... elected from candidates proposed by members of the HRC, or be appointed by the President of the HRC based on the nominations of regional groups."[128] This would give states control over the selection of the experts on both working groups since the individuals would be elected by states, be government

[123] "China," UN Human Rights Council Extranet, Institution-Building Working Groups, Working Group on Special Procedures, Expert Advice, and a Complaint Procedure, September 15, 2006, extranet.ohchr.org, accessed July 17, 2017. Point on domestic remedies being exhausted corroborated by International Service for Human Rights, *Human Rights Council Working Group on Review of Mechanisms and Mandates, Review of the Complaint Procedure*, 6.

[124] "China," UN Human Rights Council Extranet, Institution-Building Working Groups, Working Group on Special Procedures, Expert Advice, and a Complaint Procedure, oral statements, December 6, 2006, extranet.ohchr.org, accessed July 17, 2017.

[125] Ibid.   [126] Ibid.

[127] "China," UN Human Rights Council Extranet, Institution-Building Working Groups, Working Group on Special Procedures, Expert Advice, and a Complaint Procedure, oral statements, November 23, 2006, extranet.ohchr.org, accessed July 17, 2017. For similar statement, see "China," UN Human Rights Council Extranet, Institution-Building Working Group, Working Group on Special Procedures, Expert Advice, and a Complaint Procedure, oral statements, December 6, 2006, extranet.ohchr.org, accessed July 17, 2017.

[128] "China," UN Human Rights Council Extranet, Institution-Building Working Groups, Working Group on Special Procedures, Expert Advice, and a Complaint Procedure, oral statements, November 23, 2006, extranet.ohchr.org, July 17, 2017.

representatives in the Council, or be nominated from a roster of experts vetted by states. While state influence might sound harmless, it would essentially give states veto power over candidates who might be supportive of vigorous monitoring or inclined to spotlight countries for abuses. As it often did, the PRC also insisted that the working group composition be based on "equitable geographic representation," which not only reflected PRC stances underscoring the import of particular national, cultural, and development conditions, but also increased representation from nations that shared its views.[129]

In the final denouement, despite some small improvements, such as keeping the petitioner informed at each stage of the review, the PRC and a number of other countries held back any significant strengthening of the complaint procedure and ensured government influence over the groups reviewing complaints.[130] The individuals on the first working group are drawn from state-elected experts and the second working group comprises government representatives.[131] China and other states also limited possible follow-up action arising from a 1503 complaint, kept in place narrow admissibility criteria, and maintained a cumbersome and confidential two-stage review process that meant a lengthy review that often took eighteen months before consideration by the UNCHR.[132]

China also resumed the assault on the Sub-Commission that it had initiated in the 1990s along with its allies in the regime. A number of the PRC's IB statements mirror proposals it had been advancing since the early 1990s after the Sub-Commission earned China's ire when it passed two resolutions on it after the 1989 crackdown. As noted previously, the PRC and other states had already diminished this body through a series of resolutions that prevented it from considering country situations being dealt with by the Commission, restricted it from passing country or thematic resolutions that contained specific reference to specific countries, and denied it the ability to undertake new activities without the

---

[129] "China," UN Human Rights Council Extranet, Institution-Building Working Groups, Working Group on Special Procedures, Expert Advice, and a Complaint Procedure, oral statements, December 6, 2006, extranet.ohchr.org, accessed July 17, 2017.

[130] Abraham, *Building the New Human Rights Council*, 4. The Council can dismiss the complaint, keep it under review, appoint an expert to investigate, take the complaint up publicly, or recommend OHCHR technical assistance.

[131] Ibid., 4.

[132] Permanent Mission of Switzerland to the UN, *The Human Rights Council: A Practical Guide* (Geneva: Permanent Mission of Switzerland to the UN, 2014), 16. The cumbersome nature of the process and its limited effectiveness led some states to suggest eliminating this mechanism during the HRC review in 2011. Abraham, *A New Chapter for Human Rights*, 64.

Commission's approval.[133] With the IB discussions presenting a new opportunity to cripple this body and increase state control over it, the PRC argued in a September 15 statement delivered on behalf of the LMG that the Sub-Commission be "transformed into a subsidiary expert advisory group under the Human Rights Council."[134] The PRC's November 21 statement elaborated that the successor body to the Sub-Commission should

> play a think-tank role and carry out research, study on (sic) thematic human rights issues, and provide advisory opinions to the HRC as requested ... These members of (sic) should be nominated by the member states of the UN and elected by the HRC ... It should focus on thematic research, provide advisory opinions to the Council on the whole range of human rights issues, and provide input to the council (sic) in the form of studies, reports and recommendations on the subjects requested by the Council. It should not duplicate what has been taken by other human rights mechanisms. For example, it should not take up country specific situation ... it has no legislative function.[135]

In a similar vein, the PRC was among the delegations that also sought to deny the Sub-Commission the ability to engage in standard setting and in an effort to ensure a circumscribed role for this body stipulated that it should have a "clear and defined mandate."[136] As usual, Chinese diplo-

---

[133] See UN Commission on Human Rights, "Summary Record of the Fiftieth Meeting," December 11, 2000, UN Doc. E/CN.4/2000/SR.50, paragraph 74; UN Commission on Human Rights, Resolution 2003/59, "The Work of the Sub-Commission on the Promotion and Protection of Human Rights Commission on Human Rights" April 24, 2003; UN Commission on Human Rights, Resolution, 2005/53 "The Work of the Sub-Commission on the Promotion and Protection of Human Rights," April 20, 2005. There was limited leeway for the experts on this body to engage in studies and research.

[134] "China," UN Human Rights Council Extranet, Institution-Building Working Groups, Working Group on Special Procedures, Expert Advice, and a Complaint Procedure, oral statements, September 15, 2006, extranet.ohchr.org, accessed July 17, 2017.

[135] "China," UN Human Rights Council Extranet, Institution-Building Working Groups, Working Group on Special Procedures, Expert Advice, and a Complaint Procedure, oral statements, November 21, 2006, extranet.ohchr.org, accessed July 17, 2017. Corroborated by International Service for Human Rights, *Human Rights Council Working Group on the Review of the Mechanisms and Mandates, Discussion on the Future System of Expert Advice, 10–25 April 2007* (Geneva: International Service for Human Rights 2007), 6 and 10, and International Service for Human Rights, *Council Monitor, Human Rights Council Working Group on Review of Mechanisms and Mandates Discussions on the Expert Body, 2nd Session, 8–16 February 2007* (Geneva: International Service for Human Rights, 2007), 8.

[136] International Service for Human Rights, *Council Monitor, Human Rights Council, 3rd Session Daily Update, 7 December 2006* (Geneva: International Service for Human Rights 2006), 2–3. Similar views in International Service for Human Rights, *Human Rights Council Working Group on the Review of the Mechanisms and Mandates, Discussion on the Future System of Expert Advice, 10–25 April 2007*.

mats attempted to frame their positions innocuously as based on a desire to avoid "duplication between the work of the Human Rights Council and the advisory group."[137]

Beijing's proposals on the Sub-Commission also reflected its long-held positions that human rights implementation was contingent and should be based on local conditions and that states should have greater control over the regime. In a December 6 statement, the PRC asserted that "[t]he advice, reports and studies by the new body should reflect the development of human rights taking into account the diversified cultures, histories and religions."[138] It again voiced a preference for a larger body because "it did not believe that anything less than twenty-three experts would ensure respect for geographic representation [and]... representation of main legal, cultural and civilizational (sic) traditions and perspectives."[139] In an attempt to give states enhanced authority over the selection of experts, Chinese diplomats were among the state representatives asserting that the selection process should be "the sole prerogative of States, and that there was no room for the involvement of stakeholders in the pre-screening procedure [on the basis that] ... the process ... [should] be purely intergovernmental in nature."[140] As noted in reporting by the International Service for Human Rights, China, Cuba, and Algeria, speaking for the African group, felt that "the entire selection process (nomination, pre-screening and election) should be in the hands

---

[137] "China," UN Human Rights Council Extranet, Institution-Building Working Groups, Working Group on Special Procedures, Expert Body, and a Complaint Procedure, oral statements, September 15, 2006, extranet.ohchr.org, accessed July 17, 2017.

[138] "China," UN Human Rights Council Extranet, Institution-Building Working Groups, Working Group on Special Procedures, Expert Body, and a Complaint Procedure, oral statements, December 6, 2006, extranet.ohchr.org, accessed July 17, 2017. For similar statement, see "China," UN Human Rights Council Extranet, Institution-Building Working Groups, Working Group on Special Procedures, Expert Body, and a Complaint Procedure, oral statements, December 7, 2006, extranet.ohchr.org, accessed July 17, 2017.

[139] International Service for Human Rights, *Human Rights Council Working Group on the Review of the Mechanisms and Mandates, Discussion on the Future System of Expert Advice, 10–25 April 2007*, 9. See also International Service for Human Rights, *Council Monitor: Human Rights Council, 3rd Session, Daily Update, 7 December 2006*, 4–5, and International Service for Human Rights, *Human Rights Council Working Group on Review of Mechanisms and Mandates, Discussion on the Expert Body, 2nd Session, 8–16 February 2007*, 7–8.

[140] International Service for Human Rights, *Human Rights Council Working Group on the Review of Mechanisms and Mandates, Discussions on the Future System of Expert Advice, 10–25 April 2007*, 2. See also "China," UN Human Rights Council Extranet, Institution-Building Working Groups, Working Group on Special Procedures, Expert Body, and a Complaint Procedure, oral statements, September 7–8, 2006, extranet.ohchr.org, accessed July 17, 2017.

of States" rather than allowing for vetting or selection by the Office of the High Commissioner for Human Rights.[141]

The positions championed by China and these other states succeeded in shaping the Sub-Commission's replacement, the Human Rights Advisory Committee. These countries managed to keep in place the changes they had achieved previously under the UNCHR, such as restricting it to a purely advisory role, only conducting work at the request of the HRC, and curbing its mandate to addressing only thematic issues and responding to HRC requests.[142] This represented a loss since the Sub-Commission's legacy included establishing the precedent of not restricting NGO participation to organizations with UN consultative status, initiating studies to highlight important human rights trends, contributing to the establishment of specific human rights norms and standards, and calling attention to particular human rights problems.[143] The final outcome allows states to elect the experts to the Advisory Committee and other stakeholders do not have the ability to nominate candidates. While some language was included that calls on states to consult with NGOs and national human rights institutions to determine candidates for nomination, this is not a hard requirement and there is no means of enforcing it.[144] Beijing's proposed language that the Advisory Committee should consider "the diversified cultures and religions" was not included in the final text.

China employed a similar approach toward the UN special procedures system, which comprises independent human rights experts. Because of their work conducting investigations and raising awareness, the special procedures have been praised as the "eyes and ears" of the international regime. The PRC in tandem with other states challenged the special procedures system and the negotiations became a "fight ... to preserve the existing strengths of the special procedures."[145] China along with other countries that had long been critical of the special procedures was "keen to begin a review of individual mandates with a view to rationalizing and harmonizing some mandates," with the possibility that some of them would be eliminated. As a human rights NGO representative explained,

---

[141] International Service for Human Rights, *Human Rights Council Working Group on the Review of Mechanisms and Mandates, Discussions on the Future System of Expert Advice, 10–25 April 2007*, 6–7.

[142] Abraham, *Building the New Human Rights Council*, 4.

[143] On the Sub-Commission, see Olivier de Frouville, "Building a Universal System for the Protection of Human Rights," in *New Challenges for the UN Human Rights Machinery*, eds. M. Cherif Bassiouni and William A. Schabas (Cambridge: Intersentia, 2011), 241–266.

[144] Abraham, *Building the New Human Rights Council*, 17.   [145] Ibid., 25.

[T]his ... review and rationalization of the mandates ... was very dangerous because it could have led to ... well it did lead to the elimination of a couple of country specific mandates but it could have led to also the elimination of some of the thematic rapporteurs ... basically those working on civil and political rights ... and China was one of those states which were putting a lot of emphasis on the review process ... whereas western states were preferring simply renewing the list of thematic special procedure mandates.[146]

Chinese interlocutors argued that there was a "need to ensure that the mandate holders adopt a cooperative and constructive manner when approaching governments" and that a wholesale review was warranted because "some mandate holders had not conducted their work impartially."[147] Beijing further argued that "the need for the Council to review the performance of mandate holders [was needed because] ... there was no such provision for misbehavior by mandate holders."[148] China also joined Algeria and other countries seeking to expand state control by calling for a state-drafted manual or code of conduct, which human rights proponents worried could be used to curtail the independence of these experts.[149] Because the PRC felt that its views were not being incorporated in UN reports on the status of these discussions, in a November 13 nonpaper it complained that the IB Working Group facilitator was not paying due regard to these views and stated:

We are regrettable (sic) to notice that some inputs and concerns from (sic) Asia Group, Africa Group, the Like-Minded Group and OIC were not, at least not clearly reflected in this framework. Some particular groups have strongly recommended ... to elaborate and adopt a manual or operations by the Council, to set up rules of admissibility of Communications and urgent appeals, etc. We hope that the concerns and recommendations by developing countries could be duly reflected in the framework ... the working group shall consider establishing an institutional mechanism by which the performance of the

---

[146] Interview with human rights NGO representative, August 16, 2017, via Skype.

[147] "China," UN Human Rights Council Extranet, Institution-Building Working Groups, Working Group on Special Procedures, Expert Advice, and a Complaint Procedure, oral statements, November 13, 2006, extranet.ohchr.org, accessed July 17, 2017, and International Service for Human Rights, *Working Group on Review of Mechanisms and Mandates, 2nd Session, 5–16 February 2007* (Geneva: International Service for Human Rights 2007), 10.

[148] International Service for Human Rights, *Human Rights Council Working Group on Review of Mechanisms and Mandates, 13–24 November 2006* (Geneva: International Service for Human Rights, 2006), 17.

[149] Ibid., 16. The PRC also supported other states calling for "balancing thematic mandates dealing with economic, social and cultural rights (ESCR) on the one hand, and civil and political rights (SPR) on the other." International Service for Human Rights, *Council Monitor, Working Group on Review of Mechanisms and Mandates, 2nd Session, 5–16 February 2007*, 10, and 14.

mandate holders shall be reviewed, ethical performance shall be praised, and misconduct shall be addressed.[150]

Because the independence of the special procedures, which is thought to give them some immunity from state pressure, is considered one of their chief strengths human rights activists viewed this proposed manual or code and review as potentially very damaging. A human rights NGO representative elaborated that this proposal would have put "the special procedures in a situation of very large dependence on what member states wanted or didn't want ... it was limiting their capacity to make public statements and the tenor of communication was largely constrained to private communications with member states."[151] When Algeria introduced an HRC resolution on this proposed code of conduct, China backed it and supported the restrictive draft put forward by Algeria. Beijing's diplomats claimed that "instead of undermining the functioning of the special procedures, this would lead to a clearer relationship between the special procedures and the Council."[152] Chinese emissaries argued for language that would constrain the mandate holders and alleged that "some special procedures abuse their mandates, and alluded to some cases where special procedures mandate holders have used 'abusive' language with States. It felt a code of conduct was a good way to ensure that the mandate holders are held accountable."[153]

The PRC also took other positions to limit the authority and independence of the special procedures experts, lessen expectations on states to cooperate with the special procedures, and increase state influence, including over special procedure reports and the selection process.[154] Along these lines, Beijing joined other countries opposing proposals to

[150] "China," UN Human Rights Council Extranet, Institution-Building Working Groups, Working Group on Special Procedures, Expert Advice, and a Complaint Procedure, oral statements, November 13, 2006, extranet.ohchr.org, accessed July 17, 2017.

[151] Interview with human rights NGO representative, August 16, 2017, via Skype. See also International Service for Human Rights, *Human Rights Working Group on Review of Mandates: Special Procedures Highlights, Wednesday 18 April 2007* (Geneva: International Service for Human Rights 2007).

[152] International Service for Human Rights, *Human Rights Council Working Group on Review of Mechanisms and Mandates, 13–24 November 2006* (Geneva: International Service for Human Rights, 2006), 17.

[153] International Service for Human Rights, *Working Group on Review of Mechanisms and Mandates, 2nd Session, 5–16 February 2007*, 15. See also Ibid., 10.

[154] Abraham, *Building the New Human Rights Council*, 24–25. The PRC sought to give states greater control over the Office of the High Commissioner for Human Rights and "called for regular discussion of the financial and administrative aspects of the work of the High Commissioner for Human Rights," which could potentially weaken the independence of the OHCHR. International Service for Human Rights, *Human Rights Council Working Group on Agenda, Programme of Work, Working Methods and Rules of Procedure, Highlights, Monday 23 April 2007*, 8.

include standards for expected state behavior in the code of conduct, arguing that the onus should be on the mandate holder.[155] The PRC also resisted calls for states to issue standing invitations, using a November 22 nonpaper to insist that

we don't agree that every state must send standing invitation to all the special mechanisms ... Not all the special mechanisms were recognized by all states. Some special mechanisms were clearly refused and rejected at the very first day when they were born. How can a state send an invitation to some mandate that it does not even recognize (sic).[156]

PRC diplomats further sought to curb the independence of the special procedures by asserting that the terms of reference for visits should be elaborated by states, not UN experts and officials, and claimed that state-drafted terms "would help prevent 'unrealistic requirements' from the special procedures."[157] Yet, human rights experts and UN officials note that allowing states to draft the terms of reference could impede access and interfere with the independence of these experts.[158] In a bid to further increase state control, on behalf of the LMG, Beijing argued that "reports should be sent to the states concerned before making them public. The materials and comments provided by the government should be duly included."[159] According to NGO reporting, China was among the states that "stressed that the reports needed to be submitted to the concerned government before being made public, in order for it to comment on them."[160] China also joined other countries that repeatedly argued that mandate holders be elected by states, and even refused the

[155] International Service for Human Rights, *Human Rights Council Working Group on Review of Mechanisms and Mandates, 3rd Session, 10–27 April 2007* (Geneva: International Service for Human Rights, 2007), 3 and 6–8. Similar reporting in International Service for Human Rights, *Human Rights Council Working Group on Review of Mandates: Special Procedures Highlights, Monday 16 April 2007* (Geneva: Switzerland, 2007), 2, and International Service for Human Rights, *Human Rights Council Working Group on Review of Mandates: Special Procedures Highlights, Thursday, 26 April 2007* (Geneva: International Service for Human Rights, 2007), 2.

[156] "China," UN Human Rights Council Extranet, Institution-Building Working Groups, Working Group on special procedures, expert advice, and a complaint mechanism, oral statements, November 22, 2006, extranet.ohchr.org. See also International Service for Human Rights, *Human Rights Council Working Group on Review of Mechanisms and Mandates, 13–24 November 2006*, 24.

[157] International Service for Human Rights, *Human Rights Council Working Group on Review of Mechanisms and Mandates, 13–24 November 2006*, 17. See also Ibid., 22.

[158] Interview with UN official, March 17, 2017, via Skype.

[159] "China," UN Human Rights Council Extranet, Institution-Building Working Groups, Working Group on the Special Procedures, Expert Advice, and a Complaint Procedure, oral statements, September 15, 2006, extranet.ohchr.org, accessed July 17, 2017.

[160] International Service for Human Rights, *Human Rights Council Working Group on Review of Mechanisms and Mandates, 13–24 November 2006*, 26.

placement of a Office of the High Commissioner for Human Rights (OHCHR) representative on a proposed group that would develop a shortlist of candidates.[161] This method of appointment would give states an opportunity to veto candidates who might be less deferential to state preferences and more supportive of robust monitoring.

As part of its larger campaign against country-level action, the PRC called for the elimination of all country-specific special procedure mandates or at the very least the use of criteria before a country mandate could be established.[162] In October 2006, Ambassador Sha argued that

[t]he LMG believes the most serious flaw, one that is based on selectivity and has led to the greatest amount of politicization, is country mandates that proliferated under agenda item 9 of the erstwhile Commission on Human Rights. There are a number of reasons that compel the LMG to make the case for considering removing all country-specific mandates from the agenda of the Human Rights Council. Firstly, most country mandates were set up by resolutions adopted after intense and bitter negotiations and divisive votes ... Some country mandates were summarily rejected by countries concerned. Country mandates have thus been the product of excessive politicization, double standards and selectivity ... Country mandates over the years, have proven to be dysfunctional, unnecessary and controversial. They remind us how and why the Commission on Human Rights was discredited and replaced.[163]

The PRC reiterated this position in a December 5, 2006, written submission that complained that the IB group facilitator's report failed to sufficiently highlight that "country mandates ... were (sic) most politicized aspect of the Commission on Human Rights ... Many delegates have proposed that the Human Rights Council shall exercise periodical

---

[161] China's position on direct elections by the HRC was shared by Algeria, Pakistan, Bangladesh, Cuba, Egypt, Indonesia, Iran, Malaysia, the Philippines, Saudi Arabia, Singapore, and Tunisia. International Service for Human Rights, *Human Rights Council Working Group on Review of Mechanisms and Mandates, 13–24 November 2006*, and International Service for Human Rights, *Human Rights Council, Institution Building President's 2nd Open Meeting, 18 May 2007* (Geneva: International Service for Human Rights, 2007), 5–6. See also "China," UN Human Rights Council Extranet, Institution-Building Working Groups, Working Group on the Special Procedures, Expert Advice, and a Complaint Procedure, oral statements, December 5, 2006, extranet.ohchr.org, accessed July 17, 2017.

[162] International Service for Human Rights, *Human Rights Council Working Group on Review of Mechanisms and Mandates, 13–24 November 2006*, 14.

[163] Ambassador Sha reiterated the LMG's long-standing exception for the special rapporteur on Palestine because it deals with a "situation of a people under occupation." "China," UN Human Rights Council Extranet, Institution-Building Working Groups, Working Group on Special Procedures, Expert Advice, and a Complaint Procedure, oral statements, October 3, 2006, extranet.ohchr.org, accessed July 17, 2017. Corroborated by International Service for Human Rights, *Human Rights Council 2nd Session Daily Update, 3 October 2006* (Geneva: International Service for Human Rights, 2006), 3 and 5.

review over the performance of the mandate holders ... this document still does not give due attention."[164] In another move against country-level action, in early 2007, the PRC along with Malaysia "voiced their concern with the current system of country mandates, and argued that if it were to be retained, State consent was mandatory for the establishment of such mandates."[165] This requirement would render most country-focused mandates useless since the countries with the most abysmal human rights records are often those with governments that would be unlikely to consent to the creation of a relevant special procedure. This position was part of Beijing's strategy of challenging country-specific scrutiny to build support for its opposition to country-focused reso-lutions and making common cause with developing countries, which generally opposed country-specific mandates. Its efforts did not go unnoticed by its allies. Once the IB package was adopted Malaysia and Pakistan "expressed their thanks to China for its work on country mandates."[166]

In the final denouement, while some of China's positions were secured, such as the termination of the mandates for Belarus and Cuba, other stances, such as highly restrictive language on country mandates, were not adopted. Moreover, the elimination of the special rapporteurs for Belarus and Cuba were achieved because these countries had sufficient support and China's backing was not decisive.[167] Although the code of conduct had been "proposed by states aiming to limit and monitor the special procedures," including Algeria, Pakistan, China, and Russia, during the negotiations over the draft other states, especially nations from the Western European and Others Group, succeeded in

---

[164] "China," UN Human Rights Council Extranet, Institution-Building Working Groups, Working Group on Special Procedures, Expert Advice, and a Complaint Mechanism, oral statements, December 5, 2006, extranet.ohchr.org, accessed August 20, 2017. Sha also suggested that the confidential 1503 complaint procedure that the PRC had suggested should be eliminated was an adequate mechanism. He specifically said, "Thirdly, a revised but still confidential 1503 procedure would adequately address gross and systematic violations of human rights." UN Commission on Human Rights, "Summary Record of the 25th Meeting," October 3, 2006, UN Doc. A/HRC/2/SR.25 paragraphs 44–45.

[165] International Service for Human Rights, *Working Group on Review of Mechanisms and Mandates, 2nd Session, 5–16 February 2007*, 13.

[166] International Service for Human Rights, Council Monitor, *Human Rights Council, Report of the Conclusion of the 5th Session (18 June) and the Organizational Meeting of the Council (18–20) June* (Geneva: International Service for Human Rights, 2007), 6.

[167] Abraham, *Building the New Human Rights Council*, 25. A couple of interview subjects noted that other countries had secured this early victory and that the PRC did not play a key role. Luis Alfonso de Alba (former Mexican Ambassador to the UN and first President of the Human Rights Council), interview by author by Skype, August 9, 2012, and interview with Western European diplomat, May 26, 2011.

rolling back some of the worst aspects of the draft.[168] Further, a thorough review of all the special procedures mandates that states could have used to interfere with the work of the special procedures and possibly eliminate some thematic mandates was averted.[169] Although NGOs can nominate candidates, the selection process is primarily in the hands of states. A consultation group comprising member countries with input from the Office of the High Commissioner for Human Rights develops a short list of candidates. Mandate holders are then appointed by the HRC president, a position that is held by a member state, and subject to the approval of Council members.[170]

The UPR mechanism, which had been touted as a promising improvement since all states will undergo regular review, was another component of the regime that the PRC worked to dilute, especially circumscribing NGO participation; emphasizing the intergovernmental nature of the process; favoring a five-year review period, which was longer than many human rights proponents preferred; and privileging cooperation with the state, including rejecting any mandatory follow-up or any action without the consent of the state.[171] China also pushed to restrict the use of materials cited as part of the UPR, favoring state-provided reporting. In an attempt to resist a robust NGO role, China argued that the language on sources for UPR information should "read other *qualified* stakeholders."[172] It also asserted that "NGO and other information from stakeholders may not conform to the meaning of objective and reliable

[168] Permanent Mission of Switzerland to the UN in Geneva, *The Human Rights Council: A Practical Guide*, 13. The code was adopted on June 18, 2007. UN Human Rights Council, "Code of Conduct for Special Procedure Mandate-holders of the Human Rights Council," June 18, 2007, Resolution 5/2.

[169] Abraham, *Building the new Human Rights Council*, 27.   [170] Ibid., 25.

[171] "China," UN Human Rights Council Extranet, Institution-Building Working Groups, Working Group on the Universal Periodic Review, oral statements, November 22, 2006, extranet.ohchr.org, accessed July 17, 2017. See also "China," UN Human Rights Council Extranet, Institution-Building Working Groups, Working Group on the Universal Periodic Review, oral statements, February 12, 2007, extranet.ohchr.org, accessed July 17, 2017. Corroborated by interview with human rights NGO representative, August 16, 2017, via Skype. See also "Statement on Universal Periodic Review by Mr. La Yifan, Deputy Representative of the Chinese Delegation," Permanent Mission of the PRC to the UN at Geneva, http://www.china-un.org/eng/rqrd/t261293.htm, accessed January 29, 2013. A UN official noted that China was initially concerned that the Universal Periodic Review could be used to highlight PRC violations, but once it understood that all countries would receive equal treatment it dropped resistance. Interview with UN official, June 29, 2011, New York.

[172] International Service for Human Rights, *Human Rights Council Working Group to Develop the Modalities of the Universal Periodic Review, 3rd Session, 11 and 24 April 2007* (Geneva: International Service for Human Rights, 2007), 7.

information under General Assembly Resolution 60/251."[173] Instead, China favored relying on government-provided information and along with Cuba asserted that the UPR documentation "should exclude information from country rapporteurs [serving within the special procedures system] on account of their contested status."[174] In order to give the state in question greater influence, Beijing's representatives asserted that the process should be a "cooperative one and adopted by consensus with the full agreement of the state under review."[175] Chinese diplomats were also among those refusing the inclusion of assessments of state implementation of treaty body and special procedure recommendations and resisted measures to address noncompliance with UPR recommendations.[176] They urged that "the [UPR] follow-up measures should be implemented mainly through voluntary initiatives by the state under review and necessary technical assistance may be provided upon request of the state concerned."[177] The PRC elaborated that the

UPR is a cooperative mechanism, which aims to promote and protect rights … through sharing experiences instead of pointing fingers at each other. We believe that the recommendations should focus on enhancing the capacity of the reviewed country though technical assistance, not shaming and blaming … My delegation is not in favor of having a special procedure mandate, or a fact-finding mission as an outcome of the review. If a rapporteur of fact-finding mission is appointed for every reviewed country … If the mechanism is applied to only some countries, then it may easily lead to political selectivity and double standards. My delegation does not think the establishment of the OHCHR field office should be linked with UPR … The outcome of the UPR should be adopted at plenary with the full involvement of the country under review. The adoption should be based on consensus.[178]

[173] International Service for Human Rights, Council Monitor, *Human Rights Council Working Group to Develop the Modalities of the Universal Periodic Review, 3rd Session, 12–15 February 2007*, 8.

[174] Ibid., 8.

[175] "China," UN Human Rights Council Extranet, Institution-Building Working Groups, Working Group on the Universal Periodic Review, oral statements, February 12, 2007, extranet.ohchr.org, accessed July 17, 2017.

[176] International Service for Human Rights, Council Monitor, *Human Rights Council Working Group to Develop the Modalities of the Universal Periodic Review, 3rd Session, February 12–15, 2007*, 8 and 12.

[177] "China," UN Human Rights Council Extranet, Institution-Building Working Groups, Working Group on the Universal Periodic Review, oral statements, December 4, 2006," extranet.ohchr.org, accessed July 17, 2017. Deputy Representative La Yifan reiterated that the only follow-up should be "[t]echnical assistance may be provided at the request of the country concerned with a view to enhancing its capacity." "Statement on Universal Periodic Review by Mr. La Yifan, Deputy Representative of the Chinese Delegation," Permanent Mission of the PRC to the UN, www.china-un.org/eng/rqrd/t261293.htm, accessed January 29, 2013.

[178] "China," UN Human Rights Council Extranet, Institution-Building Working Groups, Working Group on the Universal Periodic Review, oral statements, February 14, 2007, extranet.ohchr.org, accessed August 20, 2017.

Beijing's diplomats also took aim at the universality of human rights, arguing that the UPR should focus on

[t]he significance of national and regional particularities and various historical, cultural and religious backgrounds must be borne in mind ... The review shall give full consideration to the cultural, religious and historical traditions and level of development of the country concerned.[179]

The PRC also linked the UPR with its long-held position to end country-focused attention by advocating that an "important objective of creating UPR mechanism (sic) is to eliminate such problems as double standards, selectivity, and politicization arising out of the consideration of country resolutions."[180]

Ultimately, the IB package resulted in numerous compromises. Although NGOs are not allowed to participate in the interactive dialogue or make recommendations for specific human rights improvements, NGO representatives can make statements in the plenary. While states can reject UPR recommendations without justification, the UPR does not rely solely on state reporting and includes compilation of information, including treaty bodies, special procedures, and other stakeholders, such as NGOs.[181] The process is also universally applied on a rotation basis. As a former PRC ambassador noted, the PRC became more "amendable" to the Council in part because the UPR is "universal, and not targeted at a small number of states."[182]

Throughout the IB process, PRC representatives continued to challenge country-specific resolutions and persisted in advancing the earlier proposal that criteria for such resolutions should be adopted and resolutions on a single country could only be introduced with the support of one-third of HRC members and passed by a two-thirds vote – a proposal the PRC had first put forward during the negotiations over the GA resolution that established the Council.[183] China's preoccupation with

[179] "Statement on Universal Periodic Review by Mr. La Yifan, Deputy Representative of the Chinese Delegation," Permanent Mission of the PRC to the UN, www.china-un .org/eng/rqrd/t261293.htm, accessed January 29, 2013.
[180] "China," UN Human Rights Council Extranet, Institution-Building Working Groups, Working Group on the Universal Periodic Review, oral statements, November 22, 2007, extranet.ohchr.org, accessed July 17, 2017.
[181] Abraham, *Building the New Human Rights Council*, 5.
[182] Chen, interview. In a similar vein, a scholar affiliated with the CCP described the HRC as a "successful reform" because "some of China's proposals were accepted" and it "prefers UPR instead of country-specific resolutions. Interview with PRC scholar, June 13, 2012, Beijing, China.
[183] International Service for Human Rights, *Human Rights Council Working Group on Review of Mechanisms and Mandates, 13–24 November 2006*, 14. Amnesty International, "Positions Taken by Countries Speaking in General Assembly Debates

ending country resolutions came to the fore in the IB Working Group on the Council's agenda, program and methods of work, and rules of procedure, where it opposed an agenda that would give the HRC the flexibility to address country-specific situations, as well as argue for restricted use of country-specific resolutions. The PRC voiced support for a structured and thematic agenda, which would leave little room for discussing country situations, even in response to emerging or intensified human rights violations.[184] Along these lines, China opposed agenda items such as "cross cutting human rights issues and human rights situations" and "other issues."[185] China endorsed Algeria's position that "'cross-cutting issues' was not an adequate term ... that such an approach would lead to a selective method of dealing with rights; and that such a term would be a 'Pandora's Box', (sic) allowing debate on any issue."[186] The PRC also rejected agenda "Item 9: Follow-up decisions of the Human Rights Council," which could have allowed the HRC to discuss specific countries, claiming that this kind of discussion "would spawn double standards."[187]

As the IB process continued and China's restrictive stance on country resolutions was not gaining acceptance, in April 2007 with the June 2007 deadline for agreement on the IB package looming, the PRC became more vocal and insistent in the working group, and resurrected

Since 11 October 2005 on the Creation of the Human Rights Council After Adoption of the September Outcome Document by the 2005 World Summit, updated November 15, 2005" (Amnesty International New York Office files), in author's possession and International Service for Human Rights, International Service for Human Rights, Council Monitor, *Human Rights Council Working Group on Agenda, Programme of Work, Working Methods and Rules of Procedure, Highlights, Monday 23 April 2007*, 17.

[184] International Service for Human Rights, Council Monitor, *Human Rights Council Working Group on Agenda, Annual Program of Work, Working Methods and Rules of Procedure, 15–19 January 2007* (Geneva: International Service for Human Rights, 2007), 1–4. To counter China's stances, the EU and the United States asserted that the more generic agenda would enable the Council to "deal with emerging issues and situations."

[185] International Service for Human Rights, Council Monitor, *Human Rights Council Working Group on Agenda, Programme of Work, Working Methods and Rules of Procedure, Highlights, Monday 23 April 2007*, 1–2 and 8. For similar PRC positions, see International Service for Human Rights, Council Monitor, *Human Rights Council Working Group on Agenda, Annual Program of Work, Working Methods and Rules of Procedure, 13–27 April 2007* (Geneva: International Service for Human Rights, 2007), 3–4 and 8.

[186] International Service for Human Rights, Council Monitor, *Human Rights Council Working Group on Agenda, Annual Program of Work, Working Methods and Rules of Procedure, 13–27 April 2007*, 8.

[187] Ibid., 10–11. Beijing also complained about "a lack of predictability and a desire to avoid political issues that might tend to get pulled into a catch-all category."

its proposed restrictive requirements for the passage of country-specific resolutions. As the International Service for Human Rights reported:

The Working Group on organizational matters ... end was quite dismal ... After progressing relatively well for most of its meetings, the stream on working methods and rules of procedure encountered a last minute initiative by China that resulted in its final 30 minutes descending into further division amid thinly disguised threats ... [...] Half an hour before the discussion was to end, China proposed a new initiative to require that resolutions relating to a specific country must be co-sponsored by a third of the members of the Council and supported by a special majority of two-thirds of the members of the Council present and voting.[188]

While China had made this two-thirds proposal previously, it had not communicated that this was a redline or that it withhold its support if it were not incorporated into the IB package.[189] As the IB package moved from the smaller working group to the HRC plenary, the PRC broke from its tendency not to "fight on the front lines" and "suddenly became very active."[190] In explaining the PRC's behavior, an Asia Pacific diplomat suggested that the PRC "realized [that the elimination of country-specific resolutions] ... was not going to happen without them."[191]

Signifying the importance of this issue to it, China approached other countries, especially its usual support base of developing countries, and urged them to support this proposal. Beijing even raised this issue with a foreign minister during a previously arranged meeting.[192] While Iran, South Africa, Bangladesh, Russia, Algeria (on behalf of the Africa Group), and Cuba had offered sympathetic comments in the working group, they refused to support China's position[193] and some of these countries even pointed out that the composition of the Council was such that China could muster the votes needed to defeat a resolution on its

---

[188] International Service for Human Rights, Council Monitor, *Human Rights Council Working Group on Agenda, Programme of Work, Working Methods and Rules of Procedure, Highlights, Monday 23 April 2007*, 1–3.

[189] Interview with human rights NGO representative, August 16, 2017, via Skype.

[190] Quote from interview with Asia Pacific diplomat, September 28, 2011, Canberra, Australia. Similar observations from interview with Southeast Asian diplomat, November 9, 2011, London; interview with UN OHCHR official, June 29, 2011, Geneva, Switzerland; interview with South Asian diplomat, June 3, 2011, Geneva, Switzerland; and interview with South Asian diplomat, May 31, 2011, Geneva, Switzerland.

[191] Interview with Asia Pacific diplomat, September 28, 2011, Canberra, Australia. Similar statement from interview with Western European diplomat, July 23, 2012, New York.

[192] Interview with Southeast Asian diplomat, November 9, 2011, London.

[193] International Service for Human Rights, Council Monitor, *Human Rights Council Working Group on Agenda, Annual Program of Work, Working Methods and Rules of Procedure, 13–27 April 2007*, 10–11 and 17.

record.[194] A diplomat whose own country concurred with the PRC that country resolutions were misused and too often aimed at developing countries noted that China's unhappiness was shared by a number of countries but described Beijing's position as "too extreme" in part because it was so unpopular with other countries, especially members of the Western European and Others Group. As a result, his country felt that "they could not back such a divisive position and preferred a compromise solution."[195] Ambassador de Alba described China as being "isolated when its usual allies" refused to back this proposal and even called on Beijing to accept the IB package.[196] Although China had considerable political and economic influence and lobbied other delegations, it does not appear to have used material incentives or other inducements and its clout did not sway other countries.[197] Beijing's position failed to garner broader support largely because other countries, especially states belonging to the Western European and Others Group, were so strongly opposed to its position and certain European countries indicated they might withdraw from the Council if the PRC proposal was accepted.[198] Beijing's insistence also risked reopening the entire IB package, thereby threatening the interests of Cuba and Belarus, which had secured the elimination of the special rapporteurs assigned to their countries and were eager to cement this agreement.

With June 18, 2007, the one-year deadline approaching, Ambassador de Alba, in his capacity as President of the HRC, negotiated with Chinese diplomats. PRC intransigence meant that the discussions

---

[194] Akram, interview, and interview with Southeast Asian diplomat, interview material in private possession of author, January 25, 2013. Akram noted that the reallocation of seats gave twenty-six out of forty-seven Human Rights Council seats to Asian and African countries, the very countries that China finds critical support from.

[195] Interview with Southeast Asian diplomat, November 9, 2011, London.

[196] de Alba, interview. He noted that the countries that would usually support China, such as Cuba, Sri Lanka, and Saudi Arabia, would not lend their support and PRC representatives were on the phone with the Ministry of Foreign Affairs getting instructions on whether to drop their proposal. Similar comments from interview with Southeast Asian diplomat, November 9, 2011, London.

[197] Interview with Southeast Asian diplomat, November 9, 2011, London, and telephone interview material in private possession of author, January 25, 2013. Sceats and Breslin offered similar findings on PRC nonuse of material leverage. See Sceats and Breslin, *China and the International Human Rights System*, 16.

[198] Richard Gowan and Franziska Brantner, *A Global Force for Human Rights? An Audit of European Power at the UN* (London: European Council on Foreign Relations Policy Paper, September 2008), http://ecfr.3cdn.net/3a4f39da1b34463d16_tom6b928f.pdf, 5. As an NGO representative noted, countries such as France and the United Kingdom each put their foot down and said, "no bloody way." Interview with human rights NGO representative, August 23, 2017, via Skype. Ambassador de Alba confirmed that some European countries indicated they might even withdraw over this issue. However, he did not describe this as a formal EU member state position. de Alba, interview.

dragged on until midnight.[199] The deadline was critical because it represented the end of the Council's first year when membership would change and, if the IB package was not agreed to, it would mean it would have to be renegotiated with a different set of states. The PRC delegation relented after Ambassador de Alba showed them news dispatches portraying it as "destroying the Council."[200] Ultimately, Chinese diplomats were left with accepting face-saving, nonbinding language that did not require but only suggested that the "sponsors of a draft resolution or decision should hold open-ended consultations on the text of their draft resolution(s) or decision(s) with a view to achieving the widest participation in their consideration and, if possible, achieving consensus on them."[201] This wording was a nod to the PRC's position but fell far short of its demands. Although China had earlier successfully employed a last-minute insistent position when it countered language in the GA resolution and World Summit Outcome Document attempting to establish membership criteria for HRC members and other proposals to strengthen the Council, in this instance its lone stance failed.

As shown above, the PRC's positions and conduct during the establishment of the HRC reveal that its attempts to constrain the regime met with some success – though these outcomes were largely achieved only when its views were shared by others. In concert with other countries, Beijing successfully prevented the Council from emerging as a more effective entity for addressing human rights, including crushing proposals to establish a high bar for membership while securing a redistribution of seats along geographic lines, which meant a greater number of potential votes to defeat scrutiny of its record. This chapter's chronological approach underscored the evolution in Beijing's conduct as it

---

[199] de Alba interview; interview with Latin American diplomat, September 5, 2011, via Skype; and interview with Southeast Asian diplomat interview, material in private possession of author, January 25, 2013, London, United Kingdom. There was also a desire to reach an agreement and meet the deadline because countries did not want to have to begin negotiations anew because "everyone might get a worse deal." Interview with Western European diplomat, June 14, 2016, Geneva, Switzerland. By some accounts, agreement was not reached until a few minutes after midnight, technically missing the official deadline.

[200] Stephane Bussard, "A Night of Madness for Human Rights," in *The First 365 Days of the Council*, ed. Lars Muller (Bern: Swiss Department of Foreign Affairs, 2007), 70. See, as an example, "China Deals Setback to the UN Human Rights Watchdog," *New York Times*, June 18, 2007, www.nytimes.com/2007/06/18/world/asia/18iht-rights.5 .6198244.html.

[201] UN Human Rights Council, Resolution 5/1, "Institution-building of the United Nations Human Rights Council," A/HRC/RES/5/1, paragraph 127. Sceats and Breslin noted that this language was meant to spare Beijing from embarrassment. Sceats and Breslin, *China and the International Human Rights System*, 11.

became more engaged when the most critical aspects of the regime were under discussion. Thus, during the IB process Chinese diplomats participated actively in discussions and were able to rout attempts to strengthen the 1503 confidential procedure; retain a limited scope for the Sub-Commission and even rename it as an advisory body, which cemented its circumscribed role; and prevent the UPR from emerging as an effective monitoring tool, such as by defeating proposals for binding follow-up and limiting NGO involvement. These outcomes were only secured because the PRC's positions were widely shared, especially among LMG countries, and when it tried to go it alone as it did in its attempt during the IB process to introduce restrictive rules on country resolutions it was not successful. Thus, although a number of Beijing's stances are in fact reflected in the final outcome, it failed on the issue that was most important to it – weakening the use of country-focused resolutions.

Conclusion

By focusing on the UN's political human rights bodies, comprising other member states, this chapter allows us to parse PRC behavior toward a highly visible UN body, one that is intended to serve as the primary venue for discussions about human rights. Because the IB package covered an expansive array of regime mechanisms, this case study provides a unique opportunity to understand China's views toward much of the substance of the human rights regime. As demonstrated in this chapter, China along with other like-minded countries was successful in getting some of their positions incorporated into the Human Rights Council. During the early phases of the talks involving the World Summit Outcome Document and General Assembly resolution, these countries successfully resisted several of the improvements recommended by the UN Secretary-General and human rights advocates, such as election by a two-thirds vote in the GA and the introduction of membership criteria.[202] During the IB negotiations, these countries were again able to influence some outcomes, including eliminating the special procedures assigned to Belarus and Cuba; preventing the advisory body from addressing country-specific issues or initiating its own studies; restricting NGO participation in the UPR process; and preventing any binding action as a result of the UPR even when troubling human rights

---

[202] Interview with Western European diplomat, June 13, 2011, Oslo, Norway, and interview with Western European diplomat, May 31, 2011, Geneva Switzerland.

abuses were uncovered.[203] At the same time, despite the efforts of China and other countries with shared human rights views, much of the regime remained intact, such as the complaint procedure and the special procedures system.

The PRC's conduct and positions were in keeping with the kinds of modifications a constrainer would seek. Although it objected to a number of the proposed improvements and challenged country-specific approaches, it did not seek to completely hollow out the regime, which would be in line with the actions of a regime breaker. For example, it did not seek to eliminate the thematic special procedures, even though some of the reports issued by these independent experts have highlighted PRC abuses. Further, despite initial reservations, Beijing backed the UPR system, which was touted as a novel procedure and an improvement since all countries would undergo examination. Its most strident and persistent efforts at constraining the regime were directed toward country-focused resolutions. The targeted and limited nature of the PRC's efforts suggests that it was seeking to constrain rather than destroy the regime. The next chapter will examine its conduct in the International Labour Organization's Conference Committee on the Application of Standards, which presented less of a threat to the PRC and therefore resulted in a different Chinese role.

---

[203] Abraham, *Building the New Human Rights Council*, 5. The special procedure mandate holder for Belarus was reinstated in 2012.

5 China and the International Labour Organization's Conference Committee on the Application of Standards: 1983–2017

Unlike its more assertive behavior in other parts of the regime, China acted as a taker toward the International Labour Organization's (ILO) Conference Committee on the Application of Standards (CCAS or Conference Committee). Over the three decades of its participation in the Conference Committee, the PRC was content to play the role of taker primarily because it received mild and infrequent scrutiny from this Committee. At the same time, there was a noticeable shift in its behavior as it evolved from an initially timid posture to a more active one in which it used this venue to speak in defense of allied countries during their reviews before the Committee. This instrumental behavior shows that even as a taker the substance of Beijing's participation in the Conference Committee did not strengthen labor rights protection. This chapter also builds on the findings of the previous case studies that unveiled the ways the PRC and other countries banded together in the regime to protect each other. I consider, in particular, the possibility of reciprocal protection in other parts of the human rights regime.

The ILO's Conference Committee is worthy of study because of its mandate and China's long record of participation in the Committee. The ILO, which serves as the leading international body to protect worker rights, was established in 1919 in order to secure and maintain fair and humane labor conditions.[1] Unlike other parts of the human rights regime, the ILO has a tripartite membership structure, which includes both governments and "social partners," specifically worker and employer representatives. In 1926, the ILO created the Conference Committee and gave it the responsibility of monitoring state compliance with ratified conventions. In order to meet this responsibility, the CCAS selects twenty-five countries of particular concern and conducts a public examination during which government officials from these countries appear before the Committee. Because the ILO's procedures for

---

[1] The ILO, which predates the creation of the United Nations, became a specialized UN agency in 1946.

protecting labor rights include bodies such as the International Labour Office, the Governing Body, and the Committee on the Freedom of Association, this chapter does not claim to capture the totality of China's interactions with the ILO.[2] However, it does provide an exhaustive examination of Beijing's behavior over the course of more than three decades in a Committee that has been described as the "heart and soul" of the ILO.[3] Although the ILO's tripartite nature means that worker and employer representatives are included, given this book's primary focus on the Chinese government's behavior. This chapter examines only PRC government statements and interventions not those of Chinese worker and employer delegates. Moreover, given the severe restrictions on civil society, PRC worker and employer representatives are extensions of the Chinese Communist Party government.[4]

This chapter begins by outlining the responsibility and functions of the CCAS and its place in the ILO's supervisory processes. The second section of this chapter turns to describing and analyzing China's participation in this Committee from 1983 through 2017. This section on China and the CCAS is divided into three subsections that address the PRC's appearances before the CCAS, its positions on the working methods of the Conference Committee, and PRC government statements during the reviews of other countries. This is followed by an analysis of Beijing's relationship with the countries it supported in the CCAS and a discussion of the possibility that these countries reciprocated in the Commission on Human Rights when resolutions on China were introduced and the Human Rights Council (HRC) during the PRC's Universal Periodic Reviews (UPRs) in 2009 and 2013.

The ILO's Conference Committee on the Application of Standards

The Conference Committee emerged out of the ILO's need to monitor state compliance and its realization that a dedicated body was necessary in order to meet the challenge of reviewing the vast number of state

---

[2] For a description of the ILO's monitoring processes, see Laurence R. Helfer, "Monitoring Compliance with Unratified Treaties: The ILO Experience," *Law and Contemporary Problems* 71, no. 1 (2008): 193–218.

[3] Ed Potter (Employer Spokesperson in the CCAS since 2005, member of the US delegation to the ILC since 1982 and participant in the CCAS, 1986–1995 and 1999–2014), interview by author by telephone, May 11, 2011.

[4] As Beja points out, the All-China Federation of Trade Unions is an instrument of the government. "Xi Jinping's China: On the Road to Neo-totalitarianism." *Social Science Research* 86, no. 1, Spring 2019, 217.

reports.[5] Thus, in 1926 the International Labour Conference (ILC) created the CCAS, charging the government, employer, and worker representatives on the Committee with the responsibility to "undertake a joint examination of the manner in which States comply with their obligations."[6] The Conference Committee is a standing committee of the ILC, the annual gathering of the ILO that attracts several thousand participants. The Conference Committee is open to all member states and ILC participants and has been one of the largest committees of the ILC, attracting several hundred individual participants. Each of the ILO's tripartite groups make up one-third of the voting, giving the governments, workers, and employers equal weight. Because the workers and employers together possess two-thirds of the voting strength, this arrangement is thought to limit the ability of governments to protect each other or themselves as often occurs in bodies made up exclusively of state representatives.[7] When the Conference Committee was established in 1926, the ILC simultaneously created a counterpart body, the Committee of Experts for the Application of Standards (Committee of Experts or COE), which as the name suggests is composed of independent experts serving in their individual capacities rather than as representatives of their respective countries. The similar names of the two committees reflect their complementary roles and responsibilities and together they form a two-tier process of assessing state compliance with ratified conventions.[8] The twenty members on the COE are drawn from every geographic region and initiate the monitoring process by reviewing

---

[5] In 1927, there were 26 ILO member states and 180 reports were reviewed by the Committee of Experts. With the expansion of the number of treaties and growing ILO membership, the number of reports now averages around 2,000 reports annually. ILO, *The Committee on the Application of Standards of the International Labour Conference: A Dynamic and Impact Built on Decades of Dialogue and Persuasion* (Geneva: International Labour Organizations, 2011), 6. Under Article 22, for fundamental and priority conventions states submit reports every two years and for all other reports every five years. ILO International Standards Department, *Handbook of Procedures Relating to International Labour Conventions and Recommendations* (Geneva: International Labour Organization, 2006), Section IV, paragraph 35.

[6] ILO, *The Committee on the Application of Standards of the International Labour Conference*, 2.

[7] Virginia Leary, "Lessons from the Experience of the International Labour Organisation," in *The United Nations and Human Rights: A Critical Appraisal*, ed. Philip Alston (Oxford: Clarendon Press, 1992), 599. Similar observation made by Paul F. van der Heijden (Chairperson of the Committee of Freedom of Association), interview by author, May 27, 2011, Geneva, Switzerland.

[8] Dame Justice Laura Mary Cox (member of the Committee of Experts and British High Court Judge), interview by author, November 9, 2011, London, United Kingdom. Cox noted that the creation of two bodies, one which comprised solely outside experts and the other comprised ILO members, reflected the ILO's desire to use outside expertise while retaining ownership and control.

reports submitted by governments, producing an annual report that highlights serious cases of noncompliance and flagging particularly egregious cases for possible CCAS review.[9]

The principal function of the Conference Committee is to conduct an in-person review of the countries engaging in the most serious violations. Using the COE report as a guide, the CCAS selects twenty-five cases of highest concern for examination during the annual ILC. This provides the government, worker, and employer representatives on the CCAS with the opportunity to express concerns, raise issues or particular cases, ask questions, request additional information, and even offer supportive comments.[10] Government representatives of the country under review appear in person, offer a presentation, and respond to questions and concerns. The ILO has often described this process as a "dialogue" during which member states can discuss the difficulties encountered in applying international labor standards and present their case, such as offering new information and highlighting areas of progress.[11] However, some countries with reports of grave labor rights abuses generate significant scrutiny, and some observers describe it as a more combative process or even a "grilling exercise."[12] An ILO official stated that the public nature of the process is intended to mobilize attention and exert "moral pressure on governments to comply with ratified conventions."[13] In a similar vein, Alfred Wisskirchen, who participated in the CCAS as a German employer delegate, argued that "[i]t is primarily the repeated, public scrutiny of a member State's observance of ILO standards which therefore exerts political and moral pressure on the government in question."[14] Following the public examination the CCAS can use a "special paragraph" in its report to highlight a country that has "seriously and

---

[9] This is done through the use of "double footnotes." Cox, interview. For less serious concerns, the Committee uses "single footnotes." The double-footnoted cases not only signal the COE's degree of concern but also officially indicate that the COE is requesting further information from the government with some degree of urgency. ILO, "International Labour Conference, 106th Session, 2017, Report of the Committee of Experts on the Application of Conventions and Recommendations, Report III (Part 1A)," 2017, www.ilo.org/public/libdoc/ilo/P/09661/09661(2017-106-1A).pdf, 15–16.

[10] Leary, "Lessons from the International Labour Organisation," 599–601.

[11] ILO, *The Committee on the Application of Standards of the International Labour Conference*, 12.

[12] Francis Maupain, "The ILO Regulatory Supervisory System: A Model in Crisis?" *International Organizations Law Review* 10, Issue 1 (2013): 120. In a similar vein, Ed Potter referred to the government under review as being in the "hot seat." Potter, interview.

[13] Interview with ILO official for workers' activities, May 24, 2011, Geneva, Switzerland.

[14] Alfred Wisskirchen, "The Standard-Setting and Monitoring Activity of the ILO," *International Labour Review* 144, no 3 (2005), 270.

repeatedly violated a Convention."[15] This paragraph, which is primarily determined by the workers and employers groups and generally includes one to five countries, is considered "the highest level of condemnation that the CCAS can use" and some have referred to it as a "blacklist."[16] Because of the seriousness it conveys and the negative attention it generates, countries included in the special paragraph "increasingly objected to it, considering it a serious form of censure."[17] Although CCAS government representatives from other countries participate in the review and are able to use their remarks to influence the tenor, including offering support for the country under review, the ILO's tripartite structure means that governments are unable to protect themselves or other countries from inclusion in the special paragraph.[18] At the same time, while the countries under CCAS review, particularly the countries included in the special paragraph, face some degree of pressure, the Conference Committee has not attracted the same level of public, civil society, and media attention as the UN Commission on Human Rights (UNCHR) and the HRC.

Not surprisingly, determining the twenty-five countries to be summoned for public examination has often been contentious as the workers and employers strive to reach consensus on the twenty-five cases to review and some countries try to avert scrutiny.[19] The workers initiate the process by developing a preliminary list of roughly forty-five countries, paying particular attention to the cases flagged in the COE report as particularly worrisome and worthy of CCAS scrutiny.[20] The Committee

[15] Wisskirchen, "The Standard-Setting and Monitoring Activity of the ILO," 275–282, and Victor-Yves Ghebali, *The International Labour Organisation: A Case Study on the Evolution of U.N. Specialized Agencies* (Dordrecht: Martinus Nijhoff Publishers, 1989), 225. See also Hector G. Bartolomei de la Cruz, Geraldo von Potobsky, and Lee Swepston, *The International Labour Organization: The International Standards System and Basic Human Rights* (Boulder, Colorado: Westview Press, 1996), 83. The special paragraph is the most severe sanction the CCAS can take before the matter is referred to the ILO Governing Body. The Governing Body has the authority to appoint a special expert to monitor the situation.

[16] Interview with ILO official for workers' activities, May 24, 2011, Geneva, Switzerland.

[17] Ghebali, *The International Labour Organisation*, 224–225, and Leary, "Lessons from the Experience of the International Labour Organisation," 599. The practice of identifying countries of significant concern following the public review was introduced in 1957.

[18] Leary, "Lessons from the Experience of the International Labour Organisation," 599.

[19] Since the early 1990s, the Conference Committee has restricted its review to twenty-five countries. Potter, interview.

[20] Interview with ILO official for employer's activities, May 27, 2011, Geneva, Switzerland and Jean-Jacques Elmiger (then-Swiss Ambassador, State Secretariat for Economic Affairs, Federal Department of Economic Affairs), interview by author, June 1, 2011, Geneva, Switzerland. The preliminary list gives governments time to prepare in the event that they are among the twenty-five cases that are examined.

of Experts determines the cases to highlight for CCAS attention based on the seriousness of the problem, particularly violations of fundamental rights; the persistence of the problem; the urgency of the situation, particularly life threatening situations or the possibility of irreversible harm; and the quality and scope of the government's response in its reports, especially cases of repeated state refusal to comply with its obligations.[21] Using the preliminary list of forty-five countries as the basis for their discussions, the workers and employers then jointly whittle the list down to twenty-five cases, with particular attention paid to the cases identified by the COE as the most egregious. They employ similar criteria as the COE, including violations of the ILO's fundamental conventions;[22] the seriousness, persistence, and urgency of the situation; previous CCAS discussions and conclusions; the quality and scope of the government's responses; comments from the workers' and employers' groups; and the likelihood that CCAS review will have a positive tangible impact.[23] Because governments are the ones potentially facing examination, the CCAS does not treat them as unbiased actors and therefore government representatives have not been involved in the drafting or finalization of the list of cases.

The Conference Committee is particularly attentive to abuses related to the eight fundamental ILO conventions, especially conventions 87 and 98, which govern the right to organize and freedom of association, respectively. As a result, "[m]ost of the cases discussed in the Conference Committee concern questions arising from the eight fundamental conventions," which include Freedom of Association and Protection of the Right to Organize Convention (87), Right to Organize and Collective Bargaining Convention (98), Forced Labor Convention (29), Abolition of Forced Labor Convention (105), Minimum Age Convention (138), Worst Forms of Child Labor Convention (182), Equal Remuneration Convention (100), and Discrimination (Employment and Occupation) Convention (111).[24] An ILO official emphasized the Committee's focus on the right to organize and freedom of association, and noted that "looking at 15 years

---

[21] ILO, "International Labour Conference, 107th Session, 2018, Report of the Committee of Experts on the Application of Conventions and Recommendations, Report III (Part A)," 2018, https://www.ilo.org/public/libdoc/ilo/P/09661/09661(2018-107-A).pdf, accessed October 15, 2018, 16.

[22] Wisskirchen, "The Standard-Setting and Monitoring and Activity of the ILO," 282.

[23] ILO, *The Committee on the Application of Standards and the International Labour Conference*, 20–21, and Wisskirchen, "The Standard-Setting and Monitoring Activity of the ILO," 280–282.

[24] Ibid., 282.

of the Applications Committee, the number of cases ... clearly the majority, deal with Conventions 87 and 98."[25]

In some instances, countries have lobbied or tried to mobilize support from other governments to avoid being among the twenty-five countries examined by the CCAS or included in the special paragraph. A Western European national trade union official who has been involved in determining the list of countries noted that in the past some countries on the workers' preliminary list of forty-five countries "lobbied to get off the list so that they are not among the 25 countries reviewed."[26] In a similar vein, according to a former employer spokesperson, "[t]here have been occasions when governments may try to lobby the Employer or Worker spokesman.... But that is relatively rare."[27] Governments also try to enlist each other's support. As an ILO official explained, "[I]n recent years, what I've seen is more lobbying among governments. 'I support you, you support me,' kind of thing ... But government solidarity is based more on the logic of international relations [meaning concerns about reciprocal support and bilateral relations] rather than ... the facts of the case."[28] Similarly, a Western European trade union official noted that "you get alliances between countries. Sometimes countries who feel somehow targeted in one way or another, might want to defend one another."[29] This kind of mutual defense among governments sometimes manifests in the form of sympathetic or supportive comments for the government in question during the CCAS review. However, because the workers and employers, not governments, determine the countries to examine and content of the special paragraph, these entreaties and lobbying do little to sway these decisions.[30]

---

[25] ILO official for workers' activities, May 24, 2011, Geneva, Switzerland. Similar statements by Andree Debrulle, (Senior Advisor to the Worker Spokesperson, Confederation of Christian Trade Unions), interview by author, March 23, 2012, Brussels, Belgium, and interview with former senior ILO official, May 25, 2011, Geneva, Switzerland.

[26] Debrulle, interview.   [27] Potter, interview.

[28] ILO official for workers' activities, May 24, 2011, Geneva, Switzerland.

[29] Stephen Benedict (Director for Human and Trade Union Rights, International Trade Union Confederation), interview by author by phone, March 16, 2012. This behavior is similar to the "authoritarian collaboration" described by von Soest. Christian von Soest, "Democracy Prevention: The International Collaboration of Authoritarian Regimes," *European Journal of Political Research* 54, 2015: 623–638.

[30] Employer and worker representatives note that while they consider the comments of other participants, including foreign governments and the explanation provided by the country, they rely primarily on the facts of the case to determine the content of the special paragraph. Potter, interview; Debrulle, interview; and Jan Dereymaeker (Development Cooperation and Education Officer, International Trade Union Confederation), interview by author, March 21, 2012, Brussels, Belgium.

Some countries, particularly non-Western nations, have occasionally criticized the Conference Committee of bias and unwarranted scrutiny. In order to redress these perceived failings, these countries proposed reforms, taking direct aim at the "special paragraph," complaining that "the list amounted to a sanction which had no basis in the ILO Constitution, [and] that the list consisted almost exclusively of developing and Socialist countries, and that technical assistance and regional study courses could have a greater effect on implementation than pointing a finger to countries in a special list."[31] During the Cold War, communist bloc countries claimed that they were selectively and unfairly targeted and called for reforms.[32] In 1974, 1977, and 1982, communist bloc countries expressed these grievances by absenting themselves during the plenary, thereby using a lack of quorum to prevent adoption of the Conference Committee's report by the ILC. Along these lines, in 1984, Eastern European countries argued that the special paragraph was of questionable legality since it gave the CCAS an almost judicial role.[33] That year, in the plenary session of the ILC the delegate from Bulgaria complained that

[t]here is another aspect of the supervisory machinery which requires adjustment and that is the day to day work of the Conference Committee on the Application of Standards. At present this Committee deals with only one-third of the cases dealt with by the Committee of Experts … We know that in some cases these criteria are predominantly political. A recent example which remains fresh in our minds is the treatment accorded to Poland and Czechoslovakia in this connection. At the same time such matters of vital importance to workers—unemployment, discrimination against women and other groups—are left in the background.[34]

Similar concerns were raised again in 2004 when Cuba, leading a group of countries belonging to the Non-Aligned Movement (NAM), pressed for changes to improve the "efficiency, transparency, and objectivity" of the CCAS.[35] That year, Malaysia, speaking as chair of the NAM, complained that

[31] Leary, "Lessons from the Experience of the International Labour Organisation," 600.
[32] Odd Bruaas (former Norwegian government official and CCAS participant), interview by author, June 13, 2011, Oslo, Norway. On efforts to alter the working methods, see Gerry Rodgers et al., *The ILO and the Quest for Social Justice, 1919–2009* (Cornell: Cornell University Press, 2009), 21, and Ghebali, *The International Labour Organisation*, 229–230.
[33] Ghebali, *The International Labour Organization*, 230–231, and ILO, "International Labour Conference, Seventieth Session, Report of the Conference Committee on the Application of Standards 70th session," 1984, www.ilo.org/public/libdoc/ilo/P/09616/09616(1984-70).pdf, accessed October 15, 2018, General Report, paragraph 21.
[34] Ibid., 16/26.
[35] ILO, "International Labour Conference Report of the Conference Committee on the Application of Standards, 92nd session" (2004), www.ilo.org/public/english/standards/relm/ilc/ilc92/pdf/pr-24p2.pdf, Part 2, General Report, 24/9. Potter suggested that

[t]he Non-Aligned Movement wishes to reiterate its concern over the current methods and procedures for supervising labour standards. We welcome international cooperation as an important contribution to the effective realization of international labour standards and, to this end, we particularly regard the effective review and improvement of the working methods of the Committee on the Application of Standards as vital for the sake of transparency and impartiality.[36]

Noting these kinds of critiques and challenges, a North American government participant observed that

there has been a long-standing 'threat' to undermine the supervisory system in order to deflect attention from serious violations. Some countries don't like the criticism and attention, and so as far back as the Cold War they started this attempt to 'reign in' the supervisory system to try to meddle with their methods of work ... it has continued, the NAM will sometimes question methods of work in the Conference Committee and the Committee of Experts.[37]

A number of Like-Minded Group (LMG) countries have criticized the CCAS's working methods. As described previously, LMG countries have been active in the UNCHR and the HRC where they have resisted country-specific scrutiny. In an attempt to address these complaints, both the COE and the CCAS note that they strive for an equitable geographic balance of cases and attempt to avoid focusing on the same nations repeatedly.[38] Despite these grievances, due largely to its tripartite structure, it has been difficult for these nations to alter the Conference Committee's working methods in ways that would dilute its ability to monitor labor rights.[39] For example, in 1984, in response to criticism from socialist countries, the employer and worker representatives pushed back, arguing that "the supervisory machinery was ... fair and effective and that questioning it too often could lead to self-destruction."[40] As a former senior ILO official noted, the Conference Committee has been "very nearly immune to pressure" from countries that have sought to weaken it and that it works much as it did in the 1960s.[41]

---

although a number of countries complain about CCAS scrutiny, "the initiators appear to be Cuba and Venezuela." Potter, interview.

[36] ILO, "International Labour Conference, Ninety-second Session, Fourth Sitting," 2004, www.ilo.org/public/english/standards/relm/ilc/ilc92/pdf/pr-11a.pdf, accessed October 15, 2018, 11/15.

[37] Interview with North American government participant, June 2, 2011, Geneva, Switzerland. See also Leary, "Lessons from the Experience of the International Labour Organisation," 601.

[38] Cox, interview; Potter, interview; Dereymaeker, interview; and Benedict, interview.

[39] Elmiger, interview and interview with North American governmental representative to the CCAS, June 2, 2011, Geneva, Switzerland.

[40] Ghebali, *The International Labour Organization*, 230–231.

[41] Interview with former senior ILO official, May 25, 2011, Geneva, Switzerland. A North American government official noted that a number of changes have, in fact, improved or strengthened the Committee's work, including an automatic registration of cases and the

The occasional ire of these countries is somewhat surprising given that the CCAS does not enjoy the same visibility as the UNCHR and the HRC. Although states included in the special paragraph faced tough questions before the CCAS and likely felt some degree of public censure since the report is presented to the entire ILC, the Conference Committee receives modest publicity and attention from NGOs and international media.[42] Even though the CCAS proceedings and report are open to the public, "well-known human rights NGOs are conspicuously absent from participation in ILO human rights activities."[43] As will be discussed in the subsequent section, this limited publicity and other institutional features, such as the Conference Committee's responsibility only for ratified conventions, inclined the PRC toward a taker posture.

China and the ILO's Conference Committee on the Application of Standards

This section on the PRC's conduct in the Conference Committee documents its role as a taker over a period that spanned more than three decades. It shows that Beijing used this part of the regime instrumentally to make protective statements for friendly states. It, then, explores ways the PRC may have benefited from reciprocal support in the UNCHR and the HRC. After providing a brief description of China's participation in the Conference Committee since the early 1980s, this section turns to tackling three key aspects of its behavior: its reviews before the Conference Committee, its stance toward the Conference Committee's working methods, and its participation in the reviews of other countries. By doing so, it not only documents the PRC's taker posture but also helps explain why it was inclined toward this role.

Committee's policy of proceeding with an examination even if a government refuses to appear before the Committee. Aside from 2012 when the Committee failed to conduct a review of cases due to a disagreement between the workers and employers over the right to strike, the CCAS has completed an annual review of cases of serious noncompliance. ILO, "International Labour Conference, Committee on the Application of Standards at the Conference, 101th session," 2012), www.ilo.org/wcmsp5/groups/public/—ed_norm/—relconf/documents/meetingdocument/wcms_183031.pdf, accessed October 15, 2018, General Report, paragraphs 6-10 and 22-23. For further inputs on the disagreement, see also Ibid., paragraphs 82–86 and 134–186.

[42] Dereymaeker, interview and Wisskirchen, "The Standard-Setting and Monitoring Activity of the ILO," 279. For similar sentiment, see also Kent, *China, the United Nations, and Human Rights*, 121.

[43] Leary, "Lessons from the Experience of the International Labour Organisation," 585.

China's involvement with the ILO corresponds with its participation in other parts of the human rights regime.[44] The PRC became an ILO member in 1971 when it was granted UN membership. Yet, as with other parts of the UN, especially bodies dealing with human rights, during the 1970s it limited its participation in the ILO. Beijing avoided ILO activities and stated that it needed "time to increase its understanding of the ILO and become familiar with it."[45] It finally assumed fuller participation in 1983 when it sent its first delegation to the annual ILC, during which Chinese representatives also attended the sessions of the Conference Committee on the Application of Standards. The ILO Governing Body, which serves as the executive body, encouraged PRC participation by forgiving its accrued debt of unpaid dues since 1971 and assisted Chinese officials in reviewing international labor standards, including those that had been ratified by the Republic of China.[46] The PRC decided to accept only fourteen of the thirty-seven conventions ratified by the Nationalist government.[47] In explaining the decision in the early 1980s to assume fuller participation, a PRC government official noted that the Chinese Communist Party government realized that there "would be issues related to China and its interests" in the ILO and therefore it had to be prepared to play a part in this organization.[48] A former US employer spokesperson pointed to similar reasoning, emphasizing that the Committee is

fairly informative and important to governments because you want to better understand the consequences of ratification and, to put it in a positive sense, how you can achieve full implementation in a better way, through the discussion as they watch other governments explain their situation ... So if you think of governments as political entities, it's pretty doggone important, and for China, I would see it as a way of really informing itself about the heart and soul of the ILO.[49]

---

[44] On China's entry into the ILO, see Ghebali, *The International Labour Organization*, 122–125.

[45] Quoted in Ghebali, *The International Labour Organization*, 125. A Chinese official explaining PRC nonparticipation prior to 1983 suggested that China was a novice that was "trying to learn and understand" the ILO and that China was still recovering from the Cultural Revolution when it had largely closed itself off to normal external interactions. Interview with Chinese government official, June 12, 2012, Beijing, China. Similar point in Ghebali, *The International Labour Organization*, 124. Similar point in *Kent, China, the United Nations, and Human Rights*, 124.

[46] Ghebali, *The International Labour Organisation*, 125. This amounted to nearly $39 million.

[47] Ibid., 123.

[48] Interview with Chinese government official, June 12, 2012, Beijing, China.

[49] Potter, interview.

Because it is the norm for ILO member countries to participate in the CCAS, Chinese officials may also have joined the Conference Committee to bring its conduct in line with other countries.[50] Unlike other international human rights bodies, where the Chinese Ministry of Foreign Affairs serves as lead agency, the Ministry of Human Resources and Social Security has the primary responsibility for Chinese participation in the ILO yet coordinates with the Ministry of Foreign Affairs.[51]

As will be detailed in the later sections, over more than three decades the PRC acted as a taker in the Conference Committee and although it has become more vocal since the late 1990s, it has continued to accept this part of the regime and has participated in a modest and low-profile manner. Other participants described China as "always … very low-key,"[52] "a good player," "respect[ing] the CCAS rules,"[53] and "not really asserting itself."[54] Ed Potter, who served as the employer spokesperson to the Conference Committee, described the PRC as "not a particularly visible country in the totality of the ILO Conference, but [also] in particular [in] the Conference Committee on the Application of Standards" and that "as a political force, they've not really asserted themselves."[55] At the same time, a Western European national trade union official had a more negative assessment, suggesting that although the PRC was not a subversive force, its approach appeared to be "We won't bother you, don't bother us."[56] As the following section will document, because the CCAS in fact has paid only minimal attention to China, including only a few uncontroversial appearances before the CCAS, the PRC has not challenged this part of the regime.

China's Reviews before the Conference Committee

In contrast to countries that received sustained CCAS scrutiny, the PRC has been examined only four times and has never been included in a special paragraph. During its examinations, the Chinese delegation has been described as "very quiet and cooperative" and "preparing and

---

[50] A North American government official noted that governments at the ILC generally try to participate in as many activities as they can and it would be unusual not to participate in the work of the ILC Committees, including the CCAS, unless there were resource constraints. Interview with North American government official, June 2, 2011, Geneva, Switzerland.

[51] Interview with Chinese government official, June 12, 2012, Beijing, China. China's Ministry of Human Resources and Social Security was previously the Ministry of Labor.

[52] Interview with North American government official, June 2, 2011, Geneva, Switzerland.

[53] Debrulle, interview.   [54] Potter, interview.   [55] Potter, interview.

[56] Dereymaker, interview.

participating in a very professional way."[57] Similarly, a former senior ILO official noted that "China has never complained about being examined and when called it has appeared before the Committee" and that it had been "compliant" and "never fights" during these reviews.[58] In a similar vein, other observers described China's appearances in the CCAS as "not controversial, not lengthy and not very interesting,"[59] "not unusual,"[60] and "a soft and constructive discussion."[61] There is also no evidence that China lobbied to be removed from the list of countries to be examined.[62] Table 5.1, which summarizes the statements made by other CCAS participants, provides further evidence that its reviews before the CCAS have been infrequent, straightforward, and not controversial. The PRC received minimal attention with only a handful of speakers representing worker groups from other countries making statements that pointed to areas of noncompliance and urged that labor standards be upheld.

The limited number of instances in which the PRC was summoned to appear before the CCAS and its mild treatment by the Committee stands in contrast with the acrimonious reviews and strongly worded interventions associated with other countries. For example, in 2005, during Myanmar's appearance before the Committee, in addition to the United States' expressions of concern, Luxembourg (speaking on behalf of the European Union), Bosnia and Herzegovina, Bulgaria, Croatia, Macedonia, Norway, Romania, Turkey, Serbia and Montenegro, Switzerland, and Ukraine delivered a statement that rebuked Myanmar, cited "no progress," and expressed regret that Myanmar ignored the ILO's calls for specific steps to improve labor conditions.[63]

---

[57] Allison Tate (Director External Relations, International Trade Union Confederation), interview by author, March 21, 2012, Geneva, Switzerland.

[58] Interview with former senior ILO official, May 25, 2011, Geneva, Switzerland.

[59] Interview with North American governmental participant, June 2, 2011, Geneva, Switzerland.

[60] Elmiger, interview.

[61] Interview with ILO official for employers' activities, May 27, 2011, Geneva, Switzerland. Similar comment from Potter, interview.

[62] Benedict, interview; interview with former senior ILO official, May 25, 2011, Geneva, Switzerland; and Potter, interview. Potter, who has been involved with the CCAS from 1986 until 2014, could not recall attempts by China to be excluded from CCAS examination.

[63] ILO, "International Labour Conference, Report of the Conference Committee on the Application of Standards, 94th session," (2005), www.ilo.org/wcmsp5/groups/public/—ed_norm/—normes/documents/publication/wcms_116491.pdf, accessed October 15, 2018, Part 3, Observations on and Information Concerning Particular Countries, Special Sitting on Myanmar, 22/8.

Table 5.1 *China reviews before the CCAS, including Hong Kong*

Year	Convention	Statements by other participants
1994	Convention 26 (Minimum Wage Fixing)	US Worker Representative: CCAS should not be satisfied with PRC's indications of how it intended to meet obligations; cited reports of low wages and unpaid wages; noted PRC repression of genuine trade unions, lack of collective bargaining and use of prison and forced labor; urged PRC to take effective action, not just announcing new laws and proposals[a]
2004	Convention 98 (Right to Organize and Collective Bargaining)	Italy Worker Representative: Expressed concern about the lack of collective bargaining; Hong Kong government has not taken recommended steps or action taken did not constitute genuine collective bargaining[b]
2007	Convention 182 (The Worst Forms of Child Labor)	Senegal Worker Representative: Degradation of women fueled trafficking in women and children; lack of any meaningful action to redress these problems; urged PRC to combat this problem and to ratify Convention 29 on forced labor
		France Worker Representative: Cited problem of forced labor in schools, including specific cases and detailed information; urged PRC government action
		Germany Worker Representative: Expressed concern about "work-study schools," "re-education through labor" camps and sexual abuse; urged PRC government to take steps to address problem and abolish forced labor among children
		US Worker Representative: Underlined the severity of child labor in China; noted link to other issues, including provision of decent work for adult population and public school fees; encouraged PRC government to take steps[c]
2009	Convention 122 (Employment Policy)	US Worker Representative: Raised reports of imprisonment, harassment and intimidation of workers who had expressed political opinions that differed from those adopted by the PRC government; expressed concern

Table 5.1 (*cont.*)

Year	Convention	Statements by other participants
		regarding lack of public education and awareness of labor-related laws; encouraged greater government consultation with public; urged greater transparency[d]

[a] ILO, "International Labour Conference, Report of the Conference Committee on the Application of Standards, 84th session," (1994), www.ilo.org/public/libdoc/ilo/P/09616/09616(1994-81).pdf, accessed October 15, 2018, Part 2, Observations on and Information Concerning Particular Countries, 25/82–25/83.

[b] ILO, "International Labour Conference, Report of the Conference Committee on the Application of Standards, 92nd session," (2004), www.ilo.org/public/english/standards/relm/ilc/ilc92/pdf/pr-24p2.pdf, accessed October 15, 2018, Part 2, Observations on and Information Concerning Particular Countries, 24/45–24/47.

[c] ILO, "International Labour Conference, Report of the Conference Committee on the Application of Standards, 96th session," (2007), www.ilo.org/wcmsp5/groups/public/—ed_norm/—normes/documents/publication/wcms_088133.pdf, accessed October 15, 2018, Part 2, Observations on and Information Concerning Particular Countries, 22/90–22/95.

[d] ILO, "International Labour Conference, Report of the Conference Committee on the Application of Standards, 98th session," (2009), www.ilo.org/wcmsp5/groups/public/—ed_norm/—normes/documents/publication/wcms_116491.pdf, accessed October 165, 2018, Part 2, Observations on and Information Concerning Particular Countries, 16/120–16/124.

The PRC has received minimal attention because the Committee's remit is restricted to ratified conventions and Beijing has only ratified four of the eight fundamental ILO conventions, including those on equal remuneration (100), discrimination (111), minimum age (138), and the worst forms of child labor (182).[64] The Chinese government has failed to ratify conventions on freedom of association (87), the right to organize (98), forced labor (29), and the abolition of forced labor (105), which are the conventions that make up the majority of the cases reviewed by the Conference Committee. As noted previously, the Committee concentrates on violations of the eight fundamental ILO conventions, with a particularly intense focus on freedom of association (87) and the right to organize (98), which comprise roughly 50 percent of the cases reviewed

---

[64] "Ratifications by Country," International Labour Organization, www.ilo.org/ilolex/english/docs/declAS.htm, accessed June 30, 2017. The PRC ratification dates are as follows: C100 Equal Remuneration, November 1990; C111 Discrimination (Employment and Occupation), January 12, 2006; C138 Minimum Age Convention, April 1999; and C182 Worst Forms of Child Labour, August 2002.

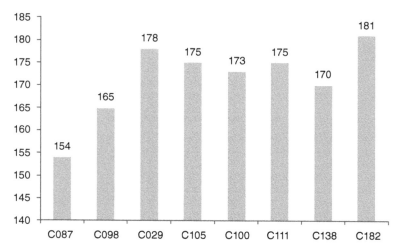

Figure 5.1 Number of countries that have ratified the fundamental ILO Conventions 87, 98, 29, 105, 100, 111, 138, and 182[65]

by the CCAS.[66] Although there are numerous accounts of labor rights violations in China, the Committee is only able to address violations related to ratified ILO conventions. As a North American government official noted, "[T]he biggest problem in terms of labor rights in China is freedom of association [but] they haven't ratified the convention."[67] As demonstrated in Figure 5.1, which shows the number of countries that have ratified the core conventions, the PRC is among a minority of countries that have failed to ratify the four fundamental ILO conventions that deal with freedom of association (87), the right to organize (98), and forced labor (29 and 105). For example, China is among the thirty-five countries that have not ratified the convention on freedom of association (87) and one of only ten countries that have refused to ratify the convention on forced labor (29).

As a result of Beijing's low ratification rate, even after the 1989 Tiananmen Square crackdown when other UN human rights bodies, such as the UN Sub-Commission on Human Rights and

---

[65] "Information System on International Labour Standards," International Labour Organization, www.ilo.org/dyn/normlex/en/f?p=NORMLEXPUB:1:0::NO:::, accessed October 15, 2018.
[66] Debrulle, interview, and interview with former senior ILO official, May 25, 2011, Geneva, Switzerland. See also Wisskirchen, "The Standard-setting and Monitoring activity of the ILO," 282.
[67] Interview with North American government participant, June 2, 2011, Geneva, Switzerland.

UNCHR, condemned the Chinese Communist Party leadership's use of force to put down the protests, Beijing did not come under increased scrutiny in the Conference Committee.[68]

As will be detailed later in this chapter, the PRC spoke in defense of other countries during their appearances before the Conference Committee, but during its examinations the PRC did not receive similar assistance. In the four instances when China was summoned before the Committee, no other foreign governments spoke on its behalf.[69] Given the PRC's mild treatment by the CCAS, this kind of assistance from other states may have been deemed unnecessary. For example, in contrast to Myanmar's contentious review described earlier, China's review was not contentious and no other foreign governments expressed concerns about suspected labor rights abuses. Thus, PRC officials likely did not request such assistance and other countries likely surmised that this help was not needed. Perhaps because it received limited scrutiny as the following section will show, China has not contested the Committee's working methods.

China and the Conference Committee's Working Methods

Beijing has not been a vocal critic or detractor of the Conference Committee. However, while China itself did not spearhead challenges or criticism, it has occasionally signed on to critical statements made by other countries, particularly countries with which it appears to have

---

[68] Ann Kent, "China, International Organizations and Regimes: The ILO as a Case Study in Organizational Learning," *Pacific Affairs* 70, no. 4 (Winter 1997–1998): 517–532. The ILO's Committee on Freedom of Association has encouraged Beijing to ratify more fundamental ILO conventions.

[69] For these reviews, see ILO, "International Labour Conference, Report of the Conference Committee on the Application of Standards, 83rd session," (1994), www.ilo.org/public/libdoc/ilo/P/09616/09616(1994-81).pdf, accessed October 15, 2018, Part 2, Observations on and Information Concerning Particular Countries, 25/82–25/83; ILO, "International Labour Conference, Report of the Conference Committee on the Application of Standards, 92rd session," (2004), www.ilo.org/public/english/standards/relm/ilc/ilc92/pdf/pr-24p2.pdf, accessed October 15, 2018, Part 2, Observations on and Information Concerning Particular Countries, 24/45–24/47; ILO, "International Labour Conference, Report of the Conference Committee on the Application of Standards, 96th Session," (2007), www.ilo.org/wcmsp5/groups/public/—ed_norm/—normes/documents/publication/wcms_088133.pdf, accessed October 15, 2018, Part 2, Observations on and Information Concerning Particular Countries, 22/90–22/95; and ILO, "International Labour Conference, Report of the Conference Committee on the Application of Standards, 98th session," (2009), www.ilo.org/wcmsp5/groups/public/—ed_norm/—normes/documents/publication/wcms_116491.pdf, accessed October 15, 2018, Part 2, Observations on and Information Concerning Particular Countries, 16/120–16/124.

shared human rights views, such as members of the LMG.[70] As a long-time CCAS participant put it, Beijing has been "rather careful in limiting criticism of the system."[71] In a similar vein, a former senior ILO official noted that China "has never tried to subvert the system by political means."[72] Again pointing to Chinese acceptance of the status quo of the Conference Committee's working methods, a PRC government official whose responsibility includes ILO matters summarized Beijing's view that as "a member of the ILO, [we] should respect established procedures and rules."[73]

The PRC was particularly cautious during its initial years in the CCAS as it remained on the sidelines of debates over CCAS monitoring. For example, in 1983 and 1984, which were the PRC's first two years attending the ILC, it remained silent as other communist countries claimed that the supervisory system victimized socialist and developing countries through selective and unfair attention and called for "democratization" of the ILO's labor rights monitoring system.[74] China's silence may have reflected the desire as a relative newcomer to avoid controversy. In 1985, there was a slight uptick in its visibility. During the ILC that year, China, along with India, Saudi Arabia, and Syria, "considered that the Committee of Experts and the other supervisory bodies of the ILO should be more flexible in their evaluation of observance of Conventions, and should take account of the particular problems faced by developing countries."[75] However, this statement was the exception rather than the norm as the PRC tended toward a low-profile role and the PRC may have signed on to this statement to demonstrate solidarity with these countries.

Nearly two decades later Beijing affiliated with a similar statement. In 2004, China signed on to a statement made by Cuba, on behalf of eighteen countries, including Algeria, Belarus, Burundi, Egypt,

---

[70] In the UNCHR, the LMG consisted primarily of Algeria, Bangladesh, Belarus, Bhutan, Cuba, Egypt, India, Indonesia, Iran, Malaysia, Myanmar, Nepal, Pakistan, the Philippines, Russia, Sri Lanka, Sudan, Syria, Venezuela, Vietnam, and Zimbabwe. See Chapter 4 for background.

[71] Bruaas, interview.

[72] Interview former senior ILO official, May 25, 2011, Geneva, Switzerland.

[73] Interview with Chinese government official, June 12, 2012, Beijing, China.

[74] For these discussions, see ILO, "International Labour Conference, Report of the Conference Committee on the Application of Standards, 70th Session," (1984), www .ilo.org/public/libdoc/ilo/P/09616/09616(1984-70).pdf, accessed October 15, 2018, General Report, paragraphs 15-16, and Ghebali, *The International Labour Organization*, 230.

[75] ILO, "International Labour Conference, Report of the Conference Committee on the Application of Standards, 71st session," (1985), www.ilo.org/public/libdoc/ilo/P/09616/ 09616(1985-71).pdf, accessed October 15, 2018, General Report, 30/5.

Ethiopia, India, Indonesia, Libya, Malaysia, Myanmar, Pakistan, Syria, Sudan, Venezuela, Vietnam, and Zimbabwe. The Cuban delegate recalled

> that at the 91st Session of the International Labour Conference, the movement of non-aligned countries ... [voiced] its concern over the working methods of the Committee on the Application of Standards and had requested a new examination of these methods ... In proposing these individual cases the Committee of Experts should take into account relative geographical balance. It shall bear in mind the need to treat fairly, equally, and on the same footing, cases from all regions of the world. The Conventions whose application is to be examined must be selected upon the basis of an adequate proportion between fundamental and technical ones (50/50).... The Conference Committee should not be approached as an inquisitorial tribunal nor a body for condemnation or confrontation.[76]

The composition of the group of countries overlaps with the LMG, which was active in resisting country-level scrutiny in the UN's human rights bodies. In addition to the complaints stated earlier, these countries also sought to give governments greater influence relative to the worker and employer groups; urged that the CCAS use clear and technical criteria in determining the countries to examine; insisted on greater geographical balance in selecting countries for CCAS review; and pushed for greater state control over the Committee's report and conclusions.[77] Within this group, Cuba, Zimbabwe, and Belarus, which were often summoned to appear before the CCAS, were – particularly vocal critics.[78] Notably, however, Beijing took a measured approach, and although it signed onto this Cuban-led effort, it was not a prominent CCAS detractor. Although the PRC itself had few gripes with the CCAS, due to Beijing's broader cooperation with these nations in resisting vigorous scrutiny and sense of solidarity, the Chinese leadership likely realized that it behooved them to join these statements. As will be documented in the following section, starting in the late 1990s, the PRC also made protective statements on behalf of some of these countries.

---

[76] ILO, "International Labour Conference, Report of the Conference Committee on the Application of Standards, 92nd session," (2004), www.ilo.org/public/english/standards/relm/ilc92/pdf/pr-24p1.pdf, 24/9–24/10, accessed October 15, 2018, Part 1, paragraphs 27–28.

[77] Ibid., Part 1, paragraphs, 27–35.

[78] Bruaas, interview; interviewee with ILO official for employers' activities, May 27, 2011, Geneva, Switzerland; interview with North American governmental representative, June 2, 2011, Geneva, Switzerland; and interview with former senior ILO official, May 25, 2011, Geneva, Switzerland.

PRC Government Participation in the Conference Committee's
Reviews of Other Countries

China's behavior in the Conference Committee is illustrative of its transformation from a timid novice that shunned participation in the reviews of other countries to a deft and shrewd CCAS participant able to use this venue to bolster select allies coming under the Committee's gaze. This subsection shows that Beijing not only acted as a taker of the regime but beginning in the late 1990s adjusted its conduct to benefit from the Conference Committee's procedures by using this venue as an opportunity to defend friendly states. This turning point in the late 1990s also coincides with its growing cooperation with kindred states in other parts of the human rights regime. For example, as chronicled in Chapter 3, China began to cooperate with Cuba, Algeria, Egypt, Saudi Arabia, Sudan, and Syria in contesting the proposed Optional Protocol to the Convention against Torture (OPCAT). In the late 1990s, the LMG coalesced and offered common positions in the UNCHR, including criticizing the use of public censure while favoring less public approaches, such as dialogue and cooperation. Moreover, an understanding regarding reciprocal support and a sense of mutual defense and solidarity may have emerged among these countries. As will be shown in a later section of this chapter, a number of developing countries whose human rights views aligned with Beijing's were also a key source of support in the PRC's ability to overcome attempts to pass UNCHR resolutions on its record.

However, prior to the late 1990s, during the PRC's early years in the CCAS, it was a subdued and quiescent participant and it did not play an active role in the public examination of other countries. From 1983 through most of the 1990s, Chinese representatives made few comments during the Committee's examinations even though PRC participants were attending the Committee's sessions and are reported to have been watching the proceedings closely. A former ILO official recalled observing PRC representatives at the CCAS proceedings in the early to mid 1980s and noted that they were attentive to the working methods and appeared to "delight" in seeing the USSR's public examination as their Soviet counterparts faced scrutiny.[79] These were the years when China regarded the Soviet Union as its major adversary, a

---

[79] Interview with former senior ILO official, May 25, 2011, Geneva, Switzerland. This was a firsthand observation by this individual.

perception that did not change until later in the 1980s.[80] Thus, as it gained familiarity with the Committee's working methods, the PRC may have been learning that the CCAS was a forum where countries could face intense scrutiny and the ways it could use its participation instrumentally.

This modest profile did not give way to a more activist one until the late 1990s when a noticeable shift occurred and Beijing began speaking in defense of a handful of countries and urged lenient ILO treatment or drew attention to areas of progress highlighted by the government in question. This behavior first manifested with a 1999 statement on behalf of Myanmar where serious forced labor abuses were reported. The PRC stated that it "hoped that the Committee would take note of the new progress achieved by the Government in the application of the Convention, as reported by the Government representative."[81] At this time, Myanmar was coming under increasing scrutiny from the ILO in response to reports of severe restrictions on freedom of association and forced labor violations. For example, the Governing Body deployed a 1998 Commission of Inquiry that found "widespread and systemic forced labour" and in 2000 the ILC passed a resolution on the problem of forced labor that mandated annual special CCAS reviews on Myanmar during the annual ILC.[82] Following this 1999 statement on Myanmar, Chinese officials delivered similar interventions and from 1999 through 2017, it voiced support for thirteen countries – Algeria, Belarus, Bangladesh, Colombia, Egypt, India, Kazakhstan, Myanmar, Pakistan, Qatar, Uzbekistan, Venezuela, and Zimbabwe. During this period, China made a total of forty statements on behalf of besieged allies. These comments generally portrayed the governments under examination as earnestly making progress, urged the CCAS to be lenient, and called on the ILO to play a supportive role by providing assistance. As an international trade union official put it, "China has been quite consistent in the kind of country cases that it spoke on ... a number of countries where the violations ... were particularly egregious ... China spoke in

[80] See, for example, Steven M. Goldstein, "Nationalism and Internationalism: Sino-Soviet Relations," in *Chinese Foreign Policy: Theory and Practice*, eds. Thomas W. Robinson and David Shambaugh (Oxford: Clarendon, 1994), 224–264.

[81] ILO, "International Labour Conference, Report of the Conference Committee on the Application of Standards 87th Session," (1999), www.ilo.org/public/english/standards/relm/ilc/ilc87/com-apd1.htm, accessed October 15, 2018, Part Two, Observations and Information Concerning Particular Countries, 23/90.

[82] ILO, "International Labour Conference adopts Resolution targeting forced labour in Myanmar," press release, June 14, 2000, www.ilo.org/global/about-the-ilo/press-and-media-centre/news/WCMS_007899/lang–en/index.htm, accessed June 2, 2017. See also Wisskirchen, "The Standard-Setting and Monitoring Activities of the ILO," 269.

defense of these governments, saying that indeed there had been some improvements."[83] Table 5.2 captures these PRC statements.[84]

Aside from the statements noted, in the majority of CCAS country examinations, Beijing usually did not intervene, including in cases where the country was ultimately included in a special paragraph. The PRC government only intervened in one to six cases annually out of a total of twenty-five cases.[85] From 1999 through 2017, there were forty-eight cases mentioned in the special paragraph and in twelve of those cases the PRC spoke in defense of the country. Table 5.3 presents a comparison of the countries that were examined and the subset of instances in which the PRC spoke to shield the country as well as the cases included in the CCAS special paragraph. This suggests that Beijing's rhetorical backing did not appear to sway the decision to include the case in a special paragraph. These findings are consistent with explanations from CCAS participants, including an ILO official who stated, "I don't think the remarks by governments ... in reality, influence the conclusions ... it is really the conclusions of the Workers and Employers that is the determining thing."[86] A former employer representative concurred, noting that "China voices rhetorical support for some countries ...

---

[83] Tate, interview.

[84] These statements reflect only PRC interventions in the Conference Committee, rather than the ILC plenary, where it also occasionally spoke for its allies. For example, in 2000, even though the PRC did not speak on Myanmar's behalf in the CCAS, it defended Myanmar in the plenary when a resolution on forced labor was considered. China complained that some parts of the ILO "still insists on the application of article 33 of the Constitution, and has carried out extreme measures against Myanmar. This has now occurred for the first time in the ILO's history. It has created a very dangerous precedent. Therefore, the Chinese Government opposes the application of Article 33 of the Constitution." ILO, "International Labour Conference, Record of Proceedings 88th session," (2000), www.ilo.org/public/english/standards/relm/ilc/ilc88/com-seld.htm, accessed October 15, 2018, Reports of the Selection Committee, 26/28. When a country refuses to fulfill the recommendations of a Commission of Inquiry, the Governing Body can take action under Article 33 of the ILO Constitution.

[85] Only in 2016 did the PRC speak on behalf of more than four countries. That year the PRC spoke out during six country reviews. ILO, "International Labour Conference, Report of the Conference Committee on the Application of Standards, 95th session," (2016), www.ilo.org/wcmsp5/groups/public/—ed_norm/—normes/documents/publication/wcms_526940.pdf, accessed October 15, 2018, Part 2, Observations on and Information Concerning Particular Countries, 16/152.

[86] Interview with ILO official for workers' activities, May 24, 2011, Geneva, Switzerland. Similar comments shared by Dereymaker, interview; Potter, interview; Debrulle, interview; Tate, interview; interview with former senior ILO official, May 25, 2011, Geneva, Switzerland; interview with North American governmental participant, June 2, 2011, Geneva, Switzerland; interview with ILO official for employers' activities, May 27, 2011, Geneva, Switzerland, and Rudi Delarue (Head of the ILO office in Brussels, Belgium and former EU Commission representative to the ILO), interview by author, March 21, 2012.

Table 5.2 *PRC statements during CCAS examination of countries*

Year	Country and convention under examination	PRC statement
1999[a]	Myanmar (29, Forced Labor)	Hoped that the Committee would take note of the new progress achieved by Myanmar
2003[b]	Myanmar (87, Freedom of Association)	Encouraged Myanmar to cooperate with the ILO
2004[c]	Colombia (87, Freedom of Association)	Noted the efforts undertaken by Colombia; hoped ILO would strengthen technical cooperation; Colombia should not appear in the special paragraph
2005[d]	Belarus (87, Freedom of Association)	Belarus was taking positive steps and had made progress; encouraged ILO and international community to provide technical assistance which was needed at this stage
	Colombia (87, Freedom of Association)	Colombia making efforts and progress to protect trade union rights; still a long way to go; praised cooperation between ILO and Colombia
	Venezuela (87, Freedom of Association)	Venezuela had made remarkable achievements in reforming its legislation and in promoting social dialogue; demonstrated Venezuela's willingness to cooperate with the social partners; should acknowledge achievements; encouraged ILO technical support
	Zimbabwe (98, Right to Organize)	Zimbabwe amending laws to address concerns; noted actions Zimbabwe had mentioned in its statement; Zimbabwe making progress and needed more time; encouraged ILO to provide technical cooperation
2006	Belarus (87 and 98, Freedom of Association and the Right to Organize)[e]	Government of Belarus was ready to apply the recommendations of the Commission of Inquiry and to follow up on the observations of the Committee of Experts, and that it had drawn up a plan of action
	Bangladesh (98, Right to Organize)	Urged the Committee to appreciate the efforts made by Bangladesh; Bangladesh fully respected international labor standards; invited the Governing Body to recognize progress made; urged ILO cooperation and allowance for latitude in design and implementation of social policy

Table 5.2 (*cont.*)

Year	Country and convention under examination	PRC statement
2007	Belarus (87, Freedom of Association)[f]	Belarus government faithfully implementing recommendations of the Commission of Inquiry; noted meaningful measures and progress; encouraged the Committee to recognize these steps; and encouraged further cooperation
	Venezuela (87, Freedom of Association)	Appreciated progress achieved and efforts made by Venezuela to cooperate with the ILO; agreed with GRULAC statement
	Bangladesh (111, Discrimination)	The principle of equality was embodied in the Constitution and the new Labor Code; Bangladesh made genuine efforts to combat discrimination and apply the Convention; asserted that Bangladesh remained an underdeveloped country and economic development was crucial to overcoming challenges; encouraged the ILO and the international community to provide assistance
2008[g]	Belarus (87, Freedom of Association)	Belarus achieved further progress through cooperation with the ILO and other steps which should be recognized by the Committee; endorsed further cooperation between ILO and Belarus
	Egypt (87, Freedom of Association)	Taken note of the Government's statement in particular with regard to the legislation adopted and the measures taken to promote social dialogue; ILO should continue to cooperate with Egypt
2009[h]	Belarus (87, Freedom of Association)	Thanked Belarus for the information provided; since 2005, the Government had been taking effective measures to improve the implementation of the recommendations of the Commission of Inquiry; Committee should recognize progress; endorsed cooperation
	Myanmar (87, Freedom of Association)	Challenges that Myanmar faced should be taken into consideration; progress towards democratization had been noted; steps taken by Myanmar reflect its will to promote human rights and protect workers; hoped ILO continue dialogue and technical assistance with Myanmar

Table 5.2 (*cont.*)

Year	Country and convention under examination	PRC statement
	Venezuela (87, Freedom of Association)	Should recognize steps taken by Venezuela to implement recommendations made by the Committee of Experts; ILO should provide technical assistance to help in capacity building in the country; ILO and Venezuela can should strengthen their mutual trust and pursue dialogue and cooperation, which will address issues and challenges
2010[i]	Belarus (87, Freedom of Association)	Belarus had paid close attention to the recommendations of the Commission of Inquiry and had made significant efforts and progress to strengthen tripartism, social dialogue and freedom of association; committee should note Belarus's sincere determination to strengthen cooperation with the ILO to improve implementation of the Convention
	Myanmar (87, Freedom of Association)	Should be acknowledged that concrete and effective measures had been taken; encouraged Myanmar to continue its dialogue and cooperation with the ILO with a view to promoting Convention No. 87
	Venezuela (87, Freedom of Association)	Venezuela taking steps; Conference Committee should recognize Venezuela's sincerity in its cooperation with the social partners and the ILO and the concrete measures it had adopted; ILO should continue its commitment and cooperation with Venezuela
2011[j]	Belarus (98, Right to Organize)	Over the last year Belarus engaged with ILO and made remarkable progress; important to acknowledge the sincerity of these efforts; hoped the ILO would strengthen cooperation
	Uzbekistan (182, Worst Forms of Child Labor)	Highlighted Uzbekistan's positive attitude; observed that proper measures were being taken; expressed support for these efforts to eradicate child labor
2012		No review conducted due to inability of worker and employer representatives in the Conference Committee to agree on list of countries to be examined due to disagreement over the COE's interpretation regarding the right to strike

Table 5.2 (*cont.*)

Year	Country and convention under examination	PRC statement
2013[k]	Pakistan (81, Labour Inspection)	Stressed that the Constitution gave autonomy to the provinces and that labor inspection powers were given to the provinces; the Government was in a transitional phase and needed time to implement legislation; ILO should provide technical assistance
	Belarus (87, Freedom of Association)	Trade union registration was improving and there had been no complaints in 2012; requested technical assistance to the Government in implement the Convention
	Uzbekistan (182, Worst Forms of Child Labour)	Highlighted the measures taken, including setting a compulsory schooling age at 12, sentencing offenders, and participating in ILO technical assistance; these achievements should be recognized by the Committee
2014[l]	Venezuela (131, Minimum Wage Fixing)	Welcomed efforts by Venezuela since 2000 to consult with social partners; hoped the cooperation with ILO would be strengthened
	Bangladesh (81, Labour Inspection)	Bangladesh had revised the Labour Act and was developing a labor law, a national occupational safety and health policy and working to improve labor inspection in the construction sector; the government's cooperation with the ILO should be recognized and improved
	Pakistan (81, Labour Inspection)	Pakistan had taken steps to improve the labor inspection system, including improving the quality and quantity of inspections, and a joint plan of action on occupational safety and health; the Government had made real efforts at implementation; Pakistan had encountered some difficulties in implementation as a developing country; ILO and international community should provide technical assistance
	Belarus (87, Freedom of Association)	Noted strengthened cooperation between ILO and Belarus; Particular mention should be made to the easing of minimum wage requirements with respect to trade unions rights, signing wage agreements, and a direct contacts ILO mission; Belarus was taking measures to implement the convention; ILO cooperation should continue

Table 5.2 (*cont.*)

Year	Country and convention under examination	PRC statement
2015[m]	India (81, Labour Inspection)	Appreciated the information and goodwill; noted the amendment to labor law ongoing; encouraged ILO to provide assistance; suggested computer system would help the independence and integrity of the labor inspectors
	Algeria (87, Freedom of Association)	The government and social partners were working to amend the labor code with ILO technical assistance; hoped the Committee would recognize this commitment and efforts; called on the ILO to continue to provide assistance; confident in Algeria's reform process
	Belarus (87, Freedom of Association)	Congratulated government on cooperation with ILO and progress; necessary to apply ratified conventions; Government had shown willingness to implement recommendation of the Commission of Inquiry; ILO should provide technical assistance
	Venezuela (87, Freedom of Association)	Expressed support for the GRULAC statement; the Government was cooperating with the ILO and had made efforts to improve legislation; countries that ratified ILO conventions should implement them; ILO should be available to assist
2016[n]	Belarus (29, Forced Labor)	Belarus had implemented numerous measures, including repealing Presidential Decree No. 9; ILO should provide assistance
	Bangladesh (87, Freedom of Association)	Commended the Government for taking a number of positive measures; the government's efforts to fulfill its obligations should be recognized and supported with technical assistance
	Kazakhstan (87, Freedom of Association)	Noted the improvements made by Kazakhstan, including formulating laws in line with international standards; it was the obligation of ratifying countries to implement labor conventions; the ILO needed to provide technical support; supported the government's efforts

Table 5.2 (*cont.*)

Year	Country and convention under examination	PRC statement
	Zimbabwe (98, Right to Organize)	Emphasized that the government had implemented the recommendation of the Commission of Inquiry; this progress should be welcomed; states were responsible for implementing ratified conventions and they needed time and ILO technical assistance; supported the efforts of the government
	Qatar (111, Discrimination)	Noted the information provided by the government on steps taken; encouraged the ILO to provide technical assistance
	Venezuela (122, Employment Policy)	Referred to the statement made by the government and GRULAC and noted that the Government had fulfilled its obligations under the convention; the government's efforts should be recognized by the Committee
2017	Bangladesh (87, Freedom of Association)	Noted the information provided by the government and progress; including revision of labour law, drafting of the Export Processing Zone (EPZ) Labour Act, increased trade union registration, and social dialogue; efforts made by the government should be recognized and the ILO should continue to provide technical assistance[o]

[a] ILO, "International Labour Conference, Report of the Conference Committee on the Application of Standards 87th Session," (1999), www.ilo.org/public/english/standards/relm/ilc/ilc87/com-apd1.htm, October 15, 2018, Part 2, Observations and Information Concerning Particular Countries, 23/90.

[b] ILO, "International Labour Conference, Report of the Conference Committee on the Application of Standards, 91st session," (2003), www.ilo.org/public/english/standards/relm/ilc/ilc91/pdf/pr-24p2.pdf, October 15, 2018, Part 2, Observations and Information Concerning Particular Countries, 24/33.

[c] ILO, "International Labour Conference, Report of Conference Committee on the Application of Standards, 92nd Session," (2004), www.ilo.org/public/english/standards/relm/ilc/ilc92/pdf/pr-24p2.pdf, accessed October 15, 2018, Part 2, Observations and Information Concerning Particular Countries, 24/26.

[d] ILO, "International Labour Conference, "Report of the Conference Committee on the Application of Standards, 93rd Session," (2005), www.ilo.org/public/english/standards/relm/ilc/ilc93/pdf/pr-22-2.pdf, accessed October 15, 2018, Part 2, Observations and Information Concerning Particular Countries, 22/24, 22/31, 22/48, and 22/57.

Table 5.2 (*cont.*)

---

[e] ILO, "International Labour Conference, Report of the Conference Committee on the Application of Standards, 95th session," (2006), www.ilo.org/public/english/standards/relm/ilc/ilc95/pdf/pr-24-part2.pdf, accessed October 15, 2018, Part 2, Observations on and Information Concerning Particular Countries, 24/21 and 24/29.

[f] ILO, "International Labour Conference, Report of the Conference Committee on the Application of Standards, 95th Session," (2007), www.ilo.org/wcmsp5/groups/public/—ed_norm/—normes/documents/publication/wcms_088133.pdf, accessed October 15, 2018, Part 2, Observations on and Information Concerning Particular Countries, 22/21, 22/55, and 22/75. Mexico's statement on behalf of the Group of Latin America and Caribbean Countries (GRULAC) noted that they "recognized the attitude of responsibility and the spirit of cooperation of the Bolivarian Republic of Venezuela with all ILO supervisory and other bodies ... The fact that the Bolivarian Republic of Venezuela had responded to all requests for information by the supervisory bodies should be taken into consideration in the Committee's conclusions." For full statement, Ibid., 22/53.

[g] ILO, "International Labour Conference, Report of the Conference Committee on the Application of Standards, 95th session," (2008), www.ilo.org/wcmsp5/groups/public/—ed_norm/—normes/documents/publication/wcms_100265.pdf, accessed October 15, 2018, Part 2, Observations on and Information Concerning Particular Countries, 19/35–19/36 and 19/53.

[h] ILO, "International Labour Conference, Report of the Conference Committee on the Application of Standards, 96th Session," (2009), www.ilo.org/wcmsp5/groups/public/—ed_norm/—normes/documents/publication/wcms_116491.pdf, accessed October 15, 2018, Part 2, Observations on and Information Concerning Particular Countries, 16/21, 16/51 and 16/86.

[i] ILO, "International Labour Conference, Report of the Conference Committee on the Application of Standards, 97th Session," (2010), www.ilo.org/wcmsp5/groups/public/—ed_norm/—normes/documents/publication/wcms_145220.pdf, accessed October 15, 2018 Part 2, Observations on and Information Concerning Particular Countries, 16/18, 16/39 and 16/60.

[j] ILO, "International Labour Conference, Report of the Conference Committee on the Application of Standards, 95th Session," (2011), www.ilo.org/wcmsp5/groups/public/—ed_norm/—normes/documents/publication/wcms_165970.pdf, accessed October 15, 2018, Part 2, Observations on and Information Concerning Particular Countries, 18/66 and 18/113.

[k] ILO, "International Labour Conference, Report of the Conference Committee on the Application of Standards, 95th Session, (2013), https://www.ilo.org/global/standards/WCMS_229263/lang–en/index.htm, accessed October 15, 2018, Part 2, Observations on and Information Concerning Particular Countries, 16/21, 16/35, and 16/134.

[l] ILO, "International Labour Conference, Report of the Conference Committee on the Application of Standards, 95th Session," (2014), www.ilo.org/wcmsp5/groups/public/—ed_norm/—normes/documents/publication/wcms_320613.pdf, accessed October 15, 2018, Part 2, Observations on and Information Concerning Particular Countries, 13/13, 13/31, 13/41, and 13/56.

[m] ILO, "International Labour Conference, Report of the Conference Committee on the Application of Standards, 96th session," (2015), www.ilo.org/wcmsp5/groups/public/—ed_norm/—normes/documents/publication/wcms_412826.pdf, accessed October 15, 2018, Part 2, Observations on and Information Concerning Particular Countries, 14/35, 14/41, 14/55, and 14/91. The GRULAC comment, which was delivered by the government of Cuba, affirmed the information provided by the Venezuelan government regarding steps taken and endorsed the government of Venezuela's argument that the events reported were unconnected with trade union activities and the exercise of the Freedom of Association. Ibid., Part 2, 14/89.

Table 5.2 (*cont.*)

[n] ILO, "International Labour Conference, Report of the Conference Committee on the Application of Standards, 95th session," (2016), www.ilo.org/wcmsp5/groups/public/—ed_norm/—normes/documents/publication/wcms_526940.pdf, accessed October 15, 2018, Part 2, Observations on and Information Concerning Particular Countries, 16/11, 16/25, 16/27, 16/59 16/123, and 16/143.

[o] ILO, "International Labour Conference, Report of the Conference Committee on the Application of Standards, 106th Session," (2017), www.ilo.org/wcmsp5/groups/public/—ed_norm/—normes/documents/publication/wcms_576287.pdf, accessed October 15, 2018, Part 2, Observations on and Information on the Conference Committee on the Application of Standards, 15/58.

Table 5.3 *Countries examined, including countries the PRC spoke on behalf of*

Year	Countries examined	Special paragraph	PRC comments
1999	Afghanistan, Australia, Bangladesh, Brazil, Cameroon, Canada, Chad, Costa Rica, Djibouti, Ecuador, Ethiopia, Guatemala, Iran, Libya, Malaysia, Mexico, Myanmar, Pakistan, Peru, Sri Lanka, Russia, Swaziland, Venezuela[a]	Cameroon, Myanmar	Myanmar
2000	Afghanistan, Australia, Brazil, Cameroon, Colombia, Djibouti, Ethiopia, Guatemala, Hungary, India, Iran, Kuwait, Mauritania, Mexico, Pakistan, Panama, Saint Lucia, Sudan, Swaziland, Tanzania, Ukraine, United Kingdom, Venezuela[b]	Cameroon, Sudan, Venezuela	No comments
2001	Belarus, Chile, Colombia, Costa Rica, Djibouti, Ethiopia, Guatemala, India, Iran, Japan, Kenya, Myanmar, Pakistan, Panama, Peru, Portugal, Spain, Sudan, Swaziland, Turkey, Uganda, Ukraine, United Arab Emirates, Venezuela[c]	Belarus, Colombia, Ethiopia, Myanmar, Sudan, Venezuela	No comments

Table 5.3 (*cont.*)

Year	Countries examined	Special paragraph	PRC comments
2002	Belarus, Colombia, Costa Rica, Côte d'Ivoire, Ethiopia, Fiji, Germany, Guatemala, Japan, Mauritania, Moldova, Myanmar, Pakistan, Paraguay, Peru, Qatar, Sudan, Swaziland, Turkey, United Arab Emirates, United States, Uruguay, Venezuela, Zimbabwe[d]	Ethiopia, Sudan, Venezuela	No comments
2003	Belarus, Cameroon, Colombia, Croatia, Cuba, Ecuador, Ethiopia, Guatemala, India, Iran, Kenya, Libya, Mauritania, Myanmar, Pakistan, Panama, Paraguay, Portugal, Serbia and Montenegro, Uganda, Ukraine, Uruguay, Venezuela[e]	Belarus, Cameroon, Libya, Mauritania, Myanmar, Zimbabwe	Myanmar
2004	Australia, Bangladesh, Bolivia, Canada, China, Colombia, Costa Rica, Dominican Republic, El Salvador, Guatemala, Iceland, Indonesia, Japan, Myanmar, Netherlands, Niger, Poland, Republic of Korea, Serbia and Montenegro, Slovakia, Sudan, Ukraine, Venezuela, Zimbabwe[f]	Myanmar	Colombia
2005	Argentina, Australia, Belarus, Bosnia and Herzegovina, Colombia, Ecuador, Guatemala, Iran, Mauritania, Myanmar, Nepal, Niger, Panama, Peru, Qatar, Romania, Russia, Saudi Arabia, Sudan, Swaziland, Turkey, United States, Venezuela, Zimbabwe[g]	Belarus, Myanmar	Belarus, Colombia, Venezuela, Zimbabwe
2006	Australia, Bangladesh, Belarus, Bosnia and Herzegovina, Central African Republic, Costa Rica, Croatia,	Bangladesh, Belarus	Bangladesh, Belarus

Table 5.3 (*cont.*)

Year	Countries examined	Special paragraph	PRC comments
	Djibouti, Guatemala, Iran, Ireland, Kenya, Libya, Mexico, Pakistan, Paraguay, Philippines, Slovakia, Switzerland, Thailand, Uganda, United Kingdom, United States, Venezuela, Zimbabwe[h]		
2007	Argentina, Australia, Bangladesh, Belarus, Bosnia and Herzegovina, Cambodia, China, Congo, Djibouti, Ethiopia, Gabon, Guatemala, India, Iran, Italy, Japan, Philippines, Romania, Spain, Sri Lanka, Turkey, United Kingdom, United States, Venezuela, Zimbabwe,[i]	Belarus	Bangladesh, Belarus, Venezuela
2008	Bangladesh, Belarus, Bulgaria, Colombia, Croatia, Czech Republic, Dominican Republic, Egypt, Equatorial Guinea, Georgia, Guatemala, Indonesia, Iran, Iraq, India, Japan, Mexico, Paraguay, Sudan, Sweden, Uganda, United Kingdom, Zambia, Zimbabwe[j]	Bangladesh, Zimbabwe	Belarus, Egypt
2009	Belarus, Chile, China, Colombia, Congo, Costa Rica, Ethiopia, Guatemala, Iran, Israel, Italy, Kuwait, Malaysia, Mauritania, Myanmar, Nigeria, Pakistan, Panama, Peru, Philippines, Russia, South Korea Swaziland, Turkey, Venezuela[k]	Iran, Myanmar, Swaziland	Myanmar, Venezuela
2010	Belarus, Burundi, Cambodia, Canada, Central African Republic, Costa Rica, Czech Republic, Egypt, Georgia, Guatemala, India, Iran, Mauritania, Mexico, Morocco, Myanmar, Peru, Russia, Sudan, Swaziland, Thailand, Turkey, Ukraine, Uzbekistan, Venezuela[l]	Central African Republic, Myanmar, Swaziland	Belarus, Myanmar, Venezuela

Table 5.3 (*cont.*)

Year	Countries examined	Special paragraph	PRC comments
2011	Azerbaijan, Belarus, Cambodia, Canada, Congo, Fiji, Greece, Guatemala, Honduras, Malaysia, Mexico, Myanmar, Nigeria, Pakistan, Panama, Paraguay, Romania, Saudi Arabia, Serbia, Sri Lanka, Swaziland, Turkey, Uruguay, Uzbekistan, Zimbabwe[m]	Congo, Guatemala, Myanmar, Swaziland, Uzbekistan	Belarus, Uzbekistan
2012	No examination conducted due to inability of the workers and employers group to agree on list of countries to examine		
2013	Bangladesh, Belarus, Cambodia, Canada, Chad, Dominican Republic, Egypt, Fiji, Greece, Guatemala, Honduras, Iceland, Islamic Republic of Iran, Kenya, Republic of Korea, Malaysia, Mauritania, Pakistan, Paraguay, Saudi Arabia, Senegal, Spain, Swaziland, Turkey, Uzbekistan, Zimbabwe[n]	Belarus, Fiji, Uzbekistan	Pakistan, Belarus
2014	Algeria, Bangladesh, Belarus, Venezuela, Cambodia, Central African Republic, Colombia, Croatia, Democratic Republic of Congo, Dominican Republic, Ecuador, Greece, Kazakhstan, Malaysia, Mauritania, Niger, Pakistan, Portugal, Qatar, Republic of Korea, Saudi Arabia, Swaziland, Uganda, United States, Yemen[o]	Belarus	Venezuela, Bangladesh, Pakistan, Belarus
2015	Albania, Algeria, Bangladesh, Belarus, Venezuela, Cambodia, Cameroon, El Salvador, Eritrea, Guatemala, Honduras, India, Italy, Kazakhstan, Mauritania, Mauritius, Mexico, Philippines, Bolivia, Qatar, Republic of Korea, Spain, Swaziland, Turkey[p]	Kazakhstan, Mauritania, Swaziland	India, Algeria, Venezuela

Table 5.3 (*cont.*)

Year	Countries examined	Special paragraph	PRC comments
2016	Bangladesh, Belarus, Cambodia, Czech Republic, Ecuador, El Salvador, Guatemala, Honduras, Indonesia, Ireland, Kazakhstan, Madagascar, Malaysia, Mauritania, Mauritius, Mexico, Nigeria, Philippines, Qatar, Swaziland, Turkmenistan, United Kingdom, Venezuela, Zimbabwe[q]	Bangladesh, El Salvador	Belarus, Bangladesh, Kazakhstan, Zimbabwe, Qatar, Venezuela
2017	Malaysia, Mauritania, Paraguay, Poland, India, Ukraine, Algeria, Bangladesh, Botswana, Cambodia, Ecuador, Egypt, Guatemala, Kazakhstan, United Kingdom, Bahrain, Sudan, Venezuela, Turkey, Zambia, El Salvador, Afghanistan, Congo, Libya[r]	No special paragraph	Bangladesh

[a] ILO, "International Labour Conference, Report of the Conference Committee on the Application of Standards, 87th Session," (1999), www.ilo.org/public/english/standards/relm/ilc/ilc87/com-apd1.htm, accessed October 15, 2018, Part 2, Observations on and Information Concerning Particular Countries.
[b] ILO, "International Labour Conference, Report of the Conference Committee on the Application of Standards, 88th Session," (2000), www.ilo.org/public/english/standards/relm/ilc/ilc88/pdf/pr-23-ii.pdf, accessed October 15, 2018, Part 2, Observations on and Information Concerning Particular Countries.
[c] ILO, "International Labour Conference, Report of the Conference Committee on the Application of Standards, 89th Session," (2001), www.ilo.org/public/english/standards/relm/ilc/ilc89/pdf/pr-19-2.pdf, accessed October 15, 2018, Part 2, Observations on and Information Concerning Particular Countries.
[d] ILO, "International Labour Conference, Report of the Conference Committee on the Application of Standards, 90th Session," (2002), www.ilo.org/public/english/standards/relm/ilc/ilc90/pdf/pr-28p2.pdf, accessed October 15, 2018, Part 2, Observations on and Information Concerning Particular Countries.
[e] ILO, "International Labour Conference, Report of the Conference Committee on the Application of Standards, 91st Session," (2003), www.ilo.org/public/english/standards/relm/ilc/ilc91/pdf/pr-24p2.pdf, accessed October 15, 2018, Part 2, Observations on and Information Concerning Particular Countries.
[f] ILO, "International Labour Conference, Report of the Conference Committee on the Application of Standards, 92nd Session," (2004), www.ilo.org/public/english/standards/relm/ilc/ilc92/pdf/pr-24p2.pdf, accessed October 15, 2018, Part 2, Observations on and Information Concerning Particular Countries.

Table 5.3 (*cont.*)

[g] ILO, "International Labour Conference, Report of the Conference Committee on the Application of Standards, 94th Session," (2005), www.ilo.org/public/english/standards/relm/ilc/ilc93/pdf/pr-22-2.pdf, accessed October 15, 2018, Part 2, Observations on and Information Concerning Particular Countries.
[h] ILO, "International Labour Conference, Report of the Conference Committee on the Application of Standards, 95th Session," (2006), www.ilo.org/public/english/standards/relm/ilc/ilc95/pdf/pr-24-part2.pdf, accessed October 15, 2018, Part 2, Observations on and Information Concerning Particular Countries.
[i] ILO, "International Labour Conference, Report of the Conference Committee on the Application of Standards, 96th Session," (2007), www.ilo.org/wcmsp5/groups/public/—ed_norm/—normes/documents/publication/wcms_088133.pdf, accessed October 15, 2018, Part 2, Observations on and Information Concerning Particular Countries.
[j] ILO, "International Labour Conference, Report of the Conference Committee on the Application of Standards, 97th Session," (2008), www.ilo.org/wcmsp5/groups/public/—ed_norm/—normes/documents/publication/wcms_100265.pdf, accessed October 15, 2018, Part 2, Observations on and Information Concerning Particular Countries.
[k] ILO, "International Labour Conference, Report of the Conference Committee on the Application of Standards, 98th Session," (2009), www.ilo.org/wcmsp5/groups/public/—ed_norm/—normes/documents/publication/wcms_116491.pdf, accessed October 15, 2018, Part 2, Observations on and Information Concerning Particular Countries.
[l] ILO, "International Labour Conference, Report of the Conference Committee on the Application of Standards, 99th Session," (2010), www.ilo.org/wcmsp5/groups/public/—ed_norm/—normes/documents/publication/wcms_145220.pdf, accessed October 15, 2018, Part 2, Observations on and Information Concerning Particular Countries.
[m] ILO, "International Labour Conference, Report of the Conference Committee on the Application of Standards, 100th Session," (2011), www.ilo.org/wcmsp5/groups/public/—ed_norm/—normes/documents/publication/wcms_165970.pdf, accessed October 15, 2018, Part 2, Observations on and Information Concerning Particular Countries.
[n] ILO, "International Labour Conference, Report of the Conference Committee on the Application of Standards, 102nd Session," (2013), www.ilo.org/wcmsp5/groups/public/—ed_norm/—normes/documents/publication/wcms_229263.pdf, accessed October 15, 2018, Part 2, Observations on and Information Concerning Particular Countries.
[o] ILO, "International Labour Conference, Report of the Conference Committee on the Application of Standards, 103rd Session," (2014), www.ilo.org/wcmsp5/groups/public/—ed_norm/—normes/documents/publication/wcms_320613.pdf, accessed October 15, 2018, Part 2, Observations on and Information Concerning Particular Countries.
[p] ILO, "International Labour Conference, Report of the Conference Committee on the Application of Standards, 104th Session," (2015), www.ilo.org/wcmsp5/groups/public/—ed_norm/—normes/documents/publication/wcms_412826.pdf, accessed October 15, 2018, Part 2, Observations on and Information Concerning Particular Countries.
[q] ILO, "International Labour Conference, Report of the Conference Committee on the Application of Standards, 105th Session," (2016), www.ilo.org/wcmsp5/groups/public/—ed_norm/—normes/documents/publication/wcms_526940.pdf, accessed October 15, 2018, Part 2, Observations on and Information Concerning Particular Countries.
[r] ILO, "International Labour Conference, Report of the Conference Committee on the Application of Standards, 106th Session," (2017), www.ilo.org/wcmsp5/groups/public/—ed_norm/—normes/documents/publication/wcms_576287.pdf, accessed October 15, 2018, Part 2, Observations on and Information Concerning Particular Countries.

[but] on the Committee the employers and workers control 66 percent of the vote so although we listen to the views of governments, government interventions are not decisive."[87] Similarly, an international labor union official noted that China's words were merely "rhetorical" and that it was almost expected that the PRC "will take the floor" in defense of these countries but that ultimately the decision regarding which countries to include in the special paragraph "is a negotiation between the employers and workers."[88] A former ILO official noted that even if the country is ultimately included in a special paragraph sympathetic comments from other countries might be mildly beneficial by softening the overall tone and providing the government in question with supportive comments that it could cite in a press release.[89]

Even if its intercessions had little impact on the content of the special paragraph, Beijing was able to use these statements to demonstrate solidarity and extend goodwill to besieged allies. According to a PRC official whose remit includes the ILO, the countries Beijing spoke in defense of approached China for "assistance" and after weighing the "merits" of the case they determined whether to make a supportive statement.[90] This same official also noted that such requests were not unusual since "countries try to gather as much help as possible" when facing this kind of scrutiny.[91] He also asserted that China "would never do … [this] in such a way that other groups in the ILO would see them as protecting wrongdoing."[92] Despite the claim that the Chinese government reviewed each request and considered the merits of the case, over the last four years this official was unable to recall a single instance when Beijing refused to make a statement when asked by another country for "assistance."[93] As explained later in this chapter, a number of CCAS participants surmised that Beijing's statements reflected solidarity and a mutual defense arrangement to come to each other's aid when facing human rights scrutiny as well as PRC bilateral interests.[94] In this vein, a former senior ILO official stressed a foreign policy dimension to the PRC's behavior and noted that, in his estimation, Chinese officials from the Ministry of Labor and Social Security officials "appeared to be speaking under instructions" and that his impression was that "when

---

[87] Potter, interview.   [88] Dereymaeker, interview.
[89] Interview with ILO official for employers' activities, May 27, 2011, Geneva, Switzerland and Delarue, interview. Delarue noted that China's comments do not directly influence the outcome, yet state comments can shape the thinking of different actors.
[90] Interview with Chinese government official, June 12, 2012, Beijing, China.   [91] Ibid.
[92] Ibid.   [93] Ibid.
[94] Dereymaeker, interview; Tate, interview; and Benedict, interview.

the Ministry of Foreign Affairs counterpart is not present, the PRC delegate will more often remain silent."[95]

As noted previously, China's support went to Algeria, Belarus, Bangladesh, Colombia, Egypt, India, Kazakhstan, Myanmar, Pakistan, Qatar, Uzbekistan, Venezuela, and Zimbabwe. Beijing's human rights views are in broad alignment with these countries and most of them have repressive political systems. Reflecting their shared human rights ideas, the majority of these countries also hail from the LMG. As has been noted previously, LMG countries embrace human rights positions that favor less robust international monitoring, including the use of resolutions to spotlight particular countries, and also espouse arguments based on cultural relativism.[96] Of the countries Beijing defended, only Colombia, Qatar, and Uzbekistan are not affiliated with the LMG. While Uzbekistan is not a member of the LMG, it along with Kazakhstan is part of the Shanghai Cooperative Organization (SCO), a regional group that includes China, Russia, Kyrgyzstan, and Tajikistan that is ostensibly focused on fighting terrorism, extremism, and separatism but also appears to work in opposition to democracy and human rights.[97] For example, according to the International Federation for Human Rights, an international NGO, Shanghai Cooperative Organization members have coordinated to forcibly repatriate individuals, even refugees, in violation of international human rights norms.[98] Other CCAS participants also pointed out that most of these countries have troubled human rights records and described them as "similarly situated dictatorships" that have "closed political systems."[99] The observations are supported by the fact that of the countries China defended, all of them except for India have been classified by Freedom House as "Not Free" or only "Partly Free."[100]

---

[95] Interview with former senior ILO official, May 25, 2011, Geneva, Switzerland.
[96] Potter, interview; Bruaas, interview; and Dereymaeker, interview.
[97] See, for example, Thomas Ambrosio, "Catching the 'Shanghai Spirit:' How the Shanghai Cooperative Organization Promotes Authoritarian Norms in Central Asia," *Europe-Asia Studies* 60, no. 8 (October 2008): 1321–1344.
[98] International Federation for Human Rights, *Shanghai Cooperative Organisation: A Vehicle for Human Rights*, (Paris: International Federation for Human Rights, 2012), www.fidh.org/IMG/pdf/sco_report.pdf, accessed September 30, 2017. At a SCO summit, Putin told President Hu, "if you do not get a grip on these NGOs in China, as we are doing in Russia, you too will have a color revolution!" David Shambaugh, *China's Future* (New York: Policy, 2016), 70.
[99] First quote from Tate, interview. Second quote from Debrulle, interview. Similar observation from interview with former senior ILO official, May 25, 2011, Geneva, Switzerland.
[100] Freedom House, "Freedom in the World: Map of Freedom, 2017," (Washington DC: Freedom House, 2017), https://freedomhouse.org/sites/default/files/FH_FIW_2017_Report_Final.pdf, accessed August 1, 2017.

These countries also appear to practice mutual defense to shield each other from human rights scrutiny and act out of a sense of solidarity that is based at least partly on a perception that Western liberal democracies unfairly and selectively target non-Western, developing countries for human rights abuses. Along these lines, a North American government participant described Beijing's interventions as "political support" that conveys a message that it was "the little guys against the western powers."[101] In a similar vein, according to US employer representative Ed Potter, China "participates in a group of countries that ... [are] driven ... by a feeling ... [among] developing countries, generally, that the supervisory process picks on them too much."[102] Ambassador Elmiger of Switzerland described this behavior as a "kind of solidarity ... China has tried to support other countries ... It is part of a political game."[103] Other participants similarly described Beijing as speaking up for "the same group of countries every year" and "always protecting its friends."[104] As a Western European national trade union representative similarly asserted, it was "always the same group of countries helping each other."[105] The PRC–Zimbabwe relationship is illustrative of this as they have long defended each other on human rights. President Mugabe backed the PRC after the 1989 Tiananmen Square crackdown and the PRC opposed sanctions against Zimbabwe, including a 2005 US–UK effort to pass a UN Security Council resolution on Zimbabwe's slum demolition campaign and a US attempt to impose sanctions following the political violence during the 2008 presidential elections.[106]

Myanmar, in particular, received vocal Chinese support. Between 1999 and 2012, Chinese representatives offered four statements on Myanmar in the CCAS, shown in Table 5.2, and nine statements during the CCAS annual special sitting on forced labor, which as mandated by a

---

[101] Interview with North American government participant, June 2, 2011, Geneva, Switzerland.
[102] Potter, interview. Potter noted as an example that during the Cold War other Communists governments would say, "The German Democratic Republic is doing a great job." According to Potter, during the Cold War these countries shielded each other so regularly that he and some of his colleagues referred to these countries as "the chorus." In discussing the list of countries, a former senior ILO official said, "the list speaks for itself" and noted the repressive nature of those regimes. Interview with former senior ILO official, May 25, 2011, Geneva, Switzerland.
[103] Elmiger, interview.
[104] Tate, interview, and interview with former senior ILO official, May 25, 2011, Geneva, Switzerland.
[105] Debrulle, interview.
[106] David H. Shinn and Joshua Eisenman, *China and Africa: A Century of Engagement* (Philadelphia: University of Pennsylvania Press, 2012), 332–334.

2000 ILC resolution were held from 2000 until 2012.[107] Table 5.4, which captures PRC statements during the special sittings, shows that Beijing spoke every year from 2004 until 2012. China's consistent support for Myanmar may have been partially driven by Chinese concern and disagreement with the intensified scrutiny Myanmar was receiving from the ILO, which as noted previously included a 1998 Commission of Inquiry and a 2000 ILC resolution that required the annual special CCAS sittings.[108] The PRC defended Myanmar in nine out of thirteen annual special sittings with the overall thrust of its interventions encouraging more lenient treatment of Myanmar, highlighting positive steps the government had taken and encouraging the ILO to take this into account. Beijing's words also put much of the onus on the ILO to provide technical assistance and capacity building. For example, in 2008, the government representative of China stated that

[h]er Government was delighted that the Government of Myanmar had been working closely with the ILO ... A referendum had been conducted in May 2008 on the new Constitution which clearly prohibited all forms of forced labour, thereby resolving the remaining legal issue. The ILO's Liaison Office was working closely with local focal points to prevent the use of forced labor. The complaints mechanism was functioning smoothly ... All these efforts indicated the Government's sincere political will to eradicate forced labour. As seen in the cooperation between the Government and the ILO, there was effective collaboration based on mutual trust for the sustained well-being of the people. Her Government hoped that the ILO and the international community would remain committed to continuing the constructive dialogue and would provide encouragement and assistance, especially in terms of infrastructure. These would help to eradicate forced labour and guarantee fundamental rights and equality of access to development and its benefits.[109]

An International Trade Union Confederation official disputed China's rosy assessment and described the situation in Myanmar as

a very serious case in terms of forced labor, and yet the Chinese representative would always portray the minute actions, maybe taken one day before the

[107] Even though in some years the PRC did not defend Myanmar during the special sitting, it often came to the junta's defense in other venues, such as in the Governing Body and the plenary of the ILC. The PRC spoke in the ILC plenary against a draft resolution on Myanmar. ILO, "International Labour Conference, Record of Proceedings 88th Session," (2000), www.ilo.org/public/english/standards/relm/ilc/ilc88/com-seld.htm, accessed October 15, 2018, Reports of the Selection Committee, 26/28.
[108] ILO, "International Labour Conference adopts resolution targeting forced labour in Myanmar (Burma)," press release, June 14, 2000, www.ilo.org/global/about-the-ilo/newsroom/news/WCMS_007899/lang-en/index.htm, accessed October 30, 2016.
[109] ILO, "International Labour Conference, Report of the Conference Committee on the Application of Standards, 97th Session," (2008), www.ilo.org/wcmsp5/groups/public/—ed_norm/—normes/documents/publication/wcms_100265.pdf, accessed October 15, 2018, Part 3, Observations on and Information Concerning Particular Countries International Labour, Special Sitting on Myanmar, 19/8.

Table 5.4 *Statements during the annual special sitting on Myanmar*

Year	PRC statement
2000	No statement
2001	No statement
2002	No statement
2003	No statement
2004	The Government of Myanmar had been making efforts to meet the obligations of the Convention; encouraged further cooperation between ILO and Myanmar[a]
2005	Myanmar's actions demonstrated commitment to eradicating forced labor; noted progress resulting from cooperation between the ILO and Myanmar; encouraged further cooperation[b]
2006	PRC supports eradication of forced labor in general; Myanmar made progress yet not sufficient for the international community; however, Myanmar moving in right direction; regretted that the previous year's conclusion of the Conference Committee had had a negative impact on cooperation between the ILO and the Government, and therefore hoped that cooperation would be strengthened[c]
2007	Myanmar making efforts; encouraged dialogue and cooperation to eradicate forced labour; encouraged Myanmar to continue to cooperate with the ILO[d]
2008	Delighted Myanmar was working closely with the ILO; Myanmar has taken concrete steps, including important legal steps and training; these efforts indicated Myanmar's "sincere political will to eradicate forced labour"; encouraged constructive dialogue and assistance[e]
2009	Commended the close collaboration between Myanmar and the ILO, which had facilitated the adoption of concrete measures; stressed that this cooperation demonstrated Myanmar's willingness to eliminate forced labor[f]
2010	Noted cooperation between Myanmar and the ILO; acknowledged forced labor as a fundamental violation of human rights; hoped the ILO would continue its assistance to Myanmar[g]
2011	Cooperation between ILO and Myanmar effective; further progress achieved, including awareness raising; forced labor a violation of fundamental rights and needed to be eliminated; encouraged continued ILO assistance and cooperation with Myanmar[h]
2012	Stressed that Myanmar had taken effective measures, including legislation and tangible results had been achieved; the good will and endeavors of the Government must be fully recognized and encouraged; ILO should provide technical assistance; sanctions against Myanmar should be listed at this session of the conference[i]

[a] ILO, "International Labour Conference, Report of the Conference Committee on the Application of Standards, 93th Session," (2004), www.ilo.org/public/english/standards/relm/ilc/ilc92/pdf/pr-24p3.pdf, accessed October 15, 2018, Part 3, Observations on and Information Concerning Particular Countries, Special Sitting on Myanmar, 3/7.
[b] ILO, "International Labour Conference, Report of the Conference Committee on the Application of Standards, 94th Session," (2005), www.ilo.org/public/english/standards/relm/ilc/ilc93/pdf/pr-22-3.pdf, accessed October 15, 2018, Part 3, Observations on and Information Concerning Particular Countries, Special Sitting on Myanmar, 22/8.

Table 5.4 (*cont.*)

^c ILO, "International Labour Conference, Report of the Conference Committee on the Application of Standards, 95th Session," (2006), www.ilo.org/public/english/standards/relm/ilc/ilc95/pdf/pr-24-part3.pdf, accessed October 15, 2018, Part 3, Observations on and Information Concerning Particular Countries, Special Sitting on Myanmar, 24/29.

^d ILO, "International Labour Conference, Report of the Conference Committee on the Application of Standards, 96th Session," (2007), www.ilo.org/wcmsp5/groups/public/—ed_norm/—normes/documents/publication/wcms_088133.pdf, accessed October 15, 2018, Part 3, Observations on and Information Concerning Particular Countries, Special Sitting on Myanmar, 22/8.

^e ILO, "International Labour Conference, Report of the Conference Committee on the Application of Standards, 97th Session," (2008), www.ilo.org/wcmsp5/groups/public/—ed_norm/—normes/documents/publication/wcms_100265.pdf, accessed October 15, 2018, Part 3, Observations on and Information Concerning Particular Countries, Special Sitting on Myanmar, 19/8.

^f ILO, "International Labour Conference, Report of the Conference Committee on the Application of Standards, 98th Session," (2009), www.ilo.org/wcmsp5/groups/public/—ed_norm/—normes/documents/publication/wcms_116491.pdf, accessed October 15, 2018, Part 3, Observations on and Information Concerning Particular Countries, Special Sitting on Myanmar, 16/7.

^g ILO, "International Labour Conference, Report of the Conference Committee on the Application of Standards, 99th Session," (2010), www.ilo.org/wcmsp5/groups/public/—ed_norm/—normes/documents/publication/wcms_145220.pdf, accessed October 15, 2018, Part 3, Observations on and Information Concerning Particular Countries, Special Sitting on Myanmar, 16/9.

^h ILO, "International Labour Conference, Report of the Conference Committee on the Application of Standards, 100th Session," (2011), www.ilo.org/wcmsp5/groups/public/—ed_norm/—normes/documents/publication/wcms_165970.pdf, accessed October 15, 2018, Part 3, Observations on and Information Concerning Particular Countries, Special Sitting on Myanmar, 18/9.

ⁱ ILO, "International Labour Conference, Report of the Conference Committee on the Application of Standards, 101st Session," (2012), www.ilo.org/wcmsp5/groups/public/—ed_norm/—normes/documents/publication/wcms_190828.pdf, accessed October 15, 2018, Part 3, Observations on and Information Concerning Particular Countries, Special Sitting on Myanmar, 19/11.

conference actually happened, as signals of great progress ... it's clearly ... a joke. It just was not progress on any level of criteria of measurement ... [these PRC statements appeared to be] purely politically protecting their friends.[110]

This international trade union official further conjectured that the negative attention Myanmar was receiving from the ILO may have fueled China's defensive actions.[111] In contrast, a Chinese official asserted that the PRC spoke in defense of Myanmar because "we noticed that there was a lot of progress made," such as legislative revisions and granting the

---

[110] Tate, interview.   [111] Tate, interview.

ILO access.[112] After 2012, following the junta's introduction of political reforms and the release of political prisoners, including Aung San Suu Kyi, the ILO lessened its scrutiny of Myanmar, which no longer faced an annual special sitting before the CCAS.[113]

In addition to Myanmar, China offered similar support to other countries, particularly Belarus, which it defended seven times, making a statement every year between 2005 and 2016. For example, in 2005, the PRC government representative noted that "the Government of Belarus was taking positive steps to give effect to the recommendations of the Commission of Inquiry and had made progress in this respect. The government had also reiterated its willingness to cooperate with the ILO."[114] In 2007, it offered even more robust backing for Belarus by asserting that

[h]is government noted with satisfaction that the Government had been faithfully implementing the recommendations of the Commission of Inquiry since the Conference in 2006. The Government had been engaged in the drafting of the Trade Union Law in cooperation with the social partners and the [ILO] Office, as well as the establishment of a tripartite dialogue mechanism and the protection of trade union rights. He considered that meaningful measures had been put in place and positive progress was being made. He called on the Committee to recognize and encourage these efforts and the progress made by the Government and its willingness to continue the ongoing cooperation with the [ILO] Office. He expressed the hope and belief that further cooperation between the Government and the [ILO] Office would promote the effective application of Conventions Nos. 87 and 98.[115]

As with Myanmar, the ILO had increased its scrutiny of Belarus, including sending a 2004 Commission of Inquiry to investigate violations of freedom of association, protection of the right to organize, and respect for the right to collective bargaining.[116] Moreover, Belarus was compelled to appear

---

[112] Interview Chinese government official, June 12, 2012, Beijing, China.

[113] The ILO Governing Body decided in March 2013 not to hold future special sessions on forced labor in Myanmar. International Labour Organization, "ILO Lifts Remaining Restrictions on Myanmar," press release, June 18, 2013, www.ilo.org/ilc/ILCSessions/ 102/media-centre/news/WCMS_216355/lang–en/index.htm.

[114] ILO, "International Labour Conference, Report of the Conference Committee on the Application of Standards, 93rd Session," (2005), www.ilo.org/public/english/standards/ relm/ilc/ilc93/pdf/pr-22-2.pdf, accessed October 15, 2018, Part 2, Observations and Information Concerning Particular Countries, 22/24.

[115] ILO, "International Labour Conference, Report of the Conference Committee on the Application of Standards, 95th Session," (2007), Part 2, Observations on and Information Concerning Particular Countries, 22/21.

[116] ILO, "Report of Commissions of Inquiry, Belarus," http://ilo.org/public/libdoc/ilo/P/ 09604/09604%282004-87-series-B-special-suppl%29.pdf, accessed October 15, 2018. On PRC interests with Belarus, see Jan Cienski, "Belarus Looks to China for Investment in Infrastructure," *Financial Times*, July 22, 2013.

before the Conference Committee eleven years in a row from 2005 through 2016. As noted previously, China is deeply critical of this kind of selective or country-specific human rights monitoring.

Beijing's interventions for the other eleven countries were similar to its protection of Myanmar and Belarus in numerous respects. First, the majority of these countries came under the repeated gaze of the CCAS. Like Belarus and Myanmar, Bangladesh, Colombia, Pakistan, Uzbekistan, Venezuela, and Zimbabwe were called before the Committee numerous times. Second, the PRC's words repeatedly drew attention to information provided by the government in question, especially any signs of progress, no matter how minute; encouraged the ILO to use technical assistance and capacity building; and advocated leniency. For example, the PRC's 2005 statement called attention to Venezuela's "remarkable achievements in reforming its legislation and in promoting social dialogue."[117] In a similar vein, the PRC's 2010 statement noted Venezuela's "sincerity in its cooperation with social partners and the ILO."[118] In the case of Colombia, in 2004 the PRC stated plainly that "Colombia should not appear in the special paragraph."[119] Chinese representatives often framed the labor violations as being due to lack of capacity or economic development while downplaying the importance of the political will of the government involved. For example, in 2007 the PRC encouraged the CCAS to keep in mind that Bangladesh was an "underdeveloped country" and further that "economic development was key to overcoming challenges."[120]

While the PRC has shielded allies, it has been careful not to overplay its protector role. Other ILO Conference Committee participants also acknowledged that Beijing was not a frequent intervener and its conduct did not amount to attempting to break or constrain the regime.[121] These impressions are an indication of the degree to which China had become adept at selectively protecting allies without doing so in a way that would

---

[117] ILO, "International Labour Conference, Report of the Conference Committee on the Application of Standards, 93rd Session," (2005), accessed October 15, 2018, Part 2, Observations and Information Concerning Particular Countries, 22/48.

[118] ILO, "International Labour Conference, "Report of the Conference Committee on the Application of Standards, Report of the Conference Committee on the Application of Standards, 97th Session," (2010), www.ilo.org/wcmsp5/groups/public/—ed_norm/—normes/documents/publication/wcms_145220.pdf, accessed October 15, 2018, Part 2, Observations on and Information Concerning Particular Countries, 16/60.

[119] ILO, "International Labour Conference, Report of Conference Committee on the Application of Standards, 92nd Session," (2004), Part 2, Observations and Information Concerning Particular Countries, 24/26.

[120] ILO, "International Labour Conference, Report of the Conference Committee on the Application of Standards, 95th Session," (2007), Part 2, Observations on and Information Concerning Particular Countries, 22/75.

[121] Potter, interview; Benedict, interview; and Tate, interview.

earn it a reputation of disrupting the CCAS. As Table 5.3 revealed, Beijing intervened in only a small minority of cases, usually between one and six instances out of twenty-five annual CCAS cases. Moreover, because of the Conference Committee's limited visibility and minimal civil society and media attention, these were low-cost PRC interventions that helped bolster its human rights allies.

Aside from solidarity or mutual protection, the PRC's protective statements may also have fostered bilateral goodwill and cemented ties with countries where it has broader bilateral interests, such as geostrategic and economic concerns, including its need to secure raw materials and energy resources.[122] For example, Myanmar's geostrategic location provides the PRC with access to the Indian Ocean, a buffer with India, and a possible source for natural gas and a site for an overland oil pipeline. [123] Venezuela, which the PRC spoke on behalf of seven times, is an important source of oil and a recipient of significant Chinese energy investment.[124] In a similar vein, Algeria, which the PRC defended in 2015, possesses oil and gas resources and it is one of Africa's largest oil producing states.[125] China's need for oil has made it the world's fasting-growing oil consumer and the third-largest global net importer. It thus has an interest in helping to develop and invest in oil resources abroad.[126]

---

[122] Several observers suspected a link between Beijing's bilateral relationships and interests and its CCAS statements. Tate, interview; Elmiger, interview; and Benedict, interview. On China's interests with the developing world, see David Zweig, "The Rise of a New 'Trading Nation,'" in *China, the Developing World, and the New Global Dynamic*, eds. Lowell Dittmer and George T. Yu (Boulder, Colorado: Lynne Rienner, 2010), 40 and 55, and Mel Gurtov, "Changing Perspectives and Policies," in *China, the Developing World, and the New Global Dynamic*, eds. Lowell Dittmer and George T. Yu (Boulder, Colorado: Lynne Rienner, 2010), 23. Similar points made by Joel Wuthnow, *Chinese Diplomacy and the UN Security Council: Beyond the Veto* (New York: Routledge, 2012), 34; Yu Zhao, "China and International 'Human Rights Diplomacy,'" *China: An International Journal* 9, no. 2 (September 2011), and Julia Bader, "Propping Up Dictators? Economic Cooperation from China and Its Impact on Authoritarian Persistence in Party and Non-party Regimes," *European Journal of Political Research* 54, no. 4 (2015): 655–672. For an account of China's use of economic leverage, see Stefan Halper, *The Beijing Consensus: How China's Authoritarian Model Will Dominate the Twenty-first Century* (New York: Basic Books, 2010), 107–119.

[123] "China Relations with Myanmar, Welcome Neighbor," *The Economist*, September 9 ,2010, www.economist.com/node/16996935, accessed October 1, 2017. See also "Myanmar Pipeline gives China Faster Supply of Oil from Middle East," *South China Morning Post*, April 12, 2017, www.scmp.com/news/china/economy/article/2086837/myanmar-pipeline-gives-china-faster-supply-oil-middle-east, accessed July 11, 2018.

[124] See also Dittmer, "China and the Developing World," 6.

[125] Shinn and Eisenman, *China and Africa*, 234.

[126] Chris Zambelis, "China's Inroads into North Africa: An Assessment of Sino-Algerian Relations," *China Brief* 10, issue 1 (2010). On authoritarian collaboration, see von Soest, "Democracy Prevention," 629, and Rachel Vanderhill, *Promoting authoritarianism abroad* (Boulder: CO, Lynne Rienner, 2013), 6.

While China's defense of these countries in the CCAS may have shored up bilateral ties and served its national interests, given the PRC's growing economic, military, and political power, it has many other tools at its disposal to advance bilateral ties, including foreign assistance aid, development loans, investment, trade, market access, military patronage, and diplomatic support.[127] China indeed deploys its foreign aid based on foreign policy considerations, including the UN voting behavior of other nations who take positions that align with Beijing.[128] Along these lines, the China–Africa Development Fund, a Chinese government vehicle, is projected to raise $5 billion and has established a number of Special Economic Zones.[129] China's largesse toward Algeria is illustrative of the range of resources China has at its disposal. Algeria has benefited from PRC military training, technology, investment ($387 million between 2000 and 2007), arms exports, purchase of exports ($4.4 billion in 2010), infrastructure development, and a strategic partnership announced by President Hu Jintao during a 2004 visit.[130] China has also been a stalwart backer of Zimbabwe since the 1980s, where it has nurtured relations through loans, trade agreements (PRC imports amounted to $246 million in 2010), investment (PRC investment was valued at $600 million in 2007), medical teams, scholarship programs, as well as a $1 billion thermal power station.[131] Along similar lines, the PRC's support to Myanmar has included providing

---

[127] For China's efforts to secure access to oil, see Chung-chian Teng, "Democracy, Development and China's Acquisition of Oil in the Third World," in *Dancing with the Dragon: China's Emergence in the Developing World*, eds. Dennis Hickey and Baoguang Guo (Boulder, Colorado: Rowman & Littlefield Publishers, Inc. 2010), 105.

[128] See Axel Dreher, Andreas Fuchs, Brad Pares, Austin M. Strange, and Michael J. Tierney, "Apples and Dragon Fruits: The Determinants of Aid and Other Forms of State Financing from China to Africa," *International Studies Quarterly* 62 (2018): 182–194, and Andreas Fuchs and Marina Rudyak, "The Motives of China's Foreign Aid," in *Handbook of the International Political Economy of China*, ed. Ka Zeng (Northampton, MA: Edward Elgar Publishing, 2019): 392–410.

[129] Kweku Ampiah and Sanusha Naidu, "Introduction: Africa and China in the Post-Cold War Era," in *Crouching Tiger, Hidden Dragon? Africa and China*, eds. Kweku Ampiah and Sanusha Naidu (Scottsville, South Africa: University of Kwazulu-Natal Press, 2008): 9.

[130] Shinn and Eisenman, *China and Africa*, 234–235. The PRC was the first non-Arab country to recognize Algerian independence in 1962. Zambelis, "China's Inroads into North Africa: An Assessment of Sino-Algerian Relations."

[131] Shinn and Eisenman, *China and Africa*, 332–333. China recognized Zimbabwe the day it gained independence. Some Chinese support to Zimbabwe has been controversial, such as high-level military exchanges and equipment, in the face of an arms embargo imposed by Western countries in 2002. Other controversial PRC support includes a 2008 arms shipment that was turned away by other African countries while it was in transit and a $98 billion loan to build the Defense College, which was repayable in diamonds.

more than $1 billion in military weapons and vetoing a 2007 Security Council resolution criticizing human rights violations in Myanmar.[132] Thus, although its laudatory statements for human rights allies were likely helpful in earning further goodwill, they were probably not Beijing's most powerful tools.

As noted earlier in this chapter, because the PRC did not attract significant CCAS scrutiny and its four reviews before the Committee were mild, it needed little help getting through its Conference Committee reviews and none of the thirteen countries Beijing defended in the CCAS offered reciprocal protective statements. However, as will be explored in the following section all of these nations – Algeria, Belarus, Bangladesh, Colombia, Egypt, India, Kazakhstan, Myanmar, Pakistan, Qatar, Uzbekistan, Venezuela, and Zimbabwe – extended support to China in the UNCHR and the UN Human Rights Council (UNHRC). This suggests that Beijing may have sought to shore up a reserve of support that it could mobilize in other parts of the regime.

Other Countries' Support to China in the UN Commission on Human Rights and the UN Human Rights Council

Beijing has benefited from support from friendly governments in other venues, particularly the UNCHR and its successor body, the UNHRC. As described in Chapters 2 and 4, Beijing often faced country-specific resolutions in the Commission after the 1989 Tiananmen crackdown and its ability to fend off resolutions was largely dependent on the backing of developing countries, including the countries Beijing defended in the ILO Conference Committee as well as the LMG. This same group of countries also delivered praise or soft comments and submitted vapid recommendations during the PRC's UPRs in the HRC since that body's creation in 2006.

Of the thirteen countries that Beijing defended in the ILO, between 1992 and 2005 all of the nations that held seats in the UNCHR voted at least once in favor of the no-action motion that China used to avert a resolution on its record in the UNCHR. As shown in Table 5.5, which captures the countries that supported no-action motions, ten countries – Algeria, Belarus, Bangladesh, Colombia, Egypt, India, Pakistan, Qatar,

---

Bronson Percival, *The Dragon Looks South: China and Southeast Asia in the New Century* (Westport, Connecticut: Praeger Security International, 2007), 39, and Gurtov, "Changing Perspectives and Policies," 23. Nondemocratic states are well aware of regional contagion effects; thus the PRC might also be especially concerned with preventing the spread of democracy in Asia.

Table 5.5 *UN Commission on Human Rights voting on PRC resolution no-action motion*

Year	Sponsor of no-action motion	Voting to prevent consideration of China resolution	Voting in favor of allowing consideration of a China resolution	Abstaining	Comments in support of China
1990[a]	Pakistan	Bangladesh, China, Cuba, Cyprus, Ethiopia, Ghana, India, Iraq, Madagascar, Nigeria, Pakistan, São Tomé and Príncipe, Somalia, Sri Lanka, Ukrainian Soviet Socialist Republic, USSR, Yugoslavia (17)	Belgium, Bulgaria, Canada, France, Germany, Hungary, Italy, Japan, Panama, Portugal, Spain, Swaziland, Sweden, United Kingdom, United States (15)	Argentina, Botswana, Brazil, Colombia, Gambia, Mexico, Morocco, Peru, Philippines, Senegal, Venezuela (11)	Cuba, Somalia
1991 1992[b]	No Resolution Pakistan	Angola, Bangladesh, Burundi, Chile, China, Cuba, Cyprus, Gambia, Ghana, India, Indonesia, Iran, Iraq, Kenya, Lesotho, Libya, Madagascar, Mauritania, Nigeria, Pakistan, Philippines, Somalia, Sri Lanka, Syria, Tunisia, Yugoslavia, Zambia (27)	– Australia, Austria, Canada, Costa Rica, Czech and Slovak Federal Republic, France, Germany, Hungary, Italy, Japan, Netherlands, Portugal, Russia, United Kingdom, United States (15)	Argentina, Brazil, Bulgaria, Colombia, Gabon, Mexico, Peru, Senegal, Uruguay, Venezuela (10)	– Cuba, Gambia, Iran, Libya, Mauritania, Sri Lanka, Syria

205

Table 5.5 (*cont.*)

Year	Sponsor of no-action motion	Voting to prevent consideration of China resolution	Voting in favor of allowing consideration of a China resolution	Abstaining	Comments in support of China
1993[c]	China	Angola, Bangladesh, Burundi, China, Cuba, Cyprus, Gabon, Guinea-Bissau, India, Indonesia, Iran, Kenya, Libya, Malaysia, Mauritania, Nigeria, Pakistan, Sri Lanka, Sudan, Syria, Tunisia, Zambia (22)	Australia, Austria, Bulgaria, Canada, Costa Rica, Czech Republic, Finland, France, Germany, Japan, Netherlands, Poland, Portugal, Romania, Russia, United Kingdom, United States (17)	Argentina, Barbados, Brazil, Chile, Colombia, Gambia, Lesotho, Mexico, Peru, Republic of Korea, Uruguay, Venezuela (12)	Cuba, Bangladesh, Iran, Malaysia, Mauritania, Nigeria, Pakistan, Sudan, Syria
1994[d]	China	Angola, Bangladesh, Cameroon, China, Côte d'Ivoire, Cuba, Gabon, Hungary, Indonesia, Iran, Kenya, Libya, Malaysia, Mauritania, Nigeria, Pakistan, Sri Lanka, Sudan, Syria, Togo (20)	Australia, Austria, Bulgaria, Canada, Costa Rica, Finland, France, Germany, Guinea-Bissau, Hungary, Italy, Japan, Netherlands, Russia, United Kingdom, United States (16)	Barbados, Brazil, Chile, Colombia, Cyprus, Ecuador, Lesotho, Malawi, Mauritania, Mauritius, Peru, Poland, Republic of Korea, Romanian, Tunisia, Uruguay, Venezuela (17)	Cuba, Iran, Mauritania, Nigeria, Pakistan, Sri Lanka, Syria
1995	China[e] (only year the no-action motion failed)	Algeria, Angola, Bangladesh, Bhutan, Cameroon, China, Côte d'Ivoire, Cuba, Egypt, Ethiopia, Gabon, India, Indonesia, Malaysia, Mauritania, Nepal,	Australia, Austria, Bulgaria, Canada, Dominican Republic, Ecuador, El Salvador, Finland, France, Germany, Guinea-Bissau, Hungary, Italy,	Benin, Brazil, Chile, Colombia, Malawi, Mauritius, Mexico, Republic of Korea, Venezuela (9)	Cuba, Bangladesh, India, Mauritania, Pakistan, Sri Lanka, South Korea, Sudan

Year	Country						
1996	China[f]	Algeria, Angola, Bangladesh, Belarus, Benin, Bhutan, Cameroon, China, Côte d'Ivoire, Cuba, Egypt, Ethiopia, Gabon, Guinea, India, Indonesia, Madagascar, Malaysia, Mali, Mauritania, Nepal, Pakistan, Peru, Sri Lanka, Uganda, Ukraine, Zimbabwe (27)	Australia, Austria, Brazil, Bulgaria, Canada, Chile, Denmark, Dominican Republic, Ecuador, El Salvador, France, Germany, Hungary, Italy, Japan, Malawi, Netherlands, Nicaragua, United Kingdom, United States (20)	Colombia, Mexico, Philippines, Republic of Korea, Russia, Venezuela (6)	Japan, Netherlands, Nicaragua, Philippines, Poland, Romania, Russia, United Kingdom, United States (22)	Pakistan, Peru, Sri Lanka, Sudan, Togo, Zimbabwe (22)	Angola, Bangladesh, Cuba, India Mauritania, Pakistan, Sri Lanka
1997	China[g]	Algeria, Angola, Bangladesh, Belarus, Benin, Bhutan, Cape Verde, China, Colombia, Cuba, Egypt, Ethiopia, Gabon, Guinea, India, Indonesia, Madagascar, Malaysia, Mali, Mozambique, Nepal, Pakistan, Sri Lanka, Uganda, Ukraine, Zaire, Zimbabwe (27)	Austria, Bulgaria, Canada, Chile, Czech Republic, Denmark, El Salvador, France, Germany, Ireland, Italy, Japan, Netherlands, Nicaragua, South Africa, United Kingdom, United States (17)	Argentina, Brazil, Dominican Republic, Ecuador, Mexico, Philippines, Republic of Korea, Russia, Uruguay (9)			Angola, Algeria, Bangladesh, Cuba, Egypt, Malaysia, Nepal, Pakistan, South Korea, Sri Lanka

Table 5.5 (*cont.*)

Year	Sponsor of no-action motion	Voting to prevent consideration of China resolution	Voting in favor of allowing consideration of a China resolution	Abstaining	Comments in support of China
1998	No Resolution				
1999	China[h]	Bangladesh, Bhutan, Botswana, Cape Verde, China, Colombia, Congo, Cuba, Democratic Republic of the Congo, India, Indonesia, Madagascar, Morocco, Mozambique, Nepal, Pakistan, Peru, Qatar, Russia, Sri Lanka, Sudan, Venezuela (22)	Austria, Canada, Czech Republic, El Salvador, France, Germany, Ireland, Italy, Japan, Latvia, Luxembourg, Norway, Poland, Rwanda, South Africa, United Kingdom, United States (17)	Argentina, Chile, Ecuador, Guatemala, Liberia, Mauritius, Mexico, Niger, Philippines, Republic of Korea, Romania, Senegal, Tunisia, Uruguay (14)	Cuba, Bangladesh, Nepal, Pakistan, Sri Lanka, Sudan
2000	China[i]	Bangladesh, Bhutan, Botswana, Burundi, China, Congo, Cuba, India, Indonesia, Madagascar, Morocco, Nepal, Niger, Nigeria, Pakistan, Peru, Qatar, Russia, Sri Lanka, Sudan, Venezuela, Zambia (22)	Canada, Colombia, Czech Republic, El Salvador, France, Germany, Guatemala, Italy, Japan, Latvia, Luxembourg, Norway, Poland, Portugal, Spain, Swaziland, United Kingdom, United States (18)	Argentina, Brazil, Chile, Ecuador, Liberia, Mauritius, Mexico, Philippines, Republic of Korea, Rwanda, Senegal, Tunisia (12)	Cuba, Bangladesh, Pakistan, Russia, Sri Lanka, Sudan
2001	China[j]	Algeria, Burundi, Cameroon, China, Cuba, India, Indonesia, Kenya, Liberia, Libyan	Belgium, Canada, Costa Rica, Czech Republic, France, Germany, Guatemala, Italy, Japan,	Argentina, Brazil, Colombia, Ecuador, Mauritius, Mexico, Peru, Republic of	Cuba, Indonesia, Libya, Pakistan Russia, Syria

Year					
		Arab Jamahiriya, Madagascar, Malaysia, Niger, Nigeria, Pakistan, Qatar, Russia, Saudi Arabia, Syrian Arab Republic, Thailand, Venezuela, Viet Nam, Zambia (23)	Latvia, Norway, Poland, Portugal, Romania, Spain, United Kingdom and United States (17)	Korea, Senegal, South Africa, Swaziland, Uruguay (12)	—
2002	No Resolution	—	—		—
2003	No Resolution	—	—		—
2004	China[k]	Bahrain, Bhutan, Brazil, Burkina Faso, China, Congo, Cuba, Egypt, Eritrea, Ethiopia, Gabon, India, Indonesia, Mauritania, Nepal, Nigeria, Pakistan, Qatar, Russia, Saudi Arabia, Sierra Leone, South Africa, Sri Lanka, Sudan, Swaziland, Togo, Ukraine, Zimbabwe (28)	Australia, Austria, Costa Rica, Croatia, France, Germany, Guatemala, Honduras, Hungary, Ireland, Italy, Japan, Netherlands, Sweden, United Kingdom, United States (16)	Argentina, Armenia, Chile, Dominican Republic, Mexico, Paraguay, Peru, Republic of Korea, Uganda (9)	Congo, Cuba, Indonesia, Mauritania, Pakistan, Russia, Sri Lanka, Sudan, Zimbabwe
2005	No Resolution	—	—		—

[a] UN Economic and Social Council, "Commission on Human Rights Report on the Forty-Sixth Session," January 29–March 9, 1990, UN Doc. E/CN.4/1990/94, paragraphs 363–369. Comments in support of China assumed to be those of countries that spoke and then voted in favor of Pakistan's no-action resolution.

[b] UN Economic and Social Council, "Commission on Human Rights Report of the Forty-Eighth Session," January 27–March 6, 1992, UN Doc. E/CN.4/1992/84, paragraphs 459–468. Comments in support of China assumed to be of those countries that spoke and then voted in favor of Pakistan's no-action resolution.

Table 5.5 (*cont.*)

Year	Sponsor of no-action motion	Voting to prevent consideration of China resolution	Voting in favor of allowing consideration of a China resolution	Abstaining	Comments in support of China

[c] UN Economic and Social Council, "Summary Record of the Sixty-Sixth Meeting," March 16, 1993, UN Doc. E/CN.4/1993/SR.66, paragraphs 54–86. Russia made comments that expressed both concern and understanding. Yet, it voted against China's no-action motion.

[d] UN Economic and Social Council, "Summary Record of the Sixth-Fifth Meeting," March 9, 1994, UN Doc. E/CN.4/1994/SR.65, paragraphs 24–35.

[e] UN Economic and Social Council, "Summary Record of the Fifty-Ninth Meeting," March 7, 1995, UN Doc. E/CN.4/1995/SR.59/Add.1, paragraphs 57–72; 1995 was the only year that China's no-action motion failed, but the resolution was defeated. It lost by one vote when Russia did not support the no-action motion but voted against the resolution. The ROK spoke of China's constructive engagement with the UN but abstained. Vote on the resolution itself was twenty in favor, twenty-one against, and twelve abstentions.

[f] UN Economic and Social Council, "Summary Record of the Fifty-Ninth Meeting," April 23, 1996, UN Doc. E/CN.4/1996/SR.59, paragraphs 31–58. India said the sponsors of the resolution seemed more motivated by political considerations than concern for human rights in China – so it would vote for China's no-action motion.

[g] UN Economic and Social Council, "Summary Record of the Sixty-Fifth Meeting," April 15, 1997, UN Doc. E/CN.4/1997/SR.65, paragraphs 48–91. The ROK noted room for improvement and advances made in the legal realm and stated that China's signing the International Covenant on Economic, Social and Cultural Rights was an encouraging sign of progress – so the delegation would abstain.

[h] UN Economic and Social Council, "Summary Record of the Fifty-First Meeting," April 23, 1999, UN Doc. E/CN.4/1999/SR.51, paragraphs 1–28.

[i] UN Economic and Social Council, "Summary Record of the Fifty-Fifth Meeting," April 18, 2000, UN Doc. E/CN.4/2000/SR.55, paragraphs 79–109.

[j] UN Economic and Social Council, "Summary Record of the Sixty-Second Meeting," April 23, 2001, UN Doc. E/CN.4/2001/SR.62, paragraphs 53–81. Russia said bilateral consultations were the best way to work on human rights in China because discussion within the UNCHR was politicized and counterproductive.

[k] UN Economic and Social Council, "Summary Record of the Fiftieth Meeting," April 15, 2004, UN Doc. E/CN.4/2004/SR.50, paragraphs 92–117.

Venezuela, and Zimbabwe – shielded China from a UNCHR resolution in at least one instance. All of the three remaining countries – Kazakhstan, Myanmar, and Uzbekistan – did not sit on the UNCHR.[133] Several other important points emerge from Table 5.5. First, a number of the countries Beijing protected in the CCAS were stalwart PRC backers. For example, during the years that they sat on the Commission, Egypt, Zimbabwe, Bangladesh, and Belarus consistently voted to block consideration of a China resolution.[134] Second, by 1999 when the PRC first began offering laudatory comments on behalf of these countries, it was prevailing in the UNCHR vote by comfortable margins.[135] As noted in Chapter 4, by the late 1990s there was also a distinct easing of human rights pressure on the PRC in the Commission on Human Rights as the EU abandoned a common position on backing a China resolution in 1997. Thus, although Beijing likely considered that making laudatory statements for these countries in the CCAS might pay dividends in the UNCHR, the support of other countries was not as critical as it may have been in the early to mid 1990s when the voting margins in the Commission were tighter. Yet, as will be discussed in the following section, Chinese leaders may have felt the need to secure a reservoir of support that could be triggered as needed.

China also benefited from friendly or mildly worded statements from these countries in the UNHRC, especially during its UPR. China is reported to have actively mobilized friendly countries to offer complementary words as a means to drown out negative comments.[136] During China's 2009 and 2013 UPRs all thirteen of the countries China assisted in the CCAS signed up to deliver statements and most of them came forth with platitudinous statements or bland recommendations and even praise.[137] In some instances, these countries asked for additional

---

[133] "Commission on Human Rights Archives, Membership," OHCHR, www.ohchr.org/EN/HRBodies/CHR/Pages/Membership.aspx, accessed July 11, 2018.

[134] Colombia also voted for the no-action motion in 1997 and 1999 but abstained six times. Colombia was on the UNCHR from 1983 through 1997 and again from 1999 through 2001. It abstained in 1990, 1992, 1993, 1994, 1995, and 1996. In 2000, it voted to bring a China resolution to the floor. Venezuela sided with the PRC in 1999 and 2001 yet voted against China's position in 2000 and abstained seven times. Venezuela was a UNCHR member from 1985 to 1996, and again from 1998 through 2003. It abstained in 1990, 1992, 1993, 1994, 1995, 1996, and 2001.

[135] Baker, "Human Rights, Europe and the People's Republic of China," 55–56.

[136] The PRC also entreated Western countries not to raise sensitive issues, such as Tibet and Xinjiang. Interview with Western European diplomat, May 26, 2011, Geneva, Switzerland.

[137] In 2009, when the speakers list was established on a first-come, first-serve basis, this resulted in queuing starting in the early morning as countries sought to secure a speaking slot. Ultimately, 115 countries signed up to speak during China's UPR, but

information on certain developments, which likely was intended to give the PRC government an opportunity to further make its case and portray even small changes, actions, policies as evidence of progress. Tables 5.6 and 5.7 capture the statements and recommendations and show that the thrust of these countries' words sympathized with the PRC, commended it, offered soft-ball comments, and even occasionally condoned human rights abuses. A number of these nations also drew attention to formulaic steps that the PRC government had taken, such as releasing a National Human Rights Action Plan, without noting growing repression against groups such as domestic human rights lawyers. Some states offered pure praise, such as Egypt, which in 2009 delivered the following statement:

Noting that China has accomplished important leaps along the path of economic development, moving in 30 years from being a poor country into becoming the third biggest economy in the world, Egypt expressed continuing support to China in its endeavour to pursue development, national unity and territorial integrity. It praised the commitment to the protection and promotion of human rights demonstrated in the new constitutional provision. It further praised China's efforts to ameliorate and promote human rights protection, taking into consideration the accompanying challenges of being a country with 1.3 billion people. It understood China's need to keep the death penalty, which it recognized is strictly controlled and applied with extreme caution and is not applied to any person under 18 or to any pregnant women.[138]

Even more troubling, some comments excused human rights violations, such as Pakistan's 2013 recommendation that seemed to give cover to repression in Xinjiang as it advised the PRC to "[c]ontinue to counter East Turkestan terrorist organizations to prevent their violent activities, and assist the ordinary people being deceived and victimized."[139] Some of these countries also offered soft or vacuous UPR recommendations that benefited China by enabling it to claim acceptance of a greater percentage of recommendations.[140] These kinds of statements also influenced the overall tenor of the review, drowning out more meaningful, incisive comments that draw attention to needed areas of reform. Noting these practices, an ambassador complained that during the UPR

---

due to time constraints, 55 countries were unable to deliver their statements. Ten of the thirteen countries China defended in the CCAS were able to make statements and three of them were not. However, all of the thirteen countries had signed up. Kinzelbach, *The EU's Human Rights Dialogue with China*, 172, and UN General Assembly, "Universal Periodic Review, Report of the Working Group on the Universal Periodic Review, China," March 3, 2009, UN Doc. A/HRC/11/25, paragraph 26.

[138] UN General Assembly, "Report of the Working Group on the Universal Periodic Review, China," December 4, 2013, A/HRC/25/5, paragraph 36.

[139] Ibid., paragraph 186, recommendation 239.   [140] Ibid., paragraph 82.

Table 5.6 *Statements and recommendations by select countries during China's February 2009 UPR*[a]

Country	Statement/recommendation
Algeria (statement)	Regretted politicization of human rights in China during the UPR; noted China's achievements toward the Millennium Develop Goals; recommended China share with developing countries its good practices; saluted the importance China gives to cooperation and exchange on human rights; recommended China continue to explore development methods and human rights implementation in harmony with its characteristics and the needs of Chinese society, including ratification of the International Covenant on Civil and Political Rights (ICCPR) as soon as possible
Algeria (recommendation)	(1) Pursue the implementation of the concept of Scientific Outlook on Development Perspectives to ensure comprehensive, coordinated and lasting development and to continue building a harmonious society marked by democracy, law, equity and justice; (2) Continue to explore methods of development and implementation of human rights in harmony with its characteristics, its realities and the needs of Chinese society; (3) Share with interested developing countries their good practices in the implementation of this concept of Scientific Outlook on Development; (4) In accordance with its imperatives dictated by its national realities, to proceed to legislative, judicial and administrative reform as well as create conditions permitting the ratification, as soon as possible, of the ICCPR; (5) As soon as possible proceed with publishing and implementing its National Human Rights Action Plan for 2009–2010
Colombia (statement)	Drew attention to China's national report; praised efforts in the area of economic and social rights; stressed importance China attached to rights of women and children; requested further information on progress and results in regard to children and development
Egypt (recommendation)	Continue its national efforts for the promotion and protection of human rights, including in the area of strengthening its national human rights architecture; In light of its national realities, continue to implement the policy of strictly controlling and applying the death penalty
India (statement)	Welcomed China's commitment to engaging in exchanges and cooperation with other countries on human rights and in promoting a non-selective approach at the international level; praised the tremendous strides China has made in reducing poverty and attaining Millennium Development Goals ahead of schedule; noted with interest the PRC government's upcoming National Human Rights Action Plan

Table 5.6 (*cont.*)

Country	Statement/recommendation
Myanmar (statement)	Welcomed the significant progress made in education, culture and public health, which is a testimony to China's political will to promote and protect human rights; praised China for "remarkable results" in improving the wellbeing of its population; reaffirmed "One China Policy," sympathized with and understood human rights challenges facing China; opposed politicizing human rights issues and using them to interfere in internal affairs
Qatar (recommendation)	Attach more importance to the protection of the rights of the child through national plans for economic and social development
Qatar (statement)	Expressed appreciation for China's development, especially on economic and social rights; welcomed the PRC's national report, including noting difficulties and challenges; appreciated accomplishments on children's rights and welcomed ratification of the Optional Protocol to the Convention on the Rights of the Child on the involvement of children in armed conflict; recommended attaching more importance to the protection of children's rights through economic and social development; and asked about plans to promote the culture of human rights among local government officials
Pakistan (statement)	Stated that China does not require external advice securing the rights of its people as it has taken concrete steps; stated that the tendency to politicize the UPR should be guarded against, noting comments about Tibet, reflected political agendas and not the situation in Tibet, which was an inalienable part of China; commented that the criminal violence in Tibet last year was due to external perpetrators; noted that the Chinese government abided by its international human rights obligations and domestic laws; noted the tremendous developments in China and China's accomplishments
Uzbekistan (statement)	Welcomed the PRC's efforts in promoting and protecting human rights, which attested to the PRC's commitment to human rights; stressed positive results related to women, children, the disabled, education and human rights, civil society, and health; drew attention to the PRC's National Human Rights Action Plan for 2009–2010
Venezuela (statement)	Commended China for attaching same importance to economic, social and cultural rights and the right to development; noted efforts to reduce poverty; encouraged China to continue poverty reduction work; noted that China put people at the center of its policies
Zimbabwe (statement)	Praised China's economic and human rights achievements; recommended that the PRC continue its poverty reduction programs and foreign language media, which would help the outside world understand China; PRC is often deliberately and grossly misunderstood

Table 5.6 (cont.)

Country	Statement/recommendation
Zimbabwe (recommendation)	Continue its poverty reduction programmes; Continue to support and encourage the further development of PRC media's use of English and other foreign languages to help the outside world better understand China, including objective coverage of China, a country that too often is deliberately and grossly misunderstood by some international media

[a] For these statements in full, see UN General Assembly, "Report of the Working Group on the Universal Periodic Review, China," October 5, 2009, A/HRC/11/25, paragraphs 26–60.

Table 5.7 *Statements and recommendations by countries during China's February 2013 UPR*[a]

Country	Statement
Algeria (statement)	Appreciated the amendment to the Criminal Procedure Law and the Law on Lawyers, broadening the range of cases open to them
Algeria (recommendation)	Continue to strictly observe the stipulations on evidence used to examine and decide on cases of the death penalty and adopt stricter standards in this regard; implement the employment priority strategy and ensure equal employment opportunities to urban and rural residents
Bangladesh (statement)	Noted that China was addressing the challenges caused by rapid social development and appreciated its cooperation with developing countries
Bangladesh (recommendations)	Strengthen efforts to promote orderly development of internet and protect the legitimate rights and interests of ordinary people while reinforcing the legislation on internet information protection and supervision; continue its international cooperation to contribute to the development of the world economy
Belarus (statement)	Welcomed measures to improve social and cultural rights and the situation of ethnic minorities
Belarus (recommendation)	Improve further means and methods for vocational education of persons in prison in order to assist in their later integration into the society; continue efforts in environmental protection and in improving living conditions
Egypt (statement)	Commended the contribution of China to achieving internationally agreed development goals through South–South cooperation
Egypt (recommendation)	Continue carrying out administrative and judicial reforms to prepare for the ratification of ICCPR; consider acceding to the

Table 5.7 (*cont.*)

Country	Statement
	International Convention on the Protection of the Rights of All Migrant Workers and Members of Their Families; continue observing its national legal safeguards surrounding the application of the death penalty as one of the legitimate tools of criminal justice; maintain its effective protection for the family as the fundamental and natural unit of society
India (statement)	Requested information on re-education through labor system, while noting China's National Human Rights Action Plan
India (recommendation)	Make efforts to ensure the participation of women in public affairs especially in Village Committees; Continue to promote economic development in ethnic minority regions and strengthen their capacity for development
Kazakhstan (statement)	Appreciated efforts for realizing the rights of ethnic minorities, including the Kazakh minority
Myanmar (statement)	Welcomed progress toward attaining Millennium Development Goals (MDGs), and noted ongoing judicial reform and subsequent changes to legislation
Myanmar (recommendation)	Strengthen institutional guarantees for the legitimate rights and interests of journalists; continue to use the platform of the All-China Federation of Trade Unions to safeguard the rights of employees to get employment, pay and social security
Pakistan (statement)	Commended promotion of economic and social development in Xinjiang Autonomous Region, ensuring freedom of belief and stability
Pakistan (recommendation)	Strengthen efforts to take action against criminals who instigate, intimidate, or help others to commit self-immolation; continue to counter East Turkestan terrorist organizations to prevent their violent activities, and assist the ordinary people being deceived and victimized
Qatar (statement)	Commended actions to protect and promote human rights implemented under National Human Rights Action Plan
Qatar (recommendation)	Continue efforts in theoretical research related to national human rights organs: improve maternity care services especially in rural areas and work to increase the percentage of women who give birth in hospitals and to decrease maternal mortality rate
Uzbekistan (statement)	Noted China's National Human Rights Action Plan, legal reforms and attention paid to social and economic development in the regions
Uzbekistan (recommendation)	Include human rights education in training programs for government officials; step up measures to bring to justice persons who instigate others to commit acts of self-immolation
Venezuela (statement)	Praised the universal social pension system, the wide-reaching medical insurance system and high voter turnout
Venezuela (recommendation)	Continue to guarantee the rights of ethnic minorities on an equal footing and in accordance with the law

Table 5.7 *(cont.)*

Country	Statement
Zimbabwe (statement)	Praised the comprehensive report, human rights programmes and the implementation of recommendations from the first UPR
Zimbabwe (recommendation)	Continue to implement policies and programmes aimed at fulfilling the interests of the disabled; continue to extend its State scholarship programmes to ensure that students do not drop out of school because of poverty

[a] UN General Assembly, "Report of the Working Group on the Universal Periodic Review, China," December 4, 2013, A/HRC/25/5, paragraphs 25–185. Bangladesh, Belarus, and Kazakhstan had signed up to speak, but were unable to deliver their statements due to time constraints.

you already begin to see signs of … horse trading, which defeats the whole purpose. You see countries approaching other countries and saying 'Please be nice to me, because I was nice in your UPR.' And I have seen … I can tell you that I have even received two requests in written form–which to me was outstanding, and astonishing–from two countries, proposing that they will behave nicely to us in exchange for us behaving nicely to them.[141]

He further suggested that the driver for this behavior appeared to be a sense of solidarity and mutual defense.

China also relied on some of these nations to shield it from a 2014 attempt by an NGO to observe a moment of silence in the HRC for Cao Shunli, a human rights defender who died in Chinese police custody.[142] During that vote, the PRC delegation lobbied vigorously and five of the thirteen countries it defended in the CCAS – Algeria, India, Kazakhstan, Pakistan, and Venezuela – were HRC members, and all five of them voted to shield China from the embarrassment of the moment of silence.[143] Commenting on the PRC's ability to secure these votes, an ambassador posted to the UN stated that

the support for China, it's a well-cemented, longstanding exercise of solidarity by a large group of countries that felt the need to support China on an issue that was

[141] Interview with an Ambassador to the UN, March 14, 2016, via Skype.
[142] For Beijing's use of foreign aid in the Council, see Andreas Fuchs and Marina Rudyak, "The Motives of China's Foreign Aid" in: Zeng, Ka. (ed.) *Handbook of the International Political Economy of China*, Cheltenham, UK; Northampton, MA: Edward Elgar Publishing, 2019, 397.
[143] Interview with Western European diplomat, June 14, 2016, Geneva, Switzerland, and interview with Western European diplomat, June 22, 2016, Geneva, Switzerland. PRC diplomats lobbied countries both in Geneva and in capitals throughout the world.

particularly important for China ... So rather than interpreting the vote in China's favor as a response to a last-minute request, I think it goes deeper into many countries' position.... And if there is an issue [of importance] to China, the rest of the room would rally behind China, and so on and so forth, because 'today is for me, tomorrow is for you.' The issue becomes secondary. The primary driver is political solidarity. So 'I support you, because you will support me tomorrow on whatever issue I want you to support me.'[144]

As he described it, this reciprocal protection meant that during China's UPR "[t]hese countries would praise, just praise, China. They will find some development, some changes, that they would praise ... particularly with fellow Like-Minded [Group] Countries, they will make sure that they will use their slot to praise the progress taking place in that particular country."[145] Thus, China's CCAS interventions for other countries appear to have translated into similar assistance in other human rights venues.

While it is customary for allied states to cooperate or coordinate, other major powers, especially the United States and European countries, have not exhibited similar behavior. As a former US diplomat put it, "[E]ven though we have lobbied, such as for resolutions on Sudan or a particular human rights theme we have never lobbied to defend ourselves ... and I don't recall European nations doing lobbying to avoid" human rights scrutiny.[146] As this diplomatic source put it, when the United States has faced criticism in the regime, "we have tried to address the issues on its merits," by explaining our position.[147] A senior State Department official concurred and further explained that the "U.S. would be unlikely to mobilize such diplomatic resources and would be more likely to shrug

---

[144] Interview with an ambassador to the UN, March 14, 2016, via Skype. During the debate over a moment of silence, the vote: in favor of moment of silence – the United Kingdom, the United States, Austria, the Czech Republic, Estonia, France, Germany, Ireland, Italy, Japan, Mexico, South Korea, Romania (13); against – South Africa, the United Arab Emirates, Venezuela, Vietnam, Algeria, Benin, China, Congo, Cuba, Ethiopia, India, Indonesia, Kazakhstan, Kuwait, Maldives, Morocco, Namibia, Pakistan, Russia, Saudi Arabia (20); abstain – Argentina, Botswana, Brazil, Burkina Faso, Chile, Costa Rica, Côte d'Ivoire, Gabon, Montenegro, Peru, Philippines, Sierra Leone (12); absent – Macedonia and Kenya (2). UN Web TV, "China, UPR Report Consideration - 41st Meeting, 25th Regular Session Human Rights Council," http://webtv.un.org/meetings-events/human-rights-council/regular-sessions/25th-session/watch/china-upr-report-consideration-41st-meeting-25th-regular-session-human-rights-council/3369309459001, accessed October 16, 2018.
[145] Interview with an ambassador to the UN, March 14, 2016, via Skype. As another diplomat put it, "China has been among the most successful LMG countries to use the group for protection, probably because they have things to give such as aid." Interview with a former US diplomat, October 28, 2019 by phone.
[146] Interview with a former US diplomat, October 28, 2019, by phone.
[147] Interview with a former US diplomat, October 28, 2019, by phone.

off UN scrutiny."[148] Moreover, given the US interagency process, the departments most keen to deflect negative human rights attention, particularly the Departments of Justice and Defense, "would have great difficulty convincing their State Department counterparts to coordinate such exchanges of support."[149]

Conclusion

This chapter examined the PRC's behavior in yet another distinct component of the human rights regime, which differs significantly from the Commission on Human Rights and the HRC covered in the previous chapter. This chapter examined a body with a more restricted mandate that encompassed only ratified ILO conventions. As a result of its narrow mandate and the PRC's refusal to ratify key ILO conventions the Conference Committee paid minimal attention to the PRC's labor rights abuses. Consequently, Beijing did not pursue changes to the Conference Committee and was content to act as a taker. Unlike its behavior vis-à-vis OPCAT and the UNHRC, in this case, even as a more familiar actor, the PRC did not shift to a constrainer role. However, it adjusted its behavior to benefit from the Committee's working methods by using it as a venue to offer protective statements for friendly countries facing CCAS scrutiny. Beijing's instrumental use of the Committee to bolster its political allies indicates that even as a taker its behavior often inched toward that of a constrainer. Yet, along the spectrum of state typologies, I argue that China operated within the realm of a taker because it did not pursue modifications to the regime and its behavior did not harm the overall functioning of the CCAS or the Committee's authority.

Thus, even as a taker of this part of the regime, its instrumental use of this venue shows that the PRC's conduct did not uphold and strengthen the purposes and intentions of the human rights regime. In fact, the PRC's interventions called on the Conference Committee to ease pressure, even in the face of reports of severe labor rights violations. Moreover, Beijing may have used its participation to advance its own interests as it responded to requests from countries for assistance, which enabled it to more firmly establish solidarity with human rights allies and shore up bilateral relationships. This behavior supports the idea that states, particularly once they have accepted the regime, might use regime

---

[148] Interview with former US Assistant Secretary of State, November 29, 2019, Austin, Texas, United States.
[149] Ibid. The Department of Defense was specifically mentioned with respect to the abuses associated with Abu Ghraib.

rules and procedures to their advantage.[150] This instrumental behavior also indicates that although Beijing acted as a taker of the CCAS, its behavior did not amount to an internalization of human rights norms. Further, the mutual defense and protection that Beijing and other countries engaged in may have weakened the normative pressure that the human rights regime is meant to exert on states to bring their practices into compliance.

---

[150] See Krasner, "U.S. Commercial and Monetary Policy," 52, and Samuel Kim, "China's International Organizational Behavior," in *Chinese Foreign Policy: Theory and Practice*, eds. Thomas W. Robinson and David Shambaugh (Oxford: Clarendon Press 1994), 431.

In the components of the regime investigated in this book, China alternated between the roles of taker and constrainer. Beijing acted as a constrainer during the drafting of the Optional Protocol to the Convention against Torture (OPCAT) and the creation of the Human Rights Council (HRC) and assumed the role of taker toward the Convention against Torture (CAT) and the ILO (International Labour Organization) Conference Committee on the Application of Standards (CCAS or Conference Committee). As suggested in Chapter 1, these roles should be viewed along a spectrum and the PRC often operated along the boundary of taker and constrainer. The finding that Beijing did not assume one constant role toward the human rights regime but rather shifted between attempting to weaken the regime and accepting it gives rise to several questions, including, What accounts for this variation? Why didn't Beijing pursue other roles, particularly that of a breaker? As outlined in Chapter 1, I offer four explanatory variables that help explain China's posture vis-à-vis the regime, including the Chinese leadership's antipathy toward scrutiny of its human rights record; Chinese officials' existing ideas that favored a Westphalian brand of sovereignty and stressed the importance of national, developmental, and cultural factors in the realization of human rights; the PRC's desire to cultivate a positive international image as agreeable and cooperative; and the PRC government's degree of familiarity with the international human rights regime.

This chapter begins with a brief discussion of the weight of these variables in the case studies, especially parsing their determinative impact on China's posture. This is followed by a detailed discussion of each of the explanatory variables, including their relative power and how the variables interacted with each other, especially in instances when they pulled Beijing in different directions. By doing so, this chapter adds to our understanding of the drivers and motivations behind Beijing's behavior, and the factors that might cause the PRC to attempt to act as a constrainer versus accepting the regime. After the discussion of these determinative variables, I consider Beijing's cooperation with other countries as a secondary influence on its conduct. I refer to this as a secondary influence because even though China's collaboration with these countries did not dictate its role, it, nevertheless, shaped Beijing's conduct in distinctive and significant ways.

The Explanatory Variables in the Case Studies

As documented in Chapter 3, China acted as a taker toward CAT and a constrainer vis-à-vis OPCAT. During the CAT discussions, Beijing's taker posture was influenced strongly by a desire to cultivate a positive global image, and to a lesser extent limited familiarity with the regime. Both of these variables pushed the PRC toward the role of taker, especially its status as a regime novice. Together these variables inclined the PRC toward a quiescent posture. For example, during its first two years in the drafting group Chinese diplomats made no statements. Even when they began expressing positions in 1984, their interventions were infrequent and they avoided holding up progress. In this case study, China's preexisting ideas that favored state sovereignty while placing limits on the reach of the international regime carried less explanatory weight. Thus, although Beijing expressed misgivings with the CAT clause on universal jurisdiction, which required states to prosecute suspected torturers and implement legislation, Chinese officials quickly relented in order to avoid obstructing adoption of the Convention. In this instance, the PRC's concern with its image trounced the import of its ideas on limiting the international human rights regime's scope. Crucially, unlike the other case studies, the drafting of CAT predated the 1989 Tiananmen Square massacre. As a result, this variable had not yet emerged as a significant influence. The absence of this as a factor meant that Beijing was much less likely to attempt to constrain the regime or vigorously resist robust monitoring of its record. In later years, this explanatory variable emerged as the prevailing variable and often caused Beijing discomfort with the regime and inclined it to act as a constrainer.

The second half of Chapter 3 documents very different behavior during the negotiations that spanned 1992 through 2002 and resulted in OPCAT as Beijing acted as a constrainer of the regime. The post-1989 timing was significant as China's aversion to human rights scrutiny became a potent force in determining its behavior. As documented in Chapter 2, Beijing loathed the public scrutiny it received, including the introduction of annual UNCHR (UN Commission on Human Rights) resolutions on its record as well as growing attention from treaty bodies and special procedures. This helps explain the PRC's insistent position against country-specific scrutiny by the Sub-Committee on the

Prevention of Torture (SPT) proposed under OPCAT. Throughout the Optional Protocol negotiations Chinese diplomats insisted that the Sub-Committee must not be able to focus on individual countries and that investigative visits must be determined on a rotational basis with the postvisit report being confidential. The post-Tiananmen timing strongly shaped Beijing's opposition to the robust investigative and reporting authority of the SPT. The CCP (Chinese Communist Party) government did not want this kind of wide access to become a norm within the international regime. China's posture was also strongly shaped by its ideas about the intersection between the state's sovereign jurisdiction and the reach of the international regime. These ideas meant that Beijing asserted positions to limit the SPT's investigative access; affirm state sovereignty by referencing respect for domestic legislation and the importance of nonintervention in internal affairs; and grant states greater control over visits, reporting, and the SPT's composition. Beijing's desire to cultivate an image as a constructive actor was a discernible though weaker explanatory variable. It did not prevent Beijing from acting as a constrainer but it did temper the degree of its resistance to OPCAT, inclining it toward a lower profile in the drafting group and moderating its opposition during the adoption process. While the PRC had become much more familiar with the international human rights regime, this did not necessarily cause it to act as a constrainer. However, greater familiarity meant that Chinese diplomats possessed the skills and ability to maneuver within the regime and play roles beyond that of a taker when the other more powerful explanatory factors inclined the PRC in that direction.

China's constrainer posture during the negotiations over the HRC was also shaped strongly by its abhorrence toward scrutiny of its human rights record. As the successor body to the UNCHR, where it faced repeated attempts to spotlight its troubled record through resolutions, Chinese diplomats sought to dilute the ability of this part of the regime to focus on any single country as a way of protecting itself. This explanatory variable also accounts for its resistance to a high bar for HRC membership, such as human rights criteria, since this would likely have increased scrutiny of its human rights violations during HRC elections and potentially barred it and many of its defenders from gaining a seat. Beijing's antipathy for scrutiny of its record also informed its more specific positions on the HRC's institutional characteristics, including its general opposition to country-specific attention, especially its attempt to introduce a rule that resolutions targeted at a single country could only be passed by a two-thirds vote; efforts to weaken the Sub-Commission and special procedures; and insistence that the Universal Periodic Review (UPR) be based on a rotational system so that it could not be used to draw selective attention to particular countries. Ideational influences also pushed Beijing in the direction of constrainer as it asserted the import of particular national, cultural, and developmental conditions in the realization of human rights and the primacy of state sovereignty. Its fidelity to these ideas meant that Beijing sought to give states greater control over the international regime, such as insisting that states elect the individual experts serving as special procedure mandate holders and members of the HRC's Advisory Committee. For example, during discussions over the composition of the Advisory Committee, which replaced the Sub-Commission, PRC diplomats articulated that this entity's work "should reflect the development of human rights taking into account the diversified cultures, histories and religions" of the world and a preference for a more expansive body to ensure "representation of main legal, cultural and civilizational (sic) traditions and perspectives."[1] Although weaker than the previous two variables, the Chinese leadership's concern with image also shaped its conduct as it moderated its constrainer behavior. These diverse influences pulled Beijing in opposing directions and meant that Chinese diplomats sought to balance their efforts to constrain the regime with a desire to project a congenial image. This meant that they often attempted to constrain the international regime through lower-profile and less-public measures. Moreover, even when the PRC ventured into more openly obstructive behavior as it did during the HRC's Institution-Building (IB) process when it sought to inhibit the use of country-specific resolutions, its concern with image caused Chinese diplomats to back down from their controversial position. As with OPCAT, the PRC's greater familiarity with the international regime was a weaker variable that did not motivate it to act as a constrainer but it did mean that it had at its disposal the skills, expertise, and strategies needed to play roles beyond taker.

As documented in Chapter 5, over the course of roughly three decades in the ILO's CCAS Beijing did not veer from its taker posture. As discussed in the other chapters, China's distaste for scrutiny of its record was a dominant factor. Yet, in this case, because China received scant attention from the Committee it was strongly inclined toward the role of

---

[1] "China," UN Human Rights Council Extranet, Institution-Building Working Groups, Working Group on special procedures, expert body, and a complaint procedure, oral statements, December 6, 2006, extranet.ohchr.org, accessed July 17, 2017, and International Service for Human Rights, *Council Monitor, Human Rights Council Working Group on the Review of the Mechanisms and Mandates, Discussion of the Future System of Expert Advice, 10–25 April 2007,* 9.

taker. Even after the CCP government used violence to end popular demonstrations in 1989, the Conference Committee did not spotlight PRC repression, even though self-organized groups of Chinese workers had joined the protests. Beijing's ideas about the authority of the state and the remit of the international regime was the second most important explanatory variable, which also disposed the PRC toward a taker posture. The Conference Committee's focus on only ratified conventions gave states a degree of control over the application of this part of the regime, which aligned with China's emphasis on state sovereignty. Beijing's concern with its global image had a subtler influence, which, as with the other case studies, tempered its conduct. Initially, this meant that from 1983 until the late 1990s, the PRC did not make interventions during the CCAS reviews of other countries and did not join other countries in complaining about the Conference Committee's working methods. Yet, even after it adopted a slightly more active posture in 1999 by beginning to speak in defense of friendly countries and joining a 2004 statement made by Cuba that criticized the CCAS's working methods, China still did so in a low-profile way that preserved its global image. In this case study, increased familiarity did not lead Beijing to abandon its taker posture. However, as demonstrated by Beijing's efforts on behalf of allied countries, its greater familiarity meant that it was able to use the CCAS instrumentally to offer protective words to other countries facing the Conference Committee's scrutiny.

The next section will parse these explanatory variables further, including their relative weight, especially in instances in which they drew China in conflicting directions. In numerous instances, the PRC's distaste for scrutiny of its record and its preexisting ideas about the international regime that were rooted in its attachment to a Westphalian version of state sovereignty and the salience of local and particular conditions inclined it to constrain the regime while its aspiration to be viewed as a cooperative and agreeable global actor inclined China to act as a taker or at least restrained its efforts to constrain the regime. The variables are discussed in order of their relative weight in descending order.

Explicating and Weighing the Explanatory Variables

PRC Aversion to Scrutiny of Its Human Rights Record

In the case studies examined in this book, the most powerful variable in determining the PRC's role was its aversion to negative human rights attention, which emerged after the 1989 Tiananmen Square protests. Beijing's experience facing international opprobrium included not just symbolic condemnation in the form of UN resolutions and increased scrutiny from the treaty bodies, the special procedures, and the High Commissioner for Human Rights but also political and economic sanctions enacted by a number of countries in the wake of the violent repression of the demonstrations. As argued in Chapter 1, the PRC experienced not just reputational costs but also considerable damage to its material and strategic interests. Consequently, after 1989 this became the most potent variable. Beijing not only attempted to thwart focus on its own record but also opposed more generally country-specific human rights monitoring, particularly complaining about resolutions and special mandates focused on individual countries. In the parts of the regime examined in this book, when the regime had spotlighted China's troubled human rights record or there were proposals to enable robust country-focused scrutiny, the PRC attempted to constrain the regime.

The impact of this variable was most apparent in Chapter 4 when Beijing acted as a constrainer during the creation of the UNHRC. Several observers noted that Chinese leaders were lukewarm to the idea of a strengthened human rights entity to replace the UNCHR because they feared this new body might be able to more vigorously spotlight its human rights abuses. Early in the reform process the PRC rejected key recommendations that proponents of reform such as Kofi Annan had advanced, particularly proposals for membership standards in the form of human rights criteria or requiring that members be elected by a two-thirds rather than simple majority of the General Assembly (GA). Beijing also used the HRC negotiations to reiterate its customary complaints about country-focused monitoring and also countered suggestions to develop other country-specific mechanisms, such as special HRC sessions on particular countries. Throughout the HRC discussions, Beijing also repeated its preference for dialogue and cooperation rather than public censure as the best means to advance human rights and had some success in getting these concepts included in the text of the GA resolution that established the HRC. Although these phrases sound innocuous, they served Beijing's broader interest in blunting country-selective attention. During the IB negotiations, this explanatory variable influenced Beijing's efforts to circumscribe a number of regime mechanisms, including country-specific resolutions, the expert body (formerly the Sub-Commission), and the special procedures; ensure that the UPR did not emerge as a mechanism to spotlight abuses but rather a process that was universal and nonselective with no binding follow-up even in the cases of serious and systemic abuses; and insist that the 1503 complaint procedure should remain confidential even in cases of reports of gross violations.[2] As recounted in Chapter 4, Beijing's aversion to UN resolutions was so vehement that it also caused PRC diplomats to hold up agreement on the IB package in June 2007 in an attempt to gain acceptance for its proposal that country-specific resolutions could only be introduced with the support of one-third of the HRC membership and passed by a two-thirds vote. This would have paralyzed the Council's ability to use country-focused resolutions. Beijing's emissaries were insistent on advancing this position even though this jeopardized their desire to cultivate an image as an agreeable international actor, another explanatory factor that is elaborated below. Its frenetic lobbying and willingness to jeopardize an agreement that had already secured the elimination of the special rapporteurs assigned to Cuba and Belarus demonstrated the importance it attached to curbing focus on its record and more generally the use of country-specific scrutiny.

This variable played a less prominent but still discernible role in influencing Beijing's constrainer posture toward OPCAT. Its aversion to country-specific scrutiny caused it to resist OPCAT and to insist that investigative country visits should be implemented on a rotational basis while repeatedly countering text that would enable the SPT to concentrate on particular countries or publicize their findings. Although ratification of OPCAT was voluntary, the PRC's resistance and attempts to dilute it likely grew out of a desire to diminish the use of this kind of robust international human rights monitoring as a commonly accepted mechanism in the regime. The post-Tiananmen timing was critical as Beijing was now wary of the international regime's reach and country-level monitoring, causing Chinese officials to resist the inspection visits and reporting proposed under the Optional Protocol.

When this explanatory variable was absent or a minimal PRC concern, Beijing was inclined to act as a taker. For example, during the CAT drafting, which predated the 1989 Tiananmen crackdown, the PRC had not yet developed an aversion to robust human rights monitoring trained on a single country. In this vein, China did not raise concerns with the CAT treaty body's authority to focus on countries or the degree of public pressure that the country reviews might generate. In a similar vein, as documented in Chapter 5, Beijing was a taker in the CCAS primarily because it received mild and infrequent scrutiny from this entity.

---

[2] Interview with Western European Diplomat, May 26, 2011, Geneva, Switzerland, and interview with UN OHCHR official, June 29, 2011, New York. Similar position confirmed by Council Monitor, International Service for Human Rights, "Human Rights Council Working Group to Develop the Modalities of the Universal Periodic Review 3rd Session, 11–24 April 2007," Human Rights Monitor Series, April 11–24, 2007, http://olddoc.ishr.ch/hrm/council/wg/wg_reports/wg_upr_03.pdf.

Aside from influencing China's particular role in the regime, Beijing's aversion to human rights scrutiny influenced its behavior in other discernible ways. First, after 1989, Beijing opposed not only resolutions on its own record but more broadly to speak out against selective country-focused human rights attention, even in the face of egregious abuses. Thus, Beijing sometimes protected other countries from scrutiny and, as documented in Chapter 5, starting in the late 1990s in the CCAS PRC diplomats began offering sympathetic comments on behalf of other nations. A Western European worker representative suggested that China intervened in CCAS cases, such as Myanmar's, because of the intense scrutiny these countries were receiving in the Conference Committee. As he put it, the PRC "considered this [sustained attention from the CCAS] ... like a precedent ... They didn't want what happened with Burma to happen to them ... I understood that more as defense position (sic) for themselves ... because they were protecting themselves from similar kinds of accusations that could be launched."[3] Echoing this sentiment, a scholar affiliated with a Chinese government think tank suggested that "when you protect someone like you, you are protecting yourself."[4] He elaborated that "China doesn't care about human rights – we just don't want to set the precedent" that spotlighting particular countries is acceptable.[5] Thus, some of Beijing's actions may have been preventive in nature as it attempted to weaken and discredit the use of selective scrutiny to protect itself. Along similar lines, scholar Courtney Fung studying the PRC's attitude toward UN Security Council intervention quoted a PRC Ministry of Foreign Affairs official as stating "when we vote on Syria, we are thinking of China."[6] Second, as analyzed in greater detail in Chapter 5, the goodwill that China gained through its laudatory comments for other countries in the Conference Committee may have translated into their reciprocal protection and assistance in other parts of the regime, such as when Beijing faced UNCHR resolutions and the HRC UPR process.

China's Human Rights Ideas

The PRC's preexisting ideas about the scope of the international human rights regime was another powerful influence on its posture. In Chapter 1, I identified two particularly salient aspects of Chinese

---

[3] Dereymaeker, interview.
[4] Interview with Chinese Academy of Social Sciences Scholar, July 12, 2013, Beijing, China.
[5] Ibid.   [6] Fung, *China and Intervention at the UN Security Council*, 2019, 2.

thinking – its assertion that the regime should not violate state sovereignty or interfere in internal affairs and its insistence on the import of particular domestic and local conditions over universal human rights norms. These ideas proved to be strongly ingrained as PRC emissaries continued to voice positions that reflected this thinking even after decades of involvement with the international human rights regime. Not surprisingly, when the regime conflicted with these Chinese views, the PRC was more inclined to attempt to constrain the regime. While these views appear to be genuinely held beliefs, Chinese officials also appear to have used them instrumentally as part of their effort to avert and deflect attention on its record, particularly in the post-Tiananmen era.

In this book's case studies, when the regime conflicted with these ideas Beijing acted as a constrainer. This factor helps to account for its constrainer role during the OPCAT negotiations, where during the decade-long drafting there was little evolution in the PRC's positions. Beijing's views on state sovereignty translated into a state-centric approach that favored giving states greater influence over the implementation and substance of the regime while diminishing the proposed international Subcommittee's authority. The chair of the informal OPCAT working group described China's main concern as "state sovereignty ... the state should decide how much it wants to open up [to the SPT] and the state should influence what comes out" of a visit.[7] Beijing repeatedly asserted that international human rights mechanisms should not contravene state sovereignty and it contested giving the international Sub-Committee "unrestricted access to all places of detention, their installations and facilities and to all relevant information."[8] This was also reflected in other positions, such as requiring state consent prior to a visit in addition to ratification, giving states leeway to deny an entire visit as well as access to a particular facility, allowing states to determine the individuals serving on the international Sub-Committee and experts assisting with country visits, pushing for inclusion of language affirming respect for domestic legislation, and attempting to enhance state influence over the postvisit report.

Likewise, the PRC acted as a constrainer toward the HRC because some of the proposals for this new entity chafed against its human rights

---

[7] Pennegard, interview. Similar statement on sovereignty from Haenni-Dale, interview.
[8] United Nations Office of the High Commissioner for Human Rights, "Optional Protocol to the Convention against Torture (OPCAT) Subcommittee on Prevention of Torture," www.ohchr.org/EN/HRBodies/OPCAT/Pages/OPCATIntro.aspx, accessed February 8, 2014.

views and it saw an opportunity to roll back certain aspects of the regime. Thus, Beijing favored increased state control over the complaint procedure, the expert advice body (the successor to the Sub-Commission), the special procedures, and the Office of the High Commissioner for Human Rights (OHCHR), including reviewing the budget and the work plan. During discussions about the fate of the Sub-Commission, which ultimately emerged as a weakened expert advice body, the PRC asserted positions such as "The advice, reports and studies by the new body should reflect the development of human rights taking into account the diversified cultures, histories and religions."[9] In a similar vein, China also insisted on a larger expert advice body because "it did not believe that anything less than twenty-three experts would ensure respect [and] representation of main legal, cultural and civilizational (sic) traditions and perspectives."[10] Beijing further sought to establish states as the primary actors in the UPR process while negating the role of nongovernmental organizations (NGOs), which again reflected its strong view of state sovereignty. As it did with the expert advice body, during the UPR discussions, the PRC used the opportunity to reiterate that "[t]he significance of national and regional particularities and various historical, cultural and religious backgrounds must be born in mind ... The review shall give full consideration to the cultural, religious and historical traditions and the level of development of the country concerned."[11]

In contrast and unsurprisingly, Beijing was inclined to act as a taker in instances when the regime aligned with its key human rights conceptions. Although China's human rights ideas were not the most prominent factor explaining its taker posture toward CAT, the alignment of Chinese ideas with a number of provisions contained in CAT, such as the use of state-provided reporting, further nudged it in this direction. Beijing may have felt some unease about being questioned by the treaty body and it expressed some reservations about universal jurisdiction, but these concerns were not significant enough to cause it to impede the Convention's adoption. Further, the voluntary nature of some of the more far-reaching clauses that gave the Committee the authority to investigate torture and

[9] "China," UN Human Rights Council Extranet, Institution-Building Working Groups, Working Group on special procedures, expert body, and a complaint procedure, oral statements, December 6, 2006, extranet.ohchr.org, accessed July 17, 2017.

[10] International Service for Human Rights *Council Monitor, Human Rights Council Working Group on the Review of the Mechanisms and Mandates, Discussion of the Future System of Expert Advice, 10–25 April 2007.*

[11] "Statement on Universal Periodic Review by Mr. La Yifan, Deputy Representative of the Chinese Delegation," Permanent Mission of the People's Republic of China to the United Nations Office at Geneva and Other International Organizations in Switzerland, www.china-un.org/eng/rqrd/t261293.htm, accessed January 29, 2013.

receive individual and intrastate complaints of torture made the Convention more palatable to Beijing since it let states opt in or out of these procedures. In a similar vein, there were several important ways that the ILO Conference Committee conformed with PRC preferences and therefore inclined it to act as taker. First, the Committee's limited jurisdiction, which was restricted to addressing only ratified conventions, dovetailed with the PRC's views on sovereignty, particularly that states should have greater control over the manner and degree in which the regime is applied.[12] Second, the CCAS review treated states as the primary actors and relied on state-provided reporting, including both written reports and an in-person review attended by government officials of the state under review.

Cultivating an Image as an Agreeable and Cooperative Actor

The PRC's desire to project an image as an agreeable and cooperative international actor also guided its conduct.[13] While not as powerful as the previous two explanatory variables, the impact of this factor was, nonetheless, discernible as a moderating influence.[14] In several instances, this variable functioned as a brake on Beijing, inclining it to be content with operating as a constrainer rather than a breaker and more generally tempering it conduct. As noted in Chapter 1, as early as the 1980s Beijing was attentive to its global image and it has aspired to be seen as a great responsible power.[15] In the human rights regime, this translated into an effort to portray itself as an engaged and supportive participant in good standing within the regime. Although this image concern is related to the strongest explanatory variable described previously in this chapter – Beijing's antipathy toward scrutiny of its human rights record – it encompasses much more. Whereas the PRC distaste for criticism of its record meant that it wanted to avoid negative attention, this variable caused Beijing to proactively attempt to cultivate a positive global image and try to give its participation in the regime the veneer of being constructive. As noted in the introductory chapter, while image is customarily associated with constructivist arguments, I argue that the PRC's concern with global image also reflects an instrumental worldview

---

[12] As a Western European trade union representative put it, China's view could be summed up as "They are sovereign [countries]. They are masters of their own country." Deremaeker, interview.

[13] Kinzelbach, "Resisting the Power of Human Rights," 174.

[14] As an Asia Pacific diplomat noted, Beijing wants "to be seen as a good international citizen." Interview with Asia Pacific diplomat, September 28, 2011, Canberra, Australia.

[15] Rabinovitch, "The Rise of an Image-Conscious China."

that views image as being linked to material interests. As argued previously, the international condemnation following the 1989 Tiananmen crackdown damaged the PRC's security and economic interests and Chinese leaders appear to have learned that a favorable global image served broader national interests and might also help allay global worries about its rise.[16] Overall, the thrust of this variable restrained Beijing's behavior and may help explain why it avoided acting as a breaker in any of the case studies. Thus, to some extent this variable worked to counter the previous two explanatory variables – the PRC's aversion to scrutiny of its human rights record and its ideas about the scope of the international regime.

In two key instances, this explanatory factor caused the PRC to back away from an obstructive position. First, as detailed in Chapter 3, in 1984 during the final stages of the discussions over CAT Chinese officials pulled back from their opposition to the language on universal jurisdiction when they realized that they were the lone holdout and this isolated position threatened the PRC's reputation. This image concern operated in a similar way in 2007 during the HRC IB process when Beijing dropped its position that country resolutions could only be introduced with the support of one-third of the members and passed by a two-thirds vote. China relented only when its opposition started to generate negative attention, including news articles that portrayed the PRC as blocking agreement on the IB package. Beijing not only conceded its position but it also downplayed its obstructionist stance by expressing support for the President's text and explaining that it had been attempting to "safeguard the credibility of the Council by putting through its proposal on country human rights situations."[17] In both of these instances, even though its preferences did not change, it retreated from impeding progress. Thus, this explanatory variable checked Beijing from venturing toward actions befitting a breaker. At the same time, Beijing's desire for a positive image was not sufficiently strong to prevent it from attempting to stymie progress in strengthening the regime.

This concern with global image also caused it to act with restraint in general, inclining Beijing's diplomats toward a more discreet, modest posture.[18] Even in instances where the PRC acted as a constrainer, as it

[16] Rabinovitch, "The Rise of an Image-Conscious China."

[17] International Service for Human Rights, *Council Monitor. Human Rights Council, Report on the Conclusion of the 5th Session (18 June) and the Organisational Meeting of the Council (18–20 June 2007)*, 4.

[18] This observation was made by a number of interview subjects, including Akram, interview; interview with Western European diplomat, October 2, 2010, Stockholm, Sweden; interview with Western European diplomat, June 13, 2011, Oslo, Norway; and interview with South Asian diplomat, June 3, 2011, Geneva, Switzerland.

did vis-à-vis OPCAT and the HRC, the moderating effect of image was evident as Chinese diplomats shied away from a prominent role and tended toward a low-key posture. As an NGO participant in the OPCAT drafting group emphasized, Chinese diplomats avoided "going out on a limb unless they felt they did not have a choice."[19] Thus, even though China retained misgivings about OPCAT, during the adoption process it did not initiate formal action to avert passage but rather took the less visible step of voting in support of blocking efforts by other countries, such as the United States, Cuba, and Japan. Image similarly tempered the PRC's behavior during the creation of the HRC. Beijing confined its opposition to reform proposals, such as criteria for membership, to private, smaller meetings while publicly making bland or vaguely supportive public comments on the idea of a body to replace the UNCHR and allowing Pakistan and Russia to take more insistent positions.[20] Citing this behavior, a Western European diplomat observed that China avoided being seen as a "prominently negative voice."[21] Even though the PRC retained reservations about a new UN human rights body, once they saw that the GA resolution establishing the Council was gaining support they dropped their resistance in order to avoid being obstructive or isolated.[22] Once the UNHRC became a reality and members embarked on the IB process, which determined key features of the Council, the restraining effect of image was less powerful as there was a slight uptick in the PRC's behavior. Chinese diplomats participated in the IB working groups actively and asserted a number of positions that were inimical to the human rights regime. Beijing took particular aim at diluting a number of Council mechanisms, including the special procedures, expert advisory body, and the 1503 complaint procedure. These more pronounced actions might be due to the fact that the Council was now a reality and the IB package would determine critical institutional details.

Among Beijing's strategies to limit image costs was varying the tone and substance of its statements based on venue and audience. Thus, Chinese officials were more circumspect in larger gatherings, especially those that were open to the public and included a record of proceedings. For example, as OPCAT moved through the UN adoption process, the PRC was cautious in larger UN bodies, such as the Third Committee

[19] Haenni-Dale, interview. Similar point made by interview with human rights expert and former member of the UN Committee against Torture, June 30, 2011, New York.
[20] Interview with UN official, June 29, 2011, New York, and interview with former US government official, October 27, 2010, Washington DC.
[21] Interview with Western European diplomat, June 23, 2012, New York.
[22] Interview with UN official, June 29, 2011, New York.

and the UN GA, which comprise all UN members. In these bodies, the PRC did not make the kinds of hostile statements offered by Ambassador Sha in the smaller UNCHR, where he called the decision to move OPCAT forward for adoption "arbitrary" and the draft "unbalanced" and threatened "negative consequences" if OPCAT were moved forward for passage.[23] In the GA, the PRC remained silent and abstained in the vote rather than being among the four countries that voted in opposition. Along these lines, an NGO participant noted that as the "margins got larger and larger, and the group of countries in opposition smaller and smaller ... China didn't want to be in a minority."[24] In a similar vein, during the early discussions over the HRC when the World Summit Outcome document and the GA resolution were being drafted, the PRC voiced firmer and more insistent positions in smaller gatherings, especially those that were limited to key states or UN officials, while simultaneously delivering vague statements or generalized support for UN human rights institutional reform in public settings. Thus, even though other diplomats and UN officials describe Beijing as resistant and being one of the last governments to agree to the HRC as a deliverable to be announced at the September 2005 World Summit, in public the PRC downplayed its misgivings and even claimed that "China is in favor of and supports the reform of UN human rights bodies."[25] As then-US Ambassador Bolton explained, Chinese representatives preferred to express their opposition to reform proposals privately in smaller, closed meetings and avoid being on record as obstructing progress.[26]

Image also modulated the PRC's conduct as a taker in the ILO's CCAS. Even though the PRC utilized this venue to offer praise or soft comments for key allies, Chinese representatives were careful not to be excessive in their interventions. The PRC itself claimed that it "would never ... [act] in such a way that other groups in the ILO would see them as protecting wrongdoing."[27] Moreover, even though numerous participants noted the protection China offered other nations with problematic labor rights records, they also described it as not attempting to break the regime and also pointed out that overall the PRC was not a frequent

---

[23] UN Commission on Human Rights, "Report of the 50th Meeting of the 58th Session, July 30, 2002, UN Doc. E/CN.4/2002/SR.50, paragraph 18 (translated from French.)

[24] Haenni-Dale, interview. For similar findings, see Alastair Iain Johnston, "International Structures and Chinese Foreign Policy," in *China and the World*, 4th ed., Samuel S. Kim (Boulder: Westview Press, 1998), 77.

[25] "Position Paper of the People's Republic of China on the United Nations Reforms, 2005/06/07," PRC Ministry of Foreign Affairs, www.mfa.gov.cn/eng/wjb/zzjg/gjs/gjsxw/t199318.htm, accessed August 5, 2011.

[26] Bolton, interview.

[27] Interview with Chinese government official, June 12, 2012, Beijing, China.

intervener.[28] As described in Chapter 5, out of twenty-five cases reviewed annually by the CCAS, Chinese interlocutors usually made protective comments for fewer than six countries. Moreover, beyond their statements in the CCAS, Chinese diplomats did not take further action, such as lobbying or pressuring other Conference Committee participants to ease normative pressure.

As suggested above, this desire for a positive global image, which generally restrained the PRC, conflicted with the previous two explanatory variables as its distaste for human rights scrutiny and its human rights ideas generally pushed Beijing toward more assertive stances or constrainer attempts. For example, when the PRC tried to weaken the use of country-specific resolutions during the HRC IB negotiations, this jeopardized its global image. PRC MFA spokesperson Qing Gang downplayed the PRC's obstinance and failed proposal by emphasizing its "constructive and cooperative manner" and claiming that

China's proposal on country human rights issues will help ensure the impartiality and seriousness of the work of the Council, prevent the abuse of country resolutions, and avoid the political confrontation in the UN Human Rights Commission in the past. China's proposal is supported by the vast majority of developing countries and many members of the Council. [29]

In this book's case studies, even though the two other variables were more powerful in determining the PRC's posture, image served as a check on Beijing's impulses toward more forceful postures. Thus, when faced with a conflict between these variables, PRC diplomats appear to have surmised that at times it was worth risking a blemished global image. Yet, ultimately, in these instances Beijing backed down from obstructing progress in order to avoid being seen as disruptive in the eyes of the global community.

The PRC's Government Level of Familiarity with the Human Rights Regime

Of the four explanatory variables, the PRC government's degree of familiarity with the regime carried the least amount of explanatory weight. This variable was more prominent when the PRC was an

---

[28] Potter, interview; Benedict, interview; and Tate, interview.
[29] "Foreign Ministry Spokesman Qin Gang's Regular Press Conference on 19 June 2007," PRC Ministry of Foreign Affairs, June 19, 2007, www.fmprc.gov.cn/eng/xwjw/s2510/2511/t331911.htm, and International Service for Human Rights, *Council Monitor, Report of the Conclusion of the 5th Session and the Organization Meeting of the Council*, June 12, 2007.

inexperienced novice with limited substantive knowledge on the regime's norms, mechanisms, and procedures. This unfamiliarity inclined it to act as a taker.[30] As indicated earlier, regime novices usually lack the skills and expertise needed to play more expansive roles. Yet, as illustrated by the case study on the ILO's CCAS, greater familiarity did not necessarily compel the PRC toward a different role and over nearly three decades of participation in the Conference Committee the PRC remained a taker even as it gained familiarity. However, I argue that enhanced familiarity meant that the PRC had at its disposal the skills and knowledge needed to play other roles when the other, more powerful, explanatory variables pushed it in that direction.

The influence of this explanatory variable was most obvious when the PRC was a new entrant in an unfamiliar international regime, which predisposed it to act as a taker. In the early to mid 1980s, which corresponded with its first few years in the human rights regime, it was a quiescent participant during the negotiations over CAT. In 1982, when the PRC first joined the CAT drafting group, it also began attending the UNCHR. Its novice status meant that Chinese diplomats refrained from offering any statements during their first two years in the CAT drafting group. Later, in the 1990s, Beijing's initial interactions as a state party to CAT provide further evidence that in the 1980s, it was unaware of how the convention would be applied to states and of the nature of the Committee's authority, and did not understand the nature of its obligations when it ratified CAT.[31] Likewise, in the CCAS, limited familiarity meant that initially the PRC made minimal interventions and tried to avoid controversy. According to a PRC official, at this point, China was "not too familiar" with the ILO, and so it was natural for it to "listen and observe and try to understand the whole organization."[32] Thus, in 1983 and 1984 when other socialist bloc countries complained that the ILO's labor rights monitoring methods were unfair and selective, the PRC remained on the sidelines of this debate. Moreover, Chinese diplomats abstained from making statements during the Conference

---

[30] Prior to 1976, not a single article dealing exclusively with human rights had been published. Hungdah Chiu, "Chinese Attitudes Toward International Law of Human Rights in the Post-Mao Era," in *Chinese Politics from Mao to Deng*, ed. Victor C. Falkenheim (New York: Paragon House, 1989), 239.

[31] As noted by Johnston, mimicking occurs when "a novice initially copies the behavioral norms of the group in order to navigate through an uncertain environment." Johnston, *Social States*, 23.

[32] Interview with Chinese government official, June 12, 2011, Beijing, China. This official noted that it was initially trying to gain "a better understanding of multilateral organizations, the rules and regulations of the organization," providing China with a "better position to participate."

Committee's reviews of other countries until 1999 when the PRC began to offer positive or bland comments to soften the CCAS scrutiny of some of its allies.

Even with greater levels of familiarity, this variable rarely played a strong determinative role on Beijing's posture. When China acted as a constrainer as it did toward OPCAT and the HRC, this was the result of other explanatory variables, particularly its distaste for scrutiny and the divergence between its human rights ideas and the substance of the regime. However, greater familiarity meant that when the other variables pushed it toward a particular role, PRC diplomats possessed skills and strategies that they could deploy. Thus, in contrast to the CAT negotiations in the early 1980s, when PRC officials were uncertain, rarely asserted themselves, and made minimal contributions, Chinese diplomats participating in the OPCAT and HRC discussions displayed diplomatic skills and relevant substantive and procedural knowledge. Greater familiarity also meant that as Beijing became increasingly conversant with CCAS rules and procedures, it was able to use this entity instrumentally to accommodate requests from friendly countries to shield them from scrutiny by making anodyne comments or delivering paeans for their allies. As will be discussed in the following section, the PRC's growing ability to cooperate with other countries was another factor – though a secondary one – affecting its conduct in the regime.

A Secondary Influence

Beijing's Ability to Align and Coordinate with Other Countries

As outlined in Chapter 1, the PRC's ability and willingness to cooperate with other countries was a secondary influence. Chapter 3 uncovered this defining development during the late 1990s in the OPCAT drafting group when Beijing began to coordinate with Saudi Arabia, Egypt, Sudan, Syria, Cuba, and Algeria. This OPCAT group has been described as the precursor to the Like-Minded Group (LMG), which was active in the UNCHR and HRC, and is further described in Chapter 1.[33] As has been noted previously, I describe this as a secondary influence because this was not a determinative variable in the sense that it did not dictate the particular role Beijing assumed. Yet, it had a discernible influence that surprisingly resulted in two contradictory tendencies. First, the presence of other similarly minded countries and Beijing's

---

[33] Interview with former Middle Eastern diplomat, May 25, 2011, Geneva, Switzerland.

cooperation with them tempered the PRC's behavior. As detailed in the section above, even when Beijing attempted to constrain the regime it preferred to let other countries take more vocal positions. At the same time and in contrast to this moderating influence, the presence of other countries with shared views may also have reinforced Chinese views on the human rights regime since China it found itself in the company of other countries echoing similar views.

China's behavior in the OPCAT and HRC case studies provide evidence of the taming effect of this secondary influence as Beijing deployed a number of strategies that enabled it to benefit from the presence and activism of other similarly minded countries. In this vein, the PRC preferred to allow other states to take a more prominent role, trumpeting shared views to curtail the international regime, and purposely stepped back when it saw that other countries were already articulating these views. For example, in the OPCAT working group the presence of Algeria, Cuba, Egypt, Saudi Arabia, Sudan, and Syria enabled the PRC to be more subdued in its opposition. An NGO participant conjectured that the existence of this group benefited China because it was put "in a position that it did not have to block [OPCAT] because others were doing it for them."[34] In a similar manner, during the HRC's establishment, Beijing benefited from the existence of countries with aligned views. For example, the PRC relied on Pakistan and Russia to take more vigorous positions against introducing HRC membership criteria. Along these lines, a diplomat noted that the PRC "was not the worst ... often they hide behind others and let others do the dirty work because they don't want to be perceived as being the real obstacle ... they never were in the lead against something and took the floor to support the ideas of others."[35] Another diplomat concurred that "it suits Beijing for others to be the spoilers" and that often "Algeria, Cuba and Pakistan do the dirty work."[36] As the chairperson of the informal OPCAT working group observed: "Because a number of other countries were more vocal on issues of importance to China, this made it possible for the PRC to hide behind these other countries and not stick out too much."[37]

The second PRC strategy involved joining group statements whenever possible rather than making its own national-level statements. During the late 1990s, in the OPCAT working group, when the above referenced

---

[34] Haenni-Dale, interview. Haenni-Dale further suggested that Beijing may have been "playing through other players." Similar views offered by Jimenez, interview, and Guillermet, interview.
[35] Interview with Western European diplomat, June 28, 2011, New York.
[36] Interview with Asia Pacific diplomat, September 28, 2011, Canberra, Australia.
[37] Pennegard, interview.

group of countries began cooperating explicitly by offering joint state-ments and written submissions as a group, Beijing signed onto these statements. By affiliating with group statements rather than making their own national-level statements, the PRC was able to avoid being seen as a prominent force obstructing progress. In a similar vein, during the cre-ation of the HRC, the PRC coordinated its constraining attempts with the LMG. Although the PRC's rotational turn serving as spokesperson for the group meant that it had a slightly more visible profile, its ability to reference the LMG enabled it to present its remarks as representing a group of countries and may also have given the PRC enhanced influence over the content of LMG statements.

Finally, the PRC often referenced the positions of other similar-minded countries to frame its positions as being shared by other states. Thus, as outlined in Chapters 3 and 4, in the OPCAT and HRC discus-sions, the PRC would often agree with or allude to the position of another country, such as Egypt, Algeria, or Cuba. Along these lines, when it stepped back from its stance seeking to limit the use of country-specific resolutions in the PRC, MFA spokesperson Qing Gang claimed that "China's proposal is supported by the vast majority of developing countries and many members of the Council." [38]

The PRC was successful in using these tactics because there were often other countries that were willing to take much more prominent roles. As a Western European diplomat put it, China "shelters behind" countries such as Russia, Egypt, Pakistan, and Cuba, which frequently took more strident positions.[39] Moreover, as a diplomat from one of the countries that often cooperated with the PRC noted, "China easily finds other countries with similar views."[40] The emergence of the LMG offers further evidence that a number of other non-Western, developing nations were in agreement with Beijing. Moreover, while the PRC benefited from this group's existence and is considered to be one of the core LMG

---

[38] "Foreign Ministry Spokesman Qin Gang's Regular Press Conference on 19 June 2007," PRC Ministry of Foreign Affairs, June 19, 2007, www.fmprc.gov.cn/eng/xwjw/s2510/2511/t331911.htm, and International Service for Human Rights, Council Monitor, *Report of the Conclusion of the 5th Session and the Organization Meeting of the Council*, June 12, 2007.

[39] Interview with Western European diplomat, October 2, 2010, Sweden, Stockholm. This point was also echoed by interview with human rights NGO representative, May 31, 2011, Geneva, Switzerland; interview with North American diplomat, June 17, 2011, Washington, DC; and interview with human rights NGO representative, June 23, 2011, by phone with author. Members of the LMG identify Cuba, India, Pakistan, and Egypt as examples of countries that have been willing to take more vocal positions. Akram, interview, and interview with Asia Pacific diplomat, September 28, 2011, Canberra, Australia.

[40] Quote from interview with South Asian diplomat, June 3, 2011, Geneva, Switzerland.

countries, it was not described as the main instigator or organizer of this group.[41] China was also not the primary leader of the group comprising Cuba, Algeria, Egypt, Saudi Arabia, Sudan, and Syria in the OPCAT working group.

In contrast to the assertion from countries that cooperated with China, including LMG members, that there was a meeting of the minds, others suspect that the PRC may confer privately with other states to ensure that its views are represented by other countries or that it might persuade others to adopt particular positions.[42] Although direct evidence is lacking, numerous UN officials, diplomats, and nongovernmental human rights representatives have speculated that during the creation of the HRC, the PRC used its influence in less visible ways by working "behind the scenes" and encouraging other countries to adopt or support certain positions and once Beijing was assured other nations would champion certain issues it could then adopt a lower profile and lend quiet support. [43] A North American diplomat conjectured that China acted as a "quiet power" behind the scenes and hypothesized that Beijing's diplomats could be "having behind the scenes conversations."[44] As a human rights NGO representative put it, "We suspect that China may have used other states to push their agenda" during the HRC negotiations.[45] Assuming these suppositions are correct (and certainly China has used such tactics in other instances), these strategies allowed China to preserve its image and obscure its obstructionist positions.[46]

[41] Interview with South Asian diplomat, May 27, 2011, Geneva, Switzerland; interview with South Asian diplomat, May 31, 2011, Geneva, Switzerland; interview with Southeast Asian diplomat, May 25, 2011, Geneva, Switzerland, and Akram, interview.

[42] Interview with former Middle Eastern diplomat, May 25, 2011, Geneva, Switzerland; and interview with Southeast Asian diplomat, May 25, 2011, Geneva, Switzerland.

[43] Quote from interview with North American diplomat, June 17, 2011, Washington DC. Similar comments from interview with human rights scholar, June 30, 2011, New York; interview with South Asian diplomat, May 27, 2011, Geneva, Switzerland; interview with Western European diplomat, June 28, 2011, New York; interview with Latin American diplomat, June 1, 2011, Geneva, Switzerland; and interview with human rights NGO representative, June 28, 2011, New York.

[44] This interview subject suggested that China might also use a variety of incentives, including aid or investment. Interview with North American diplomat, June 17, 2011, Washington DC. In a similar vein, a former North American government official described China as preferring to play an "invisible role." Interview with former US government official, October 27, 2010, Washington DC. A Pakistani diplomat acknowledged that China sometimes attempts to "exercise influence behind the scenes." Akram, interview.

[45] Interview with human rights NGO representative, May 31, 2011.

[46] Similar point made in Sceats and Breslin, *China and the International Human Rights System*, 15–16.

In contrast to this moderating influence, the existence of other countries with similar ideas also appeared to reinforce PRC human rights views. These countries provided Beijing (and each other) with a reference group, which may have weakened the impact of normative human rights pressure. For example, because of the chorus of Cuba, Algeria, Egypt, Saudi Arabia, Sudan, and Syria in OPCAT, the PRC may have been immune to the regime's ability to alter its views. As further documented in Chapter 4, the LMG came to include roughly twenty countries in the UNCHR and later over thirty members in HRC. Thus, this reference group of similarly minded countries that favored state sovereignty and the import of unique local conditions appeared to weaken the ability of the regime to alter PRC beliefs and reinforced its views.

Conclusion

While the previous chapters documented and described the PRC's behavior, this chapter helps explain this conduct by advancing four explanatory variables. I further supplement and sharpen this analysis by outlining what I term a secondary influence – China's ability to align and cooperate with other countries. By doing so, this book not only details the PRC's actions as a taker and constrainer in the human rights regime but also adds to our understanding of the motivations and drivers behind its behavior.

The findings of this chapter show the strong weight of two of the explanatory factors: the PRC's antipathy toward the regime's scrutiny of its human rights record and Chinese ideas that favored a Westphalian brand of state sovereignty and the importance of local particularities in the implementation of human rights. This underscores the 1989 Tiananmen Square crackdown as a searing experience that resulted in the Chinese leadership's abhorrence for censure of its record. As documented in Chapter 2, after 1989 a variety of the regime's monitoring mechanisms were trained on China that resulted in reputational costs as well as material losses. After 1989, China's view of the human rights regime was filtered through this lens. Consequently, Beijing not only resisted efforts within the regime to scrutinize its record but also began to propagate a broader argument that country-specific scrutiny was confrontational and counterproductive, which formed the basis of its efforts to rid the regime of all country-specific monitoring procedures and in numerous instances to act as a constrainer. In a similar vein, Chinese ideational influences proved to be unyielding as the PRC continued to espouse its Westphalian brand of sovereignty and the salience of local conditions, which inclined it to limit the reach and authority of the regime, and therefore act as a constrainer.

These two variables were particularly weighty in determining the PRC's role, yet, as noted above, they were often moderated by one of the other variables – Beijing's sensitivity to its global image. While China's yearning to be viewed as a positive and constructive global actor was weaker than the other two variables in dictating the particular role Beijing adopted, its influence was discernible as it restrained Chinese actions in general and in several instances caused it to relent from an obstructive stance. Thus, this variable may have prevented Beijing from pursuing actions in line with that of a regime breaker. The weakest variable was the PRC's degree of familiarity with the regime. This variable inclined Beijing toward a taker role during its initial years in the regime when its familiarity was limited and tipped it away from venturing toward more assertive roles.

Finally, while it did not determine the PRC's posture, Beijing's ability to coordinate and work with other countries acted as a secondary influence that manifested in two distinct ways. First, it moderated Chinese behavior in general even in instances when it acted as a constrainer. The first inkling of the effect of this secondary influence occurred during the OPCAT negotiations when Cuba, Algeria, Egypt, Saudi Arabia, Syria, and Sudan began making joint statements. Although the PRC continued to attempt to constrain the Optional Protocol, it was less pointed in its remarks and tended toward a lower profile. In a similar vein, during the establishment of HRC even though the PRC acted as a constrainer, it preferred to let other countries take the lead. Second, I argue that because it found other countries that shared its human rights views, Beijing may have been less responsive to normative pressure and the ability of the regime to alter its views. Thus, the existence of these other countries touting similar views appears to have reinforced Chinese thinking.

7   Conclusion

This book opened by recalling that prior to the 1971 UN (United Nations) vote admitting China into this international body pessimists argued that the PRC would be a disruptive presence while optimists suggested that bringing China into the UN would facilitate its acceptance of global order. China's behavior as documented in this book confounds the predictions of both of these camps. Of the possible roles of maker, promoter, taker, constrainer, and breaker, I argue that China operated as a taker and constrainer. Thus, Beijing did not attempt to hollow out or destroy the regime but it also did not embrace it and often sought to curtail its reach and authority. More specifically, the PRC acted as a taker and constrainer during the creation of the Convention against Torture (CAT) and the Optional Protocol to the Convention against Torture (OPCAT), respectively, a constrainer during the establishment of the UN Human Rights Council (HRC), and a taker in the ILO's (International Labour Organization) Conference Committee on the Application of Standards (CCAS).

As the case studies suggest, China's impact on the human rights regime is discernible. The PRC, in tandem with other countries, had some success in holding back the strengthening of the regime and its behavior affected the regime's functioning. In order to arrive at these findings, China's behavior was investigated in Chapters 3, 4, and 5, which covered varied components of the international regime. Chapter 3, which spanned 1982 through 2002, chronicled China's evolution from a quiescent and timid regime participant in the early to mid 1980s where it acted as a taker during the CAT negotiations to a more vocal and sophisticated actor able to coordinate with similarly minded countries in an attempt to constrain the regime during the negotiations over OPCAT that began in 1992 and culminated in 2002. As documented in Chapter 4, the PRC again acted as a as a constrainer during the 2004 through 2007 negotiations to establish the UNHRC, a body that was to serve as the successor to the UN Commission on Human Rights (UNCHR). This chapter also detailed the PRC's uncharacteristically prominent and controversial stance when it held up agreement on the HRC Institution-Building (IB) package in an unsuccessful effort to inhibit the use of country-specific resolutions. In contrast to its behavior vis-à-vis the HRC, Chapter 5 described the PRC's taker posture in the ILO's CCAS from 1983 through 2017. Yet, even as a taker Beijing acted instrumentally as it used the Conference Committee as a venue to speak in defense of allied countries during their reviews. Moreover, as the analysis in Chapter 5 shows, the protective PRC statements appear to have translated into reciprocal support from these countries in the Commission on Human Rights and the HRC.

Although the PRC has not been as disruptive as some observers predicted, in cooperation with other like-minded states it has been able to shape some aspects of the regime. In particular, during the creation of the HRC, China along with other countries defeated proposals to establish a high bar for HRC membership, secured greater representation for non-Western countries, resisted civil society participation and binding follow-up action as part of the Universal Periodic Review (UPR), and routed efforts to strengthen a number of the regime's mechanisms, such as the Human Rights Advisory Committee and the 1503 petition procedure. At the same time, the most damaging Chinese proposals, such as restrictive rules for the use of resolutions on a single country and a sweeping review of all of the regime's special procedures that might have eliminated some key thematic mandates, were defeated. Beijing was unable to secure the issue of greatest importance to it – hindering the use of country-specific UN resolutions – because this position was controversial and it failed to attract support from other countries, even its usual human rights allies. China also had some success as a constrainer during the creation of OPCAT. The final version of OPCAT provided for a system of inspection visits and the Subcommittee on the Prevention that was established under OPCAT had greater authority than Beijing preferred. However, some of the PRC's positions were reflected in the final text, including allowing states to reject a Subcommittee visit to a particular facility (but not an entire visit to a country), elect Subcommittee members, and refuse the inclusion of a particular expert as part of a country visit. Beijing's quest to ensure that OPCAT visits were conducted on a nonselective rotational basis rather than allowing the Subcommittee to focus on particular states also prevailed.

Beijing achieved this degree of success largely because its views aligned with other countries. As detailed in Chapter 3, during the OPCAT negotiations, China associated itself with joint statements made by Algeria, Cuba, Egypt, Saudi Arabia, Sudan, and Syria. These countries sought to make OPCAT more deferential to states and place limits on the

SPT's (Subcommittee on the Prevention of Torture) authority and access. While they were not able to prevent passage of OPCAT or secure the inclusion of language affirming state sovereignty, especially a reference to domestic legislation, as noted above, they were able to shape some aspects of OPCAT. Yet, to their chagrin, OPCAT was adopted in 2002 and the final version of it preserved robust visiting authority for the SPT, which is authorized to visit "any place under [the state's] jurisdiction and control where persons are or may be deprived of liberty."[1]

During the establishment of the HRC, particularly the negotiations over the World Summit Outcome Document and GA (General Assembly) Resolution 60/251, Beijing along with similarly minded countries, especially Russia and Pakistan, met some success as they blocked proposals to elevate the Council's status, establish human rights membership standards, or require election by two-thirds of the GA. These proposals had been recommended by proponents of UN institutional human rights reform including then-Secretary-General Kofi Annan. As a result, the Council is plagued by some of the same weaknesses as the UNCHR. During the IB process, other countries, particularly Algeria, Pakistan, Russia, Cuba, Malaysia, and Saudi Arabia, joined China in stymieing efforts to strengthen a number of the regime's mechanisms, including the 1503 procedure, the Human Rights Advisory Committee, and UPR process. Notably, when Beijing acted alone as it did when it introduced restrictive rules for country-specific resolutions that would have paralyzed the Council's ability to pass such resolutions, it was unsuccessful.

Even when the PRC acted as a taker, its ability to work with other countries enabled it to maneuver to blunt the regime's impact. In the ILO CCAS, Chinese representatives delivered protective, laudatory comments for human rights allies undergoing review before the Committee. The analysis in the chapter on the ILO further shows that Beijing appeared to have received reciprocal protective support from these countries in the UNCHR during votes on China-focused resolutions and the HRC when it was reviewed as part of the UPR process. While China and its human rights allies did not dismantle the regime, their conduct had a deleterious effect on the regime because they were able to employ political maneuvers and exchange support to shield each other from scrutiny and blunt normative pressure.

While the case studies showed varied PRC behavior, the drivers of Beijing's behavior were largely consistent. I argue that four explanatory

---

[1] Article 4, Optional Protocol to the Convention against Torture.

variables account for its posture vis-à-vis the human rights regime. In descending order of explanatory power, these variables include the Chinese leadership's antipathy toward scrutiny of its record, the Chinese government's existing ideas about protecting state sovereignty and limits on the universality of human rights norms that translated into positions to contain the scope of the international regime, the Chinese leadership's desire to cultivate a positive international image, and the PRC government's degree of familiarity with the regime. Of these, the PRC's antagonism toward human rights scrutiny was the most powerful variable. It emerged as a direct result of the international censure China experienced after using force to end the 1989 Tiananmen Square demonstrations. Beijing suffered moral condemnation, diplomatic isolation, economic penalties, and security-related sanctions, which resulted in a deep-seated PRC loathing for scrutiny. My argument emphasizes that it was not just experiencing moral judgment that caused Beijing's response but the tangible economic and strategic damage that it suffered. This episode taught the Chinese leadership that human rights scrutiny could damage its national interests. The strength of this variable meant that when the regime directed attention to Beijing's human rights violations or there were proposals to develop procedures that could be focused on it, especially mechanisms that focused on a single country, the Chinese Communist Party (CCP) government was strongly inclined to act as a constrainer. This variable also strongly accounts for the PRC's taker posture in the ILO CCAS. Because the Committee's remit is restricted to ratified conventions and China has not ratified the ILO conventions of greatest concern to the CCAS, this committee rarely scrutinized China's labor rights record, leaving the PRC content to accept this part of the international regime.

Ideational influences were another explanatory factor and the Chinese government's preexisting ideas that favored domestic sovereignty over the regime's reach and asserted the relevance of cultural, developmental, and national factors in the realization of international norms meant that China often sought to circumscribe the regime's authority and reach. In instances, when the PRC perceived the regime as encroaching on state sovereignty or the universalism of the human rights norms were emphasized without taking into account local particularities, it pursued constraining actions. For example, OPCAT rankled PRC because it perceived the investigative trips outlined in OPCAT as infringing on state sovereignty. The prominence of this variable underscores 1989 as a turning point that caused Beijing to adopt a more hostile attitude toward international scrutiny. Given that it is difficult to dissect Beijing's sincerity versus rhetorical adaptations or instrumental deployment of even sincerely held ideas, it should be acknowledged that elements of both exist in the PRC's rhetoric.

While these first two variables – China's antipathy toward human rights attention and its preexisting ideas – often inclined it toward a constrainer posture, Beijing's desire to be seen as an agreeable international actor operated as a restraint. In several instances, this variable disposed Beijing to act as a taker, tamed its constraining attempts, or at least meant that it did not take the lead in such efforts, and caused it to back away from an insistent and obstructive position. The weakest explanatory factor was the Chinese government's degree of familiarity with the regime, which initially inclined Beijing to assume the safe and uncontroversial role of taker. This was evident in the CAT drafting group in the 1980s. Yet, as the PRC's familiarity grew, this variable became weaker and other explanatory variables were more powerful in determining Beijing's posture.

Before exploring the implications of my findings, it is worth noting that the human rights regime is particularly problematic for the CCP-led government. As scholar Susan Shirk observed, "[H]uman rights was the one issue on which Chinese officials could bend the least because it was intertwined with the survival of the Communist Party autocracy."[2] Chinese leaders likely react vociferously to the regime's scrutiny of its record because they perceive this as potentially fueling domestic activism or unrest and they recall that the Tiananmen crackdown resulted in "direct costs on China in terms of trade, investments dual-use technologies, development assistance, tourist income, and a mass defection of elite students and scholars."[3] The PRC was most pointed in its reaction and counterattacks to scrutiny from the regime's public political bodies, such as the UNCHR and the HRC, when resolutions or public statements spotlighted its blemished record. Thus, while the PRC complained about the special procedures and the treaty bodies, it trained its most vigorous constraining attempts at country-specific resolutions. This type of censure is arguably the most damaging to the PRC's global reputation and perception among other nations. Thus, Beijing's posture toward the regime's mechanisms might be based less on the substantive norms involved but rather on the particular institution and form of scrutiny. In this vein, Beijing was most sensitive to highly public censure

---

[2] Susan Shirk, *China, Fragile Superpower: How China's Internal Politics Could Derail Its Peaceful Rise* (Oxford: Oxford University Press, 2008), 224. See also Zhu, "China and International Human Rights Diplomacy," 219–220, and Foot, "Chinese Power and the Idea of a Responsible State," 17.

[3] Wan, *Human Rights in Chinese Foreign Relations*, 136.

in the UNCHR and HRC, bodies comprising its peers where its interests and image could be most imperiled. The following section will consider this book's insights into China's posture toward global order, its behavior in other international regimes, and the future of the human rights regime. While it is not possible to precisely predict China's future behavior and trajectory, the following sections offer some general insights.[4]

China and the Global Order

Although this inquiry focused on China's behavior in the international human rights regime, my findings also provide insight into the broad question of the PRC's willingness to accept the international liberal order. Scholars looking at other aspects of Chinese foreign policy might find more destructive or cooperative behavior. Yet my findings suggest that while China did not seek to destroy the human rights regime, it blocked attempts to strengthen it and its behavior, such as using the ILO's Conference Committee to protect allies, negatively affected the regime's functioning. Thus, although Beijing did not pursue wholesale revisions it engaged in constraining attempts that were selective and targeted at certain parts of the regime. Beijing was especially opposed to mechanisms that applied vigorous scrutiny, such as country-focused UN resolutions. Despite Beijing's resistance to strengthening the regime, there were limits to its opposition. For example, even though it was against replacing the UNCHR with a new body, once it saw that the HRC enjoyed growing support it did not persist in obstructing reform efforts. Thus, rather than emerging as a zealous revisionist power, Beijing's conduct was closer to a careful and pragmatic actor that targeted its efforts at capping the regime's growth and authority and focusing on the parts of the regime that it perceived as most threatening to its interests.

Beijing's tendency to avoid acting as a leader or taking a prominent role also suggests that despite its status as an emerging global power there were limits to its ambitions within the regime. Rather than initiating or organizing constraining efforts, China was more often described as a core and active member of such groupings but not a leader.[5] In general, diplomats from countries that collaborated with the PRC note that

---

[4] For example, Rosen predicted that by 2015 China would move into Freedom House's "partly free" category. Henry Rowen, "When Will the Chinese People Be Free?" *Journal of Democracy* 18, no. 3 (July 2007).

[5] Interview with former Middle Eastern diplomat, May 25, 2011, Geneva, Switzerland, and interview with Southeast Asian diplomat, May 25, 2011, Geneva, Switzerland.

Chinese diplomats did not strong-arm or cajole other countries to adopt the positions held by the LMG.[6] As a Southeast Asian diplomat whose country is associated with the Like-Minded Group (LMG) explained, usually "there is a meeting of the minds" and "Beijing's views were shared by a number of other countries."[7] This suggests not only that the PRC was disinclined to pursue destructive action unilaterally but also the degree to which the CCP government's views aligned with a number of non-Western, developing countries. As noted earlier, in the instances Beijing succeeded as a constrainer this was largely because it was joined by other nations. Further, China's inability to introduce restrictive rules on the use of HRC country resolutions suggests that there were limits to its ability to effect change unilaterally.

While this might suggest that China is disinclined to attempt to upend the liberal international order and will defer a prominent, leadership role, I caveat my findings with several important points. First, the international regime's inherent weakness meant that Beijing did not need to attempt to break this regime. The human rights regime lacks strong mechanisms, such as inbuilt sanctions, to encourage compliance and is heavily reliant on the political will of other states to hold each other accountable. For example, one of the regime's most potent tools – the passage of a resolution spotlighting human rights abuses – carries no penalty beyond negative attention. The 1989 Tiananmen massacre hurt PRC interests because other nations were willing to enact national-level sanctions and in later years the PRC successfully weakened the political will of other governments to spotlight its troubled human rights record.

Second, the PRC's behavior was strongly moderated by the Chinese leadership's concern with its global image. In numerous instances, Beijing backed away from an obstructionist position to preserve its image among other states. For example, in 2002 during the adoption of OPCAT as the draft gained support and advanced to larger UN bodies the PRC dropped its resistance and no longer spoke out against it. Image also explains Beijing's decision to back away from its attempt to restrict country resolutions in the HRC when it realized that its isolated position was drawing negative attention. Yet, there are indications that under Xi Jinping the CCP government is less concerned with projecting an image as a cooperative, status quo actor. Along these lines, scholar Yong Deng coined the phrase "post-responsible power" and described "an assertive

---

[6] Interview with Southeast Asian diplomat, May 25, 2011, Geneva, Switzerland; and interview with South Asian diplomat, May 31, 2011, Geneva, Switzerland.
[7] Interview with Southeast Asian diplomat, May 25, 2011; and interview with Southeast Asian diplomat, November 9, 2011, London, United Kingdom.

and nationalist Chinese shift" in Beijing's foreign policy posture as well as a domestic turn "away from what the ruling elites call Western-style multiparty-democratic values."[8] The absence of image as a moderating force could spell bolder PRC actions that push against the liberal international order.

Finally, most of the period investigated in this book coincides with a time when the PRC was still an emerging power. As China's economy has grown and its power and influence have steadily expanded, a number of scholars see it as being more willing to exercise its power. This trend appears to have begun around the time of the 2008 Beijing Olympics and by some accounts has intensified since Xi Jinping assumed leadership. In his March 2018 address to the National People's Congress, Xi stated that "China will continue to actively participate in the evolution and construction of the global governance system. China will contribute more Chinese wisdom, Chinese solutions and Chinese strength to the world."[9] I argued in the introductory chapter that this preoccupation with its image reflected concern with social status but also that material and economic interests were at play. Yet, as China has accumulated political and economic power, its material vulnerability has lessened and Beijing is now able to use its own pressure to deflect human rights attention and is in a better position to realize its preferred vision in the regime. Thus, the full repercussions of China's rise and Xi's leadership have likely not yet been fully manifest and China's global reach might become more expansive and revisionist.

Now that it has arrived as a global power and Xi Jinping vigorously asserts Chinese interests and views, Beijing may attempt to roll back the human rights regime or at least more energetically attempt to stall its growth. The PRC's resolutions and initiatives in the HRC since 2013 in fact may be a prelude to more vigorous efforts to disseminate its ideas, play a more robust role in shaping the regime, and push back against what Chinese leaders perceive as an international regime dominated by Western concepts. As the previous chapters demonstrated, Beijing is likely to take particular aim at the ability of the regime to censure particular countries for abuses, appoint independent experts with broad authority to investigate and publicize human rights abuses, and encroach on what Beijing perceives to be the realm of domestic authorities even in

---

[8] Yong Deng, "China: The Post-Responsible Power," *The Washington Quarterly* 37, no. 4 (Winter 2015): 117–132.
[9] "Speech Delivered by President Xi at the NPC Closing Meeting," *China Daily*, www .chinadaily.com.cn/hkedition/2018-03/22/content_35894512.htm, accessed September 2019.

the face of reports of human rights violations. While Xi has articulated a desire to return China to a preeminent role, the Chinese leadership's calculus about whether to challenge the human rights regime and the extent of its efforts will likely be dependent on the degree to which it perceives the regime as threatening its interests, particularly through more intense scrutiny, and by extension threatening the CCP's continued rule. At the same time, as shown in the chapter on the HRC, despite Beijing's concerted attempts it failed to strip the regime of the ability to enact resolutions focused on a single country. Thus, the preferences and actions of other states, particularly the countries belonging to the Western Europe and Others Group, which pushed back vigorously, remain an important check on Beijing's ambitions.

China's Role in International Regimes

When China began joining international regimes in the 1980s and 1990s, this development was welcomed by the international community. Yet, as this book demonstrated, although China participates in the human rights regime, its behavior indicates that it has not internalized the regime's norms and seeks to stall the regime's growth.[10] The lens I used – of considering whether China acted as a maker, promoter, taker, constrainer, or breaker – allowed me to capture the interplay between the regime and China, including instances when the PRC resisted the regime. Although the human rights regime presents a unique challenge to an authoritarian country like China and its acceptance of this regime might lag behind other international regimes, this book provides insights that are relevant to its behavior in international regimes in general.[11] This section discusses these insights and focuses on the factors driving PRC behavior, its strategies and posture, and the regime's limited to ability to inculcate human rights norms.

One of the most revealing findings in the case studies was the PRC's concern with global image – both fostering a reputation as a cooperative

---

[10] As Nathan put it, "China's goal appears to be not to get rid of the international human rights regime ... but to cap its growth and expansion, freeze its effectiveness at the current level, shape the institutions so that they are deferential to states, and make the norms to fit long-articulated Chinese priorities." Andrew J. Nathan, "China and International Human Rights: Tiananmen's Paradoxical Impact," in *The Impact of China's 1989 Tiananmen Massacre*," ed. Jean-Philippe Beja (London: Routledge, 2010), 218.

[11] Kinzelbach acknowledges the PRC to be a "hard case" and identifies some reasons for its resistance. Katrin Kinzelbach, "Resisting the power of human rights: The People's Republic of China," in *The Persuasive Power of Human Rights: From Commitment to Compliance* (Cambridge: Cambridge University Press, 2013), 164–181.

actor and limiting criticism of its human rights record. As recounted in the case studies, this manifested in two distinct ways. First, the PRC was most intent on constraining the regime when the issues at stake involved the parts of the regime that had vigorously scrutinized its record or had the potential to do so. Second, as noted previously, the importance the PRC attached to global image often inclined it toward more cooperative behavior. This also meant that China was attentive to the size of the audience, and was more circumspect in larger, higher-profile venues, such as the UN GA where PRC representatives were more cautious in both their voting and statements.[12] These findings indicate that the PRC is likely to be most disposed toward cooperative postures in multilateral settings, especially those with a larger audience.

My findings also suggest an instrumental dimension to the PRC's behavior that might manifest in other international regimes. Chapter 5 documented Beijing's use of the ILO CCAS to advance its interests by heeding requests from friendly countries to speak in their defense. As a result, the PRC acted as a defender of countries such as Bangladesh, Belarus, Colombia, Egypt, Myanmar, Venezuela, Uzbekistan, and Zimbabwe. In turn, these countries also appear to have provided it with reciprocal support in the UNCHR, where they voted against resolutions on China and in the HRC, where they offered platitudinous or soft-ball UPR statements. These actions indicate that rather than being swayed by the regime's normative pressure, Beijing had become adept at protecting its interests.

The existence of other countries in the regime sharing Chinese human rights views had important implications for China's participation. Beijing's ability to find allies within the regime provided it with a reference group or community of nations that did not completely accept the principles and norms enshrined in the international regime. The presence of these like-minded allies and their cooperation with China on joint objectives and shielding each other from scrutiny likely dulled social opprobrium costs and the regime's normative human rights pressure. Beijing's ability to work with these countries also provided it with strategies that could be deployed in other regimes. As documented in Chapters 3 and 5, the PRC preferred to work with others nations or a group of countries especially in its attempts to constrain the regime, such

---

[12] For example, Kim noted that "China is more cooperative in a high-profile multilateral institutional or negotiating settings than in low-profile bilateral negotiations." Samuel Kim, "China and the United Nations," in *China Joins the World: Progress and Prospects*, eds. Elizabeth Economy and Michel Oksenberg (New York: Council on Foreign Relations, 1999), 81. See also Johnston and Evans, "China's Engagement in International Security Institutions," 252–253.

as in the OPCAT working group where it benefited from cooperation with Cuba, Algeria, Egypt, Saudi Arabia, Sudan, and Syria.[13] This allowed Chinese diplomats to step back from making their own strongly worded national-level statements or when they did make a statement they could frame their stance as reflecting a position shared by other nations. This cooperative behavior behooved the PRC because it enabled it to adopt its preferred lower-profile posture in the regime.

My finding that even in instances when the PRC acted as a constrainer, it tended toward a lower profile either restricting its most vigorous constraining attempts to smaller, less public meetings or working within a group of countries and relying on other states to take a more prominent role should alert us to similar strategies in other regimes. Because the PRC attempted to conceal its obstructive behavior, and often confined its more pointed stances to smaller meetings or private ones between key states and UN officials, China's behavior in international regimes might not be fully evident in the public record, such as UN reports. This underscores the importance of not relying solely on public statements, deciphering Beijing's "behind the scenes" behavior, and investigating its role within the coalitions that it joins.

While other scholars have identified ways that international regimes can alter a state's behavior and thinking, China clearly presents a difficult case in the area of human rights.[14] My findings point to potential blocking factors that might impede the internalization of norms and the paradoxical effect that increased international scrutiny after 1989 had in causing Beijing to more energetically resist normative pressure. The Chinese leadership view that external human rights scrutiny from international actors is politically motivated might also impede its acceptance of this regime. China's own instrumental use of the human rights regime is evidence of this view. When the PRC first entered into the UNCHR, it used this venue to rail against its adversaries such as the Soviet Union and Vietnam.[15] Along these lines, PRC leaders have often interpreted

---

[13] My findings track with Johnston's observation about China's tendency to build coalitions. He noted that "[s]uch a coalition not only helps muster bargaining power, but the larger it is, the lower the obstructionist behavior to China's image." Johnston, "Learning Versus Adaptation," 58.

[14] Kent makes the point about China being a least likely case in the human rights regime. Kent, *China, the United Nations, and Human Rights*, 2. On the power of regimes and international norms in general see Finnemore and Sikkink, "International Norm Dynamics and Political Change" and Keohane, "International Institutions and State Power."

[15] Rana Siu Inboden and Titus Chen, "China's Response to International Normative Pressure: The Case of Human Rights," *The International Spectator: Italian Journal of International Affairs* 47, no. 2 (2012), 49.

international human rights censure as an effort to undermine CCP rule and China's rise, not as a genuine effort to promote the cause of human rights.[16] Thus, the PRC might not fully accept the legitimacy of the regime.

As shown throughout the previous chapters, the tenacity of China ideas, especially its belief in the primacy of state sovereignty and its insistence on the salience of differing national conditions in applying universal human rights norms, translated into PRC positions that favored a circumscribed role for the international regime. There are a number of potential reasons for the persistence of these ideas that arise from inherent characteristics specific to China, its authoritarian political system, and purposeful government actions to limit the diffusion of international human rights norms. Among the chief reasons is that, unlike other international regimes, the norms and principles underlying the human rights regime pose a unique threat to the CCP's monopoly on political power and are not compatible with the PRC's political system, which is marked by a prioritization of state power over individual rights, lack of division between party and state, and the absence of meaningful elections. Along these lines, CCP ideology and "Xi Jinping Thought" espouse ideas that are inimical to the international human rights regime.[17]

Second, the PRC's historical experience when it faced subjugation by Western nations that carved up the country during the "century of humiliation" lingers and presents another potential blocking factor. As noted by International Criminal Court Judge and former PRC official Xue Hanqin, "China's experience since the Opium War ... explains why China always attaches such importance to the principle of sovereign

---

[16] Along these lines, Beijing asserted that "[t]here is also a growing tendency toward politicizing human rights or applying double standards. Some countries are using human rights as a pretext to interfere in the internal affairs of other countries." "China is Committed to a Human Rights Development Path with Chinese Characteristics 2016/12/10," Ministry of Foreign Affairs of the People's Republic of China, www.fmprc.gov.cn/mfa_eng/wjdt_665385/zyjh_665391/t1423058.shtml, accessed February 6, 2019.

[17] Xi has articulated a more state-centric approach that claims to serve the "people," yet enhances state power. Salvatore Babones, "The Meaning of Xi Jinping Thought, National Revival and Military Power," *Foreign Affairs*, November 2, 2017, www.foreignaffairs.com/articles/china/2017-11-02/meaning-xi-jinping-thought, accessed October 21, 2019, and Chris Buckley, "Xi Jinping Thought Explained: A New Ideology for a New Era," *The New York Times*, February 26, 2018, www.nytimes.com/2018/02/26/world/asia/xi-jinping-thought-explained-a-new-ideology-for-a-new-era.html, accessed October 21, 2019.

equality in international affairs."[18] Reflecting these views, Chinese diplomats have repeatedly complained that UN censure, even mere expressions of concern from UN experts and diplomats from other foreign countries, constitutes an infringement on PRC sovereignty. The PRC articulated this view in its 1991 White Paper on Human Rights, which stated that "China has always maintained that human rights are essentially matters within the domestic jurisdiction of a country."[19] In this vein, the PRC's permanent representative to the UN protested that the US 2001 draft resolution on China's human rights practices "amounted to interference in the internal affairs of developing countries and undermined their development efforts under the pretext of concern for human rights."[20]

Third, the CCP government has stoked a nationalistic response that paints international human rights scrutiny as nefarious. As Marina Svensson argued, in order to "divert attention from its own responsibilities and human rights violations [PRC leaders invoke] a powerful language of national humiliations and imperialist bullying."[21] Along these lines, Chinese leaders disparage expressions of human rights concern from external actors as arrogant, disingenuous, and aimed at sowing internal discord and division to weaken or split the Chinese nation.[22] The PRC propaganda apparatus also accuses the United States and other Western nations of seeking to foment "peaceful evolution" by advancing ideas such as individual liberty and rule of law.[23]

---

[18] Xue Hanqin, *Chinese Contemporary Perspectives on International Law* (The Hague: Hague Academy of International Law, 2012), 28.

[19] Information Office of the State Council, *Human Rights in China 1991*, Section X, Active Participation in International Human Rights Activities. PRC scholars have shared this view. See Zhou, "The Study of Human Rights in the People's Republic of China," 91.

[20] UN Commission on Human Rights, Summary Record of the 62nd Meeting, April 23, 2001, UN Doc. E/CN.4/2001/SR.62, paragraph 58. For another similar PRC statement, see UN General Assembly, Third Committee, *Summary Record of the 32nd Meeting*, February 9, 2011, UN Doc. A/C.3/65/SR.32, paragraph 62, and UN General Assembly, Third Committee, *Summary Record of the 31st Meeting*, December 31, 2010, UN Doc. A/C.3/65/SR.31, paragraph 85.

[21] Svensson, *Debating Human Rights in China*, 313. See also Robert Weatherley, "Defending the Nation: The Role of Nationalism in Chinese Thinking on Human Rights," Democratization 15, no. 2 (April 2008), 342–362, and Jessica Chen Weiss, "How China Sees the World," *The New York Times*, September 29, 2019.

[22] As Friedberg put it, "The Chinese Communist Party's use of nationalism to rally popular support and bolster its claim to a continuing monopoly on political power has been widely noted." Aaron L. Friedberg, "The Sources of Chinese Conduct: Explaining Beijing's Assertiveness," *The Washington Quarterly* 37, no. 4 (Winter 2015), 138.

[23] David Shambaugh, "Coping with a Conflicted China," *The Washington Quarterly* 34, no. 1 (Winter 2011): 11.

Fourth, unlike other international issues, where there is some evidence of Chinese experts acting as transmitters of international norms, the Chinese government has kept a tight rein on human rights scholars and experts. Moreover, groups, such as lawyers and academics, that might have been advocates of human rights or greater political liberalization have been intimidated and repressed. The Chinese government is especially sensitive about independent human rights discussions and scholarship even viewing some of the principles enshrined in the regime as subversive and potentially threatening to CCP rule.[24] Thus, an epistemic community capable of advancing new ideas and shifting the government's perceptions and interests has failed to materialize.

Finally, the PRC's status as an emerging power and its sheer size and weight, which feeds its "middle kingdom" identity and enables it to exercise economic and political leverage, is another potential blocking factor. As scholar Pu Xiaoyu suggests, socialization may be a two-way process with China being among the emerging powers that appear to be "sending a strong message to the West, 'Stop telling us how to behave.'"[25] While scholars have theorized that sensitivity to social status is an integral aspect of the socialization process and PRC leaders were attentive to image concerns, this did not appear to facilitate socialization.[26] Paradoxically, increased scrutiny and the application of the regime's procedures after 1989 caused Chinese diplomats to more energetically resist normative human rights pressure and attempt to blunt the regime's impact. Instead, the PRC's concern with its image meant that it sought to deflect human rights attention using political maneuvers and diplomatic support. Thus, PRC diplomats acted more as public relations managers than potential transmitters of norms.

---

[24] Chris Buckley, "Chinese Legal Maverick, Facing Political Gales, Bides His Time," *New York Times*, May 18, 2018, www.nytimes.com/2018/05/18/world/asia/china-rights-he-weifang .html, accessed February 11, 2019, and Mimi Lau and Guo Rui, "Chinese '709' Rights Lawyer Wang Quanzhang Stands Trial as His Wife Is Forced to Stay Away," *South China Morning Post*, December 26, 2018, www.scmp.com/news/china/politics/article/2179524/ chinese-rights-lawyer-wang-quanzhang-court-final-case-2015, accessed February 11, 2019, and Zhang Lun, "What Happens When Universities Become 'Party Strongholds,'" *New York Times*, October 18, 2018, www.nytimes.com/2018/10/18/opinion/chinas-watchful-eye-reaches-into-the-classroom.html, accessed February 11, 2019.

[25] Pu Xiaoyu, "Socialization as a Two-way Process: Emerging Powers and the Diffusion or International Norms," *The Chinese Journal of International Politics* 5 (2012): 341.

[26] See, for example, Risse, Ropp, and Sikkink, *The Power of Human Rights*, Johnston, *Social States* and Jeffrey Checkel, *International Institutions and Socialization in Europe* (Cambridge: Cambridge University Press, 2007). Foot noted "material power, demographic size, degree of openness, and political culture" as possible relevant factors. Foot, *Rights Beyond Borders*, 13.

Curiously, even though attention on China has receded, Beijing has stepped up its role in the HRC. While the PRC faces routine monitoring through a number of universally applied mechanisms, including the UPR and reviews on its ratified treaties, since the late 1990s when it convinced the EU to forego resolutions other countries have not consistently attempted to use this form of censure. Yet, since 2013 the Chinese delegation has spearheaded initiatives, such as resolutions calling for "win-win cooperation" and building a "community of common destiny" and in January 2017 President Xi Jinping addressed the UNHRC with a speech that reiterated these principles.[27] Human rights advocates complain that these concepts downplay the importance of spotlighting abuses and using public pressure to elicit state cooperation. Thus, while a desire to deflect scrutiny fueled China's initial impetus to resist the regime, Beijing now appears to have other motivations. With its increased global weight, PRC leaders may reason that they can afford to play a more activist role. China's future posture toward the regime will depend partly on the actions other states take to counter PRC efforts as well as the degree to which scholar Jack Donnelly's assertion that human rights are an important standard that nations are held to for "full membership in international society" remains an important metric for judging state behavior.[28]

The Human Rights Regime

My research also provides insights that are relevant to the human rights regime, particularly its effectiveness and functioning, the degree to which it remains contested, and its likely future trajectory. These are crucial questions, given the evidence that countries like Russia and China are detractors of the regime. Moreover, liberal democracies, which traditionally have been the principal supporters of the regime, have been struggling to counter these encroachments. The rise of nondemocratic great powers further poses a challenge to the regime.[29]

---

[27] "Work Together to Build a Community of Shared Future for Mankind," Speech by H.E. Xi Jinping," *Xinhua*, January 19, 2017, www.xinhuanet.com/english/2017-01/19/c_135994707.htm, accessed January 17, 2019.

[28] As scholar Jack Donnelly puts it, "human rights represent a progressive late twentieth century expression of the important idea that international legitimacy and full membership in international society must rest in part on standards of just, humane or civilized behavior." Jack Donnelly, "Human Rights: A New Standard of Civilization?" *International Affairs* 74, no. 1 (January 1998): 21. See also Ibid., 18

[29] Azar Gat," The Return of Authoritarian Great Powers," *Foreign Affairs* (July/ August 2007).

Because my findings stand in contrast to scholarship showing evidence of PRC internationalization of norms in other international regimes, such as arms control, this gives rise to the question of whether some issue areas and international regimes are more successful in eliciting state socialization.[30] There are important ways that the human rights regime differs from other international regimes that likely impact its power to affect state behavior and thinking. First, the human rights regime governs an area in which there is an important domestic–international nexus in which states are being held to account for their domestic policies. A nation's treatment of its own citizens is an issue area that is linked to a state's domestic political culture, system of government, and polity, likely making some nations more impervious to the regime's influence. Second, unlike other regimes, such as trade and arms control, a state's noncompliance in the human rights area does not necessarily lead to material losses for other states and is not dependent on state reciprocity.[31] Given the lack of reciprocal gains or losses, states may be less active in policing each other or using pressure to bring about norm-compliant behavior. Moreover, in terms of regime design and institutional characteristics, the human rights regime does not have strong mechanisms to encourage compliance or respond to severe violations of human rights norms.[32] As documented in this book, Chinese diplomats were often able to maneuver within the regime or use their diplomatic relationships to block passage of UNCHR resolutions and recruit other countries to help shield it from scrutiny. As a result of these differences, in the human rights regime the cost of noncompliance and the motivations driving a state to comply differs from other regimes.[33]

My findings about the PRC's ability to work with other countries provides insight into the ways that states work cooperatively to protect

---

[30] Johnston, *Social States* and Medeiros, *Reluctant Restraint.*
[31] Kent noted that the human rights regime lacks "the bargaining counter of reciprocity." Kent, *Beyond Compliance,* 25.
[32] For example, a UN official noted that the treaty body system operates at 70 percent noncompliance. Interview with UN official, May 25, 2011, Geneva, Switzerland. While the international community's response after Tiananmen showed that a damaged human rights image can hurt material interests, most of the punitive actions were not taken in the regime but were bilateral actions and the sanctions imposed were dependent on the political will of other countries.
[33] For example, Hu, Chan, and Zha argued that international regimes can create "constraints on its foreign conduct as well as incentives to adapt to prevailing norms in contemporary international relations." Weixing Hu, Gerald Chan, and Daojiong Zha, "Understanding China's Behavior in World Politics: An Introduction," in *China's International Relations in the 21ˢᵗ Century: Dynamics of Paradigm Shifts,* eds. Weixing Hu, Gerald Chan, and Daojiong Zha (Lanham, MD: University Press of America, 2000), 2.

each other from scrutiny and affect the functioning of the regime. It also underscores the degree to which China's ideas found fertile ground among other countries, primarily the non-Western, developing nations that formed the LMG. As shown in Chapters 3 and 4, China collaborated with these other countries to constrain the regime during the creation of OPCAT and the HRC, and that together these states had some success.[34] This suggests not only that Beijing's ideas fall into easy alignment with these nations but also that the regime remains highly contested. Such findings also reinforce the intuitive point that highly contested regimes are less powerful in shaping state behavior since the normative signals are inconsistent.

Given this degree of contestation and other challenges, there are growing concerns about the future of the international human rights regime.[35] While this could suggest a greater likelihood that these countries might mount a challenge to the regime, unlike other international regimes, noncompliance does not damage the material interests of other states. Thus, to damage the regime states would have to engage in more destructive actions than noncompliance. Further, the detractors would have to gain sufficient support among other nations. Additionally, as pointed out earlier the human rights regime lacks potent sanctions. Thus, while the PRC could work with other states to oppose the regime and pursue wide-ranging revisions, because of the regime's inherent weaknesses and the limited threat that it represents these states are more likely to allow the regime to survive but resist any efforts to strengthen it and continue to retard its growth.

---

[34] Similar motivation in von Soest, "Democracy prevention," 623. Thomas Ambrosio, "Constructing a Framework of Authoritarian Diffusion: Concepts, Dynamics and Future Research," *International Studies Perspectives* 11, no. 4 (2010): 376.

[35] Stephen Hopgood, *The Endtimes of Human Rights* (Cornell: Cornell University Press, 2014).

Bibliography

English Language Secondary Sources

Abebe, Allehone Mulugeta. "Of Shaming and Bargaining: African States and the Universal Periodic Review of the United Nations Human Rights Council." *Human Rights Law Review* 9, no. 1 (2009): 1–35.

Abraham, Meghna. "Building the New Human Rights Council: Outcome and Analysis of the Institution-Building Year." In Occasional Papers Geneva. Geneva: Friedrich-Ebert Stiftung, August 2007.

A New Chapter for Human Rights. Geneva: International Service for Human Rights and Friedrich Ebert Stiftung, 2006.

Acharya, Amitav. *Whose Ideas Matter? Agency and Power in Asian Regionalism.* Ithaca, NY: Cornell University Press, 2009.

Acharya, Amitav and Alastair Iain Johnston. *Crafting Cooperation: Regional International Institutions in Comparative Perspective.* Cambridge: Cambridge University Press, 2007.

Alston, Philip. "The Commission on Human Rights." In *The United Nations and Human Rights: A Critical Appraisal,* 1st ed., edited by Philip Alston, 126–151. Oxford: Clarendon Press, 1992.

"The Populist Challenge to Human Rights." *Journal of Human Rights* 9 (2017): 1–15.

"Reconceiving the UN Human Rights Regime: Challenges Confronting the New UN Human Rights Council." *Melbourne Journal of International Law* 7, no. 1 (2006): 185–224.

The United Nations and Human Rights: A Critical Appraisal, 1st ed. Oxford: Clarendon Press, 1992.

Ambrosio, Thomas. "Catching the 'Shanghai Spirit': How the Shanghai Cooperative Organization Promotes Authoritarian Norms in Central Asia." *Europe-Asia Studies* 60, no. 8 (October 2008): 1321–1344.

"Constructing a Framework of Authoritarian Diffusion: Concepts, Dynamics and Future Research." *International Studies Perspectives* 11, no. 4 (2010): 375–392.

Ampiah, Kweku and Sanusha Naidu. "Introduction: Africa and China in the Post-Cold War Era." In *Crouching Tiger, Hidden Dragon? Africa and China,* edited by Kweku Ampiah and Sanusha Naidu, 1–19. Scottsville, South Africa: University of Kwazulu-Natal Press, 2008.

Angle, Stephen C. *Human Rights and Chinese Thought: A Cross-Cultural Inquiry.* New York: Cambridge University Press, 2002.

Angle, Stephen C. and Marina Svensson, eds. *The Chinese Human Rights Reader: Documentary and Commentary 1900–2000.* New York: M. E. Sharpe, 2001.

Bader, Julia. "Propping Up Dictators? Economic Cooperation from China and Its Impact on Authoritarian Persistence in Party and Non-party Regimes." *European Journal of Political Research* 54, no. 4 (2015): 655–672.

Bailes, Alyson J. "China and Eastern Europe: A Judgment of the 'Socialist Community'." *The Pacific Review* 3, no. 3 (1990): 222–242.

Bailey, Sydney D. *The Procedure of the U.N. Security Council,* 2nd ed. Oxford: Clarendon Press, 1988.

Baker, Philip. "China: Human Rights and Law." *The Pacific Review* 6, no. 3 (1993): 239–250.

"Human Rights, Europe and the People's Republic of China." *The China Quarterly* 169 (March 2002): 45–63.

Baldwin, David A., ed. *Neorealism and Neoliberalism: The Contemporary Debate.* New York: Columbia University Press, 1993.

Barnett, Michael and Martha Finnemore. *Rules for the World: International Organizations in Global Politics.* Ithaca, NY: Cornell University Press, 2004.

Bartolomei de la Cruz, Hector, Geraldo von Potobsky, and Lee Swepston. *The International Labor Organization: The International Standards System and Basic Human Rights.* Boulder, CO: Westview Press, 1996.

Bauer, Joanne R. and Daniel A. Bell, eds. *The East Asian Challenge for Human Rights.* Cambridge: Cambridge University Press, 1999.

Bearce, David H. and Stacy Bondanella. "Intergovernmental Organizations, Socialization, and Member-State Interest Convergence." *International Organization* 61, no. 3 (2007): 703–733.

Beja, Jean-Philippe. "China since Tiananmen: The Massacre's Long Shadow." *Journal of Democracy* 20, no. 3 (July 2009): 5–16.

"Introduction to 4 June 1989: A Watershed in Chinese Contemporary History." In *The Impact of China's 1989 Tiananmen Massacre,* edited by Jean-Philippe Beja, 1–12. Hoboken, NJ: Routledge, 2010.

"Xi Jinping's China: On the Road to Neo-totalitarianism." *Social Science Research* 86, no. 1 (Spring 2019): 203–230.

Benner, Thorsten, Jan Gaspers, Mareike Ohlberg, Lucrezia Poggetti, and Kristin Shi-Kupfer. *Authoritarian Advance: Responding to China's Growing Political Influence in Europe.* Berlin: Global Public Policy Institute and Mercator Institute for China Studies, 2018.

Bloomfield, Lincoln P. "China, the United States, and the United Nations." *International Organization* 20, no. 4 (Autumn 1966): 653–676.

Bolton, John. *Surrender Is Not an Option: Defending America at the United Nations.* New York: Threshold Editions, 2007.

Booth, Ken. *Realism and World Politics.* New York: Routledge Publishers, 2011.

Boyle, Kevin. "The United Nations Human Rights Council: Origins, Antecedents, and Prospects." In *New Institutions for Human Rights Protection,* edited by Kevin Boyle, 11–47. New York: Oxford University Press, 2009.

Brautigam, Deborah. "Chinese Development Aid in Africa: What, Where, Why and How?" In *Rising China: Global Challenges and Opportunities*, edited by Jane Golley and Ligang Song, 203–222. Canberra: Australia National University Press, 2011.

The Dragon's Gift: The Real Story of China in Africa. Oxford: Oxford University Press, 2010.

Breslin, Shaun. "China and the Global Order: Signaling Threat or Friendship?" *International Affairs* 89, no. 3 (2013): 615–634.

Brinks, Daniel and Michael Coppedge. "Diffusion Is No Illusion: Neighbor Emulation in the Third Save of Democracy." *Comparative Political Studies* 39, no. 4 (2006): 463–489.

Brown, Michael E., Owen R. Cote, Sean M. Lynn-Jones, and Steven E. Miller, eds. *The Rise of China: An International Security Reader*. Cambridge, MA: The MIT Press, 2000.

Bull, Hedley. *The Anarchical Society: A Study of World Order in World Politics*. London: Macmillan, 1977.

Burgers, J. Herman and Hans Danelius. *The United Nations Convention against Torture: A Handbook on the Convention against Torture and Other Cruel, Inhuman or Degrading Treatment or Punishment*. Dordrecht: Martinus Nijhoff Publishers, 1988.

Bussard, Stephane. "A Night of Madness for Human Rights." In *The First 365 Days of the Council*, edited by Lars Muller, 70–85. Bern: Swiss Department of Foreign Affairs, 2007.

Buzan, Barry and Rosemary Foot, eds. *Does China Matter? A Reassessment: Essays in Memory of Gerald Segal*. London: Routledge, 2004.

Byrnes, Andrew. "The Committee against Torture." In *The United Nations and Human Rights: A Critical Appraisal*, edited by Philip Alston, 509–546. Oxford: Clarendon Press, 1992.

Cabestan, Jean-Pierre. "How China Managed to De-isolate Itself on the International Stage and Re-engage the World after Tiananmen." In *The Impact of China's 1989 Tiananmen Massacre*, edited by Jean-Philippe Beja, 194–205. Hoboken, NJ: Routledge, 2010.

Cardenas, Sonia. *Conflict and Compliance: State Responses to International Human Rights Pressure*. Philadelphia: University of Pennsylvania Press, 2007.

Carlsnaes, Walter, Thomas Risse, and Beth A. Simmons, eds. *Handbook of International Relations*. Thousand Oaks, CA: Sage Pubications, 2002.

Carlson, Allen. "Helping to Keep the Peace (Albeit Reluctantly): China's Recent Stance on Sovereignty in Multilateral Intervention." *Pacific Affairs* 77, no. 1 (2004): 19–26.

"More Than Just Saying No: China's Evolving Approach to Sovereignty and Intervention Since Tiananmen." In *New Directions in the Study of China's Foreign Policy*, edited by Alastair Iain Johnston and Robert S. Ross, 217–241. Stanford, CA: Stanford University Press, 2006.

Unifying China, Integrating with the World. Stanford, CA: Stanford University Press, 2005.

Chan, Gerald. *China and International Organizations: Participation in Non-governmental Organizations Since 1971*. New York: Oxford University Press, 1989.

Chan, Gerald, Pak K. Lee, and Lai-Ha Chan, eds. *China Engages Global Governance: A New World Order in the Making?* New York: Routledge, 2012.

Chan, Lai-ha, Pak K. Lee, and Gerald Chan. "Rethinking Global Governance: A China Model in the Making?" *Contemporary Politics* 14, no. 1 (March 2008): 3–19.

Chan, Steve. "Chinese Perspectives on World Order." In *International Order and the Future of World Politics*, edited by T.V. Paul and John A. Hall, 197–212. Cambridge: Cambridge University Press, 1999.

Chayes, Abram and Antonia Handler Chayes. "Compliance without Enforcement: State Behavior under Regulatory Treaties." *Negotiation Journal* 7, no. 3 (July 1991): 311–330.

The New Sovereignty: Compliance with International Regulatory Agreements. Cambridge, MA: Harvard University Press, 1995.

"On Compliance." *International Organization* 47, no. 2 (Spring 1993): 175–205.

Checkel, Jeffrey. "Theoretical Pluralism in IR: Possibilities and Limits." In *Handbook of International Relations*, edited by Walter Carlsnaes, Thomas Risse and Beth A. Simmons, 220–242. London: Sage, 2002.

Checkel, Jeffrey, ed. *International Institutions and Socialization in Europe.* New York: Cambridge University Press, 2007.

Chen, Albert H.Y. "Developing Theories of Rights and Human Rights in China." In *Hong Kong, China and 1997: Essays in Legal Theory*, edited by Raymond Wacks, 123–149. Hong Kong: Hong Kong University Press, 1993.

Chen, Dingding. "China's Participation in the International Human Rights Regime: A State Identity Perspective." *Chinese Journal of International Politics* 2, no. 3 (2009): 399–419.

"Explaining China's Changing Discourse on Human Rights." *Asian Perspectives* 29, no. 3 (2005): 155–182.

Chen, Dingding and Jianwei Wang. "Lying Low No More?: China's New Thinking on the Tao Guang Yang Hui Strategy." *China: An International Journal* 9, no. 2 (September 2011): 195–216.

Chen, Luzhi and Li Tiecheng, eds. *United Nations and World Order.* Beijing: Beijing University Press, 1993.

Chen, Nai-Ruenn. "China's Foreign Trade in Global Perspective." In *China and the Global Community*, edited by James C. Hsiung, and Samuel S. Kim, 120–139. New York: Praeger Publishers, 1980.

Chen, Titus. "China's Reaction to the Color Revolutions: Adaptive Authoritarianism in Full Swing." *Asian Perspective* 34, no. 2 (2010): 5–51.

Chen, Yu-Jie. "China's Challenge to the International Human Rights Regime." *NYU Journal of International Law and Politics* 51 (2019): 1179–1222.

Cheng, Chu-yuan. *Behind the Tiananmen Massacre: Social, Political and Economic Ferment in China.* Boulder, CO: Westview Press, 1990.

Cheng, Joseph Y.S. "China's Africa Policy in the Post-Cold War Era." *Journal of Contemporary Asia* 39, no. 1 (2009): 87–115.

"Latin America in China's Contemporary Foreign Policy." *Journal of Contemporary Asia* 36, no. 4 (2006): 500–528.

Chin, Gregory and Ramesh Thakur. "Will China Change the Rules of Global Order?" *The Washington Quarterly* 33, no. 4 (September 2010): 119–138.

Chiu, Hungdah. "Chinese Attitudes Toward International Law of Human Rights in the Post-Mao Era." In *Chinese Politics from Mao to Deng*, edited by Victor C. Falkenheim, 237–270. New York: Paragon House, 1989.

Choedon, Yeshi. *China and the United Nations*. New Delhi: South Asian Publishers, 1990.

Chow, Daniel C.K. "How China Uses International Trade to Promote Its View of Human Rights." *The George Washington International Law Review* 45 (2013): 103–124.

Christensen, Thomas J. "Chinese Realpolitik." *Foreign Affairs* 75, no. 5 (September/October 1996): 37–52.

"Pride Pressure, and Politics: The Roots of China's Worldview." In *In the Eyes of the Dragon: China Views the World*, edited by Yong Deng and Fei-ling Wang, 239–256. New York: Rowman and Littlefield Publishers, Inc., 1999.

Clark, Ann Marie. *Diplomacy of Conscience: Amnesty International and Changing Human Rights Norms*. Princeton, NJ: Princeton University Press, 2001.

Clark, Ian. *Legitimacy in International Society*. Oxford: Oxford University Press, 2005.

Cohen, Jerome Alan and Hungdah Chiu. *People's China and International Law: A Documentary Study*. Princeton, NJ: Princeton University Press, 1974.

Cohen, Roberta. "People's Republic of China: The Human Rights Exception." *Human Rights Quarterly* 9, no. 4 (1987): 447–549.

Cohen, Stanley. "Government Responses to Human Rights Reports: Claims, Denials and Counterclaims." *Human Rights Quarterly* 18, no. 3 (August 1996): 517–543.

Cole, Wade M. "Individuals v. States: The Correlates of Human Rights Committee Rulings, 1979–2007." *Social Science Research* 40, no. 3 (2011): 985–1000.

Copper, John F. "Peking's Post-Tiananmen Foreign Policy: The Human Rights Factor." *Issues and Studies* 30 (October 1994): 49–73.

Copper, John F. and Ta-ling Lee. *Coping with a Bad Global Image: Human Rights in the People's Republic of China, 1993–1994*. Lanham, MD: University Press of America, 1997.

Cortell, Andrew P. and James W. Davis. "When Norms Clash: International Norms, Domestic Practices, and Japan's Internalisation of the GATT/ WTO." *Review of International Studies* 31, no. 1 (October 2005): 3–25.

Croddy, Eric. "China's Role in the Chemical and Biological Weapons Disarmament Regime." *Nonproliferation Review* 9, no. 1 (Spring 2002): 16–47.

Davis, Michael C. "Chinese Perspectives on Human Rights." In *Human Rights and Chinese Values: Legal, Philosophical, and Political Perspectives*, edited by Michael C. Davis, 3–24. Oxford: Oxford University Press, 1995.

Davis, Michael C., ed. *Human Rights and Chinese Values: Legal, Philosophical, and Political Perspectives*. Hong Kong: Oxford University Press, 1995.

de Frouville, Olivier. "Building a Universal System for the Protection of Human Rights." In *New Challenges for the UN Human Rights Machinery*, eds. M.

Cherif Bassiouni and William A. Schabas, 241–265. Cambridge: Intersentia, 2011.

Deng, Xiaoping. "Deng Hails Armymen." *Beijing Review*, no. 24-254 (June 12–25, 1989): 4–9.

Selected Works of Deng Xiaoping (1975–1982). Vol. II. Beijing: Foreign Language Press, 1984.

Selected Works of Deng Xiaoping (1983–1992). Vol. III. Beijing: Foreign Language Press, 1994.

Deng, Yong. "China: The Post-Responsible Power." *The Washington Quarterly* 37 no. 4 (Winter 2015): 117–132.

China's Struggle for Status: The Realignment of International Relations. Cambridge: Cambridge University Press, 2008.

"Escaping the Periphery: China's National Identity in World Politics." In *China's International Relations in the Twenty-first Century*, edited by Wenxing Hu, Gerald Chan, and Daojiong Zha, 41–70. Lanham, MD: University Press of America, 2000.

Deng, Yong and Fei-Ling Wang. *In the Eyes of the Dragon: China Views the World*. Lanham, MD: Rowman and Littlefield Publishers, 1999.

Deng, Yong and Fei-Ling Wang, eds. *China Rising: Power and Motivation in Chinese Foreign Policy*. Lanham, MD: Rowman and Littlefield Publishers, 2005.

Dexter, Lewis Anthony. *Elite and Specialized Interviewing*. Evanston, IL: Northwestern University Press, 1970.

Diamond, Larry. *The Spirit of Democracy: The Struggle to Build Free Societies Throughout the World*. New York: Times Books, 2008.

Dittmer, Lowell. "China and the Developing World." In *China, the Developing World, and the New Global Dynamic*, edited by Lowell Dittmer and George T. Yu, 1–12. Boulder, CO: Lynne Rienner, 2010.

"Chinese Human Rights and American Foreign Policy: A Realist Approach." *The Review of Politics* 63, no. 3 (Summer 2001): 421–459.

Dittmer, Lowell and George T. Yu, eds. *China, the Developing World, and the New Global Dynamic*. London: Lynne Rienner Publishers, 2010.

Dominguez Redondo, Elvira. "The Universal Periodic Review of the UN Human Rights Council: An Assessment of the First Session." *Chinese Journal of International Law* 7, no. 3 (2008): 721–734.

Donnelly, Jack. "The Emerging International Regime Against Torture." *Netherlands International Law Review* 33, no. 1 (1986): 1–23.

"Human Rights: A New Standard of Civilization?" *International Affairs* 74, no. 1 (January 1998): 1–23.

International Human Rights, 2nd ed. Boulder, CO: Westview Press, 1997.

"International Human Rights: A Regime Analysis." *International Organization* 40, no. 3 (Summer 1986): 599–642.

"Progress in Human Rights." In *Progress in Postwar International Relations*, edited by Emanuel Alder and Beverly Crawford, 312–358. New York: Columbia University Press, 1991.

Dreher, Axel, Andreas Fuchs, Brad Pares, Austin M. Strange and Michael J. Tierney. "Apples and Dragon Fruits: The Determinants of Aid and Other

Forms of State Financing from China to Africa." *International Studies Quarterly* 62 (2018): 182–194.

Drezner, Daniel. "The New World Order." *Foreign Affairs* 86, no. 2 (March/April 2007): 14–28.

Drinan, Robert F. and Teresa T. Kuo. "The 1991 Battle for Human Rights in China." *Human Rights Quarterly* 14, no. 1 (February 1992): 21–42.

Economy, Elizabeth. *By All Means Necessary*. Oxford: Oxford University Press, 2014.

"The Game Changer: Coping with China's Foreign Policy Revolution." *Foreign Affairs* 89, no. 6 (November/December 2010): 142–152.

"The Great Leap Backward?; The Costs of China's Environmental Crisis." *Foreign Affairs* 86, no. 5 (2007): 38–59.

"The Impact of International Regimes on Chinese Foreign Policy-Making: Broadening Perspectives and Policies... But Only to a Point." In *The Making of Chinese Foreign and Security Policy in the Era of Reform, 1978–2000*, edited by David M. Lampton, 230–253. Stanford, CA: Stanford University Press, 2001.

Economy, Elizabeth and Adam Segal. "The G-2 Mirage: Why the United States and China are Not Ready to Upgrade Ties." *Foreign Affairs* 88, no. 3 (2009): 14–23.

Economy, Elizabeth and Michel Oksenberg, eds. *China Joins the World: Progress and Prospects*. New York: Council on Foreign Relations Press, 1999.

Edwards, Martin S., Kevin M. Scott, Susan Hannah Allen, and Kate Irvin. "Sins of Commission? Understanding Membership Patterns on the United Nations Human Rights Commission." *Political Research Quarterly* 61, no. 3 (September 2008): 390–402.

Edwards, R. Randle, John Henkin, and Andrew J. Nathan. *Human Rights in Contemporary China*. New York: Columbia University Press, 1986.

Egan, Suzanne. "Strengthening the United Nations Human Rights Treaty Body System." *Human Rights Law Review* 13, no. 2 (2013), 242.

Evans, Malcolm and Claudine Haenni-Dale. "Preventing Torture? The Development of the Optional Protocol to the UN Convention Against Torture." *Human Rights Law Review* 4, no. 1 (2004): 19–55.

Farer, Tom J. and Felice Gaer. "The UN and Human Rights: At the End of the Beginning." In *United Nations, Divided World*, edited by Adam Roberts and Benedict Kingsbury, 240–296. Oxford: Oxford University Press, 1993.

Feeney, William R. "Chinese Global Politics in the United Nations General Assembly." In *China in the Global Community*, edited by James C. Hsiung, and Samuel S. Kim, 104. New York: Praeger Publishers, 1980.

Feinerman, James V. "Chinese Participation in the International Legal Order: Rogue Elephant or Team Player." *The China Quarterly* 141 (March 1995): 186–210.

Fernandez Palacios and Juan Antonio. "The Non-Aligned Movement's Role in the Institution-Building Process of the Human Rights Council: An Approach from the Cuban Chairmanship." In *The First 365 Days of the United Nations Human Rights Council*, edited by Lars Muller, 152–161. Bern: Swiss Department of Foreign Affairs, 2007.

Finnemore, Martha. "International Organizations as Teachers of Norms: The United Nations Educational, Scientific, and Cultural Organization and Science Policy." *International Organization* 47, no. 4 (Autumn 1993): 565–597.

National Interests in International Society. Ithaca, NY: Cornell University Press, 1996.

"Norms, Culture, and World Politics: Insights from Sociology's Institutionalism." *International Organization* 50, no. 2 (Spring 1996): 325–347.

Finnemore, Martha and Kathryn Sikkink. "International Norm Dynamics and Political Change." *International Organization* 52, no. 4 (October 1998): 887–917.

"Taking Stock: The Constructivist Research Program in International Relations and Comparative Politics." *Annual Review of Political Science* 4 (June 2001): 391–416.

Foot, Rosemary. "Bush, China and Human Rights." *Survival* 45, no. 2 (January 2003): 167–186.

"China and the Tian'anmen Bloodshed of June 1989." In *Foreign Policy: Theories, Actors, Cases*, 2nd ed., edited by Steve Smith, Amelia Hadfield, and Tim Dunne, 327–347. Oxford: Oxford University Press, 2012.

"Chinese Power and the Idea of a Responsible State." *The China Journal* 45 (January 2001): 1–19.

Rights Beyond Borders: The Global Community and the Struggle over Human Rights. Oxford: Oxford University Press, 2001.

The Practice of Power: US Relations with China since 1949. Oxford: Clarendon Press, 1995.

Foot, Rosemary and Andrew Walter. *China, the United States and Global Order.* Cambridge: Cambridge University Press, 2011.

"Global Norms and Major State Behavior: The Cases of China and the United States." *European Journal of International Relations* 19, no. 2 (June 2013): 329–352.

Foote, Blythe Finke. *China Joins the United Nations.* New York: SamHar, 1973.

Forsythe, David P. *Human Rights in International Relations.* Cambridge: Cambridge University Press, 2006.

The Internationalization of Human Rights. Lexington, MA: Lexington Books, 1988.

Franck, Thomas M. *The Power of Legitimacy Among Nations.* New York: Oxford University Press, 1990.

Fravel, Taylor M. "China's Attitude Toward UN Peacekeeping Operations Since 1989." *Asian Survey* 36, no. 11(November 1996): 1102–1121.

Freedman, Lawrence. "China as a Global Strategic Actor." In *Does China Matter? A Reassessment: Essays in Memory of Gerald Segal*, edited by Barry Buzan and Rosemary Foot, 21–36. New York: Routledge, 2004.

Freedman, P.E. and Anne Freedman. "Political Learning." In *The Handbook of Political Behavior.* Vol. 1., edited by Samuel L. Long, 255–303. New York: Plenum Press, 1981.

Friedberg, Aaron L. "Bucking Beijing." *Foreign Affairs* 91, no. 5 (September/October 2012): 48–58.

A Contest for Supremacy: China, America, and the Struggle for Mastery in Asia. New York: W.W. Norton, 2011.

"Rethinking China: Competing with China." *Survival* 60, no. 3 (Summer 2018): 7–64.

"The Sources of Chinese Conduct: Explaining Beijing's Assertiveness." *The Washington Quarterly* 37, no. 4 (Winter 2015): 133–150.

Friedrich-Ebert-Stiftung and International Service for Human Rights. *A New Chapter for Human Rights: A Handbook on Issues of Transition from the Commission on Human Rights to the Human Rights Council.* Geneva: International Service for Human Rights and Friedrich Ebert Stiftung, 2006.

Friedman, Edward and McCormick Barrett, eds. *What if China Doesn't Democratize?: Implications for War and Peace.* Armonk, NY: East Gate Book, 2000.

Frieman, Wendy. "New Members of the Club: Chinese Participation in Arms Control Regimes 1980–1995." *The Nonproliferation Review* 3, no. 3 (Spring/Summer 1996): 15–30.

Fuchs, Andreas and Marina Rudyak. "The Motives of China's Foreign Aid." In *Handbook of the International Political Economy of China*, ed. Ka Zeng, 392–410. Northampton, MA: Edward Elgar Publishing, 2019.

Fuchs, Andreas and Nils-Hendrik Klann. "Paying a Visit: The Dalai Lama Effect on International Trade." *Journal of International Economics* 91 (2013): 164–177.

Fullilove, Michael. Angels and Dragons: Asia, the UN, reform and the next Secretary-General. *Lowy Institute Issues Brief*, July 2005, http://www.lowyinstitute.org/files/pubfiles/Fullilove%2C_Angels_and_dragons160306.pdf.

"Angel or Dragon? China and the United Nations." *The National Interest*, no. 85 (September/October 2006): 67–75.

"China and the United Nations: The Stakeholder Spectrum." *The Washington Quarterly* 34, no. 3 (Summer 2011): 63–85.

Funabashi, Yoichi, Michel Oksenberg, and Heinrich Weiss. *An Emerging China in a World of Interdependence.* New York: Trilateral Commission, 1994.

Fung, Courtney. *China and Intervention at the UN Security Council: Reconciling Status.* Oxford: Oxford University Press, 2019.

Gaer, Felice. "Implementing Treaty Body Recommendations: Establishing Better Follow-Up Procedures." In *New Challenges for the UN Human Rights Machinery: What Future for the UN Treaty Body System and the Human Rights Council Procedures?*, edited by M. Cherif Bassiouni and William A. Schabas, 107–121. Cambridge: Intersentia, 2011.

"A Voice Not an Echo: Universal Periodic Review and the UN Treaty Body System." *Human Rights Law Review* 7, no. 1 (2007): 109–139.

Galenson, Walter. *The International Labor Organization: An American View.* Madison, WI: University of Wisconsin Press, 1981.

Garrett, Banning and Bonnie Glaser. "Chinese Perspectives on Nuclear Arms Control," *International Security* 20, no. 3 (Winter 1995/1996): 43–78.

Gerber, Paula. "Human Rights Reform in the United Nations: The Good, the Bad, the Ugly." *Alternative Law Journal* 31, no. 22 (June 2006): 88–92.

Ghebali, Victor-Yves. *The International Labor Organization: A Case Study on the Evolution of U.N. Specialized Agencies*. London: Martinus Nijhoff Publishers, 1989.

Gilboy, George J. and Benjamin L. Read. "Political and Social Reform in China: Alive and Walking." *The Washington Quarterly* 31, no. 3 (Summer 2008): 143–164.

Gill, Bates. "Two Steps Forward, One Step Back: The Dynamics of Chinese Nonproliferation and Arms Control Policy-Making in an Era of Reform." In *the Making of Chinese Foreign and Security Policy in the Era of Reform: 1978–2000*, edited by David M. Lampton, 257–288. Stanford: Stanford University Press, 2001.

Gill, Bates and Chin-Hao Huang. "China and UN Peacekeeping." In *Providing Peacekeeping: The Politics, Challenges, and Future of UN Peacekeeping*, edited by Paul Williams, and Alex Bellamy, 139–157. Oxford: Oxford University Press, 2013.

Gill, Bates and Evan S. Medeiros. "Foreign and Domestic Influences on China's Arms Control and Nonproliferation Policies," *The China Quarterly* 161 (2000): 66–94.

Gill, Bates and James Reilly. "Sovereignty, Intervention, and Peacekeeping: The View from Beijing." *Survival* 42, no. 3 (Autumn 2000): 41–59.

Gilpin, Robert. *War and Change in World Politics*. Cambridge: Cambridge University Press, 1981.

Glendon, Mary Ann. *A World Made New: Eleanor Roosevelt and the Universal Declaration of Human Rights*. New York: Random House, 2001.

Goldman, Merle. The Importance of Human Rights in U.S. Policy Toward China." In *Greater China and U.S. Foreign Policy: The Choice Between Confrontation and Mutual Respect*, edited by Thomas A. Metzger and Ramon H. Myers, 76–83. Stanford, CA: Hoover Institution Press, 1996.

"Politically–Engaged Intellectuals in the 1990s." *The China Quarterly*, no. 159 (September 1999): 700–711.

"Politically-Engaged Intellectuals in the Deng-Jiang Era: A Changing Relationship with the Party-State." *The China Quarterly*, no. 145 (1996): 35–52.

Sowing the Seeds of Democracy in China: Political Reform in the Deng Xiaoping Era. Cambridge: Harvard University Press, 1994.

Goldstein, Avery. "The Diplomatic Face of China's Grand Strategy: A Rising Power's Emerging Choice." *The China Quarterly* 168 (December 2001): 935–964.

Rising to the Challenge: China's Grand Strategy and International Security. Stanford, CA: Stanford University Press, 2005.

Goldstein, Judith and Robert O. Keohane. "Ideas and Foreign Policy: An Analytical Framework." In *Ideas and Foreign Policy, Beliefs, Institutions and Political Change*, edited by Judith Goldstein and Robert O. Keohane, 3–30. Ithaca, NY: Cornell University Press, 1993.

Gong, Gerrit W. "China's Entry into International Society." In *The Expansion of International Society*, edited by Hedley Bull and Adam Watson, 171–183. Oxford: Clarendon Press, 1984.

The Standard of Civilisation in International Society. Oxford: Clarendon Press, 1984.

Goodman, David S. G. and Gerald Segal. *China Rising: Nationalism and Interdependence*. London: Routledge, 1997.

Gowan, Richard and Franziska Brantner. *A Global Force for Human Rights? An Audit of European Power at the UN*. London: European Council on Foreign Relations Policy Paper, September 2008.

Gurtov, Mel. "Changing Perspectives and Policies." In *China, the Developing World, and the New Global Dynamic*, eds. Lowell Dittmer and George T. Yu, 13–36. Boulder, CO: Lynne Rienner, 2010.

Gutter, Jeroen. "Special Procedures and the Human Rights Council: Achievements and Challenges Ahead." *Human Rights Law Review* 7, no. 1 (2007): 93–107.

Haas, Ernst B. *Human Rights and International Action: The Case of Freedom of Association*. Stanford, CA: Stanford University Press, 1970.

When Knowledge is Power: Three Models of Change in International Organizations. Berkeley: University of California Press, 1990.

Hafner-Burton, Emilie. "International Regimes for Human Rights." *The Annual Review of Political Science* 15 (2012): 265–286.

Hafner-Burton, Emilie and James Ron. "Seeing Double: Human Rights Impact Through Qualitative and Quantitative Eyes?" *World Politics* 61, no. 2 (April 2009): 360–401.

Hafner-Burton, Emilie and Kiyoteru Tsutsui. "Human Rights in a Globalizing World: The Paradox of Empty Promises." *American Journal of Sociology* 110, no. 5 (March 2005): 1373–1411.

Halper, Stefan. *The Beijing Consensus: How China's Authoritarian Model Will Dominate the Twenty-first Century*. New York: Basic Books, 2010.

Hampson, Francoise J. "An Overview of the Reform of the UN Human Rights Machinery." *Human Rights Law Review* 7, no. 1 (2007): 7–27.

Han, Nianlong, ed. *Diplomacy of Contemporary China*. Hong Kong: New Horizon Press, 1990.

Harding, Harry. *China's Cooperative Relationships: Partnerships and Alignments in Modern Chinese Foreign Policy*. Washington, D.C.: Brookings Institution Press, 1990.

"China and the International Order." *Remarks to the Open Forum*, Washington, D.C., April 3, 2002, http://2001-2009.state.gov/s/p/of/proc/tr/11589.htm.

China's Second Revolution: Reform After Mao. Washington, D.C.: Brookings Institution Press, 1987.

Harding, Harry, ed. *China's Foreign Relations in the 1980s*. New Haven, CT: Yale University Press, 1984.

Harris, Stuart and Gary Klintworth, eds. *China as a Great Power: Myths, Realities, and Challenges in the Asia Pacific Region*. New York: St. Martin's Press, 1995.

Hasenclever, Andreas, Peter Mayer, and Volker Rittberger, eds. *Theories of International Regimes*. Cambridge: Cambridge University Press, 1997.

Hathaway, Oona. "Do Human Rights Treaties Make a Difference?" *Yale Law Journal* 111, no. 8 (2002): 1935–2042.

He, Yin. *China's Changing Policy on UN Peacekeeping Operations*. Stockholm: Institute for Development and Security Policy, 2007.

Helfer, Laurence R. "Monitoring and Compliance with Unratified Treaties: The ILO Experience." *Law and Contemporary Problems* 71, no. 1 (2008): 193–218.

"Understanding Change in International Organizations: Globalization and Innovation in the ILO." *Vanderbilt Law Review* 59, no. 3 (2006): 649–726.

Hempson-Jones, Justin S. "The Evolution of China's Engagement with International Governmental Organizations" *Asian Survey* 45, no. 5 (September-October 2005): 702–721.

Hickey, Dennis and Baoguang Guo, eds. *Dancing with the Dragon: China's Emergence in the Developing World.* Boulder, CO: Rowman & Littlefield Publishers, Inc., 2010.

Hirono, Miwa and Marc Lanteigne. "Introduction: China and UN Peacekeeping." *International Peacekeeping* 18, no. 3 (June 2011): 243–256.

Hirschman, Alberto O. "The Search for Paradigms as a Hindrance to Understanding." *World Politics* 22, no. 3 (April 1970): 329–343.

Ho, David Yau-Fai. "On the Concept of Face." *American Journal of Sociology* 81, no. 4 (1976): 867–884.

Hollyer, James R. and B. Peter Rosendorff. "Why do Authoritarian Regimes Sign the Convention Against Torture? Signaling, Domestic Politics and Non-compliance." *Quarterly Journal of Political Science* 6, no. 3–4 (2011): 275–327.

Hopgood, Stephen. *The Endtimes of Human Rights.* Cornell: Cornell University Press, 2013.

"The Endtimes of Human Rights." In *Debating the Endtimes of Human Rights*, edited by Doutje Lettinga and Lars van Troost, 11–18. Amsterdam: Amnesty International Netherlands, 2014.

Keepers of the Flame: Understanding Amnesty International. Ithaca, NY: Cornell University Press, 2006.

Hu, Weixing, Gerald Chan, and Daojiong Zha. "Understanding China's Behavior in World Politics: An Introduction." In *China's International Relations in the Twenty-first Century: Dynamics of Paradigm Shifts*, edite by Weixing Hu, Gerald Chan, and Daojiong Zha. Lanham, MD: University Press of America, 2000.

Huang, Chin-Hao. "Peacekeeping, Sovereignty, and Intervention." In *Chinese Foreign Policy*, edited by Emilian Kavalski, 337–348. London: Ashgate, 2012.

"Strategic Adaption or Normative Learning?: Understanding China's Evolving Approach Toward Peacekeeping in Africa." *Journal of International Peacekeeping* (forthcoming).

Huang, Hua. *Huang Hua's Memoirs.* Beijing: Foreign Language Press, 2008.

Huang, Mab. "Universal Human Rights and Chinese Liberalism." In *Human Rights and Asian Values: Contesting National Identities and Cultural Representations in Asia*, edited by Michael Jacobsen and Ole Bruun, 227–248. Richmond, Surrey: Curzon Press, 2000.

Humphrey, John P. *Human Rights and the United Nations: A Great Adventure.* Dobbs Ferry: Transnational Publishers, 1984.

Ikenberry, John G. The Rise of China and the Future of the West: Can the Liberal System Survive?" *Foreign Affairs* 87, no. 1 (2008): 23–37.

Ikenberry, John G. and Charles A. Kupchan. "Socialization and Hegemonic Power." *International Organization* 44, no. 3 (Summer 1990): 283–315.

Inboden, Rana Siu. *Authoritarian States: Blocking Civil Society Participation in the United Nations.* Austin, TX: Robert S. Strauss Center for International Security and Law, 2019.

Inboden, Rana Siu and Titus Chen, "China's Response to International Normative Pressure: The Case of Human Rights." *The International Spectator: Italian Journal of International Affairs* 47, no. 2 (2012): 45–57.

Jacobson, Harold K. and Michel Oksenberg. *China's Participation in the IMF, the World Bank and the GATT.* Ann Arbor: The University of Michigan Press, 1990.

Jacobson, Linda and Dean Knox. *Policy Paper No. 26: New Foreign Policy Actors in China.* Solna, Sweden: Stockholm International Peace Research Institute (SIPRI), September 2010.

Jacques, Martin. *When China Rules the World: The End of the Western World and the Birth of a New Global Order.* New York: Penguin, 2009.

Jiang, Na. *China and International Human Rights: Harsh Punishments in the Context of the International Covenant on Civil and Political Rights.* New York: Springer, 2014.

Job, Brian L. and Anastasia Shesterinina. "China as a Global Norm-Shaper: Institutionalization and Implementation of the Responsibility to Protect." In *Implementation in World Politics: How Norms Change Practice*, edited by Alexander Betts, and Phil Orchard, 144–159. Oxford: Oxford University Press.

Johnston, Alastair Iain. "China in a World of Orders: Rethinking Compliance and Challenge in Beijing's International Relations." *International Security* 44, no. 2 (Fall 2019): 9–60.

Cultural Realism: Strategic Culture and Grand Strategy in Chinese History. Princeton, NJ: Princeton University Press, 1998.

"Cultural Realism and Strategy in Maoist China," in *The Culture of National Security: Norms and Identity in World Politics*, ed. Peter J. Katzenstein, 216–268. New York: Columbia University Press, 1996.

"Defective Cooperation: China and International Environmental Institutions, 1990–1994." Unpublished paper at Harvard University, Cambridge, MA, August 1995.

"International Structures and Chinese Foreign Policy." In *China and the World:Chinese Foreign Policy Faces the New Millennium*, 4th ed., edited by Samuel S. Kim, 55–90. Boulder, CO: Westview Press, 1998.

"Is China a Status Quo Power?" *International Security* 27, no. 4 (Spring 2003): 5–56.

"Learning versus Adaptation: Explaining Change in Chinese Arms Control Policy in the 1980s and 1990s." *The China Journal* 35, no. 1 (January 1996): 36–43.

Social States: China in International Institutions, 1980–2000. Princeton, NJ: Princeton University Press, 2008.

"Trends in Theory and Method in the Study of Chinese Foreign Policy." Paper presented at the Conference on China Studies on the Occasion of the 50th Anniversary of the Fairbank Center for East Asian Research in December 2005, Cambridge, MA, revised February 2006.

Johnston, Alastair Iain and Robert S. Ross, eds. *Engaging China: The Management of an Emerging Power.* London: Routledge, 1999.

eds. *New Directions in the Study of China's Foreign Policy.* Stanford, CA: Stanford University Press, 2006.

Jonsson, Christer. "Cognitive Factors in Explaining Regime Dynamics." In *Regime Theory and International Relations,* edited by Volker Rittberger, 202–222. Oxford: Clarendon Press, 1993.

Kalin, Walter. *"Towards a Human Rights Council: Options and Perspectives."* Institute of Public Law, University of Bern, August 4, 2004, http://www .humanrights.ch/upload/pdf/050107_kaelin_hr_council.pdf.

Kalin, Walter and Cecelia Jimenez. *Reform of the UN Commission on Human Rights.* Bern/Geneva: Institute of Public Law, University of Bern, August 30, 2003.

Keck, Margaret E. and Kathryn Sikkink. *Activists Beyond Borders: Advocacy Networks in International Politics.* Ithaca: Cornell University Press, 1998.

Kellberg, Love. "Torture: International Rules and Procedures." In *An End to Torture: Strategies for its Eradication,* edited by Bertil Duner, 3–38. London: Zed Books, 1998.

Kennedy, Paul. *The Rise and Fall of the Great Powers.* New York: Vintage Books, 1989.

Kennedy, Scott. "The Myth of the Beijing Consensus." *Journal of Contemporary China* 19, no. 65 (2010): 461–477.

Kent, Ann. *Between Freedom and Subsistence: China and Human Rights.* Oxford: Oxford University Press, 1993.

Beyond Compliance: China, International Organizations and Global Security. Stanford: Stanford University Press, 2007.

"China and the International Human Rights Regime: A Case Study of Multilateral Monitoring, 1989–1994." *Human Rights Quarterly* 17, no. 1 (February 1995): 1–47.

"China, International Organizations and Regimes: The ILO as a Case Study in Organizational Learning." *Pacific Affairs* 70, no. 4 (Winter 1997–1998): 517–532.

China, The United Nations, and Human Rights: The Limits of Compliance. Philadelphia: University Pennsylvania Press, 1999.

"China and the Universal Declaration: Breaker or Shaper of Norms?" Paper presented at the Sixth Annual Conference of the Australian and New Zealand Society of International Law, Canberra, Australia, June 19–21, 1998.

"China's Human Rights in 'The Asian Century'." In *Human Rights in Asia,* edited by Thomas W.D. Davis, and Brian Galligan, 187–211. Northampton, MA: Edward Elgar Publishing, Inc., 2011.

"China's Participation in International Organisations." In *Power and Responsibility in Chinese Foreign Policy,* edited by Yongjin Zhang and Greg Austin, 132–166. Canberra, Australia: Asia Pacific Press, 2001.

"The Universal Declaration of Human Rights and China: Breaker or Shaper of Norms?" *China Rights Forum* (Fall 1998): 4–7.

"Waiting for Rights: China's Human Rights and China's Constitutions, 1949–1989." *Human Rights Quarterly* 13, no. 2 (May 1991): 170–201.

Keohane, Robert O. *After Hegemony: Cooperation and Discord in the World Political Economy*. Princeton, NJ: Princeton University Press, 1984.

"The Demand for International Regimes." *International Organization* 36, no. 2 (1982): 332–355.

Institutions and State Power: Essays in International Relations Theory. Boulder, CO: Westview Press, 1989.

Keohane, Robert O., ed. *Neorealism and its Critics*. New York: Columbia University Press, 1986.

Keohane, Robert O. and Joseph S. Nye. *Power and Interdependence: World Politics in Transition*. Boston: Little, Brown, and Company, 1978.

Khong, Yuen Foong. "Primacy or World Order? The United States and China's Rise–A Review Essay." *International Security* 38, no. 3 (Winter 2013/2014): 153–176.

Kim, Samuel S. "Behavioral Dimensions of Chinese Multilateral Diplomacy." *China Quarterly* 72 (December 1977): 713–742.

"China as a Great Power." *Current History* 96, no. 611 (September 1997): 246–251.

China In and Out of the Changing World Order. Princeton, NJ: Center of International Studies, 1991.

China, The United Nations and World Order. Princeton, NJ: Princeton University Press, 1979.

"China's International Organizational Behavior." In *Chinese Foreign Policy: Theory and Practice*, edited by Thomas W. Robinson and David Shambaugh, 401–434. Oxford: Clarendon Press, 1994.

"China's Path to Great Power Status in the Globalization Era." In *Chinese Foreign Policy in Transition*, edited by Guoli Liu, 353–386. New York: Aldine de Gruyter, 2004.

"Chinese Foreign Policy Faces Globalization Challenges." In *New Directions in the Study of China's Foreign Policy*, edited by Alastair Iain Johnston and Robert S. Ross, 276–308. Stanford, CA: Stanford University Press, 2006.

"Human Rights in China's International Relations." In *What If China Doesn't Democratize?: Implications for War and Peace*, edited by Edward Friedman, and Barrett L. McCormick, 129–162. New York: M.E. Sharpe, 2000.

"International Organizations in Chinese Foreign Policy." *The Annals of the American Academy of Political and Social Science* 519 (January 1992): 140–157.

"The People's Republic of China in the United Nations: A Preliminary Analysis." *World Politics* 26, no. 3 (1974): 299–330.

"Post-Mao China's Development Model in Global Perspective." In *China's Changed Road to Development*, edited by Neville Maxwell, and Bruce McFarlane, 213–232. New York: Pergamon, 1984.

"Thinking Globally in Post-Mao China." *Journal of Peace Research* 27, no. 2 (May 1990): 191–209.

Kim, Samuel S., ed. *China and the World: Chinese Foreign Policy Faces the New Millennium*. New York: Columbia University Press, 1998.

ed. *China and the World: Chinese Foreign Relations in the Post-Cold War Era*, 3rd ed. Boulder, CO: Westview Press, 1994.

Kindleberger, Charles P. *The World in Depression: 1929–1939*. London: Allen Lane, 1973.

Kinzelbach, Katrin. *The EU's Human Rights Dialogue with China*. New York: Routledge, 2015.

"Resisting the Power of Human Rights: The People's Republic of China." In *The Persuasive Power of Human Rights: From Commitment to Compliance*, edited by Thomas Risse, Stephen C. Ropp, and Kathryn Sikkink, 164–181. Cambridge: Cambridge University Press, 2013.

"Will China's Rise Lead to a New Normative Order? An Analysis of China's Statements on Human Rights at the United Nations (2000–2010)." *Netherlands Quarterly of Human Rights* 30, no. 3 (2012): 299–332.

Klabbers, Jan. "Marginalized International Organizations: Three Hypotheses Concerning the ILO." In *China and the ILO Fundamental Principles and Rights at Work*, edited by Ulla Liukkunen and Chen Yifeng. New York: Wolters Kluwer, 2014.

Koh, Harold H. "Internationalization Through Socialization," *Duke Law Journal* 54 (2004–2005): 975–982.

"Why Do Nations Obey International Law?" *Yale Law Journal* 106, no. 8 (1997): 2599–2659.

Kornberg, Judith F. and John R. Faust. *China in World Politics: Policies, Processes, Prospects*. Boulder, CO: Lynne Reiner, 2005.

Miloon Kothari. "China's Trojan Horse Human Rights Resolution." *The Diplomat*. March 22, 2018. https://thediplomat.com/2018/03/chinas-trojan-horse-human-rights-resolution/.

Krasner, Stephen D. "Regimes and the Limits of Realism: Regimes as Intervening Variables." *International Organization* 36, no. 2 (1982): 185–205.

"Sovereignty, Regimes, and Human Rights." In *Regime Theory and International Relations*, edited by Volker Rittberger, 139–167. Oxford: Clarendon Press, 1993.

"Structural Causes and Regime Consequences: Regimes as Intervening Variables." In *International Regimes*, edited by Stephen Krasner, 1–22. Ithaca, NY: Cornell University Press, 1983.

"U.S. Commercial and Monetary Policy: Unraveling the Paradox of External Strength and Internal Weakness." In *Beyond Power and Plenty: Foreign Economic Policies of Advanced Industrial States*, edited by Peter J. Katzenstein, 51–87. Madison, WI: University of Wisconsin Press, 1978.

Krasner, Stephen D., ed. *International Regimes*. Ithaca, NY: Cornell University Press, 1983.

Lagon, Mark and Anthony Clark Arend, eds. *Human Dignity and the Future of Global Institutions*. Washington, D.C.: Georgetown University Press, 2014.

Lampton, David M., ed. *The Making of Chinese Foreign and Security Policy in the Era of Reform, 1978–2000*. Stanford: Stanford University Press, 2001.

Lanteigne, Marc. *Chinese Foreign Policy: An Introduction*. London: Routledge, 2009.

Lardy, Nicholas. *Integrating China into the Global Economy*. Washington, D.C.: Brookings Institution Press, 2002.

Lauren, Paul Gordon. *The Evolution of International Human Rights: Visions Seen*. Philadelphia: University of Pennsylvania Press, 2003.

"To Preserve and Build on Its Achievements and to Redress Its Shortcomings: The Journey from the Commission on Human Rights to the Human Rights Council." *Human Rights Quarterly* 29, no. 2 (2007): 307–345.

Leary, Virginia. "Lessons from the Experience of the International Labour Organization." In *The United Nations and Human Rights*, edited by Philip Alston, 580–619. Oxford: Clarendon Press, 1992.

"The Paradox of Workers' Rights as Human Rights." In *Human Rights, Labor Rights, and International Trade*, edited by Lance A. Compa and Stephen F. Diamond, 22–47. Philadelphia: University of Pennsylvania Press, 1996.

Lee, Katie. "China and the International Covenant on Civil and Political Rights: Prospects and Challenges." *Chinese Journal of International Law* 64, no. 2 (2007): 445–474.

Lee, Pak, Gerald Chan, and Laiha Chan. "China in Darfur: Humanitarian Rule-Maker or Rule-Taker?" *Review of International Studies* 38 (2012): 423–444.

Lempinen, Miko. *Challenges Facing the System of Special Procedures of the United Nations Commission on Human Rights*. Turku: Institute for Human Rights, Åbo Akademi University, 2001.

Leonard, Mark. *What Does China Think?* London: Harper Collins Publishers, 2008.

Levy, Jack. "Learning and Foreign Policy: Sweeping a Conceptual Minefield." *International Organization* 48, no. 2 (1994): 279–312.

Levy, Marc, Oran R. Young, and Michael Zurn. "The Study of International Regimes," *European Journal of International Relations* 1, no. 3 (1995): 267–330.

Li, Buyun. "Constitutionalism and China." In *Democracy and the Rule of Law in China*, edited by Yu Keping, 197–230. Leiden: Brill, 2010.

"On Individual and Collective Human Rights." In *Human Rights: Chinese and Dutch Perspectives*, edited by Peter R. Baehr, Fried van Hoof, Liu Nanlai, and Tao Zhenghua, 119–132. The Hague: Martinus Nijhoff Publishers, 1996.

Li, Mingjiang, ed. *China Joins Global Governance: Cooperation and Contentions*. New York: Lexington Books, 2012.

Li, Xin, and Verner Worm. "Building China's Soft Power for a Peaceful Rise." In *Copenhagen Discussion Papers No. 2009–28*, Copenhagen: Asia Research Centre, 2009.

Lieberthal, Kenneth. *Governing China: From Revolution to Reform*. New York: W. W. Norton and Company Inc., 1995.

Lin, T. "Beijing's Foreign Aid Policy in the 1990s: Continuity and Change." *Issues and Studies* 32, no. 1 (1996): 32–65.

Lippman, Matthew. "The Development and the Drafting of the United Nations Convention Against Torture and Other Cruel, Inhuman or Degrading Treatment or Punishment." *Boston College International and Comparative Law Review* 17, no. 2 (1994): 275–335.

Little, Richard. "International Regimes." In *The Globalization of World Politics: An Introduction to International Relations*, 2nd ed., edited by John Baylis and Steve Smith, 299–316. Oxford: Oxford University Press, 2001.

Liu, Hainian. "Human Rights Perspectives in Diversified Cultures." In *Human Rights: Chinese and Dutch Perspectives*, edited by Peter R. Baehr, Fried van Hoof, Liu Nanlai, and Tao Zhenghua, 17–24. The Hague: Martinus Nijhoff Publishers, 1996.

Liu, Nanlai. "Developing Countries and Human Rights." In *Human Rights: Chinese and Dutch Perspectives*, edited by Peter R. Baehr, Fried van Hoof, Liu Nanlai, and Tao Zhenghua, 103–118. The Hague: Martinus Nijhoff Publishers, 1996.

Liu, Yu, and Dingding Chen. "Why China Will Democratize." *The Washington Quarterly* 35, no. 1 (Winter 2012): 41–63.

Lo, Bobo. *Axis of Convenience: Moscow, Beijing and the New Geopolitics*. Washington, D.C.: Brookings Institution Press, 2008.

Long, Debra and Nicola Boeglin Naurnovic. *Optional Protocol to the United Nations Convention against Torture and Other Cruel, Inhuman or Degrading Treatment or Punishment: A Manuel for Prevention*. San Jose/Geneva: Inter-American Institute of Human Rights and Association for the Prevention of Torture, 2004.

Lu, Lianping and SZhixiang. "China's Attitude Toward the ICC." *Journal of International Criminal Justice* 3, no. 3 (July 2005): 608–620.

Lu, Xun. "On 'Face'." Translated by Yang Xianyi and Gladys Yang. In *Selected Works of Lu Hsun*, 129–132. Beijing: Foreign Language Press, 1959.

Mack, Raneta L. "China's Role on the New U.N. Human Rights Council: A Positive Shift in Its Human Rights Agenda or a Marriage of Convenience?" *Global Jurist* 7, no. 2 (2007).

Mann, James. *About Face: A History of America's Curious Relationship with China, From Nixon to Clinton*. New York: Vintage Books, 1998.

Mao, Tse-tung. *Selected Works of Mao Tse-tung: Volume 1*. Pergamon: London, 1965.

Selected Works of Mao Tse-tung: Volume 3. Pergamon: London, 1965.

Martin, Lisa L. and Beth A. Simmons, eds. *International Institutions: An International Organization Reader*. Cambridge, MA: The MIT Press, 2001.

Maupain, Francis. "The ILO Regulatory Supervisory System: A Model in Crisis?" *International Organizations Law Review* 10, no. 1 (2013): 117–165.

Mearsheimer, John J. "China's Unpeaceful Rise." *Current History* 105, no. 690 (2006): 160–162.

The Tragedy of Great Power Politics. New York: W. W. Norton, 2014.

Medeiros, Evan S. *Reluctant Restraint: The Evolution of China's Nonproliferation Policies and Practices, 1980–2004*. Stanford: Stanford University Press, 2007.

Medeiros, Evan S. and M. Taylor Fravel. "China's New Diplomacy." *Foreign Affairs* 82, no. 6 (November–December 2003): 22–35.

Mertus, Julie. "The International Labour Organization and the UN Global Compact." In *The United Nations and Human Rights: A Guide for a New Era*, 124–147. Hoboken, NJ: Routledge, 2009.

Minzer, Carl. *End of an Era: How China's How Authoritarian Revival is Undermining Its Rise*. Oxford: Oxford University Press, 2018.

Mitter, Rana. "An Uneasy Engagement: Chinese Ideas of Global Order and Justice in Historical Perspective." In *Order and Justice in International*

Relations, edited by Rosemary Foot, John Lewis Gaddis, and Andy Hurrell, 207–235. Oxford: Oxford University Press, 2003.

Mo, Jihong. "A New Perspective on Relations between Human Rights' Covenants and China." In *Construction within Contradiction: Multiple Perspectives on the Relationship Between China and International Organizations*, edited by Wang Yizhou, 196–235. Beijing: China Development Publishing House, 2003.

Morphet, Sally. "China as a Permanent Member of the Security Council." *Security Dialogue* 31, no. 2 (June 2000): 151–166.

Morsink, Johannes. *The Universal Declaration of Human Rights: Origins, Drafting, and Intent*. Philadelphia: University of Pennsylvania Press, 1999.

Moyn, Samuel. *The Last Utopia: Human Rights in History*. Harvard: Belknap, 2010.

Muller, Lars, ed. *The First 365 Days of the United Nations Human Rights Council*. Bern: Swiss Department of Federal Affairs, 2007.

Munro, Ross and Richard Bernstein. "The Coming Conflict with America." *Foreign Affairs* 76, no. 2 (March–April 1997): 18–32.

The Coming Conflict with China. New York: Knopf, 1997.

Murphy, Craig. "Global Governance: Poorly Done and Poorly Understood" *International Affairs* 76, no. 4 (2000): 789–803.

Nanda, Ved P. "New UN Initiatives for the Protection of International Human Rights." In *The Center Holds: UN Reform for Twenty-first-Century Challenges*, edited by Kevin P. Clements, and Nadia Mizner, 75–104. London: Transaction Publishers, 2008.

Narlikar, Amrita. *New Powers: How to Become One and How to Manage Them*. New York: Colombia University Press, 2010.

Narlikar, Amrita and John Odell. "The Strict Distributive Strategy for a Bargaining Coalition: The Like-Minded Group in the World Trade Organization." In *Negotiating Trade Developing Countries in the WTO and NAFTA*, edited by John Odell, 115–144. Cambridge: Cambridge University Press, 2006.

Nathan, Andrew. "China: Getting Human Rights Right." *The Washington Quarterly* 20, no. 2 (Spring 1997): 135–151.

"China and International Human Rights: Tiananmen's Paradoxical Impact." In *The Impact of China's 1989 Tiananmen Massacre*, edited by Jean-Philippe Beja, 206–220. Hoboken, NJ: Routledge, 2010.

"Is China Ready for Democracy?" In *The Global Resurgence of Democracy*, edited by Larry Diamond and Mark F. Plattner, 281–292. Baltimore: The Johns Hopkins University Press, 1993.

Chinese Democracy. Berkeley: University of California Press, 1986.

"Human Rights in Chinese Foreign Policy." *The China Quarterly* 139, no. 3 (September 1994): 622–643.

"Sources of Chinese Rights Thinking." In *Human Rights in Contemporary China*, edited by R. Randle Edwards, Louis Henkin, and Andrew Nathan, 125–164. New York: Colombia University Press, 1986.

Nathan, Andrew J. and Andrew Scobell. *China's Search for Security*. New York: Columbia University Press, 2012.

"Human Rights and China's Soft Power Expansion." *China Rights Forum*, no. 4 (2009), http://www.hrichina.org/content/3174.

Nathan, Andrew and Perry Link, eds. *The Tiananmen Papers: The Chinese Government's Decision to Use Force Against Their Own People—In Their Own Words*. New York: Public Affairs, 2001.

Naughton, Barry. "The Impact of the Tiananmen Crisis on China's Economic Transition." In *The Impact of China's 1989 Tiananmen Crisis*, edited by Jean-Philippe Beja, 154–178. Hoboken, NJ: Routledge, 2010.

Neary, Ian. *Human Rights in Japan, South Korea and Taiwan*. London: Routledge, 2002.

Nifosi, Ingrid. *The UN Special Procedures in the Field of Human Rights*. Cambridge: Intersentia, 2006.

Nixon, Richard. "Asia After Vietnam." *Foreign Affairs* 46, no. 1 (October 1967): 111–125.

Nossel, Suzanne. *Advancing Human Rights in the UN System, Working Paper*. New York: Council on Foreign Relations, 2012. https://www.cfr.org/sites/default/files/pdf/2012/05/IIGG_WorkingPaper8.pdf. Accessed September 11, 2017.

Nowak, Manfred, Elizabeth McArthur, and Kerstin Buchinger. *The United Nations Convention against Torture: A Commentary*. Oxford: Oxford University Press, 2008.

Nye, Joseph. "Nuclear Learning and U.S.-Soviet Security Regimes." *International Organization* 41, no. 3 (Summer 1987): 371–402.

Nye, Joseph S., Jr. and John D. Donahue, eds., *Governance in a Globalizing World*. Washington, D.C.: Brookings Institution Press, 2000.

O'Flaherty, Michael and Pei-Lun Tsai. "Periodic Reporting: The Backbone of the UN Treaty Body Review Procedures." In *New Challenges for the UN Human Rights Machinery: What Future for the UN Treaty Body System and the Human Rights Council Procedures?* edited by M. Cherif Bassiouni and William A. Schabas, 37–56. Cambridge: Intersentia, 2011.

Oksenberg, Michel and Elizabeth Economy. *China Joins the World: Progress and Prospects*. New York: The Council on Foreign Relations Press, 1998.

Shaping U.S.-China Relations: A Long-Term China's Foreign Affairs 2011 Strategy. New York: Council on Foreign Relations Press, 1997.

Onuf, Nicholas. "Constructivism: A User's Manual." In *International Relations in a Constructed World*, edited by Vendulka Kubalkova, Nicholas Onuf, and Paul Kowert, 58–78. Armonk, NY: M.E. Sharpe, 1998.

World of Our Making: Rule and Rules in Social Theory and International Relations. Columbia, SC: University of South Carolina, 1989.

Organski, A.F.K. and Jacek Kugler. *The War Ledger*. Chicago: University of Chicago Press, 1980.

Paltiel, Jeremy T. *The Empire's New Clothes: Cultural Particularism and Universal Value in China's Quest for Global Status*. New York: Palgrave Macmillan, 2007.

Patrick, Stewart. "China's Role in the 'New Era of Engagement'." *Council on Foreign Relations*, November 10, 2010, http://www.cfr.org/china/chinas-role-new-era-engagement/p20700.

"Irresponsible Stakeholders? The Difficulty of Integrating Rising Powers." *Foreign Affairs* 89, no. 6 (November/December 2010): 44–53.

Pearson, Margaret M. "The Case of China's Accession to the GATT/WTO." In *The Making of Chinese Foreign and Security Policy in the Era of Reform, 1978–2000*, edited by David M. Lampton, 337–370. Stanford, CA: Stanford University Press, 2001.

"China in Geneva: Lessons from China's Early Years in the World Trade Organization." In *New Directions in the Study of China's Foreign Policy*, edited by Alastair Iain Johnston, and Robert S. Ross, 242–275. Stanford, CA: Stanford University Press, 2006.

"China and the Norms of the Global Economic Regime." *China Studies*, no. 6 (2000): 147–172.

Peerenboom, Randall. "Assessing Human Rights in China: Why the Double Standard?" *Cornell International Law Journal* 38 (2005): 71–172.

China Modernizes: Threat to the West or Model for the Rest? Oxford: Oxford University Press, 2007.

"What's Wrong with Chinese Rights?: Toward a Theory of Rights with Chinese Characteristics." *Harvard Human Rights Journal* 6, no. 29 (1993): 29–57.

Pennegard, Ann-Marie Bolin. "An Optional Protocol, Based on Prevention and Cooperation." In *An End to Torture: Strategies for its Eradication*, edited by Bertil Duner, 39–62. London: Zed Books, 1998.

"Overview Over Human Rights–the Regime of the UN." In *International Human Rights Monitoring Mechanisms: Essays in Honour of Jakob Th. Möller*, 2nd ed., edited by Gudmundur Alfredsson, Jonas Grimheden, Bertran G. Ramcharan, and Alfred de Zayas, 19–66. The Hague: Martinus Nijhoff Publishers, 2001.

Percival, Bronson. *The Dragon Looks South: China and Southeast Asia in the New Century*. Westport, CT: Praeger Security International, 2007.

Permanent Mission of Switzerland to the UN. *The Human Rights Council: A Practical Guide*. Geneva: Permanent Mission of Switzerland to the UN, 2014.

Piccone, Ted. *China's Long Game on Human Rights at the United Nations*. Washington, D.C.: Brooking's Institute, 2018. Accessed September 24, 2018. www.brookings.edu/research/chinas-long-game-on-human-rights-at-the-united-nations/.

Piccone, Ted and Naomi McMillen. *Country-Specific Scrutiny at the United Nations Human Rights Council, Working Paper*. Washington, D.C.: Project on International Order and Strategy, Brookings Institution, May 2016. Accessed September 11, 2017. https://www.brookings.edu/research/country-specific-scrutiny-at-the-united-nations-human-rights-council-more-than-meets-the-eye/.

Pils, Eva. "The Dislocation of the Chinese Human Rights Movement." In *The Evolution of Law Reform in China: An Uncertain Path*, edited by Stanley B. Lubman, 585–606. Northampton, MA: Edward Elgar Publishing, 2012.

Human Rights in China: A Social Practice in the Shadows of Authoritarianism. Oxford: Polity Press, 2018.

Pillsbury, Michael. *The Hundred-year Marathon: China's Secret Strategy to Replace America as the Global Superpower*. New York: Henry Holt and Company, 2015.

Potter, Pittman B. "China and the International Legal System: Challenges of Participation." *The China Quarterly* 191 (2007): 699–715.

Power, Samantha. *Realizing Human Rights: Moving from Inspiration to Impact.* New York: St. Martin's Press, 2000.

Pu Xiaoyu. "Socialization as a Two-way Process: Emerging Powers and the Diffusion or International Norms." *The Chinese Journal of International Politics* 5 (2012): 241–367.

Puchala, Donald J. and Raymond F. Hopkins. "International Regimes: Lessons from Inductive Analysis." In *International Regimes*, edited by Stephen D. Krasner, 61–92. Ithaca, NY: Cornell University Press, 1983.

Pye, Lucian. "China: Not Your Typical Superpower." *Problems of Post-Communism* 43, no. 4 (July-August 1996): 3–15.

Qian, Qichen. *Ten Episodes in China's Diplomacy.* New York: Harper Collins Publishers, 2005.

Rabinovitch, Simon. "The Rise of an Image-Conscious China." *China Security* 4, no. 3 (Summer 2008): 33–47.

Ramcharan, B.G. "Reforming the United Nations to Secure Human Rights." In *Preferred Futures for the United Nations*, edited by Saul H. Mendlovitz, and Burns H. Weston, 193–219. Irving-on-Hudson, New York: Transnational Publishers, 1995.

The UN Human Rights Council. New York: Routledge, 2011.

Rathgeber, Theodor. "Reforming the UN Commission on Human Rights— Perspectives for Non-governmental Organisations." *Friedrich Ebert Stiftung, Briefing Papers, Dialogue on Globalization,* July 2005. http://library.fes.de/pdf-files/iez/global/50195.pdf.

Reiding, Hilde. *The Netherlands and the Development of International Human Rights Instruments.* Antwerp: Intersentia, 2007.

Reilly, James. "China's Unilateral Sanctions." *The Washington Quarterly* 35, no. 4 (Fall 2012): 121–133.

Risse, Thomas, Stephen C. Ropp, and Kathryn Sikkink, eds. *The Persistent Power of Human Rights: From Commitment to Compliance.* Cambridge: Cambridge University Press, 2013.

eds. *The Power of Human Rights: International Norms and Domestic Change.* New York: Cambridge University Press, 1999.

Rittberger, Volker, ed. *Regime Theory and International Relations.* Oxford: Clarendon Press, 1993.

Robinson, Thomas W. and David Shambaugh, eds. *Chinese Foreign Policy: Theory and Practice.* Oxford: Clarendon Press, 1994.

Rodgers, Gerry, Eddy Lee; Lee Swepston, and Jasmien Van Daele. *The ILO and the Quest for Social Justice, 1919–2009.* Cornell: Cornell University Press, 2009.

Rodley, Nigel. *The Treatment of Prisoners under International Law.* 2nd ed. Oxford: Oxford University Press, 1999.

Rorden Wilkinson and Steve Hughes, eds. *Global Governance: Critical Perspectives.* London: Routledge, 2002.

Rosenau, James and Ernst-Otto Czempiel, eds. *Governance without Government: Order and Change in World Politics.* Cambridge: Cambridge University Press, 1992.

Ross, Robert S. Beijing as a Conservative Power." *Foreign Affairs* 76, no. 2 (March–April 1997): 33–44.

"National Security, Human Rights, and Domestic Politics: The Bush Administration and China." In *Eagle in the New World: American Grand Strategy in the Post-Cold War Era*, edited by Kenneth Oye, Robert Lieber, and Donald Rothchild, 281–313. New York: Harper Collins, 1992.

Negotiating Cooperation: The United States and China, 1969–1989. Stanford: Stanford University Press, 1995.

Ross, Robert S. and Zhu Feng, eds. *China's Ascent: Power, Security, and the Future of International Politics.* Cornell: Cornell University Press, 2008.

Ross, Robert S. and Zhu Feng. "When Will the Chinese People Be Free?" *Journal of Democracy* 18, no. 3 (July 2007): 38–52.

Roy, Dennis. *China's Foreign Relations.* Lanham, MD: Rowman and Littlefield, 1998.

Rozman, Gilbert. "China's Quest for Great Power Identity." *Orbis* 43, no. 3 (Summer 1999): 384–399.

Ruggie, John G. *Constructing the World Polity: Essays on International Institutionalization.* London: Routledge, 1998.

"Human Rights and the Future International Community." *Daedalus* 112, no. 4 (Fall 1983): 91–110.

Russett, Bruce and John R. Oneal. *Triangulating Peace: Democracy, Interdependence, and International Organizations.* New York: W. W. Norton and Company, Inc., 2001.

Saich, Tony. "Globalization, Governance, and the Authoritarian State: China." In *Governance in a Globalizing World*, edited by Joseph S. Nye and Donahue, 208–228. Washington, D.C.: Brookings Institution Press, 2000.

Scannella, Patrizia and Peter Splinter. "The United Nations Human Rights Council: A Promise to be Fulfilled." *Human Rights Law Review* 7, no. 1 (2007): 41–72.

Sceats, Sonya and Shaun Breslin. *China and the International Human Rights System:Programme Report.* London: Chatham House, October 2012.

Schell, Orville and John Delury. *Wealth and Power: China's Long March to the Twenty-First Century.* New York: Random House, 2013.

Schoenhals, Michael. *Doing Things with Words in Chinese Politics: Five Studies.* Berkeley and Los Angeles: Institute of East Asian Studies, University of California Center for Chinese Studies, 1992.

Schriver, Nico. "The UN Human Rights Council: A New 'Society of the Committed' or Just Old Wine in New Bottles?" *Leiden Journal of International Law* 20, no. 4 (2007): 809–823.

Schweller, Randall L. "Managing the Rise of Great Powers: History and Theory." In *Engaging China: The Management of an Emerging Power*, edited by Alastair Iain Johnston and Robert S. Ross, 1–31. London: Routledge, 1999.

Schweller, Randall L. and Xiaoyu Pu. "After Unipolarity: China's Visions of International Order in an Era of U.S. Decline." *International Security* 36, no. 1 (Summer 2011): 41–72.

Scott, David. *'The Chinese Century'? The Challenge to Global Order.* London: Palgrave Macmillan, 2008.

Shambaugh, David. *China Goes Global: The Partial Power.* Oxford: Oxford University Press, 2013.

"Containment or Engagement of China? Calculating Beijing's Responses" *International Security* 21, no. 2 (Autumn 1996): 180–209.

Shambaugh, David, ed. *Power Shift: China and Asia's New Dynamics.* Berkeley, CA: University of California Press, 2005.

Shan, Wenhua. "Redefining the Chinese Concept of Sovereignty." In *China in the New International Order,* edited by Gungwu Wang, and Yongnian Zheng, 53–80. New York: Routledge, 2008.

Shih, Chih-yu, "Contending Theories of Human Rights with Chinese Characteristics," *Issues and Studies* 29, no. 11 (November 1993): 42–64.

Shinn, James, ed. *Weaving the Net, Conditional Engagement with China.* New York: Council on Foreign Relations Press, 1996.

Shinn, David H. and Joshua Eisenman. *China and Africa: A Century of Engagement.* Philadelphia: University of Pennsylvania Press, 2012.

Shirk, Susan. *China: Fragile Superpower.* Oxford: Oxford University Press, 2008.

"Human Rights: What About China?" *Foreign Policy* 29 (Winter 1977–1978): 109–127.

Sigel, R.S. *Learning About Politics.* New York: Random House, 1970.

Sikkink, Kathryn. "Human Rights, Principled Issue-Networks, and Sovereignty in Latin America." *International Organization* 47, no. 3 (1993): 411–141.

Smith, Steve, Ken Booth, and Marysia Zalewski, eds. *International Theory: Positivism and Beyond.* Cambridge: Cambridge University Press, 1996.

Smith-Cannoy, Heather. *Insincere Commitments: Human Rights Treaties, Abusive States, Citizen Activism.* Washington, D.C.: Georgetown University Press, 2012.

Song, Hong. "China and WTO A Process of Mutual Learning, Adapting and Promoting." In *Construction within Contradiction: Multiple Perspectives on the Relationship Between China and International Organization,* edited by Wang Yizhou, 164–195. Beijing: Zhongguo Fazhan Chubanshe, 2003.

Spence, Jonathan D. *The Search for Modern China.* New York: W. W. Norton and Company, Inc., 1995.

Stahle, Stefan. "China's Shifting Attitude towards United Nations Peacekeeping Operations." *China Quarterly* 195 (2008): 631–655.

Standing, Guy. "The ILO: An Agency for Globalization." *Development and Change* 39, no. 3 (2008): 355–384.

Steiner, Henry J., and Philip Alston. *International Human Rights in Context: Law, Politics, Morals.* Oxford: Oxford University Press, 1996.

Sullivan, Michael J. "Developmentalism and China's Human Rights Policy." In *Debating Human Rights: Critical Essays from the United States and Asia,* edited by Peter Van Ness, 120–143. New York: Routledge, 1999.

Sutter, Robert G. *Chinese Foreign Relations: Power and Policy Since the Cold War.* New York: Rowman & Littlefield Publishers, Inc., 2009.

Svensson, Marina. "The Chinese Debate on Asian Values and Human Rights." In *Human Rights and Asian Values: Contesting National Identities and Cultural Representations in Asia,* edited by Michael Jacobsen and Ole Bruun, 199–226. Richmond, Surrey: Curzon Press, 2000.

Debating Human Rights in China: A Conceptual and Political History. New York: Rowman and Littlefield Publishers, 2002.

Swaine, Michael D. and Ashely J. Tellis. *Interpreting China's Grand Strategy: Past, Present, and Future*. Santa Monica, CA: Rand, 2000.

Swepston, Lee."Human Rights Complaints Procedures of the International Labor Organization." In *Guide to International Human Rights Practice*, edited by Hurst Hannum, 86. Philadelphia: University of Pennsylvania Press, 1984.

"The International Labour Organization and Human Rights Access to the ILO." In *International Human Rights Monitoring Mechanisms: Essays in Honour of Jakob Th. Möller*, 2nd ed., edited by Gudmundur Alfredsson, Jonas Grimheden, Bertrand G. Ramcharan, and Alfred Zayas, 291–300. The Hague: Marinus Hijhoff Publishers, 2009.

The International Labour Organization: The International Standards System and Basic Human Rights. Boulder, CO: Westview Press, 1996.

Tang, James T.H., ed. *Human Rights and International Relations in the Asia-Pacific Region*. London: Pinter Publishers, 1995.

Tang, Yongsheng. "China's Participation in UN Peacekeeping Regime." In *Construction within Contradiction*, edited by Wang Yizhou, 73–98. Beijing: China Development Press, 2003.

Taylor, Ian. "China's Foreign Policy Towards Africa in the 1990s." *Journal of Modern African Studies* 6, no. 3 (1998): 443–460.

Teng, Chung-chian. "Democracy, Development and China's Acquisition of Oil in the Third World." In *Dancing with the Dragon: China's Emergence in the Developing World*, edited by Dennis Hickey and Baoguang Guo, 105–124. Boulder, Colorado: Rowman & Littlefield Publishers, Inc. 2010.

"Hegemony or Partnership: China's Strategy and Diplomacy Toward Latin America." In *China and the Developing World: Beijing's Strategy for the Twenty-first Century*. Edited by Joshua Eisenman, Eric Heginbotham and Derek Mitchell. New York: Routledge, 2007.

Terlingen, Yvonne. "The Human Rights Council: A New Era in UN Human Rights Work?" *Ethics and International Affairs* 21, no. 2 (2007): 167–178.

Thornton, John L. "Long Time Coming: The Prospects for Democracy in China." *Foreign Affairs* 87, no. 1 (January/February 2008): 2–22.

Tok, Sow Keat. *Managing China's Sovereignty in Hong Kong and Taiwan*. New York: Palgrave MacMillan, 2013.

Tolley, Howard Jr. *The U.N. Commission on Human Rights*. Boulder, CO: Westview Press, 1987.

Traub, James. *The Best Intentions: Kofi Annan and the UN in the Era of American World Power*. New York: Farrar, Straus and Giroux, 2007.

Tucker, Nancy Bernkopf. *Taiwan, Hong Kong, and the United States, 1945–1992: Uncertain Friendships*. New York: Twayne Publishers, 1994.

Tull, Denis M. "China's Engagement in Africa: Scope Significance and Consequences." *Journal of Modern African Studies* 44, no. 3 (2006): 459–479.

Tyler, Patrick. *A Great Wall: Six Presidents and China: An Investigative History*. New York: A Century Foundation Book, 1999.

Valticos, Nicolas and Geraldo von Potobsky. *International Labour Law*, 2nd ed. Deventer, Netherlands: Kluwer Law and Taxation Publisher, 1995.

Van Boven, Theo. *People Matter: Views on International Human Rights Policy.* Amsterdam: J.M. Meulenhoff, 1982.

Van Hoof, Fried. "Asian Challenges to the Concept of Universality: Afterthoughts on the Vienna Conference on Human Rights." In *Human Rights: Chinese and Dutch Perspectives*, edited by Peter Baehr, Fried van Hoof, Liu Nanlai, and Tao Zhenghua, 1–15. The Hague: Martinus Nijhoff Publishers, 1996.

Van Ness, Peter. "China as a Third World State: Foreign Policy and Official National Identity." In *China's Quest for National Identity*, edited by Lowell Dittmer, and Samuel S. Kim, 194–214. Ithaca, NY: Cornell University Press, 1993.

Van Ness, Peter, ed. *Debating Human Rights: Critical Essays from the United States and Asia.* London: Routledge, 1999.

Vanderhill, Rachel. *Promoting Authoritarianism Abroad.* Boulder, CO: Lynne Rienner, 2013.

Vincent, R.J. *Human Rights and International Relations.* Cambridge: Cambridge University Press, 1986.

Vogel, Ezra. *Deng Xiaoping and the Transformation of China.* Cambridge: The Belknap Press of Harvard University Press, 2011.

von Soest, Christian. "Democracy Prevention: The International Collaboration of Authoritarian Regimes." *European Journal of Political Research* 54 (2015): 623–638.

Vreeland, James. "Political Institutions and Human Rights: Why Dictatorships Enter into the United Nations Convention Against Torture." *International Organizations* 62 (January 2008): 65–101.

Wachman, Alan. "Does the Diplomacy of Shame Promote Human Rights in China?" *Third World Quarterly* 22, no. 2 (April 2001): 257–281.

Wan, Ming. *Human Rights in Chinese Foreign Relations: Defining and Defending National Interests.* Philadelphia: University of Pennsylvania Press, 2001.

"Human Rights and Democracy." In *the Eyes of the Dragon: China Views the World*, edited by Yong Deng, and Fei-ling Wang, 97–118. New York: Rowman and Littlefield Publishers, Inc., 1999.

Wang, Hongying. "Linking Up with the International Track: What's in a Slogan?" *The China Quarterly* 189 (March 2007): 1–23.

Wang, Hongying and Erik French. "China Perspectives in Global Governance from a Comparative Perspective," *Asia Policy* 15 (January 2013): 89–114.

Wang, Hongying and James N. Rosenau. "China and Global Governance," *Asian Perspective* 33, no. 3 (2009): 5–39.

Wang, Jianwei. "Managing Conflict: Chinese Perspectives on Multilateral Diplomacy and Security." In *In the Eyes of the Dragon: China Views the World*, edited by Yong Deng, and Fei-ling Wang, 75–81. New York: Rowman and Littlefield Publishers, Inc., 1999.

Wang, Jisi. "China's Search for Stability with America." *Foreign Affairs* 84, no. 5 (September–October 2005): 39–48.

Wang, Yizhou. "Briefing Multiple Perspectives on Relations Between China and International Organizations." In *Construction within Contradiction: Multiple Perspectives on the Relationship between China and International Organizations,* edited by Yizhou Wang, 1–46. Beijing: China Development Publishing House, 2003.

Wang, Zonglai and Hu Bin. "China's Reform and Opening-up and International Law." *Chinese Journal of International Law* 9, no. 1 (March 2010): 193–203.

Weatherley, Robert. "Defending the Nation: The Role of Nationalism in Chinese Thinking on Human Rights." *Democratization* 15, no. 2 (April 2008), 342–362.

The Discourse of Human Rights in China: Historical and Ideological Perspectives. New York: St. Martin's Press, 1999.

"The Evolution of Chinese Thinking on Human Rights in the Post-Mao Era." *Journal of Communist Studies and Transition Politics* 17, no. 2 (June 2001): 19–42.

Making China Strong: The Role of Nationalism in Chinese Thinking on Democracy and Human Rights. London: Palgrave McMillan, 2014.

Politics in China Since 1949: Legitimizing Authoritarian Rule. Routledge: New York, 2006.

Weiss, Thomas G. *Global Governance: Why? What? Whither?* Cambridge: Polity Press 2013.

Wendt, Alexander. "Anarchy Is What States Make of It: The Social Construction of Power Politics." *International Organization* 46, no. 2 (Spring 1992): 391–425.

Weng, Byron S. "Some Conditions of Peking's Participation in International Organizations." In *China's Practice of International Law: Some Case Studies*, edited by Jerome A. Cohen, 321–343. Cambridge: Harvard University Press, 1972.

Whitman, Jim. *The Limits of Global Governance.* New York: Routledge, 2005

Wisskirchen, Alfred. "The Standard Setting and Monitoring Activity of the ILO: Legal Questions and Practical Experience." *International Labour Review* 144, no. 3 (2005): 253–289.

Wisskirchen, Alfred and Christian Hess. *Employer's Handbook on ILO Standards-related Activities.* Geneva: International Labour Organization, 2001.

Wu, Edward. "Human Rights: China's Historical Perspectives in Context." *Journal of History of International Law* 4 (2002): 335–373.

Wu, Guoguang. "A Shadow over Western Democracies: China's Political Use of economic power." In *The Impact of China's 1989 Tiananmen Massacre*, edited by Jean-Philippe Beja, 221–236. Hoboken, NJ: Routledge, 2010.

Wu, Guoguang and Helen Landsdowne. "Identity, Sovereignty and Economic Penetration: Beijing's Response to Offshore Chinese Democracies." *Journal of Contemporary China* 16, no. 51 (May 2007): 295–313.

Wu, Guoguang and Helen Landsdowne, eds. *China Turns to Multilateralism: Foreign Policy and Regional Security.* New York: Routledge, 2008

Wu, Yuan-li, Ta-ling Lee, Franz Michael, Maria Hsia Chang, John F. Copper, and A. James Gregor. *Human Rights in the People's Republic of China.* Boulder, CO: Westview Press, 1988.

Wuthnow, Joel. "China and the ICC." *The Diplomat.* December 7, 2012. Accessed September 29, 2019. https://thediplomat.com/2012/12/china-and-the-icc/.

Chinese Diplomacy and the UN Security Council: Beyond the Veto. New York: Routledge, 2012.

Xia, Liping. "China: A Responsible Great Power." *Journal of Contemporary China* 10, no. 26 (February 2001): 17–25.

Xia, Yong. "Human Rights and Chinese Tradition." In *Human Rights: Chinese and Dutch Perspectives*, edited by Peter R. Baehr, Fried van Hoof, Liu Nanlai and Tao Zhenghua, 77–90. The Hague: Martinus Nijhoff Publishers, 1996.

Xiao, Hong. "Values Priority and Human Rights Policy: A Comparison between China and Western Nations." *Journal of Human Values* 11, no. 2 (October 2005): 87–102.

Xue, Hanqin. *Chinese Contemporary Perspectives on International Law*. The Hague: Hague Academy of International Law, 2012.

Yan, Xuetong. "The Rise of China in Chinese Eyes." *Journal of Contemporary China* 10, no. 26 (February 2001): 33–39.

Yee, Herbert and Zhu Feng. "Chinese Perspectives on the China Threat." In *The China Threat: Perceptions, Myths and Reality*, edited by Ian Storey and Herbert Yee, 21–42. London: Routledge/Curzon, 2002.

Yeophantong, Pichamon. "Governing the World: China's Evolving Conceptions of Responsibility." *Chinese Journal of International Politics* 6, no. 4 (Winter 2013): 329–364.

Young, Oran R. *Governance in World Affairs*. Ithaca, NY: Cornell University Press, 1999.

——— "International Regimes: Problems of Concept Formation." *World Politics* 32, no. 3 (April 1980): 331–356.

——— "International Regimes: Toward a New Theory of Institutions." *World Politics* 39, no. 1 (October 1986): 104–122.

——— "Regime Dynamics: The Rise and Fall of International Regimes." In *International Regimes*, edited by Stephen D. Krasner, 93–114. Ithaca, NY: Cornell University Press, 1983.

Yu, Keping. *China's Changing Political Landscape: Prospects for Democracy*. Washington, D.C.: Brookings Institution Press, 2008.

Yu, Keping, eds. *Democracy and the Rule of Law in China*. Leiden: Brill, 2010.

Yuan, Jing-dong. "China's Pragmatic Approach to Nonproliferation Policies in the Post-Cold War Era. In *Chinese Foreign Policy: Pragmatism and Strategic Behavior*, edited by Suisheng Zhao, 151–177. New York: M.E. Sharpe, 2004.

——— "The New Player in the Game: China, Arms Control, and Multilateralism." In *China Turns to Multilateralism: Foreign Policy and Regional Security*, edited by Guoguang Wu, and Helen Landsdowne, 51–72. New York: Routledge, 2008.

Zambelis, Chris. "China's Inroads into North Africa: An Assessment of Sino-Algerian Relations." *China Brief* 10, no. 1 (2010): 1–10.

Zhang, Yongjin. *China Goes Global*. London: Foreign Policy Centre, 2005.

——— *China in International Society since 1949: Alienation and Beyond*. New York: Palgrave MacMillian, 1998.

Zhang, Yongjin and Greg Austin, eds. *Power and Responsibility in Chinese Foreign Policy*. Camberra, Australia: Asia Pacific Press, 2001.

Zhao, Suisheng. "Beijing's Perception After the Tiananmen Incident." In *Chinese Foreign Policy: Pragmatism and Strategic Behavior*, edited by Suisheng Zhao, 140–150. New York: M.E. Sharpe, Inc., 2004.

"The Making of China's Periphery Policy." In *Chinese Foreign Policy: Pragmatism and Strategic Behavior*, edited by Suisheng Zhao. New York: Routledge, 2016.

Zhao, Ziyang. "Work Together for a Better World." *Beijing Review* 28 (November 4, 1985): 15–17.

Zheng, Bijan. "China's 'Peaceful Rise' to Great Power Status." *Foreign Affairs* 84, no. 5 (September/October 2005): 18–24.

Zhou, Wei. "The Study of Human Rights in the People's Republic of China." In *Human Rights and International Relations in the Asia Pacific*, edited by James T.H. Tang, 83–96. New York: St. Martin's Press, 1995.

Zhu, Feng. "Human Rights Problems and Current Sino-American Relations." In *Debating Human Rights: Critical Essays from the United States and Asia*, edited by Peter Van Ness, 232–254. New York: Routledge, 1999.

Zhu, Lijiang. "Chinese Practice in Public International Law: 2006." *Chinese Journal of International Law* 6, no. 2 (2007): 475–506.

Zhu, Yuchao. "China and International Human Rights Diplomacy." *China: An International Journal* 9, no. 2 (September 2011): 217–245.

Ziegler, Charles. *Foreign Policy and East Asia: Learning and Adaptation in the Gorbachev Era*. Cambridge: Cambridge University Press, 1993.

Zimmern, Alfred. *The League of Nations and the Rule of Law*. London: MacMillan and Co., 1936.

Zweig, David. "Democratic Values, Political Structures, and Alternative Politics in Greater China." *Peaceworks*, no. 44. Washington, D.C.: U.S. Institute of Peace, July 2002.

Internationalizing China: Domestic Interests and Global Linkages. Ithaca, NY: Cornell University Press, 1977.

"The Rise of a New 'Trading Nation'." In *China, the Developing World, and the New Global Dynamic*, edited by Lowell Dittmer and George T. Yu, 37–60. Boulder, CO: Lynne Rienner, 2010.

"Sino-American Relations and Human Rights: June 4 and the Changing Nature of a Bilateral Relationship." In *Building Sino-American Relations: An Analysis for the 1990s*, edited by William T. Tow, 57–92. New York: Paragon House, 1991.

Chinese Language Sources

Chen, Yue. *Zhongguo Guoji Diwei Fenxi [Analysis of China's International Status]*. Beijing: Contemporary World Press, 2002.

Dong, Yunhu. "Zhongguo renquan fazhan de yige zhongyao lichenbei" [An Important Milestone in China's Human Rights Development]. *Ren Quan [Human Rights]*, no. 1 (2002): 25.

Dong, Yunhu and Liu Wuping. *Shijie Renquan Yuefa Zonglan Xubian [A Supplement to World Documents on Human Rights]*. Sichuan: Sichuan Daxue Chubanshe, 1997.

Gao, Hongjun. "Zhongguo gongmin quanli yishi de yanjin" [The Awakening of Consciousness of Rights among Chinese Citizens]. In *Zou Xiang Quanli de Shidao [Toward a Time of Rights]*, edited by Xia Yong, 3–68. Beijing: Zhongguo zhengfa daxue chubanshe [China Politics and Law University Publishing House], 1995.

Guo, Qing. "Zhongguo zai Renquanshang de Jiben Lichang he Jiben Shijian" [The Basic Position and Practice of Human Rights in China]. *Quishi [Seek Truth]*, no. 23 (1991): 14–19.

"Guonei baokan guanyu renquan wenti de taolun zongshu" [A Summary of the Debate on the Issue of Human Rights in Domestic Magazines]. *Shehui kexue [Social Sciences]*, no. 3 (1979): 76–78.

Han, Depei. *Renquan de Lilun yu Shijian [Theory and Practice of Human Rights]*. Wuhan: Wuhan Daxue Chubanshe, 1998.

Hu, Yingxia. "Renquan yu Geren de Quanli" [Human Rights and the Rights of Individuals]. *Liaoning Faxue Xuebao [Liaoning Journal of Legal Studies]*, no. 3 (1998).

Johnston, Alastair Iain. "Meiguo Xuezhe Duiyu Zhongguo Yu Guoji Zuzhi Guanxi Yanjiu Jianshu" *[Overview of Studies on Relations between China and International Organizations by U.S. Scholars]. Shijie Jingji Yu Zhengzhi [World Economics and Politics]*, no. 8 (2001).

Li, Buyun. "Lun requan de san zhong cunzai xingtain" [On the Three Modes of Existence of Human Rights]. *Faxue Yanjiu [Studies in Law]* 4 (1991): 3–15.

Li, Buyun and Wang Xiujing. "*Renquan guoji baohu yu Guojia Zhuquan*" [The International Protection of Human Rights and State Sovereignty]." *Faxue Yanjiu [Legal Research]* 4 (1995): 19–23.

Li, Tiecheng. *Fifty Years of United Nations [Lianheguuo Wushinian]*. Beijing: China Book Press, September 1995.

Li, Zerui. "A Theoretical Study of International Human Rights Law." In *Zhongguo Guojifa Niankan [Chinese Yearbook of International Law]*, 93–116. Beijing: China Translation and Publishing Corp, 1983.

Lin, Jia. *Renquan Baiti Wenda [One Hundred Questions and Answers Concerning Human Rights]*. Beijing: Shijiezhishi Chubanshe, 1992.

Liu, Jie. "Zhongguo Canyu Guoji Jizhi de Lilun yu Shijian" *[The Theory and Practice of China's Participation in International Institutions]. Mao Zedong Deng Xiaoping Lilun Yanjiu [Studies in Mao Zedong and Deng Xiaoping Theory]*, no. 4 (2003): 80–84.

Liu, Shulin. *Dangdai Zhongguo Renquan Zhuangkuang Baogao [A Study of the Contemporary Chinese Position on Human Rights]*. Liaoning: Liaoning Remin Chubanshe, 1994.

Ni, Jianmin and Chen Zhishun. *Zhongguo Guoji Zhanlue [China's International Strategy]*. Beijing: Renmin Chubanshe, 2003.

Pan, Zhenqiang, ed. *Guoji Caijun yu Junbei Kongzhi [International Disarmament and Arms Control]*. Beijing: National Defense University Press, 1996.

Pang, Sen. *Dangdai Renquan ABC [The ABC of Contemporary Human Rights]*. Chengdu, Sichuan: Sichuan Remin Chubanshe, 1997.

Shen, Baoxiang, Wang Chengquan, and Li Zerui. "Guanyu guoji lingyu de renquan wenti" *[On the Question of Human Rights in the International Arena]. Hong Qi [Red Flag]* no. 8 (1982): 44–48.

Tian, Jin. "Guoji renquan huodong de fazhan he cunzai zhengyi de wenti" [The Development of International Human Rights Activities and Some Controversial Issues]. *Guoji wenti yanjiu Journal of International Studies*], no. 1 (January 1989): 4–7.

Tian, Peizeng, ed. *Gaige Kaifang yilai de Zhongguo Waijiao [China's Diplomacy since Reform and Opening]*. Beijing: Shijie Zhishi Chubanshe, 1993.

Wan, Erxiang, and Guo Maqiang. *Guoji Renquanfa [International Human Rights Law]*. Wuhan: Wuhan Daxue Chubanshe, 1994.

Wang, Yizhou. "Zhonguguo Jueqi yu Guoji Guize" *[The Rise of China and International Norms]*. *Guoji Jingji Pinglun [International Economic Forum]*, no. 3–4 (1998): 28–40.
    Quanqiu Zhengzhi He Zhongguo Waijiao [Global Politics and China's Foreign Policy]. Beijing: Shijie Zhishi Chubanshe, 2003.

Wang, Yuejin. *Zhongguo de Renquan Lilun [The Theory of Human Rights in China]*. Nanjing: Nanjing Renmin Chubanshe, 1998.

Wu, Jianmin. *Waijiao Anli [Case Studies in Diplomacy]*. Beijing: Renmin Daxue Chubanshe, 2007.

Xia, Yong. *Renquan Gainian Qiyuan [The Origin of the Concept of Human Rights]*. Beijing: Zhongguo Zhengfa Daxue Chubanshe, 1992.

Xiao, Weiyun, Luo Haocai, and Wu Xieying. "Makesi zenmeyang kan 'renquan' wenti" [How Marxism Views the Human Rights Question]. *Hongqi [Red flag]*, no. 5 (1979): 43–48.

Xie, Qimei and Wang Xingfang. *Zhongguo yu Lianheguo [China and the United Nations]*. Beijing. Shijie Zhishi Chubanshe, 1995.

Xin, Chunying. "Guoji Renquan Wenti Redian Shuping" [Commentary on Controversial Aspects of Human Rights Issues]. *Zhongguo Zhehuikexue [Chinese Social Science]*, no. 6 (November 1994): 132–141.

Xu, Bing. "Renquan Lilun de Chansheng he Lishi Fazhan" [The Rise and Historical Development of Human Rights Theory]. *Faxue Yanjiu [Studies in Law]* 3, no. 1 (1989): 1–10.

Xu, Jianyi. *Zhongguo de Renquan Zhuangkuang Baipishu Wenti Jieda [Understanding the White Paper of China's Human Rights Situation]*. Beijing: China Youth Publishing House, 1992.

Xue, Mouhong, ed. *Dangdai Zhongguo Waijiao [Contemporary Chinese Diplomacy]*. Beijing: Zhongguo Shehui Kexue Chubanshe [Chinese Social Sciences Publishing House], 1988.

Yan, Xuetong. *Zhongguo Jueqi-Guoji Huanjin Pinggu [International Environment for China's Rise]*. Tianjin, China: People's Press, 1998.

Ye, Zicheng. *Zhongguo Da Zhanlue [The Grand Strategy of China]*. Beijing: Zhongguo Shehui Kexue Chubanshe, 2003.

Yu, Keping. "Renquan yinlun: jinian Faguo 'Ren yu gongmin quanli xuanyan' xiang shi 200 zhounian" [An Introduction to Human Rights: Commemorating the 200th Anniversary of the French 'Declaration of the Rights of Man and Citizen']. *Zhengzhixue yanjiu [Political Science Research]*, no. 3 (1989): 30–35.

Zhang, Guangbo. "Jianchi Makesizhuyi renquanguan" [Insisting on the Marxist View of Human Rights]. *Zhongguo Faxue [Chinese Legal Science]* 4, no. 10 (1990): 10–18.

Zhang, Lili. "Zhongguo yu Guojizuzhi Guanxi de Fazhan" [Development of Relations between China and International Organizations]. In *Guojizuzhi yu Jituan Yanjiu [Study on International Organizations and Groups]*, edited by Qu Liang and Han De, 67–74. Peking: Zhongguo she hui ke xue chu ban she, 1989.

Zhou, Qi. "*Renquan waijiao zhong de lilun wenti*" [Theoretical Issues in Human Rights Diplomacy]. *Ouzhou [Europe]* 1 (1999): 4–15.

Zhu, Feng. *Renquan yu Guojiguanxi [Human Rights and International Relations]*. Beijing: Beijing University Press, October 2000.

Index

www.ingramcontent.com/pod-product-compliance
Ingram Content Group UK Ltd.
Pitfield, Milton Keynes, MK11 3LW, UK
UKHW020453010325
455719UK00016B/566